On-line/Off-line
Between
Text and Experience
Writing as a Lifestyle

WYDAWNICTWO
UNIWERSYTETU
ŁÓDZKIEGO

On-line/Off-line
Between Text and Experience
Writing as a Lifestyle

eds. Peter Gärdenfors, William Powers,
Jarosław Płuciennik, Michał Wróblewski

WYDAWNICTWO
UNIWERSYTETU
ŁÓDZKIEGO

ŁÓDŹ 2015

Peter Gärdenfors – Professor Ordinarius, Department of Philosophy
The Faculties of Humanities and Technology, Lund University, Sweden
Helgonavägen 3, Box 192, 221 00 Lund
William Powers – Laboratory of Social Machines, USA
MIT Media Lab, 77 Mass. Ave., E14/E15, Cambridge, MA 02139-4307 USA
Jarosław Płuciennik – Professor Ordinarius of the Humanities at Chair of Theory of Literature
at the Institute of Contemporary Culture, University of Łódź
171/173 Pomorska St., 90-236 Łódź, Poland
Michał Wróblewski – PhD, affiliated at Chair Theory of Literature
at the Institute of Contemporary Culture, University of Łódź
171/173 Pomorska St., 90-236 Łódź, Poland

© Copyright by University of Łódź, Łódź 2015
© Copyright for this edition by Jagiellonian University Press

All rights reserved

No part of this book may be reprinted or utilised in any form or by any electronic, mechanical or other means, now known or hereafter invented, including photocopying and recording, or in any information storage or retrieval system, without permission in writing from the publishers

Published by Łódź University Press & Jagiellonian University Press

First edition, Łódź–Kraków 2015

ISBN 978-83-7969-821-9 – paperback Łódź University Press

ISBN 978-83-233-4006-5 – paperback Jagiellonian University Press

ISBN 978-83-7969-822-6 – electronic version Łódź University Press

ISBN 978-83-233-9281-1 – electronic version Jagiellonian University Press

Łódź University Press
8 Lindleya St., 90-131 Łódź
www.wydawnictwo.uni.lodz.pl
e-mail: ksiegarnia@uni.lodz.pl
phone +48 (42) 665 58 63, fax +48 (42) 665 58 62

Distribution outside Poland
Jagiellonian University Press
9/2 Michałowskiego St., 31-126 Kraków
phone +48 (12) 631 01 97, +48 (12) 663 23 81, fax +48 (12) 663 23 83
cell phone: +48 506 006 674, e-mail: sprzedaz@wuj.pl
Bank: PEKAO SA, IBAN PL 80 1240 4722 1111 0000 4856 3325
www.wuj.pl

CONTENTS

Editors' Introduction 7

ON-LINE/ OFF-LINE

Ewa Szczęsna: *Literate Existence in the Digital Space. Contemporary Traces of Identity* . . 19
Marta Rakoczy: *Text, Writing, School in Anthropological Perspective*. 35
Lidia Gąsowska: *The Practice of Writing Fan Fiction: A Fan Fiction Writer's Tutorial*. . . 49
Agnieszka Oberc: *I Write. You Write. They Write. The Literary Works of Fandom as a Factor in Integrating the Community* 63
Karolina Sidowska: *Approaches Towards Shame in Contemporary Polish Literature*. . . . 75
Bartosz Kałużny: *People You May Know: Homosexual Men's Identity in the Time of Social Networking Services*. 89
Dobrawa Lisak-Gębala: *Contemporary Polish Essays: In Search of the Aura of Paintings and Photographs*. 115
Irena Chawrilska: *The Hybrid Work of Art as Experience* 133
Agnieszka Karpowicz: *Reincarnations of the Word: Media, Genres, Practices* 151

LITERATURE AND CONVERGENCE

Ewa Szczęsna: *Poetics in the Age of Convergence* 169
Maciej Maryl: *Convergence and Communication: Genre Analysis of the websites of Polish Writers* 189
Katarzyna Sitkowska: *Towards a Generic Analysis of the Microblog (Based on a Study of Twitter)* 209
Irena Chawrilska: *How Does the Hybrid Work of Art Exist?* 237
Irena Górska: *Liberature in Relation to the Reconfiguration of Aisthesis*. 255
Magdalena Lachman: *Literature in/of the City – Introductory Comments* 271

Contents

Natalia Lemann: *Literary Studies, History and Popular Culture – the Spaces of Convergence. Introduction* 293

Katarzyna Gutkowska-Ociepa: *Afterpop: the Almost Perfect Convergence.* 321

Beata Śniecikowska: *Transcultural Convergence? Polish Poets and Artists and the Oriental Verbo-visuality* 339

Bogusława Bodzioch-Bryła: *From an E-narrative Poem towards an Interactive Work of Art. Media Convergence Illustrated with* DOWN *by Zenon Fajfer and* The Surprising Spiral *by Ken Feingold* 371

Bibliographical notes 401

EDITORS' INTRODUCTION

Setting

The articles presented in *On-line/Off-line – Between Text and Experience* concern the status of words and literature in contemporary culture. Opinions about 'the death of words', words displaced by pictures, are no longer formulated with equal firmness as in the past. Word and image do not compete, they rather act as equally important 'ingredients' of today's culture. To revise popular judgments which reduce the meaning of the Word there is no need for detailed analysis, just observation of daily practices. The vast number of text messages, e-mails, tweets, comments, blogs' or social networking's posts written day by day confirms the strong position of words (language) in the new media and the "new new media" (as specified by Paul Levinson).

However, just as with the introduction of earlier media in the 19th and 20th centuries, a new medium influences the structure and use of the old media. For example, when movies were introduced, they were initially just filmed theatre performances. It took some time before the techniques of cutting and scene changes were developed. However, once the techniques were established they had strong repercussions on the earlier medium of writing. Many authors, for example William Burroghs, started working with cut-up-techniques in their texts. This is a clear example of how the narrative forms of a new medium influences the narratives of an earlier medium. The use of e-mail and social media has already influenced the style of writing, making it more conversational. Similarly, the ever-presence of a camera in your smart-phone has radically changed the use of visual media. An important task of literary scholars is to follow and document the cross-fertilizations between different media, their influences on narrative structures and their roles in democratic processes.

Editors' Introduction

The articles perfectly fit into the worldwide ongoing debate in humanities on the latest developments of cultural practice changing under the impact of new technologies – the way of experiencing the text, the various manifestations of "culture of participation", website genres (among which blogs and microblogs have an important place). Despite the popularity of research on digital dimensions of human existence, the presence of the word (for example in oral culture) is a subject of unabated discussion in other reaserch contexts. Thus, the object of reflection in this volume is not narrowed just to selected "on-line" phenomena, but issues from the "off-line" cultural activites. In times of rapid technological change, enthusiasts of the new often subscribe to the theory of "supersession", the idea that newer technologies supersede or vanquish older ones. But as scholar of information Paul Duguid has observed, reality is more interesting and complicated than that. In the 1950s, for instance, when television was becoming popular, there were widespread predictions of radio's imminent demise. Yet here it is 2015 and radio is not only very much alive but has thrown off vibrant digital doppelgängers of itself, in the form of internet radio stations and podcasts. In fact it seems to be more appropriate to perceive culture not in terms of radical changes and so-called 'turns', but by emphasizing the continuity and co-existence of certain cultural phenomena. Henry Jenkins – who insisted that the most valuable ability in the age of convergence is to maneuver between old and new media – can be easily regarded as a patron of such a perspective.

So it goes for all of human culture: There is really no predicting where literary culture will go next. As the articles in this collection make clear, this is especially true of writing in our time, when old and new, online and offline, are mixing, mashing up and recombining so prolifically, no single theory could ever explain it all, let alone foretell its evolution. So it's fitting that what we have in this volume is not a collection of definitive, supersession-like answers, but a multiplicity of fascinating questions explored in depth. Are microblogs a new literary genre? What happens when Japanese haiku leap across cultures? Is writing inherently an act of individuality, as we tend to believe, or is that idea just "a fruit of modernity"? Such questions will swirl around us for decades to come, and to make our way forward we will need intellectual roadmaps with the wide-ranging curiosity, high aspirations and serious intent of this one.

Themes

On 13–14 June 2013, the Interdisciplinary Conference **On-line/Off-line – Between Text and Experience** was held in Lodz. The conference was organized by the Department of Theory of Literature, Institute of Contemporary Culture – former Institute of Theory of Literature, Theatre and Audiovisual Arts – (University of Lodz) and the journal "Problems of Literary Genres" The main subjects of reflection were the aforementioned democratization and dissemination of writing as a form of human experience, communication and creativity.

Writing – or, generally 'to be with text' – became a domain of every contemporary culture's user. This is because the contemporary culture consists of literary texts, understood traditionally in terms of edition and genre background, as well as of polisemiotic hybrids, literary blogs, e-forums, e-poetry generators, posts, comments, tweets, e-mails and text messages. The ubiquity of the word (transmission of a text) despite the seemingly dominant trend of pixelation and the primacy of so called picture culture is symptomatic. It seems that the progressive technologization of the society does not affect the importance of the text and literature. Paradoxically, it acts as a stimulant in these domains, not only gaining new users for them, but also expanding their meanings.

The second part of the book, called *Literature and Convergence* consists of multiple articles about converging processes taking place amongst contemporary texts concerning culture – especially in literature. The main object of the reflection and discussion is the concept of convergence – which is extremely popular in contemporary scientific discourse. This term is used very widely: from mathematics and natural science, through to linguistics, politology and sociology, to studies in new media, communication and cultural anthropology. Are there actually so many contaminations, blendings and diffusions in cultural processes and how much does this phenomenon affect the literature and its theory? The goal of this publication is to explore and critically survey (from a literary studies' perspective) some of the cultural mechanisms and their effects characteristic for the times of digitalisation of culture and rapid technological developments. What is (or should be) the place of literature and literary studies during these changes?

The articles included here focus on a variety of problems, often presenting the research field in differing ways but relative to the initial problem. The perception of non-obviousness and the diversity of converging processes are combined here with an attempt to manage the multi-dimensionality and instability of convergence, which by definition introduces a modality, interdisciplinarity and multilingualism into text. The authors of the studies pose questions about the status of poetics in the age of convergence and the impact of digitalization processes on structures and features of genres and discourses. They analyze the ontological problems of hybrid texts and look for examples of convergence in concrete poetry, e-poetry, liberature, logo-visual texts literary blogs, social networks, historiography and the city – understood as a space of text. The infiltration of the academic fields can also be seen in the selection of research tools and methodologies – e.g. pragmalinguistics is adjacent to the genealogy, anthropology, literary theories and studies on new media. We hope that the thematic range and a variety of research perspectives make this publication an important and interesting to read (multi-) voice in twenty-first century humanities discourse on the convergence problem.

Articles

The articles selected for this volume focus on various topics and emphasize different methodological approaches towards diversified cultural phenomenons. The first part of the book has the title *On-line/off-line* and deals with characteristics of digital experience, text and status of the reader.

Ewa Szczęsna shows in her paper *Literate Existence in the Digital Space. Contemporary Traces of Identity* how the development of writing technology influences writing itself. In this paper the analysis is focused on mechanisms of reinterpretation of writing and reading in digital space, in other words, the change in experience of text. To summarize, modern media techniques make reading become writing, when writing becomes clicking (an action taken upon the texture), and clicking becomes the experience of text. Another goal is to present a special role of the texture as the tool of text's creation as well as the place of cohesion. The importance of semiotic tissue of digital text, especially in the case of digital art, is visible in the formation of intratextual relations. These relations are created in the process of working one element of texture onto another, which allow them to play an important role in the creation of textual meaning.

Marta Rakoczy's article is an attempt to reveal an anthropological structure of following categories: text and writing; the categories that nowadays require cultural, historical and institutional relativization. She maintains that the paradigm of writing as mental, individualistic creation and freely chosen way of life is a result of late modernity. Moreover, even today it is not the only paradigm and is not universally acceptable. The illustration of this that she develops in this text is an example of today's exercise books. School – as the main institution of literate initiation, including mass first contact with literature – is an institution in which the practice of writing, regulated by school breaks and specifically related to capitalist society's dual division of time, is a specific one, being a tool which is a well-defined, perceptual and social discipline. However, this discipline does not exclude creativity, as long as we leave its late-modern definition.

Lidia Gąsowska in her *The Practice of Writing Fan Fiction. Tutorial of a Fan Fiction Writer* as well as **Agnieszka Oberec** in *I Write. You Write. They write. The Literary Works of Fandom as a Factor in Integrating the Community* describe fanfiction they underline that writing fanfiction is something that fans do together. Readers discuss original texts, share their views and opinions about plot and characters, and create common interpretation that can be used by other fandom members. They also participate in creating new texts by commenting on fanficks published by other fans. Writing is not only a way to express fans opinions about their favourite books and shows, but also an opportunity to spend time with people sharing their interests. Analysis of fan-created texts shows not only its importance to individual fans, but also a vital role writing fanfiction plays in building fan communities and creating bonds between their members.

Another author, **Karolina Sidowska,** exhibits different literary approaches to the emotion of shame in *Approaches Towards Shame in Contemporary Polish Literature*. Her thesis is that literature can be perceived as a tool for overcoming feelings of shame, as it is capable of expressing even the most intimate human experiences in aesthetic terms, outside stereotypical moral judgments. From this perspective she discusses exhibitionistic tendencies on the author's part and complementary voyeuristic impulses on the part of the reader. Sidowska presents examples from contemporary Polish literature background. Also **Dobrawa Lisak-Gębala** focuses on Polish literature exploring *Contemporary Polish Essays: In Search of the Aura of Paintings and Photographs*. The article by **Bartosz Kałużny**, which divides these to papers, is related to the topic of shame and it also takes into consideration the problem of constructing an identity – this time in a social media context.

The following paper by **Irena Chawrilska** describes a hybrid work of art viewed as a form of experience. The question is how can we understand the notion of experience in relation to the work of art, and, more importantly, to the hybrid work of art. The analysis of the experience category presented here is based on the philosophical texts written by Luigi Pareyso. Hybridity is also the topic of the next article by **Agnieszka Karpowicz**. Her *Reincarnations of the Word: Media, Genres, Practices* presents the project of study of the multimedia, contemporary verbal environment. It proposes the use of the category of speech genres (Bakhtin). Focusing on the secondary genres (genres of verbal creativity) it justifies the argument that "The word is not dead. It is merely changing its skin" (Dick Higgins), and therefore in the living verbal environment we deal with the changing, heterogeneous media of verbal expression that determine, in part, the modes of functioning of particular genres and how they should be described. This paper presents performance, text and hypertext as a basic means of functioning of the verbal forms in contemporary culture; means which demand adequate categories of description and research tools in order to avoid textualization of multimedia genres and not to treat them as literature.

The second part of the book titled *Literature and Convergence* opens with another crucial paper by **Ewa Szczęsna**. In *Poetics in the Age of Convergence* she presents changes in the structure of text (its structure and ways of creation, figures in particular) in digital discourse. The identity of digital communication is premised upon existing signs, texts, and discourses; and how it develops in the process of their adaptation and reinterpretation. The Internet seems to be a really good space in which different discourses become alike. This process results in the creation of a new poetics of text and discourse. Digital media modifies rhetorical figures (especially the ontology and functions of those figures), cancels figures existing in traditional texts (for example, inversion is invalidated because no determined way of reading the text exists), and creates new ones.

Changes in contemporary Poetics are also the main concern in **Maciej Maryl**'s *Convergence and Communication: Genre Analysis of the websites of Polish Writers*. This article categorizes new forms of expressions on writers' websites as means of maintaining communication with readers. The first part is dedicated to inter- and trans-medial analyses of various multimedia materials published on such websites (e.g. biographical notes, photographs, trailers). In the second part, the website is analyzed as a hybrid text in which various types of expression are submitted to the main communicative purpose. On both levels of analysis the material is categorized in terms of the communicative function, for, as the author claims, the genre analysis of electronic discourse requires an approach which takes into consideration not only authorial intent and textual features but also the context of online utterance and the role of other partners of communication.

New media and texts likewise are the topics of the following paper about Twitter by **Katarzyna Sitkowska**. This article is an attempt to determine the place of microblogs, posted on Twitter, on the Internet or, more broadly in the multimedia genealogy. Then we can look closely at hybrid texts. **Irena Chawrilska**'s *How Does the Hybrid Work of Art Exist?* studies a relation between hybrid works of art in the background of philosophical texts by Luigi Pareyson, Jurij Łotman, Wolfgang Welsch. The main considerations focus on questions – What is the definition of a hybrid work of art? What is the impact of contemporary culture on the way of being a hybrid work of art? Do the hybrid works of art reflect the experience of contemporary reality? The reflection here is based on concrete poetry, book works, book objects and liberature.

Liberature is also a major interest in **Irena Górska**'s paper on the *Reconfiguration of Aisthesis*. This article proposes to inspect the phenomenon of liberature from the perspective of the reconfiguration of aisthesis, as described by Wolfgang Welsch. In the German researcher's approach, this consists in questioning the primacy of vision in favour of other senses, and is, first of all, an effect of the dominance of the media. However – as Górska describes – in a broader approach towards the reasons of transformations, aisthesis must be looked for in phenomena that are summarised in the formula of "new aesthetics", as proposed by Arnold Berleant. One of the significant features of this concept is the constant expansion of the area of art and the appearance of forms that stimulate the audience experience, requiring the activation of new sensory receptors. Without a doubt Górska suggests, liberature is one of those forms of art that require interactivity and a special involvement. Being a unique example of the co-existence of various types of messages (verbal, iconic and material), liberature requires a polysensory perception. This, in turn, can be a source of aesthetic satisfaction, but also a reason for an impoverishment of the aesthetic experience spanning between aisthesis and anaisthesis.

We find a different kind of approach to texts in **Magdalena Lachman**'s *Literature in/of the City – Introductory Comments*. The article attempts to describe a variety of possible ways in which literature makes itself present within the space of the city. It assumes two basic perspectives to investigate the issue. First of all, the article analyses how the city and its multiple institutions support the literature's circulation and availability for the readers. The city offers a number of venues for writers to present their works and promote them through precisely targeted events and literary festivals. The city is seen as a stage or background on which literary works and events can become fully available. Secondly, the article analyses how literary critics or more broadly philosophers and sociologists interested in urban studies use literature to understand and describe the city in its artistic and everyday dimensions. The fruitful collaboration between city as an active factor shaping artistic imagination and writers leads to developing new forms of expression as well as formulating new ideas about art. It also offers a possibility to communicate with readers in ways which are better accommodated to modern visual imagination and different forms of everyday activity.

The other kind of blending space is described *in Literary Studies, History and Popular Culture – the Spaces of Convergence. Introduction* by **Natalia Lemann**. The aim of the article is to juxtapose literary studies, literature and history as neighboring branches of humanistic knowledge. The author compares the methodologies of history and literary studies in the field of narrativity, and, in accordance with Hayden White, comprehends history as a type of fiction, historio-graphia, and literary artifact. In this view historiography and literary studies are diagnosed as forming a sisterhood relationship. When the opportunity arises it is shown that the idea of postmodern history is no novelty, since until the decline of the 18th century history and literary studies have not been opposite at all. Actually, the way of thinking about history as an (literary) art has a splendid tradition rooted in antiquity. A comparative analysis – says Lemann – leads to the conclusion, that both these "scientific" branches developed almost simultaneously (cf. feminism, gender, postcolonialism, posthumanism, animal studies). Moreover literary genres, such as the (post)modern historical novels, alternate histories or historical fantasy, opened the space of convergence between history and the literary, because of mutual fluctuation and "parasiting" of ideas, topics and poetic. The participation of popular culture makes history and literary studies more transgressive, widely open to contemporary forms of communication and more audible. In this scope, the author presents historical game books, facebook`s historical events, transmedia historical stories.

(Pop)culture is as well the field of interest of **Katarzyna Gutkowska**, who focuses on one of the newest notions in Spanish literary theory created by Eloy Fernández Porta in his work *Afterpop. La literatura de la implosion mediatica* (2007). This theorist reaches for the aesthetical accomplishments of postmodernism, avant-pop and cyberpunk in order to analyze them in the context of the new artistic mentality from the beginnings of 21st century. Juggling a multitude of literary techniques and names from various cultural backgrounds such as W. S. Burroughs, Julián Ríos, David

Foster Wallace, David Cronenberg or Michael Haneke, Fernández Porta the paper shows new criteria and new methods of recognizing the complexity and insights of intermediatic, multifaceted and polysemic, implosive "new literature".

On the other hand, the closure of *On-line/Off-line – Between Text and Experience. Writing as a Lifestyle* consists of two papers focusing on comparative studies in relation to Polish literature and literary practice. **Beata Śniecikowska** in her *Transcultural Convergence? Polish Poets and Artists and the Oriental Verbo-visuality* discusses different aspects of convergence processes of the traditional Oriental genres in the Polish culture, focusing on haiku, *haiga* and *haibun*. It examines artists' books, visual arts and the artistic websites. The theoretical frame of the research is rooted in the concept of transculturality introduced by Wolfgang Welsch. The author analyses Polish works of art employing different strategies of combining words and images, thereby showing unexpected similarities between cultures and revealing the artistic changes caused by the choice of different media. The investigation proves that the most interesting compositions uncover unexpected common elements between apparently contradictory traditions, the necessary condition is, however, at least the basic knowledge about the Other.

The figure of the Other bring us back to liberature in the last article. **Bogusława Bodzioch-Bryła**'s paper titled *From an E-narrative Poem Towards an Interactive Work of Art. Media Convergence Illustrated with* DOWN *by Zenon Fajfer and* The Surprising Spiral *by Ken Feingold*. The article, using an example of a work belonging to the literary style (*Spoglądając przez ozonową dziurę [Detect Ozone Hole Nearby]* by Zenon Fajfer) and the interactive art (the installation *The Surprising Spiral* by Ken Feingold) analyses the idiosyncracy of works positioning themselves at the borderland of media and literature, works both literary (textual, narrative and poetic) as well as media ones (changeable, iconic, set in a computer program, double-indirect), paying attention to the meaningfulness of the disciplines borderland (in this case literary and media studies). The author stresses the reasonableness of the question asked by Katarzyna Bazarnik, whether, by accident, the "Darwinian" evolution of species continues. In the author's opinion, based on her observation of works belonging to the literary style and the discussed work *The Surprising Spiral* by Ken Feingold, this question should get a positive answer. And possibly, as an effect of initiation, which has already happened, we will soon be entering the museum-gallery space not only in order to look but also to read.

Editors' Introduction

***

On-line/Off-line – Between Text and Experience. Writing as a Lifestyle considers a lot of significant issues, combining in an interesting way the specificity of the local with problems discussed in the world humanities. At the same time it gives reception to western debates and offers a number of interesting conclusions arising from the regional – Polish – experience. Therefore this publication is addressed to a broad range of readers – not only those from Poland.

On-line/Off-line

Ewa Szczęsna*
University of Warsaw

LITERATE EXISTENCE IN THE DIGITAL SPACE. CONTEMPORARY TRACES OF IDENTITY[1]

Abstract
The aim of this study is to present how the development of writing technology influences writing itself. In this paper the analysis is focused on mechanisms of reinterpretation of writing and reading in digital space, in other words, the change in experience of text. To summarize, modern media techniques make reading become writing, when writing becomes clicking (an action taken upon the texture), and clicking becomes the experience of text. Another goal is to present a special role of the texture as the tool of text's creation as well as the place of cohesion. The importance of semiotic tissue of digital text, especially in the case of digital art, is visible in the formation of intratextual relations. These relations are created in the process of working one element of texture onto another, which allow them to play an important role in the creation of textual meaning.

Key words: identity, digital space, experience of text, textual meaning, intratextual relations

Reading is writing. Writing is clicking

The topic of writing as a way of living in relation to the digital culture evoke, first of all, problems connected with the prevalence of communication in the public domain, globalization of the individual record, the changing relation between literacy and orality – shaping of the new forms of linguistic existence as well as the development of new text genres.

---

* Faculty of Polish Studies, Univeristy of Warsaw, ul. Krakowskie Przedmieście 26/28, 00-927 Warsaw e-mail: e.k.szczesna@uw.edu.pl
[1] This publication is part of the research project NN 103 398340 funded by the National Science Centre in Kraków.

The change in communicational behavior in the virtual world, transgression that takes place in text-user relation, inseparability of transciver activities – all of it significantly influence the existence of text. As a result, reading becomes writing (an action), writing becomes clicking, and clicking becomes the way of experiencing text through the texture.

Within digital culture the reception of text is a corporeal experience already at the perception level. There raises the question if clicking as a technical action, marking, selection of textual elements on the screen of computer, e.g., during reception of a hypertext novel, can be recognized as an action analogous to page turning during the reception of a novel preserved in the medium of a traditional book? At first glance, it may appear so. The opening of a book and page turning are undoubtedly **technical conditions of reading**. The counterpart of such experience in domain of digital culture is very act of clicking – I mean the act of key pushing and mouse clicking, moving cursor on the screen or marking and shifting elements on the touch screen with one's finger.

In my opinion, similarities end here. Page turning and clicking are connected with different intentions in domain of the recipient activity – the influence of a reader on the exhibition of text. Actions of turning and putting pages are connected with fulfillment of the intention of the only way of reading – by constructing text (creating record) author establishes a certain order of reading (in conventional word-composed text the order of record is the order of reading). This order, in case of e.g., a book consisted of novel text, is set by convention (various in different cultures) generated during development of writing culture along with paper information carriers. Conventionalization of the order of writing has lead to its transparency, which had been being disrupted every now and then by the creative interventions of authors. Experimental works that took degeneration from this principle as a subject of artistic activity (e.g., *Hopscoth* by Cortázar or works of Stanisław Czycz) emphasized the creative potential contained in the medium, the ability for additional textualization of the texture.

In traditional text not only author but also the reader was able (and still is) to not follow the principle of linear reception. A defiant reader or an impatient one can read selectively, fragmentalize the texture, however, in view of the current standards, such reading is still considered a fault (error in reading). Moreover, it's eradicated (especially by the school teachers who teach detailed reading with use of detailed tests regarding contents of books). Thus deviation from the reading norm comes from the readers themselves, those who cannot wait for the answer "who is the killer?" or "if he and she will live happily ever after?" and interrupt the reading in order to take a peek at the last page of a novel. Another group of defiant readers is consisted of young receivers adjusted to the culture of news, flashes, SMS, and twitts. They tend to skip the extensive description passages in multi-volume two-centuries-old novels because of lack of the reader's patience.

Still, there is another type of interference in reading order. Its example is provided by the reception of philosophical works (i.a., *Ecce Homo* of Nietzsche) which Stanisław Ignacy Witkiewicz has made[2]. It is indicated by the handwritten marking of text fragments, reader's annotations in the margins and interlines, the ironical, the mocking as well as those serious ones. Every single one of these activities indicates the existence of **reader's need to interfere in the text**, experiencing it, modeling and familiarizing someone else's text, inscribing own interpretational activity in its tissue. Witkacy in view of his reception of philosophical works (and probably not only him) was a prototype of the user.

Besides, there are books that are more or less supposed to be read selectively, not necessarily in order of following pages. I mean not only holy books, encyclopedias, dictionaries or cooking books and guides but also volumes of poetry, collections of aphorisms and sentences. No longer in principle, but more often it happens also in case of reception of dissertations and philosophical treatises. Eriksen in *Tyranny of the Moment* wrote about shortening and simplifying dictated by the quick passage of time, hegemony of fragment (Eriksen 2003), which this scholar sees as an effect of information overload and compulsion to constant actualization of it.

Fragmentalizing kind of reader, for whom reading becomes usage, remaking, therefore **text writing,** is also being shaped by contemporary mass media that are striving for his attention and competing in its appropriation. Press market should serve as good example. Semiotic method of article composition – emphasizing the most important fragments with bigger, bold font, sometimes with red color, placing them in separated, eye-catching places on the plane of newspaper page. Numerous illustrations encourage to **fragmental reading,** replacing solid, linear reading with **browsing**[3]. Selective reading performed by reader is texture modification devoid of any fixation.

---

[2] This reception was received at the exhibition *Marginalia filozoficzne* that was organized in the Contemporary Art Center in Ujazdów Castle in Warsaw (19.01–22.02.2004, curator: Paweł Polit).
[3] Browsing as a reading method is being analyzed by myself in a chapter entitled "Komparatystyka mediów. Poetyka, semiotyka, komunikacja medialna" published in a book *Komparatystyka dla humanistów* (Dąbrowski 2011: 289–312).

Specified manifestations of reading insubordination, in regard to reception in digital media, illustrate the phenomenon of perceptual and mental **overwriting** of reader's own text on the existing one (with use of this text's elements). Thus **reading becomes writing** or rather **overwriting text on another text**. It is creation of palimpsest that becomes fixated (just like in Witkacy's case but also in case of scholar's method of reading other scholar's books with pencil in a hand) or (what happens more often, even in the case of reception of magazines) is never fixated, lasting only as sort of **mental palimpsest**.

Reading mechanisms that in case of traditional book usually had a status of experiment or even aberration are set as standard in case of digital transitions. They are recognized as a principle of reading. This mainly concerns the **selection category** as well as **adding** and **commenting**. Such activities set multivariate existence of text. Meaning, choice of textual element, order of texture revealing, commenting, adding textual element – all of those are **traces of reader's presence** in text. In contrast to the traditional text, they are not vigilante actions, but become inscribed in the sender intention of the author. They are being foreseen and designed by computer.

Reader's selection of texture elements is very essence of hypertext. It's experience of written reading, reception that is writing at the same time and the texture of which stops being untouchable, but becomes a place of creative activities. Otherness of receiver activity is reflected in the category of text usage.

The text reading method changes along with development of digital culture. Research led by neurologists and perception psychologists shows that browsing internet pages, reception of text in the plane of computer screen goes in a jumping manner. Content on a computer screen is taken differently by persons shaped in the tradition of the printed book and differently by persons adjusted to tradition of the new interactive media. In the first case skipping has lesser frequency and receiver's gaze lasts longer at each fragment of text, following linear manner of its progress – in the latter case, the frequency of attention diverting rises drastically, and its span towards single elements decreases. Therefore, cause and effect thinking, coherent narratives, sequences of events development – all elaborated by the writing tradition – are replaced by associational thinking.

The issue of influence of the communication technologies on the way of how we experience text (act of constructing such experience and elaborating a certain type of perception) has been discussed many times by researchers. As an example, let's invoke thoughts of Derrick de Kerckhove, who pointed out connection between literate mind and tendency to manipulate concepts, processing information more in mind than in acting, relying more on words than on the images (Kerckhove 1985). He contrasted these features with an oral mind which he attributed (just like Ong) to associational thinking, focusing on reconstructing of imaginary, putting emphasis on memory, inventing metaphors and creating myths. Digital communication do not separate these ways of thinking. It connects them, confronts them as well, and sets in motion mutual interactions. As a result, experience of digital transmission is not only a polisensoric experience but also it reinterprets the existing epistemological order of text. Such reinterpretation appears to go beyond oralitzation and iconization of writing, literacy of speech and image[4] indicated by the scholars. Rather, it means seamless interaction of various forms of perception and orders of text structuring – though, it should be mentioned that these orders are different in view of contemporary technologies, not in the view of digitalism, for which they create coherent system and subject to the same laws.

The change in method of text reception do not necessarily mean the abolishment of **coherence** (semantic coherence), which in case of traditional text is supported by formal coherence (linear one). In case of digital transmissions the main factor supporting coherence is the kind that I define as **semiotic** coherence. The method of reading and meanings constructing in digital transmissions is quite often decided by the organization of signs of transmission on the computer screen. This coherence may be real, when sign elements are organized in such order that by determining the order of reception, they provide entirety with a specified meaning. Coherence may be illusory as well – when the order of sign elements on the screen makes semantically distant elements appear coherent for the user. It is worth noting that semiotic coherence, especially **playing with** this coherence and its **interferences,** is organizing digital art quite often.

The way of how text is presented is not a transparent medium, it becomes text itself. It is visible at the level of font. E.g., Diane Gromala has projected font of eclectic nature – its combination of various types of traditional and modern fonts. *Excretia* – that is the name of the project – has dynamic nature – the size of letters may change continually before the eyes of the viewer, participating in creation of textual meanings, which show their

---

[4] See M. Sndbothe. "Transwersalne światy medialne. Filozoficzne rozważania o Internecie", K. Krzemieniowa, tran., *Widzieć, myśleć, być. Technologie mediów*, selecion and development by A. Gwóźdź. Kraków, 2001, p. 215–222.

unstable nature already on the stratum of represented objectivities. This constantly fluctuating letters are traces of many identities that constitute every writing one.

> With Excretia, a Word processor is no longersimply a productivity tool but a reflective experience in itself. As the writer works, he sees how his biofeedback reshapeshis words. (...) Excretia makes writing truthful in the ironic sense that it reveals the writer'sbodily states. (...) Writing can be reflective interface, a mirror of the author, although not a perfect mirror because our written identity is different from who we are when we are speaking casually. In fact, we have many written identities, as we write in different voices for different audiences and different purposes (Bolter, Gromala 2005: 166, 168).

The change in reading method is physical commitment of receiver to the tissue of text. Touch, corporeality are participating in creation of texture. Receiver of traditional text in a form of a book has no ability of interference in the tissue of text. He takes text as it was proposed. His creative activity is engaged only at the level of interpretation. It is reflected in Steven Knapp's (Knapp 1993) concept of literature as well as in Martha Nussbaum's one, according to which (what Jonathan Culler notes) all literary narration techniques are eventually transforming readers into judges evaluating characters' choices, analyzing factors that were not affecting (Culler 1013).

Clicking is experiencing the text in texture and through it

In case of hypertext the attitude of "literary judge" recedes into the background, making place for attitude of "the perpetrator of the text event" and as a result, the perpetrator of the world that said text stands as. Digital transmission enables acting, even more, it **requires acting, experiencing text** and its efficacy. Clicking launches the text event and decides its way of existence. Texture gains status of textual experience object. It's experienced in physical way. It's especially evident in various projects – installations spacializing text and connecting it with receiver's body, where experience of writing is the experience of creating text with a whole body.

Written word is not only a tool of thought externalization anymore, a method of fixating them (Eriksen 2003), but it becomes an object of textual actions alone, an object of receiver's experience. Clicking is writing – causing text, organizing the way its appearing. It sets in motion performative power inscribed in linked word. A thing connected with acting is the act of immersion that researched especially in the view of video games but also – wider – in the context of narration (Ryan 2001) is described as a kind of receiving experience involving submergence in a diegetic world (Murray 1997: 98). In case of digital transmissions the semiotic layer of text along with user acts are engaged. Diegetic world becomes present yet at the level of texture, what causes immersion act to get coupled with an **aesthetic experience**.

In a digital environment the sign and text are experienced not only through eyesight and hearing but also through touch. Speaking about experiencing instead of perceiving is justified in the act of user's actions taken on the texture – both on individual signs and on whole texts.

Sign and text are analogous **relation structures**. In both cases we encounter meaning established in the act of reception, the main impulse of which is stratum of represented objectivities external to the cognizing subject. The main difference between the sign and the text is based on the degree of complexity of the elements of relations. Semiotic textures of the sign and the text differ, broadly speaking, in levels of complexity that becomes apparent in the process of meaning establishing (interpretation). The sign's stratum of represented objectivities is constructed in such way that it usually gives a single impulse to creation of meaning in the process of reception. It's different in the case of text where establishment of meanings requires determining the semantic relations that connect more complex units – aspects, events and even whole plots. An example for this may be provided by series of novels, TV series and advertising campaigns that are **politexts** where the global meaning is constituted in the interaction of many texts.

The **texture** (a **semiotic tissue of text**), is a factor of culture text perceived sensually – through sight, hearing, touch – usually somehow fixated (record, e.g., verbal, score, iconic, audiovisual one), organized in a particular way (genre-specific). The texture of a particular work is a closed set of specified elements with their own composition. In the case of conventional text this closed nature of texture remains contrasted to variously conditioned interpretation variables over time. As such texture it sets the basic boundaries of text.

There are textures that do not have any fixation by rule (e.g., musical improvisations, theatre plays) but they may be still possible to record (secondary fixation). Example may be provided by audiovisual records of sand painting uploaded to the internet (available on YouTube), we can invoke here the works of Ksenia Simonova or Ilana

Yahav[5], records of spectacles or musical improvisations. It must be noted that such record is only a remediation creating a new text.

Texture has its own **technological** and **formal** dimensions. It means that it's created with help of specified technologies – medial tools, e.g., writing, print, photography as well as audio, audiovisual and interactive technologies. Also, it means that typological information is communicated already at the level of texture – information regarding generic form of text, thus creating architext (Genette 1982).

The ability to recognize the majority of generic forms already at the level of perceptual reception are obtained by the receiver through cultural participation. In brief, already at the level of perceptual reception we can see, without any necessity to delve into the semantics of communication, that specific text is a poetic work, prose, movie poster, a comic, newspaper article, visual advertisement, a movie, theatre play, blog, a video game or a literary hypertext.

Composition of texture elements, semiotic organization and technology provide us with **indicators of generic and typological information**. E.g., the arrangement of printed words into lines and strophes (strophoids) is carrier of information telling us that we are dealing with a poem. Continuous arrangement of words with marking of dialogues and extraction of the chapters should be associated with prose. In turn, the division into columns, presence of lead, photos with captions, characteristic format of a page should invoke newspaper article. Presence of interface, links, possibility to take action on the texture while maintaining traditional generic traits indicates that conventional text has been digitally remediated.

Texture is the place and a tool used to create meanings that are formed in the active intellectual confrontation with cognizing subject. The meanings created by subject are initiated by texture (in the situation of text reading) or coded in it (in situation of text writing). Both activities are of creative nature. They are separate, but sometimes become connected as well. They cannot be opposed to each other for sure. Good example is provided by the activity of a translator, critic, cultural historian (researcher of literary text, document, iconic or musical message). Every of those activities is activity of an interpreter, who is first provided by the texture with an impulse to creation of meanings, to begin an interpretational work, then it transforms texture into text that is getting encoded in the new texture afterwards.

---

[5] See. www.sandstory.com

In a digital environment previous semiotic forms and medial structures are subjected to **remediation**. As a result, polisemiotics, multimediality, and palimpsest-like nature of digital texture confronted with previous media can be seen as elements of different systems. Subjected to remediation, in digital space they are complementary elements of a single medial system, where the foundations of said community are placed in immaterial matter of texture, ontic identity of every digitally generated texture element.

An important factor is also the change in the range of activity of a subject that stands as text in the process of texture reception. The stability of a texture is characteristic for analog culture. Except the situations regarding textual experiments, the texture is generally given to receiver in specified, single form without possibility of any change within. It is set as arbitrarily complex sign (untouchable exhibit) that provides impulse to meanings establishing. Its important feature is immutability. The only possible reconstructions and renovations are not receiver's actions but corrective proceedings aimed at restoration of the original. Receiver's activity is possible on the stratum of meanings, interpretations, thanks to which it attains its variability. Maybe it's the immobility of the texture that became the basis of theories regarding specified meaning encoded in text, meaning that is meant to be reached by the receiver.

In case of the digital transmission the receiver is **experiencing text** both at the level of meaning and texture. The important change in the ontics of texture is its mobility, the ability to make changes in texture. User's work on texture is programmed activity, where this programming concerns the existence of a set of possible actions taken on the text. Action or inaction, the order of operations, the selection of elements, appending them, adjusting and skipping – all of these remain the responsibility of the user. Causing a specified forms of texture by user – varied by users and usually different during subsequent acts of reading – is an important factor in the differentiation of meanings.

In the era of the internet the universality of daily activities on a digital texture is a necessary condition for the fortunate participation in social life – becoming a way of living itself. The economic function of the texture strengthen ups. It serves not only as a transparent medium of meaning but also as a carrier of metatextual meaning, generic information, matter of superstructural texture and a text tool. The changing form of texture, its immateriality in the world of digital media, the reinforcement of other roles beside the basic one – role of the transparent carrier of meaning, reflecting the new identity of text and its user.

Ewa Szczęsna

Texture functions in the era of a new identity of the text

Texture is still seen primarily as a transparent medium for meanings. This feature is one of the most fundamental ones, especially in the case of conventional texts. It's connected with an informational function of text, with focusing attention on communicating meanings (the invention of print, photography, cinematography, internet were associated primarily with fixation and transmission of content).

Techniques of recording, reproduction and distribution of verbal, iconic, auditory and audiovisual information are focused primarily on making the texture independent from time and space. It should be emphasized that this independence applies precisely to the texture rather than meaning, the multiple factors of which (for example, related to the predispositions of cognizing subject) are making it only partially stable. In principle, stability of texture as the impulse to creation of textual meanings is the sole guarantor of the relative stability of the text. This stability, tangibility and verifiability of texture (as opposed to variable in its essence, in many ways conditioned interpretation) was the basis of universal identification of texture with the text.

In the consciousness of an average participant of culture text is indentified with the texture (e.g., of novel, film, newspaper article or any other message), the receiver of which assigns it some specified, generally single meaning. The higher repeatability of texture form and the farther its ossification has advanced, the greater its transparency. About such transparency we should speak in case of conventional book, where repeatability of the same typographical solutions, the same principle of organizing verbal, iconic and graphic elements has led to texture becoming transparent. The idea of texture transparency is organizing a realistic art as well – in its various semiotic and medial forms – both realistic art and photography, literature and film. It also organizes methods of digital transmission, in particular, all those who are focused on the timely establishment of specified textual meanings by the receiver. News services, portals and online forums – in short, all these forms that are aimed at communicatory aspects will strive to maximize the transparency of texture while making it carrier of a generic information at the same time. Organization of texture should enable user to recognize the textual form and establish meanings through interactive interpretation.

The function of texture as a transparent medium refers to the digital textures, no less than to texts of print culture or analog audiovisuality. The difference is that in the case of interactive media, the texture of the dominant transparent medium includes within itself also interactive tools and actions. Here we encounter a peculiar paradox. On the one hand, the transparency requires simplification, reduction of texture forms, limitation of its variations so the solid forms can crystallize, on the other hand provided by digital technologies countless amount of texture modifications in the area of colors, graphic forms, arrangement of elements in the plane of screen, sound effects or kinetic forms is opposed to transparency.

Texture serves also as a carrier of matatextual meaning (a multidiscursive texture). In this case, its transparency is distorted to some extent. Multidiscursive texture calls for the attention of the recipient, stimulates him intellectually, makes him a dialogue partner, very often it introduces a game between discourses (such as *The Holy Sinner* by Thomas Mann, *Jacques the Fatalist* by Denis Diderot, *If on a Winter's Night a Traveler* by Italo Calvino, or *Fantomas contra los vampiros multinacionales* Julio Cortázar) and confronts them dialogically.

Texture's function as a genreic information carrier is realized in the fact that every texture has characteristics that are indicators of formal affiliation of the text. This includes semiotic, medial and compositional features of texture elements that already at the level of perceptual reception, without penetrating the semantic layer of text, allow us to identify the text form (generic and typological affiliation of text).

A situation where semiotic tissue of text is not a transparent medium of textual meanings, but creates an additional message, the meaning of which usually come in the interpretative relationship with semantics of the text, describes the texture, which becomes a matter of superstructural texture. A good example of implementation of such function is provided by the concrete poetry, in which the verbal texture, beyond being a carrier of a textual meanings, is also an iconic text. The same happens in the case of works of digital art. In "TextRain" (Camille Utterback, Romy Achituv) letters arrange in words that are carriers of semantic meanings, but they are also carriers of the superstructural contents – letters, falling at the body of the receiver, are arranging themselves in words, indicating in a symbolic way the participation of culture user in shaping textual meanings and text itself.

In the digital space one of the most important functions of texture is the function of the text tool. That function is performed primarily by the texture elements belonging to the tool framing of text (elements of a graphic interface) but also the elements located in text plane (e.g., linked words, icons). The greater variety and variability of textual tools' forms, the lower their transparency. In turn, the repeatability of the same tools causes the receiver to become indifferent, makes them transparent for him.

In case of texture elements that are textual tools, where texture becomes a field of user's textual operations, his focus gets shifted from looking through texture to looking at it. As Bolter writes, this shift or rather oscillation between transparency and opacity, looking "through" and "at" was present already in the print culture, in modernist literature that was moving the focus from the text as a history to the text as a structure of allusions (Volter 2011: 185).

It is worth considering the relationship between the function of the text tool and metatextual function. Both are connected by the reference not to the presented world created by the text but to the text itself. But while metatext refers to the meanings – is anchored in the act of interpretation, becoming an interpretation made present, the function of action in hypertext refers above all to the tissue of text.

When confronted with the theory of speech acts, the function of text tool (action) invokes implementing acts – performative ones that not only do not subject to the criteria of veracity but also establish facts in reality. But while speech acts demonstrate how words refer to extra-linguistic reality, the function of operations shows how words and other meaningful text elements can operate with other words and other elements of texture. Activities in hypertext, such as moving, recalling, selecting, cutting and pasting are activated by the direct actions on the texture. In case of digital communication the arbitrary elements of texture (words, icons) are stamped with function of meaning causing within the text. This makes it possible to speak about specific intratextual communication – in which communicational interactions between the texture elements within a single text take place.

The way of existence of texture in the literary hypertext leads to considerations regarding the category of **intratextuality**. The possibility of breaking apart the textual elements (atomization) setting them in motion, connecting them and hypertextually bonding reveals intratextual relations – interactions regarding elements within the text. With the development of digital communication (also digital art) the **microcosm of text** grows as well and its elements are set in motion of interaction. Microcosm of the text can be described in a confrontation with its macrocosm, which is undoubtedly constituted by the intertextual relationships – all forms of "going beyond" an individual text, establishing relationships with the other text. The example of intertextual practices, which participate in creation of text's macrocosm, are all structures of textual relations: translations, adaptations, quotations, paraphrases, allusions, parodies, travesties, pastiche – and both ones regarding content elements of text and formal elements (textual structures).

The function of communication subject is connected with text tool function. It is realized in participation in dialogical relations with the user and is inscribed into texture of programmed and simulated activity of text as a dialogical partner, interlocutor. Such dialogue is established by the rules governing specific textual form: it requires user to know the rules of using the digital texture.

The hypertext texture can cumulate functions listed above. This is especially true in the area of art open to multiple interpretations. In the literary hypertext Blueberries by Susan Gibb the words-links are transparent carriers of meanings, but at the same time its transparency is limited by the mobile color fluctuating under the influence of user's actions. Iconic elements are creating texture build up on the word, they create text of metaphoric value. Violet is associated with the image of berries appearing in the memories of heroine and the memory of sexual abuse back in childhood that is associated with them. The change in words' color into grey (after clicking them) is the symbol of futility of efforts leading to erasing of the traumatic memories. Linked words function as a medium of meanings, matter of superstructural texture and text tool. Accumulation of the texture functions, some of which are related to transparency (function of the medium of meanings) and others, on the contrary, are limiting it (a metatextual function) and cause some kind of tension, semantic and syntactic game, in which word labeled with many functions acquires the homonym status.

Semantization or even fabulariztion of semiotic tissue of text makes reading a direct experience of the presented world. Tissue of text is not a neutral medium, but a place where plot is present. The plot becomes apparent in the writing signs – in Blueberries the violet and grey words are signs of traumatic events from childhood that cannot be erased.

Even more clear exmaple of writing with body, engaging there receiver's body in texture is provided by the spacial projects – the already mentioned *TexRain* (Camille Utterback, Romy Achituv from 1999), project that is an adaptation of Zimroth's poem and inspired by concrete poetry of Appolinaire (*Il pleut* poem form 1918) or *Still Standing* (Bruno Nadeau, Jason E. Lewis from 2005)[6]. In *Tex Rain* touching letters, words, influencing their shape, the appearance of text are elements of designed user's activity. Kinetic units of text – words, letters are revealing new possibilities of meaning creation for language, writing seen as the tissue of text. While

---

[6] Both projects were analyzed by Roberto Simanowski in the context of crossing generic boundaries and playing with text (Simanowski 2007: 35–53). The *TextRain* project was analyzed also by Jay David Bolter and Diane Gromala (Bolter, Gromala 2005: 12–15).

Apollinaire in his *Il pleut* was performing reification or even iconization of words, drawing with them their meanings (rainfall painted with the word "it rains"); Utterback and Achituv are breaking words apart, saturating falling letters, words fragments with associations connected with rain. Words of the poem are becoming a rain itself. While Apollinaire's reader had to see the rain painted with word, now he has to experience the text falling with rain. Digital art is creating an intertextual **kinetic metaphor**.

The reception of a literary work means experiencing it in a physical way. It happens in interaction with texture in the process of meaning creation – reading again becomes writing. This time in the sphere of texture. In the sphere of interpretation – the authors are intentionally inscribing contextuality into the reading process. Construction of meanings has to happen in confrontation of digital project and works of Apollinaire'a and Zimroth but also in the static printed word and movable word in the digital sphere as well as experience of sense and experience of texture (in the poem by Zimroth appears a motif regarding conversation of two people that is the conversation including language of the body and language of words). In this context the reading becomes not only writing but also overwriting of meanings created as a result of confrontation between the meanings of various works, also, it becomes the experience of texture, mutual interaction of user and texture. It's stamping and constructing (or maybe cognizing) your own identity on a text in contact with the literary work.

***

In sphere of digital art signs of writing especially easily acquire status of textual actions. Subjected to iconization at the same time they become object and place of an experiment, experience of textual matter. The center of gravity is shifted from being transparent medium of content to being the matter of text – the matter to shape almost like in the case of sculpture.

Michaelo Angelo could see a shape of form in the marble blocks, a form that he – as he used to say – was only releasing from its imprisonment. Contemporary digital artists, including creators of digital literature, are noticing in letters, words, phrases a coexistence of many possible texts carrying various meanings that come together in a dialogue and are confronting each other. In such situation writing is coding multiplicity of meanings in texture, meanings that so far in traditional text could appear only in the situation of reading – at the level of interpretation. It's acknowledgment of the user's **rights to co-creation of text already at level of its tissue;** extraction of various forms trapped in texture.

Digital art by making us co-creators of text appearing on the screen allows us to redefine our identity, extract it or reconstruct in the process of text co-creation. It enables us to imprint the trace of our own identity on texture. Furthermore, by engaging us both intellectually and physically in text experiencing, it proves that the famous opposition of culture and nature is simple misunderstanding. Cultural nature of a man described by humanists is natural to us in the highest degree – and certainly not less natural and linked with corporeality just like biological aspect.

Translated by Marek Ostrowski

Bibliography

Bolter Jay D. 2011, *Writing Space. Computers, Hypertext, and the Remediation of Print*, New York: Routledge.

Bolter Jay D., Gromala Diane 2005, *Windows and Mirrors. Interaction Design, Digital Art, and Myth of Transparency*, Cambridge MA: The MIT Press.

Culler Jonathan 2006, *The Literary in Theory*, Stanford CA: Stanford University Press.

Dąbrowski Mieczysław, ed. 2011, *Komparatystyka dla humanistów*, Warsaw: Wydawnictwo Uniwersytetu Warszawskiego.

Eriksen Thomas H. 2001, *Tyranny of the Moment. Fast and Slow Time in the Information Age*, London: Pluto Press.

Genette Gérard 1982, *Palimpsests. La littérature au second degree*, Paris: Éditions du Seuil.

Kerckhove Derrick de 1985, *The Skin of Culture. Investigating the Electronic Reality*, Toronto: Kogan Page Ltd.

Knapp Steven 1993, *Literary Interest: The Limits of Anti-Formalism*, Cambridge MA: Harvard University Press.

Murray Janet 1997, *Hamlet on the Holodeck: The Future of Narrative in Cyberspace*, Cambridge MA: The MIT Press.

Ryan Marie-Laure 2001, *Narrative as Virtual Reality. Immersion and Interactivity in Literature and Electronic Media*, Baltimore and London: The Johns Hopkins University Press.

Simanowski Roberto 2007, *Digital Art and Meaning, Reading Kinetic Poetry, Text Machines, Mapping Art., and Interactive Installation*, Minneapolis – London: University of Minnesota Press.

Gwóźdź Andrzej, ed. 2001, *Widzieć, myśleć, być. Technologie mediów*, Kraków: Universitas.

http://www.youtube.com/watch?v=CamrO-9jjQo&list=PL0AE2A2A6C6249B3C

http://www.youtube.com/watch?v=heMgid4rkzU

http://www.youtube.com/watch?v=oxbHrjoNfkA

Marta Rakoczy*

University of Warsaw

TEXT, WRITING, SCHOOL IN ANTHROPOLOGICAL PERSPECTIVE

Abstract

This paper attempts to reveal anthropological structures in the following categories: text and writing; the categories that nowadays require cultural, historical and institutional relativization. The paradigm being maintained is that writing is a mental, individualistic creation and a freely chosen way of life which is a result of late modernity. Moreover, even today it is not the only paradigm and nor is it universally acceptable. This is emphasized and developed upon in the text by using examples from current school exercise books. School – as the main institution of literate initiation, where one experiences one'sfirst mass contact with literature – is an institution in which the practice of writing is regulated by school breaks and is specifically managed for capitalist society's dual division of time. Writing is specifically a tool which is a well-defined, perceptual and social discipline. However, this discipline does not exclude creativity, as long as we go by its late-modern definition.

Key words: text and writing, anthropological perspective, school, creation, exercise books

> What we understand first in discourse, as Paul Ricoeur wrote in reference to Heidegger's *Being and Time*, is not another person, but a „pro-ject, that is, the outline of a new way of being in the world. Only writing […] in freeing itself, not only from its author and from its original audience, but from the narrowness of the dialogical situation, reveals this destination of discourse as projecting the world (Paul Ricoeur 1976: 37). Writing as technology, as Walter J. Ong wrote, „is utterly invaluable and indeed essential for the realization of Fuller, interior, human potentials" […] Writing heightens consciousness. […] The use of technology can enrich the human psyche, enlarge the human spirit, intensify its interior life (Ong 1991: 82–83).

---

* Faculty of Polish Studies, Univeristy of Warsaw, ul. Krakowskie Przedmieście 26/28, 00-927 Warsaw e-mail: marta.rakoczy@wp.pl

Both cited authors have had a distinct impact on both literary studies and the theory of literacy as treated as a crucial medium for Western modernity. Both of them were zealous apologists of cultural institutions such as philosophy and literature, whose modern forms have had a decisive impact on their understanding of writing. In this article, it is argued that their understanding of writing as a creative and individualistic activity, enabling one to work in a new and more conscious way in cultural reality, and taking place between the disembodied text and the equally disembodied mind, demands relativization. This understanding is rather a result of historically and socially specific cultural conditions rather than a recognition of the very nature of writing. Therefore the aim is to examine the problems of Ricoeur's and Ong's phenomenology of writing. And consequently, to outline new, non-essentialist ways of regarding the relationship between writing, creativity and experience.

In order to bring out the relationship between writing, creating and experience, a relationship that cannot be subjected to any essentialist characteristics, it is necessary to take an anthropological examination of different practices of writing, especially their institutional, spatial, temporal and physical contexts. To put it more specifically, it is essential to begin a debate over school literate practices, practices that enable one to see in writing something more than free creativeness based on the work of an individual mind. Of course, if seen from the perspective of a participant of contemporary culture, writing texts is often associated with creativeness and a freely chosen way of life; with literary and non-literary practices, such as writing blogs, tweets or drawing graffiti. This connection is reflected in dictionaries of contemporary Polish, in which writing is defined primarily as "forming, recognizing their thoughts in writing", "communicating" as well as "creating", recording in writing literary, scientific works, composing". Only one of the four meanings mentioned these days by the dictionaries refers to the materiality and corporeality of writing, defining writing as: "plotting on paper or other material of graphic characters by hand or by copying them with machines". Others define writing by making a reference to its mental or "creative" correlates, associated with a particular communication effect, including in particular the creation of "scientific or literary works" that in the western world establishes writing as a subject of remarkable cultural ennoblement (Mały Słownik Języka Polskiego 1996: 626). In other words, writing is understood as primarily an individualistic and mental activity. The labor of an individual's mind is bound mainly with institutions in the arts and sciences, and is regarded as a prerequisite for any creativity.

It should be noticed that contemporary definitions of the word "write", in contrast to older ones, clearly separate writing from drawing. According to today's linguistic intuitions, the first one is rather opposed to the old sense of the verb "write", namely "to paint, draw, decorate with colorful strips-characters" (Bankowski 2000: 587). What becomes the medium for formation of thought as well as for communication and literate creativity are words deposited in a series of characters, but not in a line, a shape, color or a hand gesture. The very act of writing is denoted as a disembodied action which happens between an individual's mind, words and a graphic mark, whose materiality is clearly marginalized. A similar elimination of physicality and materiality occurs in terms of definitions of writing, which state, for instance, that the latter is "a form of human communication by means of a set of visible marks related, by convention, to some particular, structural level of language" (http://www.britannica.com/search?query=writing, 20.02.14) or "a system of signs, used for preserving or replacing spoken language by writing" (Encyklopedia PWN 1985: 548). Writing is reduced therefore to specific content and is specific, it is detached from body and matter, it is visual and clear. To the same extent the separation from bodily and material practices develops "text" which is defined by modern dictionaries as "the verbal content of any oral or written statements" (Mały Słownik Języka Polskiego 1996: 935).

Such a conceptualization of writing is the result of a long and varied cultural evolution but is dependent on cultural background. In order to illustrate the fact, it is useful to recall André Leroi – Gourhan, who, in contrast to literacy theorists such as Walter J. Ong, analyzed the origins of alphabetic writing not so much in terms of creation of the most economical system of representation, a system which allows, like other writing systems, to create "texts" in today's meaning of the word, as in terms of abandonment of the bodily and non-verbal specificity of prehistoric graphism. The latter, involving, *inter alia*, paintings on a rock, incisions on objects, as Leroi-Gourhan claimed in *Le Geste et la parole*, was based on a completely different form of alphabetic writing, which was radiant, non-linear and consisted of the rhythmic organization of meanings (Leroi – Gourhan 1964–1965). It was not an "autonomous discourse" in the sense employed by Ong, not a text equipped with meaning irrespective of the context of its implementation. It was not a text at all, but a trace of action, a phenomenon, whose culmination was a process which comprehensively involved a human being, rather than its intellectual and communicative effect.

Graphism, it should be added, subsequently originated in western culture. The separation of writing and drawing were extraneous to each other; separation which is still absent in the cultures of the Far East, where both actions, as Tim Ingold notes in the book *Lines. A Brief History*, used the same materials and similar criteria for evaluation (Ingold 2007: 131–136). The fact that there was no clear distinction between these actions was the cause, according to Leroi – Gourhan, of the fact that graphism was independent with respect to verbal language, breaking through its limitations as a tool of expression. Expression, which was not identified with the expression of thought, but with the medium of overall, cognitive, emotional and bodily experience as an alternative to the symbolism of speech. Indeed, relationships between thoughts and words and words and graphic signs, as we know already from the works of Lev Vygotsky, are not universal and all the more they are not innate (Vygotsky 1989: 407). They have a cultural character and this means that they are subjected to historical and social programming.

In other words, the changing of historical, cultural and institutional contexts allows one to see the specificity of the modern conceptualization of "writing" and "text". This means that the category of creativity is itself poblematic. As noted by Elisabeth Hallam and Tim Ingold in the introduction to the book *Creativity and Cultural Improvisation*, categorization currently prevails as part of the global consumption market where creativity "begins to be seen as the main driving force of economic growth and social well-being", appearing in the titles of numerous scientific books, especially relating to business, education and management (quotation from Hallam, Ingold 2007: 2). The authors discuss two opposing conditions as ways to understand creativity which are imposed by specific cultural and historical conditions, namely: innovation and improvisation (2007: 1–24). The first one consists of identifying creativity with individuality, the breaking of social conventions, expression, and also with a radical rejection of the past. An identification such as this is a typical product of Western modernity, one that promotes individualism, one that gives a clear dichotomy of the social and individual as well as the positive valuation of the present, the future and change. It is aimed at effect and is not transparent. As Hallam and Ingold write:

According to these authors, the category of creativity should be widened significantly, and should not be identified withunconventionality but rather with improvisation. Improvisation does not have to mean deliberate, aimed at change, or a transgression of rules. It is the essence of every act, because there is no reproductively implemented scenario of cultural and social life (Hallam, Ingold 2007: 1). Each system of conventions only provides general guidelines that one should put into context and adapt to a particular situation which is always unique (Hallam, Ingold 2007: 2). The identification of creativity and improvisation as stipulated by the authors is undistinguishably about understanding creativity as a process: a kind of "happening" that goes on not so much in the mind of an individual but in the mutual interaction between things endowed with agency, people and the environment. It allows one to see the creative potential in such inconspicuous activities like walking on a crowded street, or, to focus on the practices of writing, filling in official forms, tax returns or workbooks.

Adherence to these methodological demands leads to many consequences. One of those is the possibility of dethroning the modern institution of literature, to deprive it of a monopoly in the field of literate creativity (Karpowicz 2012: 36–49). Another consequence is a deeper, anthropological problematization of the categories such as text and writing, which are still largely seen as a reflection on literature understood in a modern way, yet criticized by Ingold.

By focusing on the concept of writing, for example in the culture of ancient Greece the verb *graphein* originally meant scraping letters, the word associated with writing is not so much an intellectual activity but a physical activity which required a great amount of effort to work, using a sharp tool with tough materials. (Harris 1986: 29). Similarly, in ancient Egypt, where the occupation of a writer or a scribe was contrasted with the occupation of a farmer or a craftsman, not because it was identified with that of an artist, but as a labor less physically tiring, cleaner and giving more social advantages (Kuckenburg 2006: 210).

Similar relativization can be applied to the category of text, whose cultural and historical concretizations do not come under one particular definition (Majewski 2013: 31–32). Apart from the fact that the category relates us to so many different artifacts such as literary texts, recipes, tombstone inscriptions or spontaneous writings on a wall, one should remember that for many centuries and in many institutional and cultural contexts texts were usually heard collectively in a controlled way rather than read silently by a single and relatively free reader. They were not subjected to a more or less arbitrary process of interpretation. They were rather subjected to memorizing, and to the internalization of patterns and values that they comprised of. For example, in the time of Plato, materials for learning how to read and write the first strings of letters were pieces of classical poetry. Reading those had nothing in common with interpretation as in today's school meaning, which is a reconstruction of an authorial intention accompanying the text and nor with a more modern, though originating in medieval biblical hermeneutics, way of reading (Olson 2011). Text primarily served at moralizing aims, while simultaneously being an accumulation of positive patterns (Ford 2003: 26).

Despite the late-modern discourse which associates writing as a free activity, in particular with a process which is not so much physical as mental, and one which consists of the direct externalization of thoughts on to paper, writing in ancient Greece was accompanied by completely different connotations. Writing was often associated as an activity that was not only physical, but also and most of all, socially disciplining. Writing did not involve creation in silent thought but specified, subsequently externalized contents, which comprised of physically reproducing ready-made graphical forms. Traces of this way of thinking can be found in Plato's *Protagoras*, where he compares state law enforcement with enforcing a line that a teacher sketches on a plate for a child who is learning how to write its first letters. The link between the requirements of the law and the letters written by a teacher, letters which the child does not write by himself but which he copies with his own hands and the accompanying note, stating that "he who transgresses them, is to be corrected ", are quite significant (Plato's *Protagoras*: 326e). Plotting the first letter is clearly opposed to the concept of free artistic and intellectual activities and identified with the disciplining reproduction of an imposed pattern. Needless to say, that this way of understanding writing is positively valued by Plato. Identifying it with a style of life would have been, for Plato, not only incomprehensible, but simply disastrous.

Therefore, the idea of writing as creating in silent thought and a freely chosen lifestyle is a fruit of modernity. Evidently the historical and cultural reasons for this are complex. Firstly, the identification of writing as primarily a mental activity, with direct conversation with one's own mind transferred to paper, was, at least in part, the result of a specified conception in order to facilitate writing, namelystationery which reduced the physical act of writing in order to benefit intellectual activities. It should be kept in mind that writing in ancient times was quite hard work, requiring not only the drafting of letters on parchment, a resistant material, but also scraping and smoothing the latter (Ingold 2007: 142–143). Thus, in the time of Thomas Aquinas intellectual creation was rather associated with speaking/dictating than with standalone writing; a noteworthy example of the fact is *Summa*, being dictated by him.

Additionally, the concept of writing understood as creativity required a particular concept of text, based on the assumption that the latter is a representation of an individual mind, not memory support; such a concept reached its apogee in the modern age (Olson 2011: 273–293). In the days of Plato reading and writing were not activities involved with the reproduction of texts as external and independent media. It was a way of creating and reconstructing supports for memory, which means that they were to be, under the attention of authority, internalized, and used later in various social and political contexts associated with oral communication oriented at the community of polis and its moral bonds (Ford 2003: 25–26). The concept of text as a representation required the development of their own graphic and semantic devices allowing independently, and therefore in the absence of its author and the institutions responsible for the "correct" understanding, to interpret a text in terms of its illocutionary power. This is associated with Walter J. Ong's observations that writing a text that "speaks for itself" (Ong 2011: 131–132) was not present at the beginnings of literacy. Such an ideal would have required finding that writing is not at all a perfect tool for the representation of spoken language. Consequently it requires the invention of punctuation, a theory of mind accompanied by adequate vocabulary which signals the intentions of the author and a dictionary would be used containing verbs such as "assume", "doubt", "argue", " assume ", etc. (Olson 2011: 180).

The transition from the notion of a text as memory support to the notion of the latter as representation is clear enough, especially if we compare medieval and modern tracts. If the case is that medieval *questiones* retain agonic structure of medieval scholastic debates and vague references to other texts, it is not only a result of the form as such. There are a small number which are preserved, the manuscripts are without pagination and thus preven us from precisely locating citations. This is primarily the result of the fact that the participants of those discussions shared the same memory, that they had internalized those texts. Modern tracts have lost their agonic structure, since they are imitations of a process undergone in an individual's mind rather than a course of common conversation and include precise references to other texts: references possible in print culture only, but also caused by the fact that a writer and a reader do not share any common memory. They are organized in a way that is proof of following the idea of a text understood as a representation, a text made for analytical, independent reading, meaningful in the absence of the author and any institutionalized interpretative community. Therefore a paradigmatic contemporary tract, Spinoza's *Ethics, Demonstrated in Geometrical Order*, begins with the definition of basic concepts and axioms supporting further reasoning and then a series of statements accompanied by evidence, possible explanations and footnotes that support the reading of the main text. It is no coincidence that it also contains many references intrinsic to the text, providing the reader with detailed ways enabling them to navigate independently through the text. Thus the text is understood as the result of "creative" activity and exceeds the tradition of single minded labour.

It is worth noting that the modern identification of writing as individualistic, or rather understood as innovative, unfolding along the lines of creation and ultimately alongside lifestyle was related to the democratization of literacy. In the Middle Ages, when literacy was basically a monopoly of the clergy, serving mainly the dominant institutions such as the church or the state, it could not become a tool of individual expression. Of course, the aforementioned democratization cannot be explained exclusively by the emergence of print and individualism as a modern value. It cannot be explained even by the emergence, in the eighteenth and nineteenth centuries, of public literate education and this is because: firstly, in every European country literate education is often accompanied by other assumptions and values (Graff 1987b), and secondly, not always and not everywhere did democratization meant the concept of, as was already rasied herein as, writing as creativeness. For example, a very high level of literacy in eighteenth century Sweden certainly related to its democratization, the latter, however, did not entail any democratization of writing as an act of individual expression. Such literacy was achieved in the context of religious, created for the needs of the Protestant church, general education. What was emphasized was not writing as an act of creating definitive texts, but selective and controlled reading (reading the catechism, the Bible). Moreover, this kind of reading, we should add, favored memorizing certain content, rather than interpretation (Chartier, 2007: 455).

Moreover, although the identification of writing as an individualistic, mental and creative activity, involving a crossing of a certain textual tradition, is of late-modern origins, it has never been a binding identification in all late-modern cultural institutions. A good illustration of the fact are today's early-school practices of writing and communing with text. School, as the main institution of literate initiation, including the first mass contact with literature, is an institution in which the practices of writing have been, for a relatively long time, rather closer to ritual operations (Holthoon von 2007: 439). In this case communing with the text here does not involve free, solitary and critical reading. It consists of shared, strongly established, subjected to interpretative control and re-reading (Olson 2009: 571–572).

Let us examine early-school literate practices. Before the act of writing becomes a tool to generate one's own independent content, it must be internalized. This first exercise, of a remarkably carnal quality, is not socially neutral. For it consists in associating the activity of writing with a number of cultural meanings as well as values and forming a culturally specific kind of perception. This training, left out of the classical theory of literacy and research on the social functioning of texts, is associated with certain, culturally specific ways of attention management. As such, it influences the organization of subsequent experience.

It should be noted that in the case of graphomotor exercises, writing does not have the character of intentional communication, nor is it a tool for individual expression or individual thought. It is, inherently, a bodily function, precisely: an originator of the body to specific gestures. These gestures, like the ritual ones, are not yet an instrument of consciously achieving by an individual their own particular purposes. And as such, they are not so much instrumental as symbolic and theybecomes expressions of belonging to the world of adults: a token of literary competence as determinants of power and knowledge. Of course, the use of a strong anthropological tradition of categories of ritual to graphomotor exercise requires some justification. More precisely, it requires extraction from a classical and fairly narrow understanding of ritual as a reproductive, reserved for the sacred, primitive communities and involving more or less a mechanically reproduced tradition and phenomenon. After all, in broader and more frequently used terms, for example by Eric Rothenbuhler (Rothenbuhler 2003), and in relation to the school by Peter McLaren (McLaren 1986), ritual may be secular, modern and creative. For collective action which consists of, depending on the specifics of a particular situation, adhering to certain collectively codified rules does not preclude creativity as improvisation. On the contrary, it is a necessary condition.

Of course, the difference between literacy school rituals and traditional rituals is that participants of the former are subject to continuous, individual evaluation. This evaluation, however, also has a symbolic character. The entire process of training preserves the ritual character, because child activities are not undertaken due to the calculation of measures and targets, but for the reason that others do so, and "one should do so" because of exactly the same reasons that cause ritual actions of the adults. Performed as a part of initial education writing exercises are collective practices, embedded in non-neutral time and space. They are difficult to interpret, if we focus only on the manner in which they exercise the body and mind of a single child. Writing consists in collective actions carried out simultaneously in socially structured and hierarchical, subjected to supervisory authority, space. They are performed in time centrally regulated by bells, more precisely, by the dual division of time (work / lesson versus rest / pause), characteristic of capitalist society. It is not identical with a style of life, with the form of action characteristic of the modern individualism. Like any given ritual it serves, to recall Peter McLaren's expression, "psychosocial integration" (McLaren 1986: 45), to be exact: providing individual mental and bodily activities with common meter associated with evoking a certain symbolic sphere. Like any ritual, writing, in this case, is standardized and repeatable, consistent with ready-made, arbitrarily fixed scenarios. Last but not least it is a kind of performance. In contrast to performance art, it is not about showing individual competence. It is rather a bond-creating action, collectively evoking atoken of belonging to a particular community.

Graphomotor exercises have yet another function. They serve as a particular type of social programming of perception, and hence programming a certain kind of experience. More importantly, this kind of programming does not involve "knowledge that": explicit knowledge, linguistically articulated and revised in subsequent, non-school individual development, knowledge which is provided by reading at a later stage of education. It concerns, to use Michael Polanyi's category, tacit knowledge: embodied and not disclosing in any form of explicitly expressed patterns or values. Knowledge, which affects our experience, although does not allow to shape the latter more or less freely.

One of the key elements of graphomotor exercises is the acquisition of skills needed for accurately reproducing templates of each of the letters printed on the start line of the workbook, and then independently imitated by a student. The method of acquiring this competence is not transparent, and what is interesting, it varies depending on the type of writing and the accompanying cultural area. For values preferred in the western, alphabet calligraphy, which is based on a certain kind of hand-eye coordination are, as Tim Ingold points out, constancy, stability and eye-centering.

It is clear when school Western calligraphy is compared with Chinese calligraphy. As in the latter, children learn to perform an ideogram performing the associated hand gesture in the air. These exercises in western schools are used only incidentally and much more difficulty is placed on the act of writing in motor, not visual, memory. In addition, classical Far Eastern calligraphy tracts teach that by observing things an excellent level of handwriting lines is possible to achieve. It is not aimed at modelling with a shape of an ideogram, a constant, enduring essence of the thing it denotes. The idea is to imitate with a hand gesture its mobility and volatility. This means that again, excellence in calligraphy is not a fixed formconnected to the product of writing. Intentional bodily expressions hidden behind, which seen from the point of view of western calligraphy is calligraphy that focuses on certain body disciplining, subordinated to the idea of visual precision and is something completely unnecessary (Ingold 2007: 131–136). From the point of view of the western literate initiation, Chinese calligraphers' words cited by Ingold, say how they attained perfection in performing certain ideograms by the gestural mimicking of the movement of flying birds, playing rats or a waterfall falling into the abyss seem completely incomprehensible (2007: 131–133). In western graphomotor activities a specific gesture itself is removed from the scope of intentional action. In contrast Far Eastern calligraphy becomes a transparent medium for producing/copying specific content, whilst in the previous one it is a non-transparent tool filled with content expression, and as such is subjected to intentional control and gradual improvement.

Of course, graphomotor exercises are hardly creative, if that term is to be reserved for innovative actions and understood in accordance with the modern and individualistic paradigm as criticized by Ingold. However, if we mean by creativeness improvisation, then we see that the performance of these exercises can be identified by creative adaptation to a specific situation and to the rules provided by an authority. As Hallam and Ingold write:

> In writing with the pen, nothing the tip save the movement of the hand and fingers with their characteristic penhold. The line rendered on paper is the trace of an ongoing gestural improvisation. Though we may have been taught the "correct" ways to form letters by copying models, a person's handwriting is as distinctive and recognizable an aspect of their being, as it issues forth into the world, as is their voice. […] The personal style is not planned or designed, but emerges through a history of improvisation, above all in finding ways to connect letters in the cursive script in the interest of speed and efficiency. In "joined –up" writing we fashion the joins, each in our own way, as we go along. (Hallam, Ingold 2007: 13)

Therefore the practices used in early school education, are practices of embodiment which can hardly be recognized as passive practices of reproduction. Although not a 'lifestyle', they remain a tool for creating and maintaining a particular social and perceptual experience.

In fact, insight into the specifics of the early-school literacy practices can not tell us what is writing as a specific cultural practice. On the contrary, it only allows us to problematize a number of his traditional definitions presented not only in Ong's and Ricoeur's writings, but also in popular thinking. There is, as I think, not one legitimate definition of writing, just as there is no single characteristic of his relationship with creativity, experience and individuality. There is rather a lot of literacy practices and its institutional contexts. Consequently, an understanding of the entire continuum of literacy policies and logics is waiting for the next generation of lieracy anthropologists.

Bibliography

Antropologia pisma. Od teorii do praktyki 2010, eds. P. Artières, P. Rodak, Warsaw: Wydawnictwa Uniwersytetu Warszawskiego.

Bańkowski Andrzej 2000, *Etymologiczny Słownik Języka Polskiego*, vol. 2, Warsaw: PWN.

Carruthers Mary J. 1990, *The Book of Memory: The Study of Memory in Medieval Culture*, Cambridge: Cambridge University Press.

Chartier Anne Marie 2009, *The Teaching of Literacy Skills in Western Europe. An Historical Perspective*, [in:] *Cambridge Handbook of Literacy*, ed. D. R. Olson, N. Torrance, Cambridge: Cambridge University Press.

Connerton Paul 2012, *Jak społeczeństwa pamiętają*, trans. M. Napiórkowski, Warsaw: Wydawnictwa Uniwersytetu Warszawskiego.

Creativity and Cultural Improvisation 2006, eds. T. Ingold, E. Hallam, New York-Oxford: Berg.

Encyclopedia Britannica, "Writing", (http://www.britannica.com/search?query=writing, entered 20.02.14).

Ford Andrew 2003, *Where Literacy Counts: Schooling*, [in:] *Writing Texts and the Rise of Literate Culture in Ancient Greece*, ed. Y. Harvey, Cambridge: Cambridge University Press.

Godlewski Grzegorz 2008, *Słowo – pismo – sztuka słowa. Perspektywy antropologiczne*, Warsaw: Wydawnictwa Uniwersytetu Warszawskiego.

Goody Jack 2012, *Mit, rytuał i oralność*, trans. O. Kaczmarek, Warsaw: Wydawnictwa Uniwersytetu Warszawskiego.

Goody Jack 2011, *Poskromienie myśli nieoswojonej*, trans. M. Szuster, Warsaw: PIW.

Goody Jack, Watt Ian 2007, *Następstwa piśmienności*, trans. J. Jaworska, [in:] *Almanach antropologiczny: oralność/ piśmienność*, eds. G. Godlewski, A. Karpowicz, I. Kurz, A. Mencwel, P. Rodak, Warsaw: Wydawnictwa Uniwersytetu Warszawskiego.

Goody Jack 2006, *Logika pisma a organizacja społeczeństwa*, trans. G. Godlewski, Warsaw: Wydawnictwa Uniwersytetu Warszawskiego.

Graff Harvey J. 1987, *The Legacies of Literacy: Continuities and Contradictions in Western Culture and Society*, Bloomington: Indiana University Press.

Graff Harvey J. 1979, *Literacy Myth: Literacy and Social Structure in the Nineteenth Century City*, New York: Academic Press.

Harris Roy 2009, *Rationality and the Literate Mind*, New York: Routledge.

Harris Roy 1986, *The Origin of Writing*, London: Duckworth.

Havelock Eric A. 2006, *Muza uczy się pisać. Rozważania o oralności i piśmienności w kulturze Zachodu*, trans. P. Majewski, Warsaw: Wydawnictwa Uniwersytetu Warszawskiego.

Havelock Eric A. 2007, *Przedmowa do Platona*, tłum. P. Majewski, Warsaw: Wydawnictwa Uniwersytetu Warszawskiego.

Holthoon von Frits 2009, *Literacy, Modernisation, Intellectual Community and Civil Society in Western World*, [in:] *Cambridge Handbook of Literacy*, eds. D. R. Olson, N. Torrance, Cambridge: Cambridge University Press.

Ingold Tim 2007, *Lines. A Brief History*, Routledge, Taylor & Francis Group, London, New York.

Ingold Tim 2000, *The Perception of the Environment. Essays on Livelihood, Dwelling and Skill*, London, New York: Routledge.

Karpowicz Agnieszka 2012, *Proza życia. Mowa, pismo, literatura*, Warsaw: Wydawnictwa Uniwersytetu Warszawskiego.

Kuckenburg Martin (2006), *Pierwsze słowo: narodziny mowy i pisma*, transl. B. Nowacki, PIW, Warszawa.

Leroi-Gourhan André 1964–65, *Le geste et la parole*, Paris: Albin Michel.

Majewski Paweł 2013, *Pismo, tekst, literatura. Praktyki piśmienne starożytnych Greków i matryca pamięci kulturowej Europejczyków*, Warsaw: Wydawnictwa Uniwersytetu Warszawskiego.

McLaren Peter 1986, *Schooling as a Ritual Performance: Towards a Political Economy of Educational Symbols and Gesture*, New York: Routledge & Kegan Paul.

Olson David R. 2011, *Papierowy świat. Pojęciowe i poznawcze implikacje piśmienności*, trans. M. Rakoczy, Warsaw: Wydawnictwa Uniwersytetu Warszawskiego.

Olson David R. 2009, *Literacy, Literacy Policy and the School*, [in:] *Cambridge Handbook of Literacy*, eds. D. R. Olson, N. Torrance, Cambridge: Cambridge University Press.

Ong Walter J. 1991, *Orality and Literacy. The Technologizing of the Word*, London, New York: Routledge & Kegan Paul.

Mały Słownik Języka Polskiego 1996, ed. E. Sobol, vol. 1, Warsaw: PWN.

Plato, *Protagoras*, http://www.gutenberg.org/files/1591/1591-h/1591-h.htm [entered: 20.02.14].

Ricoeur Paul 1976, *Interpretation Theory: Discourse and the Surplus of Meaning*, Fort Worth: Texas Christian University Press.

Rodak Paweł 2009, *Pismo, książka, lektura. Rozmowy: Le Goff, Chartier, Hebrard, Fabre, Lejeune*, Warsaw: Wydawnictwa Uniwersytetu Warszawskiego.

Rothenbuhler Eric 2003, *Komunikacja rytualna. Od rozmowy codziennej do ceremonii medialnej*, trans. J. Barański, Cracow: Wydawnictwo Uniwersytetu Jagiellońskiego.

The National Literacy Campaignes. Historical and Comparative Perspectives 1987, eds. Harvey J. Graff, R. F. Arnove, New York: Springer.

Vandendorpe Christian 2008, *Od papirusu do hipertekstu, Esej o przemianach tekstu i lektury*, trans. A. Sawisz, Warsaw: Wydawnictwa Uniwersytetu Warszawskiego.

Lidia Gąsowska*
University of Warmia and Mazury

THE PRACTICE OF WRITING FAN FICTION: A FAN FICTION WRITER'S TUTORIAL

Abstract
The aim of this article is to define fanfiction as a cultural phenomenon rooted in the literary field and created by readers in relation to works published and recognized by the audience itself. Fan confabulation, dreams and planned intrigue is supported by techniques created by the use of new media and aesthetics expressinga desire for brevity, and on the other hand – communication ecstasy. Fanfics creation may be a unique literary experience which also includes debates and discussions as well as the exchange of information on literary forums and chat rooms. It forms a part of the sphere of cultural participation mediated by the media.

Key words: fanfiction, practice of writing, media, new media, readers

The practice of writing fan fiction and tutorials for fan fiction writers is situated in its broadest of contexts by the creation of fan fiction published on the Internet. It applies to the reception which the texts receive from the pop culture circle, often under the sign of the bestseller. These „steps" can be seen as the practice of reading and writing about the works published and recognized amongst the readers. The effects of fansite interpretive work exceed the wildest of expectations. Amateur short stories, poems, video clips which somehow spring up around the original work, complement it, function as errata or an afterword. Fansite text takes the quality of an individualized presentation of source reception and demonstrates its importance for the fan. It turns out that the prototype stirs the imagination

---

* University of Warmia and Mazury, Humanistic Faculty, ul. Kurta Obitza 1, 10-725 Olsztyn e-mail:lidiagasowska@wp.pl

to such an extent that one has to "rewrite" it anew, deepen the selected plots, unveil some mystery, change the viewpoint, accept a perspective of a supporting character. The author of fan fiction wishes to live the story once again but on his own terms, which creates a contextualized reading of the original.

The work within fan fiction is proof of creative and critical reading at the same time (Jenkins 2008, 12.09.2013). Its results – fan fiction stories, in the sense of – proof from reading, are posted on literary forums and in blogospheres. Fans – both authors and critics, have developed their own vocabulary to talk about them. In many of the comments it is visible how strongly the legitimacy of the text and its implied opposition to the source text is negotiated as well as how complex conditions a fan fiction text must meet. This complexity is nothing new. It is the transposition of the rules of the real world, on the correct, i.e. communicative writing, to the virtual world.

Fans of heroes from popular books (*Harry Potter* by JK Rowling and Stephenie Meyer's *Twilight*) and their stories, fans of the TV series, Japanese cartoons (anime) and comics (manga), video games, movies or current media phenomena (such as, for instance One Direction boys band or Justin Bieber) create their own completion, to participate personally in the events depicted in a favorite fictional world. They take handfuls of resources from pop culture combining the plots from various cultural texts, giving resistance to patriarchal visions of the world, opposing the mainstream ways of reading works.

Agata Wlodarczyk and Marta Tyminska perceive *fan fiction* as a literary and cultural phenomenon (Włodarczyk, Tymińska 2013, 12.09.2013). Also Przemysław Czaplinski, characterizing the community of fiction fans (Czapliński 2013), draws attention to the awakened cultural activity of the fandom. He combines its achievements with "poaching" (Jenkins 2007: 45), which has developed the skills of "grabbing the mass text " to create an alternative group of fans and most importantly, it created methods and tools to transform what is ready and set in "unfinished, incomplete, requiring creation" (Czapliński 2013, 12.09.2013.). Fans remake mass culture into their own mold trying to find the benefits for self-expression in it and recognizing the possibility of showing the power of their own imagination. They unscrupulously pirate, sometimes gracefully, sometimes awkwardly, violate the original text.

Fan confabulation, dreams and planned intrigue is supported by techniquess created by new media and aesthetics expressing a desire for brevity, and on the other hand – communication ecstasy. They become a popular form of expression and "infect" the ideas about literariness, creating a type of literature and reading what Mary Hopfinger calls "literary communication" (Hopfinger 2010: 47). This type of communication indicates the relationships of participants in the dialogue (in our sense – fans), their active participation in the media and literary culture (Internet access and writing fan fiction as coexistence) as well as in communication (multiple relationships on the Web). For the purposes of our argument communication presented by the researcher of the new media of communication will be called a fansite. I am going to introduce the requirements of such communication, showing the action of so called fans' analysis and the work of a beta-reader on the websites gathering fansite prose.

Anna Soczawa, a very young, only twelve years old (at her debut) writer, once said in an online interview: "I never tried to write by force. I was waiting for inspiration to come by itself and if it took too long, I attempted with fan fiction which always helps me" (Soczawa 2012). This confession, in various forms, appears as a topic on the forums devoted to amateur textual production. To simplify this, the most common tip and encouragement is this: if you do not know what to write, fan fiction can help you with ideas for "creating living characters" and "rapid action" (Schmidt 2008, 12.08.2013). Lively and enthusiastic audience reactions are usually transmitted in the form of an encryped entry, such as "Great .^.^ Quickly write 4 part. x]]]". Emoticons depicting cyber speech fulfill an ornamental as well as a rhetorical function and are posted in the comments to some fan fiction. Readers' waiting for the next chapters of the story written anew is the best motivation for continuing their work.

Fanfics creation may be a unique literary experience which also includes debates and discussions as well as the exchange of information on literary forums and chat rooms. It forms a part of the sphere of cultural participation mediated by the media. According to one of the online guides there are two factors which aid survival in the world of fandom: firstly, to write well and secondly, to create both an interesting and recognizable character – one that is compatible with the original (The Brat Queen 2013). Ironically, it might be summarized as: the first and the last step are the most difficult ones. Principles of text composition, knowledge of spelling rules and punctuation as well as the linguistic and stylistic correctness are rarely the strong points of fan fiction writers.

A text must meet various requirements in order to be placed on a proper site collecting fan fiction. Website administrators set the rules by themselves and they are often biased and therefore harm the linguistic or stylistic accuracy of fan fiction. The selection of texts as well as the control of them is not very good. A proofreader (called a beta-reader) attempts to bring law and order into the world of prose. Such a person is responsible for the text analysis for linguistic errors.Higher standards of grammar and style, therefore, depends on the skills of the proofreader. "Pirated academies of writing" suggest there are eight principles in order to create a good piece of fan fiction[1].

The first step (1) is the choice of a book, movie or TV series which stirs the imagination[2]. Step Two (2) concerns accurately rethinking of the construction of the presented world. One should keep in mind the principle that recipients of fan fiction are fans who are generally very familiar with the original characters, the source plots which we may want to parody and sometimes turn into a travesty or pastiche[3]. We must therefore rely on the characteristics of the created character on accessibility and read the canon of work, unless the story is set in an alternate world, but even there, if we use the canonical form of the work, which for example does not have legs, we should not write that the character "was kneeling" or "had his or her feet cold" (Leavell [Ms. Nitpicker] 2002, 12.09.2013). These are errors that even the best writers have not avoided. Moreover, fans know other people's amateur stories very well, hence the principle of a fanfictioner, both a passive reader and an active writer, is to read and comment. That also leads to learn from the mistakes made by others, from "ruined" and inept stories posted on the Web (Schmidt 2008, 12.08.2013). We should refer at least to some of the "ff" of the genre chosen by us (e.g. slash) because a lot of stories (many of the "paired" crafted characters and plots) have already been exhausted. Fanfics should not be duplicated – and cannot be "overwritten" because it defeats the purpose of fan fiction entertainment.

The fundamental principle is to include work which is appropriate to the fandom, hence an important role is assigned to searching for plots and formig an analysis. It is also important as to who will be the recipient: young people or adults. In the latter case, works which contain erotic scenes must be denoted.

---

[1] *How to Write a Fanfiction*, http://www.wikihow.com/Write-a-Fanfiction, [02.06.2013]. cf. L. Gąsowska, *Moda na fan fiction, czyli jak fan tworzy fikcję i jak jej używa*, [in:] *Mody w kulturze i literaturze popularnej* 2011.

[2] "It can be anything – from your current favorite paperback novel to the old TV cartoons you used to watch as a child", *How to Write a Fanfiction*, http://www.wikihow.com/Write-a-Fanfiction.

[3] "Remember – people read fanfiction because they are fans of the original work, and they would like it to be accurate to the original work – otherwise known as «canon» fanfiction", Ibidem.

Step three (3) is the selection of a character that we want to "fanficate". This can be a hero borrowed "at a source", but we can try to change its characteristics, in other words, we can build the so-called *out of character* (OOC in the language of fandoms – these acronyms frequently occurring in "fans' speech" are a contribution to the thesis about the digitization of communication on the Internet) (Kamińska 2011) – someone nice will become cruel or we can introduce a completely new, imaginary character – original character (in the language of fandoms – OC). At this stage, one should avoid the creation of a type of great Mary Sue who can expose the writer to expressive criticism.

Step four (4) is to think about the content of a fanfic. Questions which create a fan's text can take the form: "What if ___ is not dead?", "Why ___ feels this to ___?", "What would happen if ___ married ___? We can set the story in our times, in the past or in the future, thus, adding new facts, changing the canon, we build an alternative world (*an alternative universe,* in the language of fandoms – AU).

Step Five (5) – is to form the mood of the story. This principle might be understood as generating a background in which everything will be presented, additionally it will allow the text to direct its interpretation. Of course it all depends on the creator of *fan fiction* as to whether it will be dark or joyful.

Step Six (6) – "Start writing!" This tip means preparing a plan or at least a sketch of the plot and selecting the viewpoint, whether we are going to engage emotionally in the story and choose the creation of a first-person narrator or whether we will tell the story as an event by keeping a distance.

Step Seven (7) – self-correction, and/or using a beta- reader is one of the best methods. One should always make sure that the story is written well which means answering the question as to whether we edited spelling and grammatical errors. The practice of publishing grammatically or stylistically underdeveloped stories on the Internet is frowned upon. Sometimes it is sufficient that the work submitted for online publication is checked by a friend or another writer who might have a good, critical look at the whole text. An additional tip is: always listen to the two types of comments to your fan fiction: those which are extremely flattering as well as those which are disapproving.

Step Eight (8) – publication in the fandom. The author of the "eight-steps" tutorial *How to Write a Fanfiction* reminds writers that fanfics exist because there are fans who want to read them, therefore, it is a good idea to sign your work. It is in accordance with a rule: "now that you put effort into writing this, be responsible" (Leavell 2002, 12.09.2013). If fanfic is good, then comes the creation of a writing brand and its reputation in an amateurs' production.

These skills are useful in any type of critical reading and analysis, including academic exegesis of the literature. Writing fan fiction on the Web arouses interest in literary analysis and comments which can more or less be considered professional streamline the text's editing and facilitate its edition. Their reading imposes the idea of participation in the (un)ordinary workshops of creative writing. Unfortunately, the practice of fan fiction also permits so-called scribblers.

It is hard to argue with the thesis that a significant part of fan fictions is a literary "waste", but if only the reader or the pragmatically oriented author are willing to devote some time for searching, then they can find examples which surprise – even leave behind professionally published works. Moreover, it must be remembered that the appearance of what may be considered general ("all fanfics are graphomania") and herding (how one can be moved by the "scribbling of a school-girl" or by the view of a pink unicorn kicking in the moonlight as a *fan art*), will lead every phenomenon to banality.

When expanding the tutorial, we learn about the existence of other, non-negotiable basics such as this, that the spelling of the name of the main character should be fixed (Schmidt 2008, 21.08.2013)[4]. Further, that the description must be attractive and appealing with its richness of detail. One of the tips is: "Readers do not know what is going on in your mind. The more adjectives you provide, the more they will «see» what you think" (Schmidt 2008, 21.08.2013). On English websites there is a piece of advice to post information before the text that we do not expect financial payments for "ff" written and published on the Web.

Another piece of advice relates to the linguistic construction of fanfics of which in this field there are indeed the most failures. Some fanfics are simply impossible to be read out by sensitive recipients. Lazy and ignorant authors will be quickly reprimanded or even excluded from the circle of "ff" writers, but bad rumors that they are ungrammatical and misspelled "nonsense" will remain.

Many tips apply to the construction of a dialogue which should be learnt from the masters, not the other fans. Characters should speak a liv-

---

[4] "Give each character a name that starts with a different letter of the alphabet. This helps the reader keep them separate. A useful technique for this is to write the alphabet vertically down a sheet of paper and create a last name starting with each letter. Repeat this process for first names. If you run out of letters you've got too many characters" (Schmidt 2008: 4).

ing language, they cannot be as if made of "paper". While giving tips to the authors who are the beginners of "ff ", they warn:

"Remember that in real life we use many abbreviations and slang and seldom we give long and heavy lectures in fancy terminology to our interlocutors" (Schmidt 2008, 21.08.2013). Besides, one should use correct and complete sentences. Sentences vary in length. Keep long ramblings for "people sitting in the evening by the fire" but when we create the sequence of fights or a chase, we need to add variety and boost our story with single, short sentences which depict uncertainty and rapid action (Schmidt 2008, 21.08.2013).

It is good to pay attention to two simple messages which are presented to the participants of the network workshops who write fan fiction: "Do not tell us what happened – show us" and "Avoid telling us too much" (Schmidt 2008, 21.08.2013). The first piece of advice is about a construction of a dialogue and the description of an action[5]. If our hero is to play the role of an intermediary, we must provide readers with the knowledge on what was his reaction to the news about the mission, show his feelings and present them through facial expressions or body language. The reader must know the answer to the question whether the hero had any doubts about the participation. The author should know what the character will tell when he arrives at the destination. Should he bring something from there? Will he be armed? Is he going to have a long conversation there? Is he angry, amused or worried? "Give us the whole scene instead of a few summarizing sentences" (Leavell 2002, 12.09.2013).

In Polish fanfics there are often blatant phrases such as: "[…] Brown-haired [LG] could not resist and grabbed [Naruto – LG] the front of his T-shirt", "blonde's mouth [LG] slammed on her neck with gentle kisses and marked it with red dots from time to time" (Rebelos). The nouns which refer to the color of the heroes' hair are an awkward attempt to avoid repetition and reference to significant elements of the canonical story from which the protagonists were taken or they are a calque (a loan translation) from the English language such as "the small brunette said look at the blond" (Ritszka and Hoshi) and then in translation their authors miss the linguistic feeling because, as Ms. Nitpicker would write this, (in Polish this phrase would mean "Ms. Seeker Holes in the Whole" or "Mrs. Biting"): "And since when blond hair has any importance when you want to show your feelings?" (Leavell 2002).

---

[5] "Don't TELL us what happened –SHOW us, with dialogue and action", J. Leavell [Ms. Nitpicker], *How to Write Almost Readable Fan Fiction*.

If a fanfic takes place in a haunted house, "one doesn't have to devote a few pages to the description of its four walls"[6]. Readers usually ignore boring and long passages. Let the atmosphere of terror increase with the plot development and the found secret documents relating to the act of home ownership, mysterious e -mails, silent phone calls, chats with the neighbors will tell more about the place than the static written presentation on a number of pages, as it is advised by Ms. Nitpicker on the page bearing a suggestive title which can be translated in this way: How to write almost good fanfics or How to write almost readable fan fiction (in the original: *How to Write Almost Readable Fan Fiction*). We also learn that you should write in such a way so that the story is understood. You should avoid the arguments of the Old Testament as who was whose son. And of course you have to remember that dialogues are good "scissors" for a description that is too long (Leavell 2002, 12.09.2013).

A scenes feature should be constructed in such a way so that the reader knows where and when the hero is and at what time the action takes place. If the scene is set in an old warehouse, it is good to write how to get there and give details which appeal to our senses, which would remind us of the tips given to the Masters of Games in RPG s: What smell do we feel? What sounds do we hear? What do we see?

The meanings of words which are not understood should be avoided. At one of the meetings with Ewa Białołęcka, who is engaged in the *fan fiction* movement, gave an example of such a writing, when the hero of the story "has wrapped up tightly with ottoman "has actually cropped up". Probably at home, "he rests on a mantle", as Białołęcka summed it up.

Ms. Nitpicker warns us against mixed metaphors and similes which perplex, although at the same time it is recommended to move away from cliché phrases: "as white as a ghost", "as white as a sheet". The author of a set of guidelines deals with samples of failed metaphors: "the eyes that were like coals, casted ominous lightings" (Leavell 2002, 12.09.2013). He jokingly asks whether anybody has ever seen "a storm in the rack on the grill?" (Leavell 2002, 12.09.2013). One should also avoid descriptions in which the hero, though "stands still" is waving his hand. In the narrator's statements one should also be careful with the words which only sound smart. If "an opal eye" is to glance at us, it is good to make sure if it was not better to write just about blue eyes.

---

[6] "We live in fast-paced times where action is valued over description. Use action phases to describe instead of adjectives which just tell", (Schmidt 2008).

In the English language such an overblown style is called *purple prose*. If the story reads like a romance with lots of tousled hair, crimsons, deep sighs and looks, sulky mouth and eyes full of tears, certainly "the style is of purple color" (Leavell 2002, 12.09.2013). A quasi-baroque style of *purple prose* abounds in sentimental rhetorical figures, it does not avoid exaggeration, pathos and draws attention with flowery sentences and verbal ornamentation.

Fan fiction guides just repeat what is traditionally taught at schools. Writing should always be logical and coherent (a writer should not attack the reader's attention with "a sword from behind", as it is stated in a Polish tutorial *About Characters Description*[7], since each event has its cause) and he should not demonstrate general knowledge. Authors involved in the promotion of fan fiction often share information about a real police investigation or the rules prevailing in a real emergency room at the hospital, which helps to avoid the records that the hero shot in the heart and dead from a quarter suddenly woke up and fired at enemies (unless he is a zombie). The pages including the tips often post not only links to spell-checkers and grammar dictionaries but also to the dictionaries of the police or medical slang, the history of the Middle Ages "in a nutshell".

The writer needs to choose a point of view (POV – point of view, a common abbreviation used by fanfic writers), a specific character and stick to him in the presented scene. Traditionally speaking, it is he who enables us to look at the world through the character's eyes. Juggling with the points of view in prose (like overusing the passive voice) this introduces a general confusion and the text becomes "unbearable for reading". When "we become" Bella from *Twilight*, when we think and feel like she does, and if for a moment (in the same scene) we are moved into the world seen through the eyes of Edward, it is a nuisance for our reading memory. The addressee of such confusedly constructed scenes cannot familiarize with neither the one nor the other character since he does not remember anything of what they think, feel and see.

Typically, novice authors usually receive advice not to publish a story on the Web if they are not going to finish it. If we do not have an idea for an ending, we should not even start writing because it is as if one has promised children gifts for Christmas and has deceived them by "canceling Christmas" (Leavell 2002, 12.09.2013). Hence, practical and yet another linguistic and compositional advice is: "Sketch a plan of a whole, then you

---

[7] *O opisywaniu postaci*, http://piorem-feniksa.blog.onet.pl/2,ID300034991,index.html [12.05.2012].

can actually use the present tense" (Leavell 2002, 12.09.2013). The sequels are also inadvisable before completing the story since you do not have to shred the plots excessively.

"You have to read" – most of the tips that introduce beginners of fan fiction into the world of digital fanfic stories which can be summarized in this way. You do not have to read classics but something more than the presentation of a film on the Filmweb and a summary of a TV series. People who introduce beginners into writing "ff" ensure that "what you read, looks at you", so if we read clumsily written fanfics, we will be bad writers.

Practicing fan fiction, fans – creator and fans – critics come in a variety of modes: they praise, reprove their writing samples, share tips on the composition of "ff", analyze the language of the originals playing, with a smaller or greater freedom, the role of literary theorists (nonetheless, their quality and level are highly diverse, although sometimes it goes beyond information from secondary school.

The possibility of free amateur production corresponds to an artists' "desire", satisfies the needs of self-realization and provides cultural development. In order to create culture, you no longer have to be a traditional musician or a writer. A lot of its objects derive from people who simply think unconventionally and are often guided by their emotions in relation to some existing product of culture, they have not received formal artistic education but yet they act creatively. It is achieved owing to a number of technologies which enable them "to make movies", "to make music" and to distribute their "achievements ". Although the type of work in which these comments have been posted enforces the use of quotation marks as conceding that these are not, however, Great Works and Achievements, Movies and Music in the academic sense, nonetheless they deserve recognition since they are a manifestation of amateur culture, in the circle of which there are the living ideas of democratization, equality, egalitarianism, shared fun and carnival that are distractive from the deadly serious Reflections upon the Importance and Interpretation and equally serious sums received for Their Creation. It brings to mind an old right to mint coins in the kingdom. Only kings had such power and roughly from the early twentieth century, "each owner of Edison [phonograph brand – LG] or aeolian [pianola brand]" (Lessig 2008: 37–39).

These observations are confirmed by a smart thesis by Gregg Gillis who argues that we live in a "remix culture", or "In the times of appropriation when every primary school pupil has Photoshop and he can download the image of President George Bush and freely "convert" his face and then send its alteration to his friends" (Lessig 2008: 37–39). The practice of fan fiction is the essence of free culture of which the concepts have been convincingly laid out in a book by Lawrence Lessig. Ensuring that freedom is an important legal aspect when we think of fan fiction. According to Lessig, the creation of fan culture cannot be prohibited.

The existence of fan fiction tutorials is not merely a contribution to the thesis that Web 2.0 triggers creativity and certifies directly predominant "originality" and widely understood amateur "manufacturing". Users are becoming creators of online communications (Olcoń-Kubicka 2010: 129–132). They create the content of the pages, categorize them ("tag" the content) using keywords – they create their own names and unexpert categories by the *fanspeak*[8]. They exchange opinions on particularly valuable resources. They create knowledge (fanon) in a dynamic way, but from the bottom up, they decide what is valuable (the Facebook "Like").

The practice of fan fiction is logging in to the culture of participation which "the guides for writing" try to regulate. Participation blurs the line between the consumer and the producer. Manufacturers give consumers space so that they can create their own product. It sounds optimistic, although Andrew Keen is right when he presents this type of culture as an amateurishness, mass culture vulnerable to manipulation (Keen 2007). The scholar predicts a collapse of culture based on professionalism in which the truth disappears (good and beauty have landed on a scrap heap a long time ago), in which "intellectual theft and plagiarism lead to a disgrace of the idea of original authorship and intellectual property" Olcoń-Kubicka 2010: 129).

All stories prove one truth: humanity is a narrative genre, as Paul Levinson says. We differ from others by the fact that we are able to weave a plot with ourselves, what is more, we differ in the types of stories that we create. The material is everything that the external environment provides us with. If external stimulus is not enough, we add our expectations, more or less relevant concepts that are sufficient to complete the story (Levinson 2007: 47). Their detailing occurs due to the existence of literary experience in which allusions, both direct and indirect, play an important role. Looking at the literariness as at a mode of our internal phantasmatic life, it is somehow reminiscent of the fun in recalling to mind the specific

---

[8] E.g. OOC, POV, AU.

scenes from your favorite movies and processing their storylines (Janion 1991: 181). A story understood in such a way will never end. In the world of electronic media it has been accepted that the last version of a narrative is always true and the best but what if it is still the same story but told in a different language?

Electronic media are helpful and unusual as it is another tool to meet the need of storytelling, creating "new" stories, repeating the well-known ones and their transformations. Thanks to various games and with the support of personalization techniques, we may have the impression that we are the participants of the stories. Finally, as Anna Martuszewska puts it, it is a substantial element of the affinity of new media with literature (Martuszewska 2007: 34). It is a vast area for potential plots and the many possible ways of their presentation, which are created with the aid of means from many arts using computer technology[9].

Bibliography

Czapliński Przemysław 2013, „Piracka akademia pisania", *Gazeta Wyborcza*, http://wyborcza.pl/magazyn/1,130290,13257727,Piracka_akademia_pisania.html [14.03.2014].

Hopfinger Maryla 2010, *Literatura i media po 1989 roku*, Warsaw: Oficyna Naukowa.

Janion Maria 1991, *Projekt krytyki fantazmatycznej. Szkice o egzystencjach ludzi i duchów*, Warsaw: PEN.

Jenkins Henry 2008, *How Fan Fiction Can Teach Us a New Way to Read Moby-Dick (Part One)* http://henryjenkins.org/2008/08/how_fan_fiction_can_teach_us_a.html [14.03.2014].

Kamińska Magdalena 2011, *Niecne memy. Dwanaście wykładów o kulturze Internetu*, Poznan: Galeria Miejska Arsenał.

Keen Andrew 2007, *Kult amatora. Jak Internet niszczy kulturę?* trans. M. Bernatowicz, K. Topolska-Ghariani, Warsaw: WAiP.

Lessig Lawrence 2008, *Remiks. Aby sztuka i biznes rozkwitały w hybrydowej gospodarce*, trans. R. Próchniak, Warsaw: WAiP.

Leavell Jane [Ms. Nitpicker] 2010, *How to Write Almost Readable Fan Fiction* http://littlecalamity.tripod.com/HowTo2.html [14.03.2014].

Levinson Paul 2007, *Miękkie ostrze: Naturalna historia i przyszłość rewolucji informacyjnej*, trans. H. Jankowska, Warsaw: Spectrum.

---

[9] Fan fiction as a form of literature in its own right may have reached a watershed point, fueled in recent years by two factors: the seemingly bottomless devotion of fans of the Harry Potter and Twilight series, and technology. *Is Fan Fiction Ready to Go Mainstream Thanks to Fifty Shades of Grey?* http://www.tor.com/blogs/2012/03/is-fan-fiction-ready-to-go-mainstream-thanks-to-fifty-shades-of-grey [retrieved: 03.06.2012].

Martuszewska Anna 2008, *Radosne gry*. O grach/zabawach literackich, Gdańsk: słowo/obraz terytoria.

Olcoń-Kubicka Marta 2010, *Kulturowe wymiary Internetu*, [in:] *Wirtual. Czy nowy wspaniały świat?*, ed. K. Korab,Warsaw: Scholar.

Schmidt Wayne 2008. *Amateur to Amateur: A Non-expert's Guide to Expert Writing* http://www.waynesthisandthat.com/writefanfic.htm [14.03.2014].

Włodarczyk Agnieszka, Tymińska Marta 2013, *Fan fiction a literacka rewolucja fanowska. Próba charakterystyki zjawiska*, http://depot.ceon.pl/bitstream/handle/123456789/2252/Wlodarczyk_Tyminska_Fan_Fiction.pdf?sequence=1 [14.03.2014].

Agnieszka Oberc*

University of Wroclaw

I WRITE. YOU WRITE. THEY WRITE.
THE LITERARY WORKS OF FANDOM
AS A FACTOR IN INTEGRATING THE COMMUNITY

Abstract

Fanfiction is a fiction based on situations and characters that have been created by someone else. It is written by fans who use original texts to create their own art and culture. Writing fanfiction is something that fans do together. They discuss original texts, share their views and opinions about plot and characters, and create common interpretation that can be used by other fandom members. They also participate in creating new texts by commenting on fanficks published by other fans. Writing is not only a way to express fans opinions about their favourite books and shows, but also an opportunity to spend time with people sharing their interests. Analysis of fan-created texts shows not only its importance to individual fans, but also a vital role writing fanfiction plays in building fan communities and creating bonds between their members.

Key words: fanfiction, fan communities, fandom, writing and reading

Fanfiction is defined as stories set in worlds or using characters created by other authors. The fans write to fill the gaps in original texts, continue familiar stories, or create alternative universes. Most fanfiction is written within fandom, that is, communities of fans gathering around given works of fiction. Fandom is a subculture whose existence is based on other people's creations; the members take their creations, and use them to create their own artifacts, as well as build group traditions. The fans rewrite source texts to adapt them to their own needs; they actively participate

---

* Insitute of Polish Philology, University of Wrocław, Plac Nankiera 15, 50-140 Wrocław, e-mail: agnieszka.oberc@gmail.com

in culture, and create their own art. Fandom creativity can take different shapes and forms. Apart from works of fiction, one can find examples of visual arts ("fanart"), music ("filk"), and audiovisual arts ("fanvid"). Regardless of form, all fandom's creations are based on the source text, which is usually refered to as "canon". Canon is what binds fans as a group, giving them creative space within which they can act. In a way, canon is the source of group identity, since most fans identify with the groups within which they create. Saying: "I'm a Star Trek fan" means declaring oneself as a member of a group that has its unique traditions, different, for example, of those cultivated by Harry Potter fans – although, of course, there are many elements that both groups share.

While some people are satisfied with belonging to just one fandom, others eventually start discovering other texts as well. Through broadening the scope of canon texts, a fan becomes a member of a community described by Henry Jenkins as *media fandom* (Jenkins 1992: 1). What is specific to this group is focusing not on one text, but on multiple texts at once: movies, TV shows, anime, comics, computer games, and popular literature.

It is generally understood that one becomes a fan of a text due to genuine fascination. After familiarizing oneself with a text and becoming drawn to it, a potential fandom member starts seeking contacts with other enthusiasts, gradually becoming more and more involved in fan culture. In *media fandom*, however, another phenomenon is observed: wanting to become a part of a specific fandom is a key factor in choosing texts to read. For example, fans can start watching a TV show not because they particularly enjoy the premise, but because there is a lot of good fanfiction in the show's fandom, or because an author they enjoy writes in more than one fandom.

Fanfiction is always a re-creation depending on the source text on which it is based. On one hand, this allows the fanfic writer to ommit certain elements of world-building, because their readers, familiar with the canon, understand hints just as well as direct statements. On the other hand, the reader can only fully comprehend a piece of fanfiction if they are familiar with the source text. Some works of fanfiction require in-depth knowledge of the canon, for others it is enough to be familiar with a few basic facts, but in any case, consuming fanfiction always needs to be related to the source text. In result, a fan can have a few favorite source texts which they can analyze, and they can have a few otherswhich they only know well enough to read fanfiction and participate in discussions. Due to the sheer size of fandom it is difficult to cite exact numbers, but from observing users' profiles on fanfiction.net one can conclude that there is a tendency to read fanfiction in multiple fandoms, while only creating in a few of them.

In this context, one should pay particular attention to the role of writing fanfiction in identifying with fandom. According to Sheenagh Pugh, fandom as a whole is a federation of independent republics rather than a kingdom (Pugh 2005: 116). Every single fandom can have its own area of interest, and in some cases, a particular fandom might have little in common with the other, but the activity of fanfiction writing goes beyond fandom borders. Writing might be only one of many examples of fandom activity, but for groups writing and commenting on fanfiction, the creative process is very closely linked to binding the group together, which, especially in *media fandom*, helps to create a common culture based on many texts.

Fanfiction as interpretation

When considering fanfiction, one should first and foremost look at the reception of source text, because in the case of fanfiction, reception and creation seem to be inseparable processes. Canon text is not only an inspiration, but also a material from which a new work is fashioned. Most fans consume source texts alone, reading or watching in their homes (however, there are examples of groups gathering to watch movies or TV shows together). What separates a fan from a casual viewer is that, after consuming a text, they enter a discussion with other fans. Jenkins describes reading as a "social process through which individual interpretations are shaped and reinforced through ongoing discussions with other readers" (Jenkins 1992: 44).

One could say that discussion is the very basis of fandom. During conversations held on internet forums, as well as reading and commenting on other fans' stories fandom engages in a continuous debate about the source text. One of the aims of this discussion is the exchange of information. On many discussion forums there are special threads in which fans can find information about characters or worlds. A good example can be The Harry Potter Zone (Strefa Harry'ego Pottera) on Mirriel forum, where various pieces of information (including facts from minor characters' lives, characters' birthdays, wand cores etc) can be found.

However, the main aim of fans' interactions is to interpret the canon. Jenkins describes fandom as a critical environment, classifying fanfiction as a form of a critical text (Jenkins 1992: 88), while Kristina Busse and Karen Hellekson in *Work in Progress* notices similarities between fandom and academia. Those statements seems to be confirmed by the way fans approach the canon: they analyze it with care and great attention to detail, and their works tend to absorb multiple theories; complimentary as well as mutually exclusive ones. On the other hand, fannish interpretation is often very different from one that could be expected in academic discourse. Fandom analysis goes beyond the source text, allowing the fans to add events that do not take place in the canon. They do not just analyze what happened; they are also interested in what could have happened, and what, according to them, should have happened. Very often they emphasize elements that are marginal in the source text (minor characters, undeveloped plots). The main difference between fandom and academia is the intimate relationship between the fan and the text, which breaches the distance between a work of art and its recipient. The line between the fictional and the personal is blurry, because the metatext created around the source text can be based on personal experience, which broadens the scope of analysis. Fandom discussions can be focused on the personal (for example using the fan's failed relationships to explain what is happening between characters), which means that fictional events can be helpful to interpret what is happening in one's personal life.

The aforementioned lack of distance is one of the reasons why fans are often accused of not being able to tell the difference between fiction and reality. However, it is worth remembering that distance or lack of thereof are merely strategies a reader can choose while approaching the text. Neither is inherently superior to the other, and the recipient is allowed to change their approach according to their needs. Most fans are capable of consuming their favorite texts both with distance and with great emotional investment. On one hand, they are interested in how a particular text came to be: they read interviews with writers, producers or actors, they familiarize themselves with filming techniques, special effects, or changes in scripts. They take a text apart to see how an illusion is created. On the other hand, they allow themselves to be invested in personal worlds, treating the characters like real people whose stories and emotions can be analyzed. "Fans see the fictional characters and their actions as simultaneously "real" and "constructed", adopting a strategy of "double viewing" that treats the show with both suspended disbelief and ironic distance." (Jenkins 1992: 67).

Another aim of fandom discussions is exchange of personal information between participants. It is common to combine a personal chat with a discussion of the canon, which allows analysis to be conducted as well as building relationships at the same time. Thanks to the internet, the fans are no longer limited to local communities, but they can meet people from all around the world. Face-to-face encounters remain important in fandom life, but in case of people living on different continents, they are not always possible. Exchanging personal information during fandom discussion is, therefore, even more important, because it allows the fans to get to know each other.

Due to interactions between fandom members, individual opinions start to melt into common interpretations. This is how fanon, defined as a collection of all fanmade elements, is created. Fanon includes interpretations as well as elements of the canon world. Fans discuss the source text, read each other's stories, comment, and sometimes even include other fan's ideas in their own fanfiction. Some ideas are elaborated on, others are not met with much interest. As a result, established ways of perceiving events and characters are created. Of course the size of fandom prevents it from proposing readings every single member would subscribe to; instead, it creates a set of common interpretations.

A good example of this phenomenon is fandom's ways of describing Ronald Weasley in fanfiction based on the Harry Potter universum. Ron is often presented as Harry's best friend who accompanies him in his adventures, but it is equally common to focus on his traits that suggest that he is merely an immature brat who is jealous of his friend's fame. This leads to two basic versions of Ron (positive and negative) being created. It seems particularly interesting that those two interpretations, despite being schematic, are immensely popular, which shows how subjective fannish interpretation can be. Both views are firmly based on canon events, but they emphasize them differently, thus creating two completely different characters. Most fanfiction including Ron subscribes to one version or the other.

Those basic interpretations are then used by fans, who develop them by adding more elements. Due to interpretations being very schematic one could conclude that any resemblence between particular depictions are purely coincidental. However, I would argue that established "versions" of characters do, indeed, exist, because every such reading is accompanied by a set of typical "additional features". For example, a meek, reasonable Remus Lupin is often a chocolate addict, while Remus the Werewolf's eyes turn amber when he is angry. None of those elements is relevant to the plot, but they appear often enough to attract the reaserscher's attention.

Fans use not only those pieces of information regarded as common property (i.e. interpretations, or such elements of canon texts that have lost its connection to the author). They also utilize other fans' creations in their artistic expression. A writer can introduce an original character created by another writer, or set their story in an alternative universe produced by other fans. Every fan-created text belongs to a complicated net of texts which are its source as well as its context.

Fanfiction as literature

A story idea is usually discussed between friends, and as a result, it often happens that two writers decide to write together, but even if the author writes alone, the story is always influenced by many people. One of the most prominent people involved in production of fanfiction is a beta-reader. The term itself derives from the word "beta-tester", which is used to describe people who use beta-versions (that is, working, but not completed versions) of computer software to check it for quality, efficiency and stability before it is released. The relationship between the author and their beta-reader is that of cooperation. The beta-reader's task is to point out potential mistakes and problems, and to suggest solutions. The author attempts to take those into consideration, then the story is discussed again. The whole process bears resemblance to negotiations, and ideally, it should lead to creating a text both the author and the beta-reader deem good. The scope of beta-reader's suggestions varies from author to author. In some relationships, beta-readers suggest major plot changes or removing whole scenes; in others, they just make cosmetic changes.

In her article about the role of beta-reader, Angelina Karpovich notices that a beta-reader combines the functions of a reader, a critic, and an editor. They definitely can influence the text, even if not directly – after all, the final decision lies with the author. Despite that, it is common practice in fandom to name beta-readers when publishing a story, which means that they are considered at least partially responsible for the text.

Of course the audience can also have some degree of influence on "professional" literature. E-mails, blogs, meetings with fans and various conventions allow fans to express their opinions and wishes. However, their influence is somehow limited because of the distance that exists between the author and the audience. In fandom, the situation is quite different. By definition participants are not divided into writers and readers, because many of them are both at once. Additionally, the internet allows for immediate and direct communication between fans through comments posted under stories. The main difference between this and traditional literary criticism is that "professional" criticism is usually created after the work is published, when fans can follow a story while it is being created.

As it was already mentioned, the fans' interpretation very often goes beyond the scope of the original text; it diminishes some of the distance between the text and its reader, and is based on personal experience. Fans often use the same approach when analyzing texts written by other members of fandom. People who comment on and talk about their impressions. They often compare the fic writer's interpretation with their own, accepting it as believable or rejecting it. Since the fans know each other, one can often notice allusion to common experiences, texts read etc. It can be assumed that this is a form of discussion of an interpretation of canon presented by the fic writer. At the same time, however, fanfiction is not only an interpretation, but also a piece of literature in its own right. Commenting on a fic, fans also pay attention as to how it was written. Language, plot, character-building, tension – all of this is noticed and described, like in Zoe's comment on a crime story under construction:

> I love crime stories and Mrs Christie, and Hercule Poirot has my undying love. This is why I really, really love the idea of Tuesday Meeting Club. A few ladies watching a movie, then guessing the ending. I immediately imagined a big university building, the professors and their wives, the suburban atmosphere (…)
>
> But… Unfortunately, there is a "but". Too much. There is too much of all this! At the very beginning, you introduced a few new characters, and it's hard to keep track of them. I can't remember their names or their husbands' jobs. All those details really slowed the pace – if they aren't necessary for the plot, maybe it would be better to get rid of some of them? (Zoe 2011, access: 21.05.2012).

This clearly shows that fans not only pay attention to their own feelings or impressions, but also on technical solution that could improve the text. If readers point out inaccuracies or errors, they expect them to be fixed in the following chapters. In some stories, one can see big discrepancies in style between chapters because of changes suggested by readers. Of course not all comments include technical suggestions, or even constructive criticism. A majority is just an expression of positive feelings towards the story. The purpose of this kind of comment is to maintain a relationship between reader and writer. It makes authors feel that their work is appreciated by other fans, but it does not influence the writing process because it lacks constructive feedback. Because of this, on some forums the moderators attempt to force the users to include constructive criticism in their comments.

Fans who comment on a story usually expect the author to react; either by saying a few words in the introduction to the next chapter, or by creating a separate post. There is a constant discussion about the text, during which both sides exchange opinions about how it should be shaped.

> I don't buy your James, either, and most of all, I don't buy your Remus. I'm sorry, but they seem like spoiled brats here, I'm thinking mostly about James, but Remus is also very "un-Remus-like".
>
> As for James and Remus, well, let's start with Potter. I must admit that I never liked him very much, and the way he was depicted in fanfiction always seemed too idealized to me. I think that's why I went in the opposite direction, making him into… well, a spoiled brat who has some serious issues. (Cattysxx 2006, access: 21.05.2012]

Comments by both readers and writers also have an additional function. Fanfiction obviously is not an independent text; it needs canon in order to exist. Therefore when reading a fic, the fan needs to remember the original. Sometimes, however, there are questions that neither canon, nor fanfiction answers. Holes in the canon are filled by fanfiction, but holes in fanfiction are dealt with differently. Some of them are also developed into separate stories; either by the author, who writes multiple stories in the universum they created, or by other writers, who "tag along". However, it often happens that fans ask questions about details of world buildings or the characters' behavior. Author's replies allow them to create a coherent image of the fictional reality. It also means that comments are even more important in fanfiction research, because they often include important information.

One of the more interesting ways of letting the readers join the creative process is creating polls in which they can decide what will happen next. An example of such an experiment can be *The Powers That Be* written by CrowNoYami (CrowNoYami 2010, access: 20.05.2013). It is a Harry Potter / Buffy the Vampire Slayer crossover focused on Spike. In this story, Spike returns to the magical world (his real name here is William Malfoy), and searches for his destined partner. However, when Spike arrives to England, he does not know who this person is. As it turns out, neither does the author. At first in the author's notes, she informed that the story would be a slash fic (a story featuring a homosexual relationship), but the pairing was not yet established. In author's notes to chapter five, CrowNoYami included information about a poll that was supposed to decide who would be Spike's partner. Harry, Snape, Remus and Draco were featured among the possible choices. The fans were also free to suggest other characters, although the author made some restrictions (it had to be a man, and not Dumbledore). Eventually Harry won, but the author promised to write short scenes with other popular choices as a consolation prize.

> It is hard to judge this kind of behavior. On one hand, it can be interpreted as the author's inability to solve the plot, and shifting the responsibility on the readers instead. However, another interpretation of her motives is also possible. She clearly had a well-established story idea. The poll only appeared in chapter five, and it was open for quite a long time. In the meantime, further chapters were written, in which the partner's identity did not play any part. The story is entirely focused on Spike, and the author seems indifferent towards the choice of partner. She let the fans decide what they wanted to read, while she herself fulfilled her goal: to write a story about Spike in the magical world.

Polls are common practice in fandom. One of the main reasons why fanfiction is written is because the fans want more than the canon can offer them. They might want to read about what happened next, or take a look at the elements of the canon that were not fully utilized. Sheenagh Pugh describes those expectations as an opposition between wanting "more of" and "more from the text" (Pugh 2005: 19). Many stories are written simply because the fans would like to read them. It leads to all kinds of different fests during which fans ask for stories that meet specific criteria. An especially nice variation of this custom is gifting each other stories for birthdays or Christmas:

> This story was written as a gift for Mithiana, after I overdosed her stories and that one song she likes. I'm sorry in advance if anyone feels disappointed.
>
> Thank you, Micia. Happy birthday.
> Semele (Semele 2005, access: 15.05.2012)

Fanfiction can also be treated as fun and a chance to test one's abilities. An example of such an approach can be games developed in fandom, mostly realized as challenges that can be entered by authors. On fanfiction.net, there is an established practice of authors creating "challenges". The author establishes criteria (for example genre, characters, specific plot elements) that have to appear in stories, and invites people willing to participate to write. The most famous challenge like this was one created by Severitus (Severitus 2012, access: 23.05.2013). He called for stories in which it turns out that Snape is Harry's biological father. Apart from this, a few other elements had to be included (Lupin had to be present, Harry's appearance had to be altered etc). The challenge became so popular that all stories in which Snape is Harry's father are commonly called "severitus", even if they do not meet the other criteria of the original challenge.

A more formalized form of writing challenge are duels on Mirriel. The person creating a challenge establishes the condition. After someone accepts the challenge, both authors write stories, who are afterwards asessed by other users in the following categories: idea, style, meeting the criteria of the challenge, canon-compliance, and general impression.

Conclusion

The main element integrating a fan community is the original text, because it is what cements the fans as a group, and gives them material to create their own art. Fanfiction, thanks to its relationship to the canon, is also a part of creating this cultural community. At the same time, however, it is more that just that. Fans not only write stories based on a shared canon; they also create them together, using elements both from the canon and from other fanmade stories. Being a part of fandom is approaching the text in a specific way as well as interacting with other fans. When looking at fanfiction, one needs to pay attention to the fact that in creating a text (from interpreting the source text to presenting the final product) there is a whole group of people involved, and writing a fic is not over when it is posted. A fic is constantly rewritten by other fans, who comment on it or use it in their own writing. In this context, it seems appropriate to describe fanfiction, following Busse and Hellekson, as an eternal "work in progress". Every separate story, as well as the whole body of fanfiction, constantly grows, transforms, and redefines. At the same time, writing fanfiction is a chance for the fans to discuss both personal matters and scientific problems. It lets the fans learn from one another, have fun together, and communicate on a level different from a casual conversation. In the 1960s, fandom created a statement: Fandom is a way of life". It seems, however, that for the fans creating fanfiction it is writing that became a way of life.

Bibliography

Busse Kristina, Hellekson Karen 2006, *Introduction. Work in Progress*, [in:] *Fan Fiction and Fan Communities in the Age of Internet*, Jefferson: McFarland & Company Inc. [Kindle Edition]

Coleman Susanna 2010, *Making Our Voices Heard: Young Adult Females Writing Participatory Fan Fiction*, [in:] *Writing and the Digital Generation. Essays on New Media Rhetoric*, ed. H. Urbański, Jefferson: McFarland & Company Inc.

Coppa Francesca 2006, *A Brief History of Media Fandom*, [in:] *Fan Fiction and Fan Communities in the Age of Internet*, eds. K. Hellekson, K. Busse, Jefferson: McFarland & Company Inc. [Kindle Edition]

Derecho Abigail 2006, *Archontic Literature: A Definition, a History and Several Theories of Fan Fiction*, [in:] *Fan Fiction and Fan Communities in the Age of Internet*, eds. K. Hellekson, K. Busse, Jefferson: McFarland & Company Inc. [Kindle Edition]

Gąsowska Lidia 2009, *Fan fiction, czyli złoto dla zuchwałych. Pomiędzy pragnieniem narracji a realizacją opowieści*, [in:] *Kody kultury. Interakcja, transformacja synergia*, eds. H. Kubicka, O. Taranek, Wrocław: Sutoris.

Hellekson Karen 2010, *History, the Trace, and Fandom Wank*, [in:] *Writing and the Digital Generation. Essays on New Media Rhetoric*, ed. H. Urbański, Jefferson: McFarland & Company Inc.

Jenkins Henry 2007, *Everybody Loves Harry*, http://henryjenkins.org/2007/05/everybody_loves_harry.html

Jenkins Henry 2007, *Kultura konwergencji. Zderzenie starych i nowych mediów*, Wydawnictwa akademickie i profesjonalne, Warszawa.

Jenkins Henry 2006, *Fan Fiction as Critical Commentary*, http://henryjenkins.org/2006/09/fan_fiction_as_critical_commen.html

Jenkins Henry 2006, *Can One Be a Fan of Hight Art?* http://henryjenkins.org/2006/07/can_one_be_a_fan_of_high_art.html

Jenkins Henry 1992, *Textual Poachers. Television Fans & Participatory Culture*, New York: Routledge.

Kaplan Deborah 2006, *Construction of Fan Fiction Character Through Narrative*, [in:] *Fan Fiction and Fan Communities in the Age of Internet*, eds. K. Hellekson, K. Busse, Jefferson: McFarland & Company Inc. [Kindle Edition]

Karpovich Angelina 2006, *The Audience as Editor: The Role of Beta Reader in Online fan Fiction Communities*, [in:] *Fan Fiction and Fan Communities in the Age of Internet*. eds. K. Hellekson, K. Busse, Jefferson: McFarland & Company Inc. [Kindle Edition]

Pugh Sheenagh 2005, *The Democratic Genre. Fan fiction in a Literary Context*, Glasgow: Bell and Bain Ltd.

R. D. M. 1996, *First Fandom*, http://www.jstor.org/stable/4240563

Southard Bruce 1982, *The Language of Science-Fiction Fan Magazines*, http://www.jstor.org/stable/455177

Wooley Christine 2001-2002, *Visible Fandom: Reading The X-Files Through X-Phile*, http://www.jstor.org/stable/20688369

Agnieszka Oberc

Fanfiction

Cattysxx 2006, *Re: Lód w sercu*, http://forum.mirriel.net/viewtopic.php?f=2&t=17450 [access: 21.05.2012].

CrowNoYami 2010, *The Powers That Be*, http://www.fanfiction.net/s/6229179/1/The_Powers_That_Be [access: 31.05.2012].

Semele 2005, *Nibylandia*, http://forum.mirriel.net/viewtopic.php?t=1839 [access 15.05.2012].

Severitus 2012, *Severitus Challange*, http://severitus.livejournal.com/5823.html [access: 10.05.2012].

Zoe 2011, *Re: Romantyczna kryjówka*, http://forum.mirriel.net/viewtopic.php?f=2&t=15021 [access: 21.05.2012].

Karolina Sidowska*

University of Lodz

APPROACHES TOWARDS SHAME
IN CONTEMPORARY POLISH LITERATURE

Abstract
This article focuses on literary approaches to the emotion of shame. My thesis is that literature can be perceived as a tool for overcoming feelings of shame, as it is capable of expressing even the most intimate human experiences in aesthetic terms, outside stereotypical moral judgments. From this perspective I discuss exhibitionistic tendencies on the author's part and complementary voyeuristic impulses on the part of the reader. In this context I then consider the phenomenon of literary provocation and its function to then analyse two examples from Polish contemporary literature: *Polka* by M. Gretkowska – a literary journal of pregnancy – and *Lovetown* by M. Witkowski. Both, in my opinion, offer interesting aesthetic views on intimate but relevant aspects of everyday life.

Key words: aesthetics, shame, contemporary Polish literature, experience

In her famous essay *Reading for Life* Martha Nussbaum proposes a theory stating that reading is an ethical act which holds significant implications for the reader's entire life and functioning within the community. (Nussbaum 1990) The essay title might therefore be understood as a summons to apply the knowledge and experience gained from reading in order to live a better, fuller, more responsible and conscious life. Another interpretation is that Nussbaum places reading on the same level as processes and activities indispensable to maintaining life in its basic, biological form; to paraphrase – that there is no life without reading. Or, at least, no life worthy of the name. Undoubtedly, despite distressing reports on the decrease

---

* German Philology, Univesity of Lodz, ul. Pomorska 171/173, 90-236 Lodz, e-mail: karolinasidowska@wp.pl

of readership, there still are people for whom this high-minded statement rings true and who indeed cannot imagine a day without reading. For them, reading is a way of life. This phenomenon, or more broadly, readers' reception of literary works, has been a subject of interest to literary scholars – professional readers, who endeavour to explain the phenomenon of reading from a scientific perspective, but still not without certain personal sentiments.[1]

The scope and range of readership studies illustrates the scale and importance of the phenomenon of reading. Writing, as much as it remains a complementary counterpart of reading, seems to be a less egalitarian pursuit – or, at least, this has been the case until recently. The circle of writers has always been considerably narrower than that of readers, even if we include the scores of journals, memoirs and poems written purely for personal pleasure or stored in desk drawers; works that never made it into public consciousness. In the era of websites, blogs and Internet forums, reaching potential readers is simple enough, which presents an opportunity for many new writers, including amateurs or so-called 'scribblers', whose creations would not previously have passed editorial filters. One could question the value of this artistic democratisation, or repeat after Julian Tuwim: *"Blessed is he who has nothing to say and does not put this fact into words"*. (Tuwim 1987) Finally, one could conclude that just as writer's block exists, there also exists a certain imperative to write (or in some cases, an imperative to self-promote, if one was to treat the phenomenon less warmly). This desire for expression, for marking one's presence or even for bringing intimate experiences and reflections into the light includes an element of exhibitionism. We are all exhibitionists and voyeurs by nature – those are natural instincts, which only become a pathology when they turn into an obsession: "Every human being is motivated by that deep desire to be seen, to have attention paid to them, to be noticed and to be heard." (Carr-Gomm 2012: 198) Furthermore, is it possible to imagine creative activity without those instincts? Is not every author an exhibitionist in a way, one who – to follow the Latin etymology –

---

[1] Diverse texts can be placed in this category – philosophical studies, such as Roland Barthes' *The Pleasure of the Text*; literary studies by scholars such as Anna Burzyńska (*Lekturografia. Filozofia czytania według Jacques'a Derridy*, in: "Pamiętnik Literacki" 1/2000, *Literatura jako sztuka uwodzenia: przyczynek do tematu* in: "Teksty Drugie" 4/1998; *Ciało w bibliotece* in: "Teksty Drugie" 6/2002; *Teoria i lektura: niebezpieczne związki*, "Pamiętnik Literacki" 1/2003) or Ryszard Koziołek (*Maski czytania*, in: *Intymność wyrażona*, ed. M. Kisiel, M. Tramer, University of Silesia Press, Katowice 2006) or essays and literary takes on the subject such as Alberto Manguel's *A History of Reading* or – from the Polish corner – *Młodszy księgowy* [The Junior Clerk] by Jacek Dehnel, WAB, Warsaw 2013.

exhibits, shows, uncovers in public? Not perhaps by undressing in public, but quite on the contrary – by dressing truths up with words and literary conventions? In this model of exhibitionism, uncovering is complemented by covering, and what we are shown only appears to be a faithful representation of what lurks in the creator's soul. Searching in a literary work for a direct expression of the creator's experience, as Dilthey would have done, over a century after the anti-Positivist turn would be a slightly amusing andnaïve anachronism. A limited degree of trust is advisable; even more limited, if the text seems to be a "sincere" autobiographical account with first-person narration. In reality, as Erazm Kuźma points out – "pisanie jest zawsze zdradą wnętrza, zdradą w tym sensie, że to, co uchodzi za prawdziwe wnętrze, zastępuje się sztucznym." [English: "writing is always a betrayal of the inner sphere as much as what seems to be the real inner sphere is replaced by an artificial construct"] (Kuźma 2006: 11).

The artist's exhibitionistic impulse can take the form of a provocation – a conscious and deliberate infringement of accepted norms. Frequently such actions are motivated by nothing more than marketing; the aim is to create a media buzz and increase sales. It would, nevertheless, be an oversimplification to say that there can be no other dimensions to it. Provocative texts can function as doors, through which the reader can access those areas of reality which otherwise remain off-limits, on the margins of consciousness, never articulated. By dealing with taboo subjects they enrich knowledge, deepen understanding and are a school of sensibility. Thanks to those literary provocations, those not calculated solely to create a media shock, but in order to communicate valid truths, some experiences and phenomena can trickle down from the realities of life into the realm of acceptable literary subject matter. As a result, not just the readers' horizons open up, but language itself is enriched – even if those more conservative among us tend to view this as pollution of discourse. We can trace this paradigm to the sexual revolution which took place in the second half of the twentieth century and has lead to enriching literature and deepening artistic and ethical sensibilities, largely due to artists' rejection of stale social models and conventions (cf. Sadkowski 1987). Naturally, literary provocation is not an invention of the 20th and 21st centuries: throughout history, authors of scandalous works have faced considerable sanctions, including a ban on publication and imprisonment.[2] Today's courts of justice rarely get involved, unless a book is seen as offensive towards a specific, personally offended

---

[2] Probably the best-known case is that of Marquis de Sade's lengthy imprisonment in the Bastille for offending public morality.

individual. Literary criticism has liberalised along with its subject matter; the limits of its influence has narrowed. Large numbers of readers consume that which is fashionable and trendy. The public, accustomed to drastic scenes and images present in the media, politics, arts, reacts to provocative gestures and words with a decreased sensitivity. This natural reaction is akin to a "blasé" condition – a result of long-term and intense nervous stimulation, described by Georg Simmel already at the beginning of the 20th century. (Simmel 2006: 120) These days' authors are rarely accused of propagating immoral attitudes or breaking the rules of good taste. Therefore we should ask if there is still anything a writer is not "supposed to do"? Do any taboo subjects or off-limits aspects of reality exist? Does the depiction of any sphere of life require a courageous transgression of universally accepted norms, or a certain "shamelessness" in depicting a given theme? Is the lack of shame to be understood in a positive sense, as a kind of openness and sincerity (not without its own problems)?[3] These questions belong to the field of creativity psychology rather than literary studies. Therefore on the following pages I will attempt to look not at the psychology of authors, but at selected contemporary literary texts which tackle "shameful", intimate, overlooked themes and examine the function – or functions – of literary works of this type. How is shame (or shamelessness) depicted in literature? Can one talk about known 'shameful' motifs and what are the implications of their existence in everyday, non-literary reality?

Shame is an emotion that appears at the moment of realising that one has infringed upon the norms or conventions adopted in a given environment. (Demmerling/Landweer 2007) These norms and rules vary, of course, with each time period, geographic location or social class, which is why many researchers treat shame as a cultural phenomenon. However, its universal presence – despite varying forms of expression – suggests the need to situate the ability to feel ashamed in the basic anthropological human toolset. An important, but not indispensable factor is the pres-

---

[3] It is worthwhile mentioning that the differentiation between sincerity and authenticity in existential philosophy; for instance, in Sartre's view sincerity, as a way of adopting a specific identity, "being something", is a priori ill-intentioned as an escape from the irremovable duality characterising being-for-itself, which must constantly define itself against the surrounding beings. Therefore „autentyczność musi być projektem znacznie bardziej radykalnym, wyjściem poza krąg złudzeń wspieranych przez szczerość, zaakceptowaniem własnej nicości jako jedynej cechy przysługującej podmiotowi." ["authenticity must be a project more radical, a step outside the circle of illusions supported by sincerity, an acceptance of one's nothingness as the sole characteristic."] (Warchala 2006: 11).

ence of witnesses: they personify the unchanging nature of rules that have been broken. Still, even if a witness, judge or prosecutor is not present, the norms and prohibitions are always present in the consciousness – or subconsciousness – of the transgressing individual. The gaze of the Other, in which, to quote Sartre, the experience of being is realised, is a constant of being, even if the Other is not given in its physical form: "Thus shame is *shame of oneself before the Other*; these two structures are inseparable. But at the same time I need the Other in order to realize fully all the structures of my being. The For-itself refers to For-others."[4] (Sartre 2003: 246) Max Scheler, author of an exhaustive study on the feeling of shame, derives it from the duality of human nature, which comprises of a spiritual component, a reflective component and the bodily, organic component which places human beings close to animals. It is the things that are fragile, mortal, subject to the laws of biology and therefore opposed to human values and ideas that most frequently cause shame and repulsion. (Menninghaus 2009: 177) A quick look at the repertoire of most popular 'shameful' literary motifs across the centuries confirms this: we are most often ashamed of nudity, bodily anomalies and diseases, physiological processes, sex and old age. Naturally shame can also have a moral dimension, a social dimension, it can result from an inadequate skill or incompetence, unethical behaviour, treason etc. Such a definition of shame, related to a personal sense of honour, appears in the writings of Artistotle and Plato, and dominates practically until the end of the 19th century, at which time it began to be associated mainly with the body and sexuality, especially female. (Frevert 2013: 24) Puritan upbringing and control was intended to tame the sexuality of women, who in Scheler's view are characterised by a less acute (than in men) sense of shame. (Scheler 2003: 32) Since the 1850s these trends have been countered by emancipatory movements, strengthened between the world wars and then blossoming within the feminist wave of the 1960s. Feminist literary criticism directed public attention not only to stereotypical and patriarchal renditions of women, but also to the absence of any literary depictions of numerous vital aspects of female existence – especially those related to the body and female physiology, 'impure' and

---

[4] Cf. the following passage: "Every look directed toward me is manifested in connection with the appearance of a sensible form in our perceptive field, but contrary to what might be expected, it is not connected with any determined form. Of course what most often manifests a look is the convergence of two ocular globes in my direction. But the look will be given just as well on occasion when there is a rustling of branches, or the sound of a footstep followed by silence, or the slight opening of a shutter, or a light movement of a curtain." (Sartre 2003: 281)

unfit for print. The literature of the end of the 20th and the beginning of the 21st centuries makes up for those deficiencies and refuses to be reduced to the derisive genre of "menstruatory literature"[5]. (Nęcka 2006)

One of the most important women's experiences – pregnancy and birth – has only recently become a major theme in Polish literature, making its appearance in Anna Nasiłowska's *Domino. Traktat o narodzinach* (Dominoes. A Treatise on Birth) and *Księga początku* (Book of the Beginning) by the same author, as well as in *Polka* by Manuela Gretkowska. Gretkowska, labelled the provocateur of Polish literature since her debut in early 1990s, does not shock in her pregnancy journal as much as she surprises the reader with the directness and simplicity of description, not devoid of physiological or anatomical detail, but not seeking to needlessly impose them on the reader. Few situations justify concentrating on bodily sensations and signals as much as pregnancy does. This particular diary of pregnancy may not have been written for personal purposes, but with readers in mind, nevertheless the impression of sincerity is most suggestive. The author-narrator reveals herself in two ways – by describing her fears, doubts, and thoughts and by describing how her body changes shape. Notably, however bold and striking the images, the narrator points out: "Intimate things are those in one's head". (Gretkowska 2012: 276) This statement, as indeed the entire journal, draws new boundaries of the intimate – and consequently, new boundaries of shame, even if the feeling is not unknown to the protagonist in the most commonplace of situations:

> Nie poślizgnąć się, nie poślizgnąć. Docieram do sklepu. Z koszyczkiem obchodzę półki. W naszym bezzapachowym sklepie wykręca mnie odór wody. Flejtuchowaty pijak wybiera cukierki. Odwracam się ze wstrętem, chyba za ostentacyjnie. Znowu się na niego natykam przy warzywach. I nagle... Prrr – elegancka dama z koszyczkiem rozpierdza się. Nie mogę powstrzymać nagłej eksplozji. Pijak spogląda na mnie z rozbawieniem. Nie rozepnę kożucha i nie pokażę sprawcy, naciskającego spust gazów. Wstyd okropny. (Gretkowska 2012: 244)

> [Note to self: do not slip, do not trip. I reach the store. I circle the shelves, shopping basket in hand. In our odourless shop I am repulsed even by the smell of water. A grubby drunk chooses sweets. I turn my back with disgust, a little too ostentatiously, perhaps. I bump into him again by the vegetables. And suddenly... Prtt! – elegant basket lady farts: I can't stop a sudden explosion. The drunk looks at me with amusement. I won't undo my overcoat and present the culprit who pushed the trigger. Dreadful embarrassment. (Gretkowska 2012: 244, English translation by the author of the article]

---

[5] Term coined by Jan Błoński.

The *faux pas* may have had natural causes and been unavoidable, still the feeling of shame is automatic. Its source is not just the transgression of accepted standards of behaviour, but also the loss of control over one's body and the observation of cultural constructs quickly perishing in confrontation with biological processes:

> Człowiek strasznie stara się być człowiekiem. Nie posikać się, nie posrać, nie zarzygać. Udawać cywilizowanego czyścioszka, panującego nad odruchami. Człowiek jest chyba bardzo znerwicowany sobą samym, tak zaciskając zwieracz i pęcherz. Biegnę do łazienki. (Gretkowska 2012: 272)

> Humans try so hard to be human. Don't pee yourself, don't shit yourself, don't puke. Pretend to be squeaky clean, civilised and in control over your instincts. Humans must be very stressed, clenching their orifices all the time. I run to the bathroom. (Gretkowska 2012: 272, English translation by the author of the article)

More similarly self-reflective passages can be found in *Polka*, and they should not perhaps be reduced to questioning shame or rejecting it as baseless. The originality lies rather in the openness towards discussing it, surprising in the case of an emotion which tempts us to hide from the inquisitive gaze of others. To admit to feeling ashamed or embarrassed, even to oneself, and to conduct a detailed analysis of potential causes is to disarm and neutralise the sensation. The ability to see oneself from a certain distance is also important, even if – in the most extreme cases – it displays traits of a split personality: "The pure ego, unstained by physiology has escaped somewhere towards the top of my head. From there it watches the body contorted by disgust and shame" (Gretkowska 2012: 66, English translation). Similarly in another passage: "I get up at night with a bad taste in the mouth. Self-disgust. I run to the toilet. How does one like someone, for whom the only goal is getting up and having a pee? I've caught myself having this sole need at three in the morning, the rest of me is sleeping or mocking me." (Gretkowska 2012: 147) Similarly, often very intimate revelations are usually accompanied by a healthy dose of self-irony, expressed in explicit phrases typical for Gretkowska: "I feel like a female about to spawn" (Gretkowska 2012: 342), or: "The body pushes out what it can: haemorrhoids, nosebleeds. A general rehearsal before pushing out Pola." (Gretkowska 2012: 331)

Humour and wit have for centuries successfully neutralised shame, especially that relating to the sphere of the body. An example of this can be the entire genre of medieval and Renaissance picaresque literature. Laughter liberates all those engaged in a shameful situation: the offender as well as witnesses of the shameful act, often highly embarrassed themselves. A humorous approach or witty convention creates a healthy distance and weakens the *gravitas* of the offense, as well as, possibly, the severity of any sanctions. On the other end, socially adopted rules and adherence to them lose their power in situations of extreme closeness, governed primarily by the rules established by the partners in a given intimate relationship. Paradoxically, intimacy does not exclude humour, but rather widens its context. In Gretkowska's book both remain in a state of balance. The personal experience of pregnancy (from an anthropological point of view – a key human experience), frequently eliminated from public discourse, receives a treatment devoid of false modesty or embarrassment, but also devoid of stereotypical pathos. Acceptance for the biological, animalistic dimension of this experience, expressed in colloquial and occasionally vulgar expressions,[6] does not diminish its metaphysical dimension – on the contrary, underlines the complexity of experience and constitutes a step forward in literary explorations of important regions of human existence.

It would be difficult to assess Gretkowska's book as scandalous and therefore shameless; evaluations of this kind were evoked in 2004 by the appearance of the "first Polish gay novel"[7] by Michał Witkowski. I refer of course to the infamous *Lovetown*, in which the author's intent was to be a new *Decameron*, a "Great Atlas of Polish Faggots". We might treat those arrogant declarations with a pinch of salt, still their forcefulness proves the author's unrestrained approach to the "slippery" subject of homosexuality. It also invokes the long tradition of depicting homosexuality in the history of literature. The deliberate openness with which Witkowski describes the life of aging gay men is reminiscent of a literary *coming out*. We have here a clear aim to end the demonisation of homosexuality, to revise conservative, small-town patterns of thinking, and a yearning for the possibility of free expression, for life without shame. This state of no shame would then represent not a moral downfall, but a utopian idea of return to the state of paradise-like innocence, when human beings knew nothing

---

[6] Cf. Sadkowski's remarks on style related to the sexual revolution: "Coraz jaśniejsze staje się natomiast, że unikanie dosadności językowej tam, gdzie jest ona zasadna, gdzie jest odzwierciedleniem i ewokacją rzeczywistości językowej i psychologiczno-obyczajowej, jest artystycznym fałszem." [It is becoming clear that avoiding frank language where it is justified, where it is a reflection and evocation of linguistic, social and psychological reality, is artistic falsity.] (Sadkowski 1987: 337)

[7] This label has been attached to Witkowski's book somewhat hastily. Polish literature dealing with similar themes has previously existed, for instance the 1980 *Rudolf* by Marian Pankowski.

of sin or moral evaluations. It would therefore mean a return to honesty and natural behaviour, as it occurs in children and animals. Such a vision stands however in stark contrast with the theatricality and artificiality of the twisted poses of the characters of *Lovetown*, who anyway do not identify with any slogans calling for emancipation of sexual minorities in the political debate about equal rights. Acting naturally feels alien to them and they do not wish to be natural any more than they wish to gain social acceptance or care for unambiguous, universal social standards. They do not care for authenticity:

> Neither has ever heard of plastic surgery or sex-change operations. They get by with a flourish or two of their plain black satchels, which they call 'handbags'. (...) All they have to do is hold their cigarettes a little differently, shave every day, and put their words, their language, to use. For their power lies in their words. They have nothing; whatever they do have they've had to make up, lie up, sing up. (...) They don't want to be women at all; they want to be swishy men. That's how they like it, how they've been their whole lives: pretend femmes. To actually be a woman would be beside the point. What's exciting is the pretending; to actually satisfy their imagination would be... (Witkowski 2011: 12)

The source of excitement is not just the rough sex appeal of "grunts"[8], but also the act of pretending, masquerading and an ever-present risk factor. Assuming roles and constantly oscillating between different realities and identities defines Witkowski's characters:

> Lucretia poses like a dowager countess deprived of her fortune by the vicissitudes of war. She crosses her legs (a pale calf, tattooed with a web of veins, appears between her sock and the cuff of her brown trousers), lights a cigarette, holds the smoke in for a moment, then releases it with a deep sigh, a lady lost in revery. They put on their favourite Anna German record. (Witkowski 2006: 14)

Embarrassment and modesty is just another part of the game, even if it is pretend modesty, fussing and affectation. Shame signals a rule has been broken, marks an awareness of having transgressed the rules in force; it is the very act of breaking rules and social taboos that gives the characters

---

[8] Cf. the following passage: "Grunt is what gives our lives meaning. A grunt is a bull, drunken bull of a man, a macho lowlife, a con man, a top, sometimes a guy walking home through the park, or passed out in a ditch or on a bench at the station or somewhere else completely unexpected (...) Grunt can be homosexual, too, as long as he's simple as an oak and uneducated – because if he finishes school he isn't a real man any more, he's just some intellectual. Grunt can't be someone who puts on airs. He has to have a mug like a thigh – a box covered with hide, the last place where anything can be expressed, least of all feelings!" (Witkowski 2011: 11)

a shot of adrenalin and excitement. Bataille describes similar experience of transgression in the categories of ecstasy and fear (Bataille 2007: 42), still it seems that shame plays a significant part, too, as a feeling related to fear. In essence shame is a type of fear – fear of exclusion, of rejection by one's environment, but also of betraying oneself (when one breaks the rules which define us in our own eyes). It is a reaction against losing self-control, control of our bodies, emotions or words.[9] In that sense it serves a protective role for the most internal and intimate sphere of the individual, guarding its boundaries and preventing behaviours contradictory to the essence of a given individual (cf. Chu, de las Heras 1994). At the same time shame has an important cognitive significance. The emergence of the emotion of shame lets us recognise the moment in which we cross a taboo – the moment when transgressing the norm makes it all the clearer in our consciousness. Along with other emotions it is an element of the internal 'early warning system': thanks to it, the rules are constantly confirmed. And only where rules are known, playing the game is possible.

Notably, the oppressive character of the shame experience, its objective unpleasant character, for the protagonists of *Lovetown* seems to present a value. A masochistic tendency for self-humiliation is characteristic for Patricia and Lucretia: they derive a perverse pleasure from acting weak, submissive and used: "Patricia realizes she's called herself a 'bag lady' and she's delighted at her new joke. Somewhere deep down it contains a trickle of indignity, and Patricia is already planning to drink it, to lick it up like a drop of eggnog from the bottom of a glass. Tonight." (Witkowski 2011: 8) In this context, the feeling of shame loses its negative overtone, it indeed gets questioned. Do the characters really experience shame, or has it been replaced by role play? When they do feel ashamed, it is in entirely different situations and for reasons different from what's expected. *Lovetown*, picturing just a specific, self-encompassing gay scene – with aging actors past their prime, living on the reminiscences of the past – appears not to concern the psychological inhibitions of the homosexual characters or the author, but instead to be directed at pushing the reader to battle his or her own prejudices and feelings of shame (which the reader may feel "for" the depicted characters). Often enough this kind of shame felt "for" someone else causes offensive and aggressive behaviour, in this case – homophobic. At the same time, Witkowski demonstrates that demonising behaviours

---

[9] Cf. "Bezwstydem jest zamęt, który sprawia, że nie panujemy nad ciałem, że tracimy trwałą i wyraźną osobowość." (Bataille 2007: 21)

and upholding taboos results in demonstrating perpetual blindness to the heart of the problem. The narrator of *Lovetown* lounges on the beach and comments:

> I entice them for their stories… I want them to become my storytellers, like the ones in Pasolini's Salo. And every day they'll tell an even more perverted tale for the State, standing at the piano, in front of the burning doors. It's a faggot Decameron I'm trying to turn out here. The only problem is there's no such a thing as sin any more. It's vanished, soaked up by the sand like a couple of drops they've flicked off themselves after coming out of the sea. Where did it vanish? When? (Witkowski 2011: 81)

If in Gretkowska's work the sensation of shame is rarely called by name, in Witkowski's prose this word possibly never appears; still, in the reader's reception, both texts hugely concentrate on getting accustomed to, taming and overcoming this emotion. In Gretkowska and Witkowski's work, a significant role is played by irony, humour and distance towards the problems described – despite opting for first-person narration, which tends to bring the reader closer. The author hides behind the narrator, juggling autobiographical allusions from a safe distance. The convention of openness and honesty legitimises the use of colloquialisms and vulgarisms. Thus, not just the subject matter, but also the language of the discussed novels might be described as "shameless" – that is, falling outside the boundaries of good taste, even if such assessments seem naïve and anachronistic. Social and aesthetic norms, even if liberalised, remain in force, ergo transgression and provocation are still possible. Although these days we are increasingly ashamed not of breaking rules, but of shame itself and its automatic appearance. Feelings of shame accompany the readers who, with pleasure bordering on the perverse, devour especially texts viewed as obscene, scandalous, forbidden, and indecent and inducing both embarrassment and excitement. If the writer displays exhibitionistic inclinations, the reader is by nature a voyeur, a nosy onlooker (cf. Anz, 1998) especially interested in things intimate and hidden. As Agata Bielik-Robson points out: "Podglądanie innych w sytuacjach, które filozofia określa jako graniczne – narodziny, miłość i śmierć – okazuje się potrzebą nieodpartą, zdradzaną już przez osobniki najmłodsze, co nieomylnie wskazuje na jej niezmienny, uparcie naturalny charakter. [Watching others in situations defined by philosophy as thresholds – birth, love and death – turns out to be an irresistible need, exhibited already by the youngest individuals, which clearly points to its unchanging, stubbornly natural character]" (Bielik-Robson 2000). The transgressive experiences mentioned above are closely linked to the bodily dimension of existence and belong to the set of motifs traditionally viewed as shameful. Their attractiveness and almost magical appeal results from the fact that they reveal "a fragment of peculiar and untamed being (…) that which we do not understand, that which crosses the boundaries of our understanding" (Bielik-Robson 2000). The thirst for knowledge to which Bielik-Robson refers may be, thanks to literature, satiated within safe, aesthetically defined boundaries. The exhibitionist-voyeur game played by author and reader rests outside the commonplace moral assessments and its shamelessness becomes its virtue.

Bibliography

Anz Thomas 1998, *Literatur und Lust. Glück und Unglück beim Lesen*, München: dtv.

Bataille Georges 2007, *Erotyzm*, trans. Maryna Ochab, Gdansk: słowo/obraz terytoria.

Bielik-Robson Agata 2000, „Podglądanie, czyli głód rzeczywistości", *Tygodnik Powszechny Magazyn Kulturalny* no. 6 (44).

Carr-Gomm Philip 2012, *A Brief History of Nakedness*, London: Reaktion Books.

Chu Victor, de Las Heras Brigitta 1994, *Scham und Leidenschaft*, Zürich: Kreuz Verl.

Demmerling Christoph, Landweer Hilge 2007, *Philosophie der Gefühle*, Stuttgart: Metzler Verl.

Dilthey Wilhelm 1974, *Przeżycie i poezja*, trans. O. Dobijanka, [in:] *Teoria badań literackich za granicą. Antologia*, ed. S. Skwarczyńska, t. II, Cracow: Wydawnictwo Literackie.

Frevert Ute 2013, *Vergängliche Gefühle*, Göttingen: Wallstein Verl.

Gretkowska Manuela 2012, *Polka*, Warsaw: WAB.

Kuźma Erazm 2006, *Od wyrazu do intymności*, [in:] *Intymność wyrażona*, eds. M. Kisiel, M. Tramer, Katowice: Wyd. Uniwersytetu Śląskiego.

Menninghaus Winfried 2009, *Wstręt. Teoria i historia*, trans. Grzegorz Sowiński, Cracow: Universitas.

Nasiłowska Anna 1995, *Domino. Traktat o narodzinach*, Warsaw: OPEN.

Nasiłowska Anna 2002, *Księga początku*, Warsaw: WAB.

Nęcka Agnieszka 2006: *Granice przyzwoitości. Doświadczenie intymności w polskiej prozie najnowszej*, Katowice: PARA.

Nussbaum Martha C. 1990, *Love's Knowledge. Essays on Philosophy and Literature*, New York: Oxford University Press.

Psychologia emocji 2005, eds. M. Lewis, J. Haviland-Jones, Gdansk: Gdańskie Wydawnictwa Pedagogiczne.

Sadkowski Wacław 1987, „Wzlot i upadek. Rewolucja seksualna od Henry Millera do Wiliama Burroughsa", *Literatura na Świecie*, no. 5–6.

Sartre Jean Paul 2003, *Being and Nothingness: An Essay on Phenomenological Ontology*, Oxford–New York: Routledge Classics.

Scheler Max 2003, *O wstydzie i poczuciu wstydu*, [in:] *Wstyd i nagość*, ed. M. Grabowski, Toruń: Wydawnictwo Uniwersytetu Mikołaja Kopernika.

Simmel Georg 2006, *Mentalność mieszkańców wielkich miast*, [in:] *Most i drzwi*, trans. Małgorzata Łukasiewicz, Warsaw: Oficyna Naukowa.

Tuwim Julian 1987, *Aforyzmy i limeryki*, Warsaw: Wydawnictwo Artystyczne i Filmowe.

Warchala Michał 2006, *Autentyczność i nowoczesność. Idea autentyczności od Rousseau do Freuda*, Cracow: Universitas.

Witkowski Michał 2011, *Lovetown*, trans. W. Martin, London: Portobello Books.

Bartosz Kałużny*

University of Lodz

PEOPLE YOU MAY KNOW: HOMOSEXUAL MEN'S IDENTITY IN THE TIME OF SOCIAL NETWORKING SERVICES

Abstract
In the following article several key points are highlighted from a doctoral thesis entitled *Gay Men, Social Media and Self-presentation: Managing Identities in Gaydar, Facebook and Beyond* written by Elijah M. Cassidy at the University of Technology in Queensland, Australia. The dissertation focuses on the ways in which homosexual men, who use both niche and mainstream Social Network Services (SNS), manage their identities therein. The research uncovers the entanglements of various practices employed in both spaces and presents complex privacy concerns. It also refers to manifold peculiarities of Internet-mediated communication and the ambivalent impact of mainstream and niche SNSs on the sense of collectivity of the researched group. Having presented the main ideas of Cassidy's research I determine the connection between his conclusions and those drawn from two Polish studies which recently treaded the relatively uncharted waters of this research area.

Key words: internet-mediated communication, identity, queer studies, social media

My interest in how homosexual users of Social Networking Services shape and manage their identities was sparked by a doctoral dissertation entitled: "Gay men, social media and self-presentation: managing identities in Gaydar, Facebook and beyond" written in 2013 by Elija M. Cassidy at the University of Technology in Queensland, Australia. In my paper I would

---

* The Department of Transatlantic and Media Studies, Faculty of International and Political Studies, University of Lodz, ul. Lindleya 5a, 90-131 Lodz, e-mail: bartosz.aegee@gmail.com

like to take a closer look at this research and consider the relevance of an Australian academic's questions in a Polish context. The following abbreviations will be used in the course of this paper–SNS (*Social Networking Service*), RL (*Real Life,* situations which are not Internet-mediated, offline), FB (Facebook) and GD (Gaydar). Having acknowledged the adequacy of the term "research participants" in the case of the Australian qualitative research, due to linguistic aptness I will be using it interchangeably with the term "respondents".

The research question raised by Cassidy was supposed to investigate "how do the cultures and practices surrounding identity management on Gaydar[1], as an example of an existing, community-specific SNS, fit into the broader ecology of its users' engagements with newer mainstream SNSs, such as Facebook, and their identity management processes in this space" (Cassidy 9). In other words, Cassidy aimed to research how homosexual men between 18–28, living in the city of Brisbane, use two types of SNSs in the process of identity management and what similarities and differences of activities within these two spaces can be observed. In terms of recognizing oneself as a positioned subject Cassidy considers himself an "observant participant" rather than participant observer (Cassidy 2013: 27) since he, just like his respondents, is a homosexual man who used to be a user of both Gaydar and Facebook.

The research employs two main methods of data collection. The first one is participant observation which is mediated through Gaydar profiles (7500 accounts) and various FB profiles and fanpages associated with the gay community in Brisbane (over 50 profiles and fanpages). The observation allowed for the analysis of gay men's self-presentations in both SNSs as well as for investigation of digital infrastructure of FB and GD as the

---

[1] As the author argues Gaydar, the SNS targeted at homosexual men, is extremely popular in most English-speaking countries. It offers two types of membership (a free guest account and a commercial membership account). It was established in 1999 in London and gained its popularity in Australia few years later. Cassidy notices that FB was launched in 2004 and its popularity increased in Australia at the turn of 2007 and 2008 when several magazines commented on social changes brought by this SNS. Thus, some participants had been using GD before they started using FB. In general Cassidy distinguishes two types of SNSs: the niche one (targeted at a specific group of people and revolving around particular interest or activity) and the mainstream one (unspecialized, not aimed at any specific group). Although there are some technical differences between various SNSs, most of them provide similar facilities such as: profiles (private, public or semi-public), contact lists, chats or messengers, photo albums and others. Most SNSs also allow for commenting and sharing various content (such as music, videos etc.) (Cassidy 5; as cited in boyd and Ellison 2007: 2, Albrechtslund 2008: 2, Livingstone 2008: 394).

environments within which the self-presentations operate. Cassidy examined how users design their presentations in terms of physical aspects, what kind of information users share with others, whether they celebrate or reject markers of gay identity etc. He also analyzed how users present and practice their group affiliations and what modes of interaction they employ. It allowed Cassidy to take into account the specificity of various templates and technical solutions which are offered to SNS users and of which they can take advantage.

In order to cope with the very problematic matter of private and public sphere division in cyberspace Cassidy adopts the perspective of continuum located between two opposite extrema–the public one (available to everyone with no limits, also for non-registered users) and the private one (strictly controlled by the author who precisely manages the visibility of given content and allows selected users to have access to it) (Cassidy 21; as cited in Sveningsson Elm 2009: 135). Cassidy locates SNSs within the semi-public sphere since privacy settings of different users may vary significantly. However, as the unobtrusive observation (which does not require any consent on the part of the observed) was to be carried out, the author needed to cope with the privacy concerns related to such observation. Thus, Cassidy assumes that public sphere for such observation includes spaces which can be accessed by every registered member[2] of a given SNS (Cassidy 24; as cited in Danet, Ruedenberg-Wright and Rosenbaum-Tamari 1997). The author indicates similarities between such a method of data collection and an offline observation which was employed during the research on nightclubs and shopping centers during the 1990s (Cassidy 24; as cited in Thornton 1996, Lewis 1990).

Another stage of Cassidy's study included individual semi-structured interviews and focus groups (FGI) with the users of both SNSs. Participant observation (site analysis) and individual interviews generated data which suggested questions for further exploration within focus groups. It allowed respondents to comment on the researcher's observation and hypotheses. In order to analyze the generated data Cassidy mobilized discourse analysis and used the QSR Nvivo program. Having analyzed the data he turned to SNSs again and studied profiles and groups within GD and FB, since hypotheses were still to be verified. Overall research which was carried out between 2009 and 2010 included a study of 7500 Gaydar profiles and over 40 Facebook groups and fanpages (related to homosexual men in Brisbane) of that time. A total of 30 respondents (homosexual

---

[2] It uncludes a non-commercial membership in GD.

men of different ages living in Brisbane, users of both FB and GD) took part in FGI and interviews.

In the self-reflexive part of his dissertation, the author admits that he used Social Networking Services for several purposes, such as exploring the "gay world" and trying to locate his identity within, following and assisting real-world LGBT events and bonding with peers. He also considered it a source of information and social capital. Cassidy's perspective on SNSs and their complex role in self-presentation inspired the analysis which brought various conclusions.

First, it seems that GD provides digital infrastructure and interface which may strengthen certain stereotypes of homosexual men[3]. The domination of the stereotypical model, from which most respondents distance themselves, leads to isolation and participatory reluctance. The latter is manifested by taking disapproving and dismissing attitudes towards other GD users and GD itself. However, such a negative stance does not stop those who are reluctant from participating in GD life. Reluctant participants consider themselves and their motivations as very different from the dominant ones. According to the respondents Facebook, in comparison to Gaydar, provides greater possibilities for self-presentation and self-expression in less stereotypical ways.

The participants indicated three premises which contribute to their skepticism about GD. Their reasons can be summarized as follows:

> nothing but casual sex can be found on GD; GD users are men who are looking for casual sex and who fit squarely into certain stereotypes of homosexual men; there is no real alternative to GD within niche SNSs.

The first reason stems from the participants' perception of GD as a place where they cannot find what they are mainly seeking–a monogamous and long-term relationship (they also quest for gay city guides, flatmates, gym buddies etc.). Most participants consider themselves an exception to the rule. On the one hand, the researched often mobilized the "myth of cyberspace" (Cassidy 85; as cited in Baym 2010) which divides the reality into separate spheres: the offline (the more "real", "important", "normal" or "authentic" one) and online (a kind of substitution for meaningful relations with other people) spheres. Such remarks correspond with the respondents' belief that GD is a place where nothing but casual sex (a superficial substitution of a relationship) can be found.

---

[3] Hedonistic and promiscous white, young, middle-class, homosexual men living in big cities with a strong interest in clubbing and designer clothes (Cassidy 91).

Furthermore, the very site, like all technologies, is far from ideologically neutral (Cassidy 85; as cited in Akrich, 1992; Latour, 1997; Lessig, 2000). A visit to GD is accompanied by adverts, competitions and various graphic elements which suggest the sexual and "superficial" (respondents' term) character of the site. Though sometimes ads related to LGBT or LGBT-friendly venues can be found, most commercials come from porn sites and have pornographic content. Home page and sign-out screens also include erotic graphics. The profile construction includes explicitly suggestive elements too: the possibility to send naked photographs, indicate penis size, circumcision status, sexual role preference, attitude towards safe sex, fetishes or sexual activities. All those indications appear as key words in a given profile. The very problematic question of fixed categorization and limited possibilities of control over identity performance is increased by *menu-driven identities* (Nakamura 2002) based on tick-box categories and drop-down menus. Drawing on other scholars' writings (Light, Fletcher and Adams 2008) Cassidy indicates (87) that homosexual men are considered to be less concerned about sex and selling of sex (which is offered in commercial GD membership). However, the group studied seems to contradict this.

Cassidy notices, that respondents' attitudes towards the site and other GD users is a very complex issue which is viciously cyclical. The respondents interact (or not) with other users and evaluate them with lowered expectations. At the same time the group being studied uses their stereotyped attitudes (for instance that GD is not a polite site) to justify their behavior, such as ignoring received messages or negative evaluation of other users on the basis of how they behave (even though the respondents behave in the same or similar way). The illustration of this paradoxical situation is a debate on the parts of profiles which are left blank. The respondents explained that the blank spaces in their profiles were a sign of resistance to the sexualized character of the site. However, when they commented on other users' blank profiles, they concluded that it is because these men use their accounts only to gain access to erotic materials and look for casual sex.

Nonetheless, the respondents' comments on the sexualized character of GD and its users do not seem unjustified. Besides the aforementioned erotic content of the site Cassidy presents some conclusions drawn from the observation and informal talks with older GD users. Older GD members admitted that they are unwilling to connect and stay in touch with the younger GD generation since they tend to chat infinitely and do not seem to strive for a meeting in RL. Older GD users consider such relationships a waste of time. In order to explain the generational shift Cassidy provides some wider sociopolitical context.

Taking into account the content of LGBT magazines and publications the Australian scholar concludes that with the passage of time gay identity, which used to be interwoven with political liberation and decriminalization of homosexuality, became more connected to a specific lifestyle and consumption. It seems that gays who became adults in the late 20th century no longer considered LGBT right movements as fundamental to their identity as older generations used to do. A new identity, named by Alan Sinfield (1998) as the metropolitan model, was closely linked to the consumption of particular goods and urban life of white, young, middle-class, homosexual men (Cassidy 91). The ever-expending mass media paved the way for the gay image to be associated with a camp aesthetical style[4], hedonism, promiscuity, clubbing, drug overuse and love of designer clothes. Its popularity was fueled by the phenomenon of *cybercarnality* (Cassidy 89; as cited in Mowlabocus 2010: 58) which refers to the pornographic mediation of the gay male body and the fact that for decades it was precisely the gay porn sphere where homosexual relations and practices had been validated and seen as normal. Elsewhere a very heteronormativite attitude towards sexuality had prevailed[5].

Cassidy fairly argues that since 2004 significant changes can be noticed in mainstream cinematic productions. Movies such as *Brokeback Mountain*, *A Single Man* or *Beginners* present a completely different from the metropolitan model image of homosexual mento wide audiences. Changes can also be observed in public sphere–coming outs which have become increasingly popular amongst famous athletes, movie stars, musicians and TV celebrities. They provide distinct images of homosexual men as they appear on the screen together with their partners and families. The flagship example seems to be Elton John and his husband. As Cassidy's research suggests another of Sinfield's (1998) suppositions that the new, internally diverse post-gay identity will appear in the 21st century was correct. Sinfield claimed that post-gay could not be defined in terms of particular lifestyle, interests, tastes, involvement in political struggle or even the sexual orientation itself.

---

[4] Which in general can be characterized by theatricality, exaggeration, exaltation and ostentation. Camp style is said to be provocative, impudent and somehow disruptive. As Susan Sontag writes (1964): "Many examples of Camp are things which, from a <<serious>> point of view, are either bad art or kitsch".

[5] Further explanation of *cybercarnality* available at: http://vimeo.com/31857570.

The participants' conviction that GD users strive for nothing but casual sex affects not only their attitude towards the site but also their self-perception. As they employ the mechanism of *cognitive simplification*[6] they tend to think of themselves as more normal, more real, more honest and happier than other GD users. The characteristics which respondents attribute to other GD users correspond with those which constitute the metropolitan model. Those in this study group do not wish to be identified with that model since to them it appears unfamiliar and limiting.

Taking the above-mentioned into consideration, the question which remains unanswered is why the participants use GD at all. All respondents, mostly at the age of 18, created their GD accounts since they did not know any other homosexual men (for various reasons such as living in the suburbs, attending boarding schools etc.). Even though the respondents admit that they made some friends via GD and they attended events sponsored by GD they also argue that GD did not provide them with any sense of belonging to a gay community. Facilitated interaction seemed outweighed by "counterproductive" elements of the site (Cassidy 100).

The participants do not publish their naked photos and they ignore sex offers (as well as money-for-sex offers usually sent by older users) they receive. They also declare that having explored several profiles of other users they usually felt discouraged to meet those men in person, for instance during some LGBT events. However, they do not seem to know that the number of young, frustrated and isolated GD users who are looking for a long-term relationship and who distance themselves from the metropolitan model is greater than they might expect. Cassidy claims that it is not necessarily a participants' ignorance or *misperception which leads to such a situation*. GD's interface imposes limited typology (exemplified by Twink and Bear[7] categories) which strongly restricts the possibilities of GD users' self-presentations. Then, even if the participants' intention is to leave blank spaces to mark their opposition to fixed categorizations offered by GD, the sexualized character of the site may suggest the wrong interpretation whenever such actions are taken by other users.

Drawing on Judith Butler's idea of *performativity* (1990) Cassidy notices, that GD users got involved into hitherto existing discourses on gay

---

[6] Which allows for distinguishing oneself from others and creating a positive self-definition (Cassidy 96; as cited in Buckingham 2008: 6).
[7] These are just two examples of a restrictive typology. Whereas Twink stands for a more "effeminate", young homosexual man who has a slim build and youthful look Bear seems to embody "masculine" traits as he is large, hairy and a bit crude.

identity. Those discourses which were shaped by previous generations and which became embodied and represented by GD digital infrastructure led to respondents' isolation and frustration. Besides some positive effects were already mentioned, GD does not seem to meet expectations which worked as a motivation for the participants to start using the site. GD does not provide a sense of belonging to some community, neither does it demarginalize respondents' identities (Cassidy 161; as cited in McKenna and Bargh 1998).

When asked about FB[8], the respondents took different attitudes and their comments and observations are somehow ambivalent. First, it seems important for the participants that FB does not require from its users any information which is directly related to sexual preferences[9]. In other words, there is no obligation to define oneself in terms of any sexual orientation. The respondents indicate (or not) their preferences and relations with other people in a variety of modes, which seemed to be a very different experience than simple self-definition offered by GD. The participants noticed that even when they indicate their interest in men, the more neutral character of interaction within FB made such indication much less less sexualized. Furthermore, as there is no particular goal or interest on which FB members are focused, the site does not impose any specific "model" of homosexuality. Also, the possibility to set one of many relationship statuses (including 'married' even if it is not legally admissible where a given person resides) extends users' freedom of self-presentation.

During FGI the respondents paid attention to another crucial aspect. Within FB they do not feel defined exclusively through the prism of their sexual orientation and the way they present themselves to the world is more open and changeable. The everyday information which is shared with others, such as movies, music or comments can be interwoven with posts about a night out in a gay club. The homosexual orientation is no

---

[8] It is worth reminding here that FB is the first mainstream SNS which in 2012 was awarded by GLAAD (*Gay and Lesbian Alliance Against Defamation*) with the Special Recognition Award for its involvement in anti-bullying campaigns and for various efforts to reach an inclusive representation (exemplified by the possibility to set same-sex relationship statuses).

[9] Although FB users do not specify their sexual orientation Cassidy received several invitations from companies or institutions which had been previously present on GD as well as from some unknown gay men from all over the world. Moreover, in the 'people you may know' column Cassidy noticed familiar faces he recognized from the local, offline LGBT events. Hence, there seem to be a growing convergence between digital gay culture and mainstream SNSs.

central issue and it is not precisely framed. The same is true for hetero- or bisexuality which makes all these statuses equal. The more neutral FB interface eliminates the conviction that other gay men present on FB are looking for nothing but casual sex. The group studied stopped positioning themselves in opposition to the imagined others and they ceased to consider themselves as more normal or more real. Thus, their feeling of isolation reduced. Also, the equal terms of self-presentations through a stream of information[10] available for all FB users allow a more natural narrative to be constructed. Borrowing from Anthony Giddens (1991: 54) Cassidy (106) draws attention to this creative potential which makes "a particular narrative going" and composes a continuous story about a self. In the case of FB the narrative is not sexualized or reduced to restrictive typologies/stereotypes, which is appreciated by the participants.

Another important remark on FB is that the general transparency and lack of anonymity within the site increases users' authenticity and strengthens the conviction that their self-presentations correspond with who they are in RL[11]. According to the participants, the very popular practice is to leave in GD a notice about the FB profile (for instance by sharing an e-mail address) so that a given user can find one on FB. In this way the participants avoid inscribing themselves into the restrictive GD template. Also, due to the wider stream of information[12] FB allows for compatibility verification and facilitates the selection of people with whom the respondents would like to stay in contact. Looking through somebody's friends list seems to be a useful source of information. Not only does it suggest what kind of person one is but also some more or less complicated relations with other people can be noticed (as Cassidy argues [133] somebody's "history" is of utmost importance for minority groups residing in smaller

---

[10] Which includes posting various remarks, liking, commenting, partaking in different events [LGBT ones too], joining interest groups and many others.

[11] On the one hand, self-presentations in online spaces are rarely honest (Cassidy 42; as cited in Baym 2010: 121). However, Cassidy fairly notices (42) that the debate over authenticity leads to the question of anonymity seen as disembodiment and liberation from stigmatized identities (as for disabled people) or demarginalization of identities (McKenna & Bargh 1998, Morahan-Martin 1999, Tyler 2002, McIntosh and Harwood 2002). The more pessimistic vision of online anonymity suggests the possibility of social isolation and problems with the interaction in RL (Cassidy 42; as cited in Kiesler, Siegel and McGuire 1984, Beninger 1987, Parks and Floyd 1996).

[12] One participant provided an example of information about religious and political beliefs. Although there is a possibility to reveal one's religious and political beliefs in GD the participant argues that FB allows to learn more about somebody's attitudes due to the variety of information shared.

areas). Checking a FB profile which belongs to somebody the respondents know from GD and screening one's friends serves as a "virtual compass" (Cassidy 130; as cited in Donath and boyd 2004). It helps avoid interaction with those whom the participants cannot tolerate as their friends.

The wide variety of information which can be shared on FB is considered by the participants as a huge advantage[13]. However, Cassidy (125) borrows from Fiske and Taylor (1984) and their concept of *cognitive miser*[14] and draw on some research (Ellison, Heino and Gibbsa 2006) which indicates that in technologically-mediated environments cognitive misery is heavily increased when compared with offline milieu. In the case of SNS (Cassidy 126; as cited in Baym 2010: 119) the very fragmented information (particular photos, quotes, shared interests etc.) are used to fill the blanks in our knowledge about other users. Consequently such simplified images are built upon social cues which are very distinct from those processed in face-to-face interaction. Such phenomena are present despite the amplified range of information shared on FB.

Still, it seems that FB plays an important role in reducing participants' sense of isolation through interaction with other homosexual users who join particular LGBT-friendly places, events or interest groups. The respondents were almost unanimous in their claims about contacting other like-minded gay men with similar interests. They argued that these relations were just normal and fit their way of living[15]. Cassidy notices that becoming members of various groups, partaking in different events and general interaction within FB is not experienced by the group studied as belonging to the gay community but to the "normal" or "open" one. Their resistance to the metropolitan model offered by GD appears even more explicitly here.

The conclusions drawn from the observation of local LGBT groups on FB correspond with respondents' critical comments on GD. Those groups

---

[13] Cassidy (124) indicates that the self-disclosure, which is possible on FB, is connected with what Caroline Haythornthwaite (2005) calls *media multiplexity* (MM). MM stands for people's tendency to employ more media in relationships as people grow closer. That is another reason why it is FB and not GD, which is used by the respondents to maintain the acquaintances made offline.

[14] This term refers to people's tendency to use mental shortcuts and minimize their cognititive effort while making sense of the world around. Because of efficiency reasons people employ the least complicated (and not the most accurate) approach in order to solve a provlem. As a result huge volumes of information are extrapolated on the basis of minimal social cues.

[15] For instance, one respondent used FB to find and join a local LGBT swimming squad.

which revolve around sexual orientation itself (such as "Gay Brisbane") are less active and less numerous in comparison to groups associated with various activities or hobbies. Moreover, at the time of observation out of 133 members of "Brisbane Gay Men's Facebook Chat Group" 126 users were over 30 years old which confirms respondents' (who were between 18 and 28 years old) claims that their attitude towards sexuality and its role in identity formation is connected with generational shift. The participants were eager to join groups associated with various events and interests associated with LGBT people[16] rather than groups which just gather homosexual people.

The question concerning the future existence and usefulness of such sites as GD in the present form evoked discrepant opinions. Participants debated whether GD (as a necessary evil) is indispensable for young gays to become familiar with some part of gay culture (even if they reject it) or it is detrimental as it strengthens the domination of the metropolitan model. The general conclusion drawn was that the advent of mainstream SNS, which are not targeted at any specific group of people, enables the users to present themselves in a more unrestricted manner and thus makes younger generations more critical about GD-like sites.

As Cassidy underlines, privacy concerns and identity management are inseparably linked. Keeping the balance between the information which is revealed and concealed is central to identity formation (Cassidy 145; as cited in Goffman 1959, Schlenker 1980, Baym 2010, Quercia et al. 2012). The decision about a disclosure of particular information lies at the very heart of various relationships (Cassidy 145; as cited in Altman and Taylor 1973, Chan and Cheng 2004) and lets distinct roles to be taken on in different interactions. Naturally, what is considered private is socially negotiable and depends on a wide spectrum of factors and circumstances such as historical context and social expectations (Cassidy 145; as cited in Prost et al. 1991) affected by race, sexual orientation, social status, religious beliefs and many others (Cassidy 145; see more: Gilbert, Karahalios and Sandvig 2008, Chang et al. 2010, Quercia et al. 2012, Tufekci 2012).

To draw a line between various contexts or types of interaction in RL seems easier than to do it in cyberspace. Online communication mediated by SNS is constantly endangered by *context collapse* (Cassidy 13; as cited in Hogan 2010, Marwick and boyd 2011) and *privacy trainwreck* (Cassidy 48; as cited in boyd 2008) since the users need to face the fact that the information they share can be re-shared, commented and received in very different con-

---

[16] For instance "Top the Chef: Gay Cooking Club" (Cassidy 121).

texts in real-time. The awareness of what the norms of a given interaction are and who participates in the interactional situation in cyberspace is lower[17] and so is the accuracy of measures employed. The successful interaction requires not only participants' awareness of this fact but also their *technological literacy* (Cassidy 146; as cited in boyd and Hargittai 2010) which allows for the proper management of privacy settings and information visibility.

Cassidy argues that GD privacy arrangements are simple, stable, intuitive and user friendly. GD privacy policy includes regulations of account privacy (external access to the profile, its visibility in search engines, visit tracking), protection against unauthorized use of private content (picture watermarking), LGBT-friendly police, options to block a given user from one's account and many others. Whether one prefers full transparency (with profile's visibility in search engines and one's real name[18]) or invisibility, the accessibility to all functions offered by GD remains the same (the same functions are also available to the users who have no friends added or are not members of any groups).

For most respondents the chance to recognize somebody offline (during different events) who they already knew from GD improves their comfort and confidence as the site users. Often the reversed situation–discovering that somebody respondents knew in person was present on GD–was a catalyst in relationships (particularly those with neighbors, flatmates or colleagues). Another positive aspect is a facilitated interaction online after even the most coincidental encounter offline and vice versa. In both cases the initiation of conversation was easier. Moreover, in spite of the negative opinion on GD in general, one of the respondents argued that his sense of isolation reduced significantly after he had discovered that there are so many homosexual men living in Brisbane (it is worth noticing that discovering the very number of homosexual men living in Brisbane does not translate into positive evaluation of these people).

Several privacy concerns refer to offline encounters with GD users with whom the participants only had online contact. The respondents highlight *non-gay contexts*, such as a chance meeting in a store during work. Some better or worse relations which stem from previous online interaction seem to be valid only in that specific context and cannot be easily transferred into the offline situation between a customer and a shop assistant. The participants also draw attention to the impression they could

---

[17] In comparison with offline situations. Face-to-face interaction is usually limited to a specific audience and takes place in a given space.
[18] Which is not required.

not dispose of and which made them feel uncomfortable. They tended to create negative images of GD users on the basis of what they had observed online and could not change such unfavorable perception while seeing these people offline.

On the other hand, Facebook privacy concerns are far more complex. Cassidy elaborates on multiplicity of options and extended regulations. He also notices that for an ordinary user it can be really time-consuming to become familiar with all the details of constantly changing privacy policies (default settings after each change do not provide the highest privacy protection). FB's insistence on transparency with its requirement of real-name profiles (successfully circumvented by some users) appears as a place where users are encouraged to reveal as much information as possible. Such elements of digital infrastructure as the Timeline which is expected to present the story of a lifetime or various applications which summarize specific periods of users' life are quite suggestive examples.

By offering and somehow imposing such transparency and openness, Facebook subscribes to a "nothing to hide, nothing to fear" style of rhetoric. It divides people into those who may be afraid to freely express themselves in some contexts and those who have no (or little) reason to fear. It does not come as a surprise that the respondents have their doubts about the policy which is conducive to *context collapse*. Reduced control over the shared information increases the possibility of being received by audiences which are not the addressee. Drawing on other scholars' writings (Cassidy 167; as cited in Hogan 2011, boyd 2011) Cassidy also notices that the potential decontextualization[19] somehow violates the right to free speech which is context-specific[20].

In general, privacy concerns related to FB are definitely much greater. One of the most troublesome questions is the possibility that the information shared within FB can reach close family (and not some unknown people as in the case of GD) to whom it is not addressed (Cassidy 169; as cited in Livingstone 2008). The researched were concerned about the unwanted mixing of information on their orientation with those from professional, domestic and other spheres. Even those participants who openly identified themselves as gay in all possible contexts did not want their homosexuality to be "rubbed in the face" of their families (Cassidy 170).

---

[19] Which can happen when the information is re-shared or shared with new (or edited) comments added.
[20] Since people are free to say what they want to the audience they chose and in the specified situation they are aware of.

Due to participants' inability to control all the information via privacy settings, some of them resort to self-censorship whereas others rely on the idea which resembles Goffman's civil inattention (Cassidy 170; as cited in Goffman 1963). In other words, they assume that some gay-oriented content they share would be ignored or misunderstood by those to whom the information is not addressed. However, those participants who could not count on civil inattentiveness (since, for some reasons, they could not come out to all possible audiences at a particular moment) employed alternative strategies for protecting their privacy.

The most popular tactic seems to be the limitation of FB friends (realized in many different ways–by the upper limit, personal/offline acquaintance, probation period, according to common interests etc.). Some participants create special codes for their gay friends or gay locations (so that they could be understood only by specific audiences). As Cassidy notices (172) coding, as a method based on social knowledge and not on structural access, has been also noticed by other researchers (Marwick and boyd 2011: 2) who studied the usage of SNS by teenagers and parental surveillance. Another tactic is "lagging" (sharing information about different activities with such delay that people who live in the respondent's hometown cannot keep track of his life), untagging photos from LGBT events or deleting suggestive comments. One of the respondents decided to only post such information which he considered proper to be viewed by all SNS members, which Cassidy calls (Cassidy 173; as cited in Hogan 2010) *the lowest common denominator approach.*

Cassidy notices further negative implications of FB transparency for the researched group. Some self-restrictions which respondents impose limit their access both to online socializing (when they stop being members of some LGBT groups due to the possible leak of such information) and offline integration (when they stop attending offline LGBT events due to the possible leak of photos and the unsolicited linking to one's FB profile). The phenomenon of *facestalking* (undesirable following and monitoring somebody's profile on FB often connected with intimidation or harassment) was also mentioned as a serious privacy concern for those who use simultaneously FB and GD.

It seemed that some of the participants' privacy concerns are quite justified. Out of 30 respondents 3 were outed[21] to their families via FB, which caused family conflicts. The participants also indicated offline stalking

---

[21] When a person is outed it means that one has been discovered as a homosexual without one's persmission or intention.

(which can be facilitated by FB transparency) as particularly threatening due to the relative low number of homosexual men in Brisbane and few physical places (which along with events can be traced online) where they meet.

What seems important for further SNSs analysis is the fact that the participants (despite the employment of various preventive measures) do not appreciate the very basic features of information located in cyberspace. Drawing on other scholars' writings (Marwick and Boyd 2011: 9) Cassidy (177) itemizes four important properties of such information:
- *persistence*
- *replicability*
- *scalability*
- *searchability*

All these properties have a significant influence on the users' safety, specifically when users are not too familiar with how to configure their privacy settings. The flagship example are pictures from LGBT events which in pre-SNS era (or even before the Internet gained such popularity) appeared in paper magazines[22] targeted and usually read by a specific audience. It was not possible to multiply the materials infinitely and at the great speed or seek them in real time with the help of search *algorithms*. The control over information on FB is also weakened since the re-sharing destabilizes its placement. As a result, pictures from a local gay club in Brisbane appear not only to those who look through the fanpage but also to those who follow it (as they receive a notice in their newsfeed) or those who are tagged in the photos[23]. It is also seen by friends of the user who are not in the photo but simply shared it.

When it comes to comparison of privacy concerns related to FB and GD, the former evokes definitely more doubts. Facebook as a space where the information can be shared and re-shared, commented, multiplied,

---

[22] Instead of 400-500 digital pictures which circulate in the web out of control in various contexts there were 4-5 photos in a given issue.

[23] It is worth noticing that whether a given user requires to check and accept tags before they appear on one's timeline or not they are visible in the SNS anyway. When some of our friends recognize us in the photo and tags us in the comment, this comment redirects others to our profile. Sometimes several comments start a whole discussion which could be followed both by friends of the users tagged in the photo (or in the comments) and by those who follow a given fanpage or simply look through it. After several re-sharings the photo together with the comments which accompany it can appear completely out of context. The user who is in the photo can be unaware of a potential homophobic bulling until he or she logs in FB (and reads a notification) or discovers the photo oneself.

received in various contexts by unknown audiences which makes the interactional situation somehow unpredictable and results in context collapse. Due to the growing popularity of FB and its expanding outreach more and more people use this SNS as their regular work tool which complicates the matters even more. On the other hand, less abstruse privacy settings and no real-name policy in GD results in minor concerns. The possible identification of a GD user is usually connected with two negative phenomena[24]: one's homosexuality is revealed (those users who did not come out in all spheres of life) or/and one is inscribed into the metropolitan model (those users who came out but do not wish to be identified with such a model).

Apart from privacy and safety concerns related to each SNS the respondents indicate some interconnections between FB and GD in terms of both safety and functionality. The majority of participants (27 out of 30) claimed they use simultaneously both SNSs due to practical reasons. They initially search for other homosexual men in GD and then they turn to FB to gain more information on that user (for instance by using one's e-mail address). Such a strategy, as reported by respondents, often helps avoid "dramas"[25] (Cassidy 183). Sometimes, using FB, they also follow places and events, wherein a given user declares to appear, and arrange encounters. However, in a reversed situation the respondents express serious concerns about such *facestalking*.

On the other side, before the advent of FB, GD users could only be recognized by some skillful observer from GD. FB allows you to not only find a user's real name but also to discover a lot more or less personal information which is circulating within the SNS. It discourages GD users from setting their faces in profile pictures or from using FB or MSN as communicators[26]. The latter practice used to be a regular one not only because of ideological reasons (trying to keep off of GD as much as possible) but also because of technical premises. The chat offered by GD is said to be problematic for the non-commercial user.

While drawing more general conclusions Cassidy (192) quotes Kris Schmidt (2011), the gay blogger who argued that "no one has benefited more socially from the Internet than the gays. The Internet opened up an entire world to let gay people know we're not alone; that there is hope

---

[24] Gaydar is used mainly by other homosexual men, hence the possibility of homophobic bullying or purposeful spread of orientation-related information is more unlikely. The amount of personal data and the opportunity to trace someone is very limited in comparison to FB, therefore the danger of stalking is reduced too.

[25] The engagement into unworthy relations.

[26] MSN reveals user's e-mail address which can be used to search for more information in FB.

and help out there; and that you're perfect just the way you are". Referring to the Australian research (Hillier, Kurdas and Horsely 2001) Cassidy (12) underlines that chats used to play an important role in homosexual youth's lives. Interaction with like-minded others, facilitation of offline relations with same-sex-attracted young people, reduction of a sense of isolation, provision of a sense of community and safe spaces for discussion are just some of the benefits of chats. Thus, the very fact that the participants in Cassidy's research indicated several privacy concerns seems important not only due to the long history of LGBT people's engagement in social media and Internet communication. It seems also significant since this demographic is considered to be skilled at identity management and equilibration of disclosure and concealment of personal information in various contexts, also those technologically-mediated (Cassidy 188; see more: Gross 2007: vii–x).

However, the role of SNS in gay digital culture is crucial not only because this demographic has been long involved in SNSs usage or due to the groundbreaking opportunities to interact with other non-heteronormative people provided by SNSs and Internet communication. It is also the struggle for the legalization of same-sex-marriages, combating stereotypes and counteracting against homophobic bullying which is carried out within places such as FB, Twitter or Youtube. The SNSs' contribution to the reduction of homophobic bullying will be commented in the further part of this article.

Cassidy's dissertation provides rich, qualitative data which reveals various motivations, strategies and dilemmas connected with identity management in two different SNSs. The study becomes an important source of knowledge not only for academics but also for SNS and other digital space designers. As the research was focused mainly on FB and GD some questions related to other SNSs, such as Grindr or Hornet were not elaborated upon. Undoubtedly, respondents' remarks encourage further explorations in this direction.

Also, taking into account LGBT youth's higher level of anxiety and depression (Cassidy 194; as cited in Leonard et al. 2012) as well as a higher rate of suicidal thoughts and behaviors[27] (Cassidy 194; as cited in National LGBTI Health Alliance 2010, Suicide Prevention Australia 2009: 20) the study seems to be a source of key information on privacy concerns, fear of homophobic bullying or a sense of collective belonging and isolation. The latter respondents experienced this within a part of the LGBT community

---

[27] In comparison to the heteronormative youth.

rather than outside of it (Cassidy 194). Such observation can be crucial for LGBT organizations which cope with matters of mental health.

The study provokes further questions about the anxiety and its intensity when it comes to disclosure or concealment of sexual orientation of those non-heteronormative SNS users who are closeted or partially out. Cassidy underlines, that not all participants, who were out in every possible context, approved of FB full transparency. It seems that a different degree of users' sensitivity to unwitting outings and their vulnerability to such situations is of a very complex nature. The identification and examination of various factors and contexts which can increase the users' anxiety, such as specificity of a given workplace or friends' beliefs and ideological convictions may contribute to the modification of SNSs policy as well as to wider social changes.

The generational shift which seems to have taken place among homosexual men is another important aspect of Cassidy's research. Fear of being perceived through the prism of specific stereotypes, the opposition to sexualization and the metropolitan model as well as the wish for normalization[28] indicate an important change which was brought by the new generation. Cassidy's conclusions are not based solely on his research. He underlines that the necessity for redefinition of gay identity was publicly highlighted in 2012, when the founder of *Hello Mr.* magazine, Ryan Fitzgibbon, wrote about the misrepresentation of homosexual men (Cassidy 196; as cited in Fitzgibbon 2012). This shift is related to the new generation's distinct experience of gay history and culture since particular problems, values and priorities of previous generations have been replaced by new ones. Such a problem might be solved with LGBT organizations' further efforts to promote variety and less restrictive identity models. It could decrease a sense of isolation and respondents' feelings of inadequacy (as Cassidy underlines the participants' sense of isolation did not stem exclusively from the discovery of being homosexual but from the lack of correspondence between their behaviors, attitudes and longings and the dominant metropolitan model).

Finally, the research draws attention to the growing role of SNSs in identity management in general, not only for non-heteronormative users. Cassidy draws attention to the growing pressure to partake in SNS life and all users' need to face privacy breach and context collapse. The online environment with its constantly expanding options, novel techno-

---

[28] Achieved through the increased diversity of homosexual men representation which finally leads to the equalization of various orientations.

logical solutions and changing goals is where identities are being shaped to a higher extent (Cassidy 191; as cited in James et al. 2008: 15). The interdependent and colliding practices of identity management in different online spaces are likely to play an increasingly important role.

Bearing in mind the relevance of the Australian research it seems that the current state of LGBT studies and digital culture studies in Poland suggests the increased demand for common efforts aimed at developing interdisciplinary projects of this kind. As the literature review lies beyond the scope of this article my intention is to refer to some Polish research which cope with similar matters and to comment on the possibilities of further explorations. In recent years dynamic developments of Polish studies in digital culture and its various aspects can be noticed. Within the field of digital culture one can find research which corresponds with Cassidy's study. The results of the first one are presented in a paper entitled "Connecting to reality–Polish gays in the Internet/Polscy geje w internecie" (2006). The study was carried out by Marta Klimowicz from the University of Wroclaw. The results of the second study are presented in the article entitled "The influence of the Internet on relations in groups of homosexual men in the city of Torun/Wpływ internetu na relacje w grupie osób homoseksualnych w Toruniu" (Lewandowski & Kobylska 2011). The research was undertaken by a group of students from the Nicolas Copernicus University in Torun. Even though both studies are analytically less advanced in comparison with Cassidy's full doctoral dissertation, they set an interesting direction for further exploration.

The Torunian research, just like the Australian one, examined two types of data: the content of SNSs and in-depth interviews with eleven homosexual men (of different age) from Torun. The report presents remarks on the impact of digital and web environment on relationships among Torunian gays, which means it is not focused exclusively on SNSs. Klimowicz also analyzed two types of data: the content of gay blogs and sites (she employed both qualitative and quantitative measures) as well as standarized interviews and replies to queries posted on gay forums. Thus, her study does not analyze SNS directly as she focused on a kind of online collectivity which is constituted by homosexual men in Poland and on a role which virtual spaces play in their lives. On the other side, the Torunian project (which draws on Klimowicz's study) aimed to explore how the Internet affects homosexual men on a collective and individual level and in terms of internal communication. Both studies share an interest in interrelations between offline and online interactions of homosexual men.

While writing about this field of research in Poland and Australia it is worth commenting on some sociopolitical circumstances which are common for both places. First, there was little or no positive representation of homosexual men in the mainstream media in the period before 1990. Despite the fact that officially homosexuality ceased to be penalized in Poland in 1932, it was still persecuted during the communist period. Any official and open LGBT activity was hampered and the very question of non-heteronormative people situation became marginalized (the authorities' refusal of official recognition of the Warsaw Gay Movement in late 1980s, the Operation Hyacinth and others). In Queensland homosexuality was decriminalized in 1990 (Cassidy 72) which suggests the specificity of LGBT people's situation beforehand. Cassidy comments (72) on governments' endeavors to block any consolidation of LGBT milieu. The sociopolitical atmosphere in Poland and Australia before 1990 resulted in homosexual people's invisibility on one hand and to their consolidation (paradoxically, as counter-reaction) on the other.

The very brief description of the Torunian environment of homosexual men and its transformations brings into perspective the changes brought on by the advent of the Internet. The authors start with an overview of the pre-1989 period when informal (and illegal) gay gatherings/cruisings (Pol. *pikiety*) were a popular form of contact with other gays. Relations started during such meetings and were usually passing acquaintances of a sexual character. Any information about meetings circulated within narrow circles and was confidential. The period after 1989 was the time when the first gay bars and clubs appeared[29]. Also, the first official LGBT organizations and magazines[30] were founded. The changing situation increased group consciousness and boosted the development of symbolic communication and linguistic metaphors (Lewandowski & Kobylska 201). It also reduced anonymity. The sources of gay identity were to be found in personal interactions with other homosexual men but also in official publications on LGBT matters. The role of stereotypes and heteronormative knowledge started to be diminished. However, as Klimowicz fairly argues (308) the representation of homosexual men in Polish media was (and still is) scarce and biased when compared with, for instance, American discourse.

---

[29] The research describes Torunian reality of that time. Generally in Poland before 1989 pubs in which homosexual men were gathering existed in disguise. The informal gay pubs are referred to by Krzysztof Tomasik in his book *Gejerel. Sexual minorities in the People's Republic of Poland/Gejerel. Mniejszości seksualne w PRL-u* (2012).

[30] The situation was similar in Queensland where the very first local LGBT publication, *Queensland Pride*, was issued in 1991 (Cassidy 72).

The identity formation, as inextricably linked to the accessibility of information, was therefore significantly affected by the advent of new media[31]. Both Polish (Lewandowski & Kobylska 202) and Australian (Cassidy 159) studies reveal that new media and web communication significantly increased group consciousness and LGBT people's interaction. Cyberspace permits secure and comfortable searches for various content and facilitates the exchange of experiences and interaction with like-minded people. Cyberspace also affects the coming-out process and speeds it up (Lewandowski & Kobylska 211). Klimowicz (317) underlines that gay blogging also reduces the sense of isolation and loneliness due to the free exchange of experiences and thoughts. The information shared by other users (via forums, blogs or other spaces) provides a base for the negotiation of behavioral patterns, norms or solutions to interactional pitfalls (321). Thus, further studies on sexual minorities' identity formation and digital, web-based environment appear extremely necessary.

One of the most interesting of Klimowicz's conclusions is that in spite of the increased LGBT-related content in traditional media (for instance the growing number of cover stories on LGBT matters in mainstream magazines, see more: Oliwa 2012: 113) cyberspace is considered to be more representative of reality than the offline world. Moreover, the respondents argue that initiating a long-term relationship on the Internet is perfectly normal and valuable. Besides, they believe that cyberspace allows the tightening of the relation and getting to know the other party better (Klimowicz 320). It stays in partial but apparent contradiction with the Australian research (Cassidy 85) where the aforementioned *myth of cyberspace* was alive[32].

On the other side, the advent of the Internet and new media led to a kind of disintegration of the Torunian group of homosexual men. It seems that such disintegration overlaps with Cassidy's conclusion since the extension and dispersion of young homosexual men's identities was sparked in both groups. The participants do not feel obliged to adopt, for instance, the metropolitan model. Also, they do not consider being homosexual men as inseparably connected with partaking in cruising, going

---

[31] Beforehand this information was much more limited. The scarce and biased representation of homosexual men in the mainstream media and growing, but still limited, interaction of Torunian gays prevailed.

[32] As the *myth of cyberspace* was mobilized only in the context of Gaydar it cannot be extended over the whole online environment.

out to gay bars or being engaged in political struggle. Internet-mediated interaction allowed young men to define themselves as gays on different terms (Lewandowski & Kobylska 202). The growing diversity and emerging subgroups (revolving around various interests, ways of life etc.) are parts of the same process within which the resistance to the metropolitan model is located. The experiences of isolation and the growing diversity of gay identity in Poland promotes further examination.

Attention should also be paid to the question of anonymity, which according to Torunian authors (Lewandowski & Kobylska 205) is highly appreciated by the respondents and motivates them to use niche SNSs for gays. Does the anonymity affect these users' involvement in mainstream SNSs? Do gay SNS users consider transparency disturbing or useful in reducing homophobic bullying and hate speech? What are the interrelations between using mainstream and gay SNSs in the Polish context? How does the specific sociopolitical context influence the participation in online communities?[33].

I believe that a comparative research which explores how two demographics (different generations of homosexual men with similar sociometric parameters) manage their identities online while using SNSs (both niche and mainstream ones) could be realized with mixed methods of data collection and analysis (such as content analysis of secondary data available online and multiple FGI or IDI with subjects of both demographics). Such research could reveal how different generations of homosexual men are affected by the growing participation in SNS and the increasing importance of online spaces.

Urgent questions which could be studied within such projects are privacy concerns (specifically those related to coming outs) and the diversification of gay identity. The research would also provide some clues about SNSs' role in promoting equality. Finally, it could be verified how the *Parasocial Contact Hypothesis* (PCH) resonates with the presence of

---

[33] Polish context seems specific for at least two reasons. First, the history of mainstream SNS usage is relatively shorter and has its peculiarities. Second, two main Polish gay-targeted SNSs (*Kumpello* and *Fellow*) seem less sexualized when analized in the manner employed by Cassidy. One of the first options offered to newcomers in *Kumpello* is the possibility to set a filter on sexually offensive content. Neutral ads (bookstores, banks) can be noticed in the background. The site offers various interest groups or place-related groups. *Fellow* seems to be more sexualized–there can be noticed half-naked models in the background, however, the pictures cannot be labeled as pornographic or even erotic since they could be easily presented on *Men's Health* cover. *Fellow* also offers a more extended template of sexual preferences.

non-heteronormative people in mainstream SNSs[34]. Cassidy (69) pays some attention to PCH while noticing that common interests, friends or places visited can build positive relations and reduce homophobic bias[35]. The variety of information shared via FB and the multifaceted interaction in the site (for instance hetero- and non-heteronormative users' participation in the same interest group etc.) can be seen as a kind of parasocial contact and may reduce the homophobic bias or facilitate mutual understanding of heteronormative and non-heteronormative users. It can also normalize their interactions by making sexual orientation a non-issue. In order to gain better answers to such questions it would require engaging both homosexual and heterosexual respondents.

Generational differences seem to have various implications, ranging from technological literacy, through to distinct sociopolitical (or socio historical) experiences, ending up with a variety of problematic coming outs. The latter issue seems particularly important for those men who stayed in the closet for several years (sometimes decades) because of unfavorable circumstances of the past which had shaped their family or professional situations (Lewandowski & Kobylska 214). Contrasting participants for whom SNSs and online interaction are inseparably linked with their lives (and thus play a naturally greater role) with homosexual men whose identities were also being shaped in the pre-Internet era would provide a more holistic image of this still relatively unexplored field of research.

Bibliography

Akrich Madeline 1992, *The De-scription of Technical Objects*, [in:] *Shaping Technology/building Society: Studies in Sociotechnical Change*, eds. W. Bijker and J. Law, Cambridge (MA): MIT Press.

Albrechtslund Anders 2008, "Online Social Networking as Participatory Surveillance", *First Monday* No. 13(3).

---

[34] PCH aasumes that the indirect/mediated contact with positive images of minorities can result in bias reduction. In practice PCH could be verified, for instance, by tracing the influence of the positive representation of Tomasz Raczek (Polish film critic and journalist who, together with his partner, was awarded Gala Roses 2008 for the most beautiful couple of the year) on the mitigation of homophobic attitudes.

[35] In terms of PCH it seems that due to the basic properties of Internet communication the information can be considered as more "real" or les ideologically burdened (no central distribution of information, the possibility to post critical comments and to share information freely etc.).

Altman Irwin, Taylor Dalmas 1973, *Social Penetration: The Development of Interpersonal Relationships*, New York: Holt.

Baym Nancy K. 2010, *Personal Connections in the Digital Age*, Malden (MA): Polity.

Beninger James R. 1987, "Personalization of Mass Media and the Growth of Pseudocommunity", *Communication Research*, No. 14.

boyd danah 2008, "Facebook's Privacy Trainwreck: Exposure, Invasion, and Social Convergence", *Convergence*, No. 14(1).

boyd danah, Ellison Nicole B. 2007, "Social Network Sites: Definition, History, and Scholarship", *Journal of Computer-Mediated Communication*, No. 13(1): http://jcmc.indiana.edu/vol13/issue1/boyd.ellison.html

boyd danah, Hargittai Eszter 2010, "Facebook Privacy Settings: Who cares?", *First Monday*, No. 15(8).

boyd danah, Marwick Alice 2011, *Social Privacy in Networked Publics: Teens' Attitudes, Practices, and Strategies*, paper presented on 22nd August during the Oxford Internet Institute Decade in Internet Time Symposium, available at: http://www.danah.org/papers/2011/SocialPrivacyPLSC-Draft.pdf.

Buckingham David 2008, *Introducing Identity*, [in:] *Youth, Identity, and Digital Media*, Cambridge MA: The MIT Press.

Butler Judith 1990, *Gender Trouble: Feminism and the Subversion of Identity*, New York: Routledge.

Cassidy Elija M. 2013, *Gay Men, Social media and Self-presentation: Managing Identities in Gaydar, Facebook and Beyond*, doctoral dissertation written at Queensland University of Technology, available at: http://eprints.qut.edu.au/61773/

Chan Darius K. S, Cheng Grand H. L. 2004, "A Comparison of Offline and Online Friendship Qualities at Different Stages of Relationship Development", *Journal of Personal and Social Relationships*, No. 21(3).

Danet Brenda., Ruedenberg-Wright Lucia, Rosenbaum-Tamari Yehudit 1997, "'Hmmm... Where's That Smoke Coming From?'. Writing, Play and Performance on Internet Relay Chat, *Journal of Computer-Mediated Communication*, No. 2(4).

Donath Judith, boyd danah 2004, "Public Displays of Vonnection", *BT Technology Journal*, No. 22(4).

Ellison Nicole, Heino Rebecca, Gibbs Jennifer 2006, "Managing Impressions Online: Selfpresentation Processes in the Online Dating Environment", *Journal of Computer-Mediated Communication*, NO. 11(2), available at: http://jcmc.indiana.edu/vol11/issue2/ellison.html

Fiske Susan, Taylor Shelley 1984, *Social Cognition*, Boston (MA): Addison-Wesley.

Fitzgibbon Ryan 2012, "About the Magazine", *HelloMr.*, available at: http://hellomrmag.com.

Giddens Anthony 1991, *Modernity and Self-Identity: Self and Society in the Late Modern Age*, Stanford: Stanford University Press.

Goffman Erving 1959, *The Presentation of Self in Everyday Life*, Carden City, N.Y.: Doubleday Anchor.

Goffman Erving 1963, *Behaviour in Public Places: Notes on the Social Organization of Gatherings*, New York: Free Press.

Gross Larry 2007, *Foreword*, [in:] *Queer Online: Media, Technology and Sexuality*, eds. K. O'Riordan, D. J. Phillips, New York: Peter Lang.

Haythornthwaite Caroline 2005, "Social Networks and Internet Connectivity Effects", *Information, Communication and Society*, No. 8(2).

Hillier Lynne, Kurdas Chyloe, Horsley Philomena 2001, *'It's just easier': the Internet as a safety-Net for same sex attracted young people*, Melbourne: Australian Research Centre in Sex Health and Society, La Trobe University, available at: http://apo.org.au/node/15390

Hogan Bernie 2011, *Real Name Sites Are Necessarily Inadequate for Free Speech*, post from 08.08, available at: http://people.oii.ox.ac.uk/hogan/

Hogan Bernie 2010, "The Presentation of Self in the Age of Social Media: Distinguishing Performances and Exhibitions Online", *Bulletin of Science, Technology and Society*, No. 30(6).

Kiesler Sara, Siegel Jane, McGuire Timothy W. 1984, "Social Psychological Aspects of Computer-mediated Communication", *American Psychologist*, No. 39(10).

Klimowicz Marta 2006, *Connecting to reality – polscy geje w internecie*, [in:] *Re: Internet – społeczne aspekty medium*, eds. Ł. Jonak, P. Mazurek, M. Olcoń, A. Przybylska, A. Tarkowski, J. M. Zając, Warszawa: Wydawnictwa Akademickie i Profesjonalne.

Latour Bruno 1997, *Aramis, or the love of technology*, London: Routledge.

Leonard William, Pitts Marian, Mitchell Anne, Lyons Anthony, Smith Anthony, Patel Sunil, Couch Murray, Barrett Anna 2012, "Private Lives 2: The Second National Survey of the Health and Wellbeing of Gay, Lesbian, Bisexual and Transgender (GLBT) Australians", *Monograph Series*, No. 86, Melbourne: The Australian Research Centre in Sex, Health and Society, La Trobe University, available at: http://www.glhv.org.au/files/PrivateLives2Report.pdf.

Lessig Lawrence 1999, *Code and Other Laws of Cyberspace*, New York: Basic Books.

Lewandowski Piotr, Kobylska Joanna 2011, „Wpływ Internetu na relacje w grupie osób homoseksualnych w Toruniu", *Nowe Media*, No. 3, available at: http://apcz.pl/czasopisma/index.php/Nowe_Media/article/view/NM.2012.010/218

Lewis George H. 1990, "Community through Exclusion and Illusion: The Creation of Social Worlds in an American Shopping Mall", *Journal of Popular Culture*, No. 24.

Light Ben, Fletcher Gordon, Adam Alison 2008, "Gay Men, Gaydar and the Commodification of Difference", *Information Technology and People*, No. 21(3).

Livingstone Sonia M. 2008, "Taking Risky Opportunities in Youthful Content Creation: Teenagers' Use of Social Networking Sites for Intimacy, Privacy and Selfexpression", *New Media and Society*, No. 10(3).

McIntosh Wayne, Harwood Paul 2002, "The Internet and America's Changing Sense of Community", *The Good Society*, No. 11(3), available at: http://muse.jhu.edu/journals/good_society/toc/gso11.3.html

McKenna Katelyn Y.A., Bargh John 1998, "Coming Out in the Age of the Internet: Identity 'Demarginalization' through Virtual Group Participation", *Journal of Personality and Social Psychology*, No. 75.

Morahan-Martin Janet 1999, "The Relationship Between Loneliness and Internet Use and Abuse", *Cyber Psychology and Behavior*, No. 2.

Mowlabocus Sharif 2010, *Gaydar Culture: Gay Men, Technology and Embodiment in the Digital Age*, Surrey UK: Ashgate.

Nakamura Lisa 2002, *Menu-Driven Identities: Making Race Happen Online*, [in:] *A Review of Cybertypes: Race, Ethnicity, and Identity on the Internet*, New York: Routledge.

National LGBTI Health Alliance 2010, *Suicide and LGBTI People (Information Sheet)*, available at: http://www.lgbthealth.org.au/briefingpapers

Oliwa Radosław 2012, *Z szafy do ramówki, Sytuacja społeczna osób LGBT. Raport za lata 2010 i 2011*, eds. M. Makuchowska i M. Pawlęga, Warsaw: Kampania Przeciwko Homofobii.

Parks Malcolm R., Floyd Kory 1996, "Making Friends in Cyberspace", *Journal of Computer-Mediated Communication*, No. 1(4), available at: http://jcmc.indiana.edu/vol1/issue4/parks.html

Prost Antoine, Ariès Phillippe, Vincent Gerard 1991, *A History of Private Life: Riddles of Identity in Modern Times*, Cambridge (MA): Harvard University Press.

Quercia Daniele, Las Diego, João Casas, Pesce Paulo, Stillwell David, Kosinski Michal, Almeida Virgilio, Crowcroft John 2012, *Facebook and Privacy: The Balancing Act of Personality, Gender and Relationship Currency*, [in:] *Proceeding of the Sixth International AAAI Conference on Weblogs and Social Media*, available at: http://aaai.org/ocs/index.php/ICWSM/ICWSM12/paper/view/4613.

Schlenker Barry 1980, *Impression Management: The Self-Concept, Social Identity, and Interpersonal Relations*, Monterey (CA): Brooks/Cole.

Schmidt Kris 2011, "Gay 'Dating' Online: A User's Guide", *Popingay*, available at: http://popingay.com/post/2818824999/gaydating-online-a-users-guide

Sinfield Adam 1998, *Gay and After*, London: Serpent's Tail.

Sveningsson Elm M. 2009, *How Do Various Notions of Privacy Influence Decisions in Qualitative Internet Research?*, [in:] *Internet Inquiry: Conversations about Method*, eds. N. Baym, A. Markham, New York: Sage.

Thornton Sarah 1996, *Club Cultures: Music, Media, and Subcultural Capital*, Hanover: University Press of New England.

Tomasik, Krzysztof (2012), *Gejerel. Mniejszości seksualne w PRL-u*, Warsaw: Wydawnictwo Krytyka Polityczna.

Tyler Tom R. 2002, "Is the Internet Changing Social Life? It Seems the More Things Change, the More They Stay the Same", Journal of Social Issues, No. 58(1).

Dobrawa Lisak-Gębala*
University of Wrocław

CONTEMPORARY POLISH ESSAYS: IN SEARCH OF THE AURA OF PAINTINGS AND PHOTOGRAPHS[1]

Abstract
When an essay, as a specific form of writing, is conventionally compared to travel, the latter is understood not only as a model of translocation but also as a literary genre. The parallel between essays and travel writings identifies their numerous common elements in text, for instance a movement between the topics, the observer's visible distance, an intellectual journey (the last term was introduced by Walter Pater in his pioneer reflections on the essay in 1893). The listed similarities encourage the writer of this article to formulate a rudimentary statement: both real and literary travel and the act of writing an essay are usually undertaken to discover a thing worth one's attention and interest; a thing that, even if commonly known, should be, firstly, experienced, and secondly, depicted in a way that would cast new light on it.

Key words: literary genre, essay, act of writing, experience, real and literary travel

Theodor W. Adorno in his work entitled *The Essay as Form* describes the specific happiness of unconstrained essayistic exploration: "the object of essay is the new as something genuinely new, as something not translatable back into the staleness of already existing forms", and later adds, that essay "becomes a compelling construction that does not want to copy the object, but to reconstruct it out of its conceptual *membra disjecta*" (Adorno 1984: 169). As a consequence, in a model form of a travel essay (which is

---
* Institute of Polish Philology, Univeristy of Wroclaw, Plac Nankiera 15, 50-140 Wroclaw, e-mail: dobrawa_lisak@o2.pl
[1] The project was financed by NCN and contributed under the number DEC-2011/01/N/HS2/00510.

a distinctive subgenre of essay writings) the described search of novelty should be certainly taken into account. Supposedly, what seems the most attractive for authors of travel essays are the excursions to unknown regions intriguingly labelled *"ubi leones"*. Experiment, risk, originality, individual experience – all those elements are repeated in various preliminary definitions of an unstable, protean essayistic form (e.g. Bense 2012, Atkins 2005, Sendyka 2006).

Considering contemporary Polish travel essays, an important question might be asked: how to discover this individual voice and the novelty of the essay's object when the traditional place of an artistic pilgrimage comes to be the destination of a real journey, described subsequently in the text. The great amount of eminent Polish travel essays (Zbigniew Herbert's *Barbarzyńca w ogrodzie* [*Barbarian in the Garden*], Jarosław Iwaszkiewicz's *Podróże do Włoch* [*Travels to Italy*], Wojciech Karpiński's *Pamięć Włoch* [*The Memory of Italy*] and Ewa Bieńkowska's *Co mówią kamienie Wenecji* [*What Do the Stones of Venice Say*]) treat Italy – a land described by innumerable writers (Goethe, Byron, Madame de Staël, Stendhal, Chautebriand and John Ruskin among the others); a land full of works of art that are inevitably perceived not only by essayist-erudite's own eyes, but also through the prism of some famous authors' accounts[2]. Apparently one could believe that there is nothing new to find in this country. Wojciech Karpiński in the 1982 *credo* of his Italian pilgrimage, resists such a melancholic feeling of surfeit which he compares to blindness, a paralysis of sensitivity, and suggests that the kind of journey he describes is the best treatment for acedia, a way to reintegrate one's personality and to refresh one's insight (Karpiński 2008: 17). The redundancy of external stimuli, of remembered descriptions and cultural associations does not necessarily have to be treated as a burden, especially when the feeling of connectedness with the European tradition is strong and when the project of penetrating the visited place and its art is based on an individual plan of interpretation followed by the construction of the essay. It becomes evident why Adam Szczuciński claims that writing about Italy becomes "making notes on the margins of the others' works" (*"pisanie o Włoszech [...] jest [...] zapiskami na marginesach cudzych dzieł"* – Szczuciński 2008: 61).

---

[2] In case of other notable travel essays by Herbert (*Martwa natura z wędzidłem* [*Sill Nature with a Bridle*]) and Karpiński (*Amerykańskie cienie* [*American Shadows*], *W Central Parku* [*In the Central Park*]), although those texts present different areas and not Italy again, it can be claimed that they are equally supported by library readings and visits to the museums.

But the same intertextual origins can be found in case of Montaigne's *Essays*: the work that, in the 20th century reflection on essay, has become an archetype of a typically modern inscription of an individual, processual experience (e.g. de Obaldia 1995: 37–38; Lopate 1994: XLIV). As Phillip Lopate argues, although "the whole modern essay tradition sprang from quotation" (Lopate 2012: 131), nowadays the most influential position in essay writing is not preoccupied by common literary culture but by personal experience and an individual voice. This diagnosis, transplanted to the context of Polish travel essays on paintings, expresses the need to underline an individual way of experiencing the work of art, revealed indirectly in numerous ekphrases and often defined *explicite* in autothematic commentaries describing the circumstances of looking at pictures, the events preceding and following the moment of admiring these paintings. Analysing those components, we can build specific, individual maps of chosen essayists' intellectual journeys.

Nevertheless, many well-read writers seem to be completely unable to travel alone, as numerous records of this culturally recognized *Grand Tour* to Italy, created by authors representing various countries and periods, are indeed very often mentioned and quoted in the above-mentioned Polish travel essays. However, the abundant repertoire of others' interpretations is usually treated as a preparatory course, rather than as an obstacle. A cultural background seems to be necessary for the beginners before their actual visit to Italy, because other travellers' writings can even teach diligent novices how to find their singular mode of art's experience. As an illustration, Iwaszkiewicz and Karpiński openly establish an imagined conversational community of travellers admiring the same works of art in different times and circumstances, and, at the same time, these two authors underline their individual experience of those pictures. Iwaszkiewicz, after listing famous artists (Eugène Delacroix, Jan Matejko, Stanisław Wyspiański, Zygmunt Krasiński and Cyprian Norwid) who, just like him, viewed the Venetian *Assunta* by Tiziano notes: "And each one of us saw his own Assunta", and then, starting a discreet game with an epiphanic model of art's reception, adds: "Should I say: his own Assumption?" (*"A każdy z nas widział swoją Assuntę. Czy mam powiedzieć: «swoje wniebowzięcie»?"* – Iwaszkiewicz 2008: 14). Karpiński in turn, while reporting his contact with Signorelli's frescos in Orvieto, admits his lasting memory of other authors' interpretations stratifying on the surface of image and shows advantages of the unsolitary experience of art. After mentioning Iwaszkiewicz, Miłosz, Herbert (three Polish writers which were older than him), he notes: "When I stood in front of Signorelli I remembered about those meetings. Not only did they not disturb me, but they helped me see the work on my own" ("*Gdy stałem przed Signorellim, pamiętałem o tamtych spotkaniach. Nie tylko nie przeszkadzały mi patrzeć, lecz pomagały w zobaczeniu dzieła na własną rękę*" – Karpiński 2013: 130–131). This replication of delight in art, on the one hand confirms the essayist's participation in the European cultural tradition and in the community of persons that, due to their sensibility and connoisseurship, are able to appreciate works really worth one's attention (and not necessarily the most famous ones). On the other hand – such a repetition of delight would not be of much importance if it did not contain also the unpreceded trait of individual experience ("to see on my own").

Contemporary Polish essays on paintings present diverse types of image reception. For example, a reception can be focused on formal, artistic features, or concentrated around developing some extravisual associations by either considering the original context or the picture's resemblance to today's reality. In this article, I would like to distinguish another important type of reception which is an essential element of travel essays on paintings: the one based on the viewer's experience of a picture's aura. Such an experience allows us to observe some significant convergences of the reception of art with the model form of an essay and idea of travel accounts, as has been mentioned in the initial part of this inquiry. The auratic experience is linked to the notion of an experiment and risk. Additionally, in the field of this interesting type of reception the object, even one veiled with a web of citations, should be still able to show its novelty. The term "aura", introduced by Walter Benjamin, is understood as the distinctiveness of the work of art, based on its uniqueness and originating from a particular place and time. According to the philosopher's description, aura is "a strange weave of space and time; the unique appearance or semblance of distance, no matter how close it may be" (Benjamin1998: 518). It becomes evident why searching for the aura could be easily connected with two important strategies of overcoming the cultural and historical distance which are distinctive of Polish travel essayists. Those strategies are: actual journeys to historical sites and imaginary time travels. Moreover, the experience of a painting's aura reveals the writer's personal voice and often results in an emotional and artful ekphrasis. Such a subjective description about an especially attractive picture works as a mirror for the essayistic "self", as a medium of self-cognition and self-presentation (Sendyka 2009).

An attempt at creating one's virtual collection – a specialized gathering of auratic images, individual impressions and quotes from the writings of predecessors – often becomes a preferred starting point for inventing a refreshed essayistic insight and singular mode of experience. According to Karpiński's suggestion, the full experience of Italy "requires a delicate balance between ignorance and pedantry, between distraction and speculation" („*wymaga delikatnego wyważenia między ignorancją a pedanterią, między nieuwagą a spekulacją*" – Karpiński 2008: 70). This balancing "in-between" resembles the typical situation of essayist who is a writer that chooses a form characterised by tension between art and science, between subjectivity and objectivity, between freedom and discipline (Atkins 2005: 112). Adorno claims that an essayist should be a dilettante and amateur suspending his erudition. Moreover, an essayist's choice of both the beginning and the end of his exposition should be made wilfully with "childlike freedom" (Adorno 1984: 152). Since Montaigne's essay seems to be a form which opposes the narrow ideals of a dogmatic system, a predictable order or completeness, it is clear why this form of writing is often presented as antiscientific. The essay's "in-betweeness" appears to be a kind of an "unmethodical method" (Atkins 2005: 114). Analysed travel essays prove this hypothesis because, while their authors make supposedly spontaneous choices, meanwhile, they reveal certain purposeful attitudes: essayists' searching for the aura indeed give the impression of a kind of an "unmethodical method", it is both deliberate and random, both carefully arranged and free spirited. It is rooted in a strictly specified cultural and historical area but dependent on some changing circumstances.

In order to experience the aura, the mentioned essayists concentrate mainly on bringing an imaginary revival of lost time and place, of a certain point from the past from where the work of art originates. Herbert quotes "Goethe's wise dictum: *Wer den Dichter will verstehen, muss in Dichters Lande gehen*" and openly declares: "As the fruits of light, paintings should be viewed under the artist's native sun. Sasseta seems out of place even in the most attractive American museums. Hence the pilgrimage to Piero della Francesca" (Herbert 1985: 149). It can be that claimed the author of *Barbarian in the Garden* travels to Italy in order to find the experience of aura, and many other essayists act likewise. Karpiński intends to see Italian towns and cities through the prism of great amount of various historical sources combined altogether: he includes paintings, the pieces of knowledge about particular past events, biographies, architecture, literary texts, politicians' treatises and the way of exercising the power. Ewa Bieńkowska similarly develops her project of "historical anamnesis", which means an attempt at rediscovering the history of collective imagination of the Venetians from *cinquecento*, *seicento* and *settecento*, the metamorphoses of their spirituality hidden in the paintings. A description of an auratic experience of art can also appear in the essay in a less methodical form, rather capriciously, without previous announcement. This is the case with Jarosław Iwaszkiewicz's *summa vitae* – *Travels to Italy*. In the introductory commentary the writer underlines his will of distinguishing himself from other travellers thanks to the autobiographical impulse which binds the texture of his essay. As a consequence, *Travels to Italy* turn out to be a mosaic self-portrait of the artist. Due to this almost egotist perspective some random and unpredictable circumstances appear as the necessary conditions of an auratic experience of some chosen pictures. Not only intersubjectively available details, like the historical character of a place where a picture is exposed or the advantages of a work itself, seem to be an adequate ground for the bloom of aura. Such an unusual experience, according to Iwaszkiewicz, also requires an appropriate viewer's mood, it depends on his recent sensations and even on the weather. Hence the revelation of aura, although sought in the Italian cultural treasuries, does not have to be fulfilled.

An important problem is that in 20th and 21st essayistic travel records we can find numerous fragments which describe the progressive vanishing of aura and enlist some obstacles that hinder the full contact with Italy treated as the artistic zone. Those commonly denigrated interruptions are connected with some seemingly extraneous details and civilizational forms: the institution of museum and practices of art exposing, mass tourism, the modernisation of city areas, which may collectively be recognized as the signs of all changes found in the valuable historical space that the essayist would still love to see as an untouched preserve of ancient Italy's aura, just like it probably appeared in the times of Goethe or Stendhal.

According to all discussed essayists, in the case of paintings originally housed in churches moving them to art galleries becomes a main reason of an irreversible loss of aura. Iwaszkiewicz, who visited Italy many times since 1924, could observe and judge many such changes. He argues, for example, that the famous fresco *Triumph of Death* from Palermo was received in an absolutely different manner in its natural surroundings of monastery walls than in the museum where "cleaned and isolated counts only on immediate visual effect" (*oczyszczony i odosobniony, obliczony jest już tylko na bezpośrednie działanie malarskie* – Iwaszkiewicz 2008: 10). This conclusion illustrates how practically Malraux's idea of *le musée imaginaire* is realised: the "religion of art" replaces the traditional cult; in the "imaginary museum" items originating from different traditions are equalized as the objects meant to make impression only thanks to their sensual impact (Malraux 1967). No wonder that Herbert complains: "The rapid swallowing of paintings (in large doses) is as pointless as the swallowing of kilometres" (Herbert 1985: 73), while in the gallery full of equally treated exhibits viewers are forced to face the overwhelming surplus of stimuli. Iwaszkiewicz describes the Venetian Galleria dei Belle Arti as a "storehouse of needless pieces of junk" ("*skład niepotrzebnych rupieci*") and states bitterly: "Our museums are not Epicur's gardens" ("*Nasze muzea nie są ogrodami Epikura*" – Iwaszkiewicz 2008: 31). In the opinion of this author, museums do not offer a background for cultural cruciate, neither guarantee the refuge for the values of European culture. As Katarzyna Szalewska argues, an institutional gallery is valued ambivalently by Polish travel essayists; on the one hand, according to Herbert, Bieńkowska and Karpiński, a museum provides an opportunity for individual contact with art that integrates the "self"; on the other hand, a museum is often perceived as an empty storage of lifeless history (Szalewska 2012: 316). As a result, the supposed pilgrimage often turns into a tedious effort of passing numerous rooms which is hardly salvaged by the minor prize of discovering some fascinating experience. While the structure of the museum reproduces some demarcations, typologies introduced by art historians ("scholarly insects" as Herbert calls them), such critical diagnosis of institutionalised galleries is linked clearly with antiscientific attitudes of essayists. For instance, Bieńkowska claims that an encounter with art at the museum is a situation rather intellectual than experiential – annihilating the chance of any imaginary restoring scenes from paintings back to life, expunging any illusionistic interpretations of picture (Bieńkowska 2002: 247). Essayists' very selective collecting of especially attractive paintings could be observed at the level of their texts' composition. Probably during actual museum visits those authors also choose only few adorable works to join their "imaginary collection". This selectiveness of essayists' preferences seems to be an advantageous strategy of dealing with the structure of huge galleries, because such a critical attitude, linked with ignorance of the majority of exposition, enables the chance to catch several revelations of aura.

Ewa Bieńkowska presents herself as a very sensitive viewer. Her criticism embraces not only the institution of a museum, but also some exhibitory practices met in old Italian churches, places by their nature predestined to be auratic. The authoress of *What Do the Stones of Venice Say* notices many civilizational changes diminishing the historical character of sacred interiors. Bieńkowska, as a writer fixed on the mysticism of light, underlines the unsuitable impact of electricity, called by her "an abstractive nakedness" ("*abstrakcyjne obnażenie*" – Bieńkowska 2002: 181), and presented as distant from twinkling candle flames which seem full of life. It reminds us of Iwaszkiewicz complaints on the exhibition of Giorgione's masterpiece (he found *The Storm* guarded by heavy glass which hindered any perception of painting) or on the technique of renovation that transforms precious pictures – ancient and auratic in their deterioration – into loudly coloured, glittering objects which had already lost all features caused by their age. According to the two above-mentioned essayists, such achievements of civilisation as the stable, homogenous light, glass protecting the masterpiece or modern techniques of renovation may effectively annihilate aura, although those innovations were arranged either to keep the works safe or to facilitate the perception of art.

Another important thematic area is connected with the contemporary shape of historical sites. Essayists writing about their Italian tours often endeavour to extend the successfully discovered aura towards the scenery of cities and their surroundings, since these authors describe panoramas in a highly painterly way, similar to depictions of old artworks. A figure transforming distinguished views into potential pictures could be called an "imaginary ekphrasis" (John Hollander's term: Hollander 1998). However, the modernisation of urban spaces again turns out to be a main obstacle on the way to recognize alleged prototypes of landscapes known from famous paintings or at least of some that resemble artful Italian pictures. Iwaszkiewicz seems to be a tireless seeker of the latest civilizational modifications, plenty of which are discredited by him as bringing dissonance in the experience of a traveller searching for the anterior aura. New styleless buildings, traffic and the crowd are usually listed in analysed essays as disadvantages of 20th century urban life. Whereas such complaints, especially about cars, could be also found in publications from two initial decades of 20th century: in Paul Muratow's travel writings often quoted by Polish essayists (in addition: since the Polish translation in 1969 Muratow's texts established in Poland a certain paradigm of the genre), this criticism might be treated as a recurrent *topoi* of such essays. Moreover, the myth of 19th century Italy as an uncontaminated preserve of aura shaped by famous romantic travellers still seems to be a point of reference. The phenomenon that could not have been observed by Muratow is mass tourism which history dates from *circa* 1925. In Iwaszkiewicz's *Travels* Americans sitting in the squares of Rome are treated with some dose of friendly tolerance and called "hippies", although sometimes they are given some features similar to Rousseau's "good savage". This author notices also with a bit of satisfaction the presence of Japanese tourists. Herbert instead is less forbearing:

> Loud guides drive herds of tourists. Sweating farmers from a distant country film every piece of wall which the guide shows them and obediently manifest enthusiasm by touching ancient stones. They are so absorbed with producing copies that they have absolutely no time to see. They will visit Italy at home: colourful moving pictures that have nothing to do with reality. No one has any desire to study things as they are. A tireless mechanical eye multiplies emotions as thin as film. (Herbert 1985: 68–69)

This kind of pointing out the incompetence of a passive consumer might be inscribed in the wider frame of criticism towards mass culture (Shallcross 2002: 47). As many commentators claim, this disapproving attitude is typical for contemporary essays as niche and exclusive forms proudly opposing the "private, idiosyncratic voice" to omnipresent "anonymous babble" (Sanders 2012: 124).

After enlisting diverse difficulties met in the alleged sanctuaries of aura it is vital to present some positive strategies of contemporary Polish travellers to Italy, some alternative procedures that overcome melancholic mourning of this land's historical atmosphere seen as lost forever and unavailable. Those projects usually resemble the advice from a tourist guidebook, but interpreted *a rebours*, beginning with reversing recommended places and seasons. As an illustration, Iwaszkiewicz admits that he usually travels in November, during the month when tourists are almost absent in Italy. The act of detecting some asylums and artworks abandoned by mainstream functions as a source of great delight as well. Herbert, having left the main touristic routes, rediscovers the aura of a less known masterpiece by Piero della Francesca – Madonna dell Parto – housed in a little chapel in Monterchi (Herbert 1985: 153–154), while Iwaszkiewicz, during his visit to the Venetian Basilica of San Marco, ignores the splendid interior and concentrates on the small side chapel of San Isidore, because it reminds him of the intimate atmosphere of Polish village churches (Iwaszkiewicz 2008: 22). Also Bieńkowska and Marek Zagańczyk (a travel essayist from the younger generation) often describe their magnificent discoveries hidden in out-of-the-way places that are usually closed and not meant for tourists. For example, Zagańczyk admires a picture found in some "stuffed sacristy" (Zagańczyk 2005: 39).

All observed circumstances connected both with a textual and extratextual world incline the writer of this article to ask whether there could be found some traces of exhaustion in the seemingly institutionalised discourse of Italian artistic travels; such a hypertrophy of others' commentaries and of civilizational obstacles that make the full, immediate experience of paintings more and more difficult. In other words, is it true that while intending an affirmative description of a famous Italian picture and its surroundings it is increasingly troublesome not to write about some banal commonplaces, or not to develop some bitter critique? Certainly, the answer cannot constitute an authorized thesis, especially when referred to the future, but it is still worth to search for it because, considering the two more recent pieces of essay writing about visits to Italy (Adam Szczuciński's *Włoskie miniatury* [*Italian Miniatures*] and Marek Zagańczyk's *Droga do Sieny* [*The Track to Siena*]), an important transformation of travel discourse becomes evident. Although in these texts Italy still seems to be a land permeated by art and is treated as a preserved sanctuary of the past, the directly declared aim of the excursion is no longer to see and admire art in itself or to gain the auratic and individual experience. In this sense, the two above-mentioned younger authors seem to continue the sneakiness of Iwaszkiewicz's statement formulated almost 50 years earlier: "Travelling in order to watch flowers is as good as travelling in order to watch the architecture or paintings" (*Podróżowanie po Włoszech «po kwiatach» jest równie dobre jak każde inne, «po architekturze» czy «po obrazach»* – Iwaszkiewicz 2008: 12). As this writer claims, when someone stubbornly intends to create another (usually boring) description of an Italian tour, speaking on any other subject would be the best thing to do. But Szczuciński and Zagańczyk are much more consistent than Iwaszkiewicz. Zagańczyk tries to apply an alternative perspective by looking through the "other's eyes" (Zagańczyk 2005: 8), while searching for his *idée fixe* – the beloved view of a valley, an adorable hybrid of combined landscapes remembered from paintings or imagined when reading famous travel accounts. Szczuciński is looking for some trails of eminent writers that visited Italy, for instance, he presents Josif Brodsky's travel to Venice. The intertextuality is a typical feature of this kind of essay writing (or even of essays at all) but in the case of these two authors it is exceedingly intensified. It can be demonstrated by the fact that, for example, in a part of an essay that is usually dedicated to presenting highly subjective descriptions of paintings, accounts that express the essayist's personal voice, in Zagańczyk's book the reader finds some quotations of the other authors' ekphrases. The usual "seeing on my own" essay strategy (mentioned by Karpiński, and practiced by Herbert, Bieńkowska, Iwaszkiewicz and many others) is replaced by "seeing through the other's eyes". Consequently, the one of fundamental ideas of travel writing, in which the accounts should be based on one's search for unconstrained individual experience of art, is clearly absent in the latest Polish essays mentioned in this paragraph.

During the last decade, next to the slightly transformed model of Italian tour distinctive of Zagańczyk and Szczuciński's books, another important tendency could be observed in the field of Polish essayistic travel writing, while there has been established an alternative route towards the South of Europe. The latter phenomenon does not concern the journey undertaken by a man from the North going South in order to pass the cultural initiation or to regain his creative powers. This route is directed rather towards the East. The most representative literary examples are Andrzej Stasiuk's books (*Jadąc do Babadag* [Going to Babadag] and *Dziennik pisany później* [Diary Written Afterwards]); essayistic records from the excursion in search of the mythic Central Europe, grounded in the archaic past. The institutionalisation of two distinguished oppositional types of discourse could be easily observed. "Zeszyty Literackie" in the series called "Travels", edited by Marek Zagańczyk, publishes traditionally oriented cultural and artistic travel writings (the new original pieces, but also some re-editions or translations, including the classic realisation of Italian travels – Muratow's *Images of Italy*). "Czarne" owned by Stasiuk has its travel series too. It is called "Sulina" and presents the accounts of unusual journeys through forgotten corners of Europe. An essential feature of Stasiuk's essay is a very specific identity of the "self": it is far from both the ideal citizen of Europe and from "barbarian in the garden" defined by Herbert as a traveller from a poor, isolated country, but who aspires to join the great European society with its high culture. For Stasiuk the Mediterranean tradition and masterpieces of art definitely are not a positive point of reference. He identifies himself with the inhabitants of Central Europe; he declares his allegiance to Ukrainians and people from Balkan countries. His myth of a Central European identity (and Polish identity as well) is formed by the category of the "outcasts of the West, traitors of the East" ("*wyrzutki Zachodu, zdrajcy Wschodu*" – Stasiuk 2011: 160). Travelling through Central Europe locations, he trails not only the atmosphere of the past but also intends to feel the authenticity of life or even some horror.

The comparison of the traditionally arranged travels to Italy with Stasiuk's excursion to the unknown regions of Central Europe might be interesting and seemingly it is not ungrounded, while the project of Stasiuk' travelling was thoroughly criticized by Marek Zagańczyk, one of the advocates and admirers of Mediterranean heritage:

> Świat Stasiuka kończy się tam, gdzie mój zaczyna, i jest odległy od tego, co sam dla siebie wybrałem (…). Nie ma u Stasiuka miejsc rzeźbionych wspólną pamięcią. Nie ma tak ważnego dla mnie splotu natury i kultury. Jest to zapis rozpadu, obraz świata w zaniku. Gubię się wśród nazw węgierskich, albańskich, rumuńskich. Żadna mapa mi nie pomoże (Zagańczyk 2005: 77).

> Stasiuk's world ends where mine begins and it is far from what I have chosen for myself [...]. There are no sites sculpt by collective memory. There is no entanglement of nature and culture which has been of such importance for me. It is a record of destruction, a picture of vanishing world. I feel lost amongst Hungarian, Albanian and Romanian names. No map can help me. [translation by the author of the article]

Notwithstanding this antagonism, although the two types of travel essays present themselves as alternatives, it is possible to point out some features shared by both projects. These common elements are: the distance to globalization and mass culture, diving into the past, searching for some inspiring experience, and the mighty desire for freedom (also because of leaving Poland). Summing up, those elements could be described as a specific kind of escapism, often demonstrated in one's longing for the preserved mythic past, the search of which is an act based on many idiosyncratic choices. And maybe this escapism has something to do with the essayistic form itself since Carl H. Claus concludes: "So it might be said that above all else essayists conceive of the essay as a place of intellectual refuge, a domain sacred to the freedom of mind itself" (Claus 2012: XXI). In travel essays the free movement of thoughts is accompanied by an actual translocation and escaping from todays' reality, so it is a multiplied refuge.

The above hypothesis constitutes an adequate background for interpretation of another pair of essayistic books published by "Czarne" – Wojciech Nowicki's *Dno oka* (*Fundus of the Eye* from 2010) dealing with the subject of old photographs and *Salki* (*The Attics* – published in 2013) where an excursion similar to the one undertaken by Stasiuk is depicted: including an analogous destination (Ukraine and Balkan countries) and the search for intriguing otherness. In Nowicki's texts the act of translocation is apparently connected with time travelling, realised in two forms: as telling a story about old photographs and people presented in those pictures (in *Dno oka*), and also as looking for places where time has seemingly stopped (in *Salki*). Additionally, this convergence of travelling and an interest towards old photographs is present in *Going to Babadag* as well. Stasiuk claims that his plan of travelling and writing a book was born due to his former enthusiasm for Andre Kertesz's work presenting a blind violinist: "Wherever I go I search for its [photograph's] three-dimensional, coloured versions and I often feel that I find them" (*Dokąd się nie wybiorę, szukam jego [zdjęcia] trójwymiarowych i barwnych wersji, i często wydaje mi się, że je znajduję* – Stasiuk 2004: 210).

When two books by Nowicki are treated as complementary texts, it is vital to say that they contain several basic elements that turned out to be essential for the construction of classical essays about Italy mentioned in the initial part of this article. The common features of all these essays are: the narrative frame of a travel, reference to visual arts and the most important one – searching for asylums of auratic experience. Nowicki presents himself as a seeker of "gatherings from the borderland of a circus, science and pornography" (*zainteresowanie zbiorami na pograniczu cyrku, nauki i pornografii* – Nowicki 2013: 157). On the margins of description of some forgotten, province museum in Central Europe, he gives a large critique of the Western institution of famous galleries like the Louvre (called by him "bombastic Ford Nox of art with marble and canvas instead of gold"; *bombastyczny Luwr, ten Fort Nox sztuki z marmurem i płótnem zamiast złota* – 158). Therefore he repeats, although in a highly radical form, one of the stereotypes of Polish travel essays on Italy. Nowicki depicts the contemporary, grotesque religion of art with irony:

> Muzeum staje się miejscem obowiązku, opresji, tu trzeba dygać grzecznie przed płótnami wymalowanymi na hektary, przed podpisami, przed nazwiskami. A te małe zakurzone zbiory na obrzeżach świata, w rzadko odwiedzanych muzeach są mnie wymuskane, pokazują rzeczy gdzie indziej już nieoglądane, kolekcję krawatów, okulary i syjamskie bliźnięta. Są esencją kraju, który je wydał, ledwie wydobywającego się z błota. (Nowicki 2013: 158)

> The museum has become a place of duty and oppression. One has to curtsy politely in front of kilometres of painted canvas, in front of signatures, in front of names. While those little dusty gatherings at the margins of the world, housed in rarely visited museums are less smoothed but they show things that could not be seen anywhere else yet: a collection of ties, glasses and Siamese twins. They are an essence of a country that bore them, hardly peeking from mud. [translation by the author of the article]

An unusual collection of this type occupies also Nowicki's "imaginary museum" which, as an effect, starts to resemble a cabinet of curiosities. With no doubts are such "dusty gatherings" of objects recognized by this author as *par excellence* auratic – bound with particular place and historical moment.

Despite his above-quoted denigration of the commonly favoured expositions of masterpieces, in two noticeable excerpts the author of *Salki* surprisingly presents a testimonial of an auratic experience of paintings by George de La Tour. The first fragment is about admiring *The Cheat with the Ace of Diamonds*, (*nota bene* this painting is housed in the Louvre) and contains an ekphrasis filled with enthusiasm ("the one of those unbelievably deliberately projected explosions of painter's virtuosity, the profusion of colours [...]" – *stanąłem przed [...] jednym z tych nieprawdopodobnie przemyślanych rozbłysków malarskiej wirtuozerii, tej feerii kolorów* – 162). This description could be easily ascribed to the already analysed essay writing created by the effective defenders of values of European art and culture, like, for instance, Herbert or Karpiński. But in *Salki* this affirmative reception of a picture is immediately confronted with an earlier and evidently different experience of another La Tour's painting – housed in the State Art Gallery in Lviv:

> Na obraz La Toura natknąłem się niespodziewanie i właściwie nie był to obraz, ale czarny prostokąt, spękany i wybrzuszony, ledwie wtedy czytelny. Nie potrafiłem odejść. Nokturn La Toura był pokryty dodatkową patyną, oprócz historii malarza i mojej z nim przygody nakładała się nań historia malatury. Wiele przeszła, raz za razem poddawana różnorakim torturom, aż wzdęła się i załamała pod sczerniałym werniksem, gotowa odpaść. Doczytywałem się obrazu pod tą maskującą siatką, przypatrywałem chaosowi spojrzeń, które wzajem do siebie prowadzą i zdradzają nie tylko gwałtowny charakter tego malarstwa, ale też – po raz kolejny – jego przemyślaną strukturę. La Tour z Lwowskiej Galerii Sztuki doskonale oddaje historię miasta, które przechowuje to płótno: w sali pomalowanej na brudnozielono, z zaciekami wody, w kącie wisiało dzieło niewątpliwie warte podróży. (…) Nawet tutejsze muzea były jeszcze jak dotknięte gangreną, opryskliwe i wzbudzające strach. (Nowicki 2013: 163)

> I unexpectedly came up against La Tour's picture and it wasn't exactly a picture but a black rectangle, chapped and bellied, hardly readable. I couldn't leave. Nocturne by de La Tour was covered with an additional patina, alongside the history of the painter and my adventure with him there was a coating of history of painted overlay. It had experienced a lot, from time to time it had been tortured till it became inflated and broke under the blackened varnish, ready to fall down. I tried to read an image under this camouflage net, I looked at the chaos of glances that led one to another and revealed not only the violent character of this art but also – again – its purposefully considered structure. La Tour at Lviv gallery perfectly presented the history of city that kept the canvas: in the corner of a dirty green room, with some damp patches, there was a work undoubtedly worth travelling to. […] Even local museums were still like affected with gangrene, harsh and terrifying. [translation by the author of the article]

Undoubtedly, this work presents itself as full of aura but the most important fact is that this desired quality is grounded due to the damage of the picture (at the same time it sounds similar to Iwaszkiewicz's complaints on excessive renovation of old works as a practice that annihilates aura). Nowicki wrote in an analogues way about his experience of Antonello da Messina's *Crucifixion* housed in Brukenthal Museum in Sibiu: "the version from Brukenthal is full of cracks and bellied, and that is why it is touching, as a testimony of the fate of this city, this country, all those countries, as an accidently created map of damages" (*ta wersja od Brukhentala jest pełna spękań i wybrzuszeń i właśnie przez to poruszająca, jako świadectwo losów tego miasta, tego kraju, tych wszystkich krajów, jako przypadkowo powstała mapa zniszczeń* – 161–162). The aura is developed here not due to a picture staying in the original location where it was created, but due to its in-separable relation with the history of the city where the painting was housed for years. All the events that the painting was exposed to, left their traces in its ruined materiality which brings the uniqueness of the object marked by history.

What is essential for my analysis, is that when Nowicki in his collection of essays entitled *Dno oka* writes about the aura of old, damaged photographs, he presents the identical approach. As he claims, in case of fractured prints or abortive images "the aura is created by time that has passed since their creation because it has damaged and torn the paper, which means it has weaved them with insinuation. [...] For all those photographs, primarily those unworthy anyone's attention, the entropy is a salvation, a spring into the cosmos of images which are singled out from garbage by the hand of a curator (a collector, an author of a text) and placed on the pedestal" (*aurę tworzy czas, jaki upłynął od ich wykonania – bo zniszczył, podarł papier, czyli osnuł niedopowiedzeniem. (…) Dla tych pierwotnie niewartych uwagi fotografii entropia jest ratunkiem, skokiem w kosmos obrazów, które ręka kuratora (zbieracza, autora tekstu) wyławia ze śmietnika i wystawia na piedestał* – Nowicki 2010: 173). The essayist openly declares: "All this writing is caused by one reason only: to stand aside those real, and therefore harsh, pictures" (*Całe to pisanie po to właśnie: żeby stanąć po stronie obrazów rzeczywistych, więc chropawych* – 177). He discredits smooth copies or virtual images which are separated from the past and drift without any chance for another rooting. Nowicki's attitude towards old photographs entails an approval of their inevitable fading, and of their disintegration in the end. Moreover, it also means permission for forgetting about pictured persons and places, for their alleged nonexistence. It is worth noticing that, although Benjamin, who created the notion of aura, is famous for disfavouring photographs as serial, undistinctive reproductions, he underlined auratic appearance of the earliest, long-exposed portraits.

When contemporary Polish essays on paintings and those on photographs are considered together as a specific kind of discourse, their association could be regarded in the context of historical metamorphoses. I tried to show that in case of famous, aged masterpieces an essayist seeking an auratic experience of images meets numerous obstacles (crowds of tourists in galleries, the overwhelming repertoire of other authors' interpretations). As a consequence of this situation, the essays on old photographs could be interpreted as a serious alternative: a kind of asylum for an experience of aura in the field of visual objects. Nowicki's writings and the essayistic ekphrases by Jacek Dehnel, gathered in an artful volume *Fotoplastikon*, might be treated as a literary proof of this daring hypothesis.

The strategy of collecting images in order to build a private "imaginary museum", so characteristic for essayists interested in paintings, could be easily detected in texts on photographs. Nowicki and Dehnel often recall a story about circumstances of acquiring particular chosen prints: about visiting flea markets, antique shops or about internet auctions. Objects in their collections, according to Nowicki's words, are "singled out from garbage". In the travel essays on paintings there is a counterpart of this narration about discovering adorable pictures, while Herbert, Karpiński, Bieńkowska or Iwaszkiewicz also tend to describe exhaustively the road they had to take to experience a view of a certain masterpiece. In both types of essays, on the margins of accounts of discovering a fascinating picture, there is often a reflection on the role of chance and destiny, on mysterious entanglement of factors which led to noticing an outstanding image.

Dehnel and Nowicki perform a kind of a time travel, because they are interested mostly in the photographs dating from *circa* 1880 to 1950. However, when a private collection is meant to be build the adequate age of a print is not the only one decisive factor. What counts the most is a poignant detail causing the specific anxiety of sensitive viewer (the Roland Barthes' term *punctum* is often used to describe this feeling). Again it results in a search of singular experience and for an exciting novelty or otherness. In practice the pursuit of aura repeatedly turns out to be a tendency of selecting phenomena that differ from today's sensibility and sometimes seem to be a bit strange (just like in Nowicki's and Stasiuk's travel essays). In *Fotoplastikon* the catalogue of those provocative motives is very ample and it could be alleged with aesthetics of "camp" (Sontag 1966). The writer concentrates on the mentality of *belle époque* and the times of two world wars and selects photographs attitudinized, made for the shows, in costumes. Jacek Dehnel as a "colonial connoisseur" (Zalewski 2010: 263) tests various borders of otherness: picks up pictures of deformed bodies, trails the race differences or sexual differences and acts of discrimination. He wants to know the story of persons from a photo and thanks to the work of imagination and free speculations he often brings chosen pictures "back to life".

Summing the above inquiry up, the evident anachronous impulse and imaginary time travelling commenced due to a certain visual stimulus, as the tendency that let me to draw a parallel between travel essays on historical paintings and essays on old photographs, encircles a large area of potential models of experiencing images and some of these models do not have many features in common with a simple admiration of a masterpiece. The project of searching for auratic experience sometimes means transgressing the kind of perception related to alleged beauty or perfection of a picture (however it does not exclude such an approach). Other interesting outlooks come into play, also as far as the contact with painting is concerned, for example: fascination with otherness, strangeness, horror. A certain historical sense seems to be a key element of all the presented essays, but it is different from the attitude that resulted in establishing the institution of museum. It is a very selective historical sense: a singular voice of an essayist.

Bibliography

Adorno Theodor W. 1984, "The Essay as Form", trans. B. Hullet-Kentor, F. Will, *New German Critique*, No. 30 (Spring – Summer).

Atkins G. Douglas 2005, *Tracing the Essay. Through Experience to Truth*, Athens and London: The University of Georgia Press.

Barthes Roland 1981, *Camera Lucida: Reflections on Photography*, trans. R. Howard, New York: Hill and Wang.

Benjamin Walter 1968, *The Work of Art in the Age of Mechanical Reproduction*, [in:] *Illuminations*, ed. H. Arendt, London: Fontana.

Benjamin Walter 1999, *Little History of Photography*, trans. E. Jephcott and K. Shorter, [in:] *Walter Benjamin: Selected Writings*, ed. M. Bullock and M. W. Jennings, vol. 2, part 2, 1931 – 1934, Cambridge: The Belknap Press of Harvard University Press.

Bense Max 2012, [From *On the Essay and Its Prose*], trans. E. Sampson, [in:] *Essayists on the Essay*, ed. C.H. Claus, N. Stuckey-French, Iowa City: University of Iowa Press.

Bieńkowska Ewa 2002, *Co mówią kamienie Wenecji*, Gdansk: słowo / obraz terytoria.

Dehnel Jacek 2009, *Fotoplastikon*, Wydawnictwo WAB, Warsaw.

Obaldia Claire de 1995, *Essayistic Spirit. Literature, Modern Criticism and the Essay*, Oxford: Laredon Press.

Essayists on the Essay 2012, ed. C.H. Claus, N. Stuckey-French, Iowa City: University of Iowa Press.

Herbert Zbigniew 1985, *Barbarian in the Garden*, trans. M. March and J. Anders, Manchester: Carcanet.

Hollander John 1988, "The Poetics of Ekphrasis", *Word & Image*, No. 4.

Iwaszkiewicz Jarosław 2008, *Podróże do Włoch*, Warsaw: Państwowy Instytut Wydawniczy.

Karpiński Wojciech 2013, *Twarze*, Warsaw: Fundacja Zeszytów Literackich.

Karpiński Wojciech 2008, *Pamięć Włoch*, Warsaw: Fundacja Zeszytów Literackich.

Klaus Carl H. 2012, *Toward a Collective Poetics of Essay*, [in:] *Essayists on the Essay*, ed. C.H. Claus, N. Stuckey-French, Iowa City: University of Iowa Press.

Lopate Phillip 1994, *Introduction*, [in:] *The Art of the Personal Essay*, ed. Ph. Lopate, New York: Anchor-Doubleday.

Lopate Phillip 2012, *What Happened to the Personal Essay?*, [in:] *Essayists on the Essay*, ed. C.H. Claus, N. Stuckey-French, Iowa City: University of Iowa Press.

Malraux Andre 1967, *Museum Without Walls*, trans. S. Gilbert, F. Price, New York: Doubleday.

Nowicki Wojciech 2010, *Dno oka. Eseje o fotografii*, Wołowiec: Wydawnictwo Czarne.

Nowicki Wojciech 2013, *Salki*, Wołowiec: Wydawnictwo Czarne.

Pater Walter 2012, [From *Dialectic*], [in:] *Essayists on the Essay*, ed. C.H. Claus, N. Stuckey-French, Iowa City: University of Iowa Press.

Sanders Scott Russel 2012, [From *Singular First Person*], [in:] *Essayists on the Essay*, ed. C.H. Claus, N. Stuckey-French, Iowa City: University of Iowa Press.

Sendyka Roma 2006, *Nowoczesny esej. Studium historycznej świadomości gatunku*, Cracow: TAiWPN Universitas.

Sendyka Roma 2009, „Esej i ekfraza (Herbert – Bieńkowska – Bieńczyk) ,,, *Przestrzenie Teorii*, No.11.

Shallcross Bożena 2002, *Through the Poet's Eye. The Travels of Zagajewski, Herbert and Brodsky*, Evanston: Northwestern University Press.

Sontag Susan 1966, *Against Interpretation and Other Essays*, New York: Straus & Giroux.

Stasiuk Andrzej 2004, *Jadąc do Babadag*, Wołowiec: Wydawnictwo Czarne.

Stasiuk Andrzej 2011, *Dziennik pisany później*, Wołowiec: Wydawnictwo Czarne.

Szalewska Katarzyna 2012, *Pasaż tekstowy. Czytanie miasta jako forma doświadczania przeszłości we współczesnym eseju polskim*, Cracow: TAiWPN Universitas.

Szczuciński Adam 2008, *Włoskie miniatury*, Warsaw: Fundacja Zeszytów Literackich.

Zagańczyk Marek 2005, *Droga do Sieny*, Warsaw: Fundacja Zeszytów Literackich.

Zalewski Cezary 2010, *Pragnienie, poznanie, przemijanie. Fotograficzne reprezentacje w literaturze polskiej*, Cracow: TAiWPN Universitas.

Irena Chawrilska*

University of Gdansk

THE HYBRID WORK OF ART AS EXPERIENCE

Abstract
This article focuses on the hybrid work of art viewed as a form of experience. The issue taken into consideration is hybrid work of art viewed as a form of experience from the perspective of how Dewey wrote about art which can be perceived as a form of experience. How can we understand the notion of experience in relation to a work of art, and, more importantly, to a hybrid work of art? The analysis of the experience category is based on the philosophical texts written by Luigi Pareyson. The question explored is whether hybrid works of art portray the experience of contemporary reality. The poems of Paula Claire (ES-SENSE and Hymns to Isis) and the artistic book by Jim Butler (A.M.D.G) are taken into consideration.

Key words: hybrid work of art, experience, Luigi Pareyson, contemporary reality

The reference in the title of the following article to John Dewey's work entitled *Art as Experience* is naturally not accidental. The question being explored is concerned with what type of thought about art was suggested by Dewey. He opposed the divisions according to which the aesthetic sphere is divided from the sphere of cognition or morality. We could even say that he hoped, similarly to the Avant-garde representatives, that the world can be filled up with the salutary power of art. The philosopher claimed that every cognitive experience has its own aesthetic component, and contrary to Kant's postulations, we should acknowledge that even morality is not deprived of aesthetic aspects. Dewey emphasized that:

---

* Philology Department, University of Gdansk, ul. Wita Stwosza 55, 80-952 Gdansk, e-mail: i.chawrilska@gmail.com

"(…) any practical activity, provided that it is integrated and moves by its own urge to fulfillment, have esthetic quality" (Dewey 2005: 41). Dewey regarded the aesthetic experience to be a complete experience which cannot be described in purely psychological terms from the perspective of the evaluating subject. The philosopher found that the real object, which serves as basis for the experience is equally important. Dewey believed that different things can evoke such reactions. However, he emphasized that the modern world is not favorable if we want to experience reality deeply. As Dewey said:

> Zeal for doing, lust for action, leaves many a person, especially in this hurried and impatient human environment in which we live, with experience of an almost incredible paucity, all on the surface. No one experience has a chance to complete itself because something else is entered upon so speedily. What is called experience becomes so dispersed and miscellaneous as hardly to deserve the name (Dewey 1975: 57).

Surely it is not hard to agree with Dewey's statements, nevertheless these remarks can be considered trivial by the following article's readers. If we wanted to use a simplifying outline, we could say that aesthetic experience in the modern world is no longer experience in general, as perceived by Dewey, (the experience which can refer to art and other elements of reality), but it can also describe the mental and physical dimension of experiencing the world. Wolfgang Welsh defines this process as the reconfiguration of *aisthesis*:

> Furthermore, a reconfiguration of *aisthesis* can today be observed. For instance, one of the consequences of media dominance is the challenging of the primacy of vision which has shaped occidental culture since the Greeks, and which culminates in the television age. Contemporary critique of ocularcentrism has other reasons too, but the experience of media constitutes an important factor (Welsch 2005: 126).

The reconfiguration of *aisthesis* is a result of changes in modern culture, with developing media technologies at its head. However, it is also an expression of changes occurring in art itself. The newly evoking artistic forms require from their recipients the type of perception in which none of the senses is still dominant.

Generally, working on the problem of experience may turn out to be inconclusive, and potential conclusions can be futile. This problem raises extreme opinions in terms of both its importance and aptness when taken into academic considerations. It is not easy to get clear conclusions from scholars who are interested in this issue. It has not been declared how we should understand the notion of experience and neither by Martin Jay, author of *Songs of Experience: Modern American and European Variations on a Universal Theme*, nor in Poland by Dorota Wolska in her book *Odzyskać doświadczenie. Sporny temat humanistyki współczesnej*. (To Regain Experience: a Disputable Problem of Contemporary Humanities). However, even scholars, who are most skeptical about the experience and who question its significance for any scholarly activity, admit at the same time that it is extremely difficult not to refer to this sphere of human life in humanities studies. Surely, the notion of experience is fairly common in everyday life, and people must be very familiar with it while living in the world. All this could be confirmed by remarks made by Roger-Pol Droit in his article *The Magnitude of Experience*, which is known to Polish readers thanks to the translation published in the magazine *Teksty Drugie (Second Texts)*:

> Of course we could try to build a term for experience <<in general>>, but it would be pretty unclear. I do not wish to penetrate the thicket of philosophical considerations on experience because we are both fortunate and unfortunate to deal with the term which has always had an undetermined meaning, and which is one of the most common terms (it has been a good experience, I haven't experienced it before etc.); and which possesses a wide range of theoretical meanings – in its proper sense – in philosophers' works. (...) I am afraid that we will not achieve anything in next years if we analyze the problem from the standpoint of its genealogy (Droit 2006: 106–107).

Droit claims that every experience has a binary nature: passive and active, it is always felt and "given" (cf. Droit 2006: 107). From the standpoint of the following deliberations, the issue of "giving" experience, which of course influences the other aspect – feeling, is more significant. How does it happen then that the experience of an author becomes contained in the work? Is it justified to think that the hybrid work, existing in the borderline between literature and visual arts, is a consequence of experiencing the modern world? Does the structure of hybrid works reflect in a specific way the multi-layered complexity and simultaneity, the vagueness of the postmodern reality? What makes artists choose a hybrid form, and not another one? We could hazard a guess that hybrid works are structured in a way which enables them to communicate that it is impossible to grasp the sense on the level of reality. The aporetic nature of reality can be seen through the visuality integrated with the word. The first thing we should ask is what kind of works can be considered hybrid.

Irena Chawrilska

Hybrid nature of the work of art

As users of modern culture we live in the space which is more and more frequently filled with heterogeneous works, consisting of two or more carriers of sense. What we have in mind is visual poetry, concrete poetry, cybernetic and digital poetry, the artistic book, and liberature. Each of the enumerated types of work operating on the borderline between literature and visual arts is somehow hybrid in nature. It is easy to notice that some of the numbered artistic forms are thought to be a part of the world of works of arts, supposing we still acknowledge works of art to be a valid category, whereas some of them are considered to be literary works.

Seemingly the problem does not sound complicated. On account of genre concrete poetry can be derived from the tradition of visual poetry, dating back to antiquity and various avant-garde movements, starting from parole in libertà of Marinetti, through to calligrammes by Appolinaire, ending at *A Throw of the Dice will Never Abolish Chance* by Mallarmé; and we can consider it a literary experiment. An artistic book, which is the foremost recognize museum piece in the Polish tradition, can be easily acknowledged as art. Liberatic authors call their works literary ventures, thus we could count them among literary works of avant-garde provenances. Surely it is more difficult to immediately classify the works which come to life through so called new media. However, we can frequently hear that what we deal with here are literary works involved in the context of multimedia. After having this simplified we can see that new artistic phenomena can be easily recognized as something secondary which only takes advantage of a new or different medium.

In hybrid works it is of utmost importance that there are two ontological orders joined together, that is to say: the physical sphere of the work as well as its intentionality in terms of Ingarden's ideas. At this point I am referring to the Ingarden's theory because there we can clearly see that the task performed by the matter is reduced to registering, it does not play an important part. The material sphere of the literary work enables us, in Ingarden's opinion, to reach the intentionality included in the work in the process of specification. In the case of hybrid works their materiality does not cause the depreciation of their intentional sphere if we wanted to use Ingarden's terminology, and the process of specification includes the non-language aspects. The crucial part is played by the physical space of the work because the matter itself performs an important semantic function as well. The category of hybrid works indicates the individual character of a particular work. Thanks to the mythological references it presents some kind of cognitive uneasiness which is felt by the recipient after he or she encounters the work in which a visual sign is integrated with a verbal sign. In the case of hybrid work the disturbing quality is its heterogeneity, putting together various elements which do not surprise us individually, but when they are pieced together, they form a being: a strange, disturbing, and not existing as claimed by Aristotle, being[1].

The term; hybrid work, similarly to Higgins' term; intermedia, enables us to put works in the right order from the borderline between literature and visual arts, and we do not have to decide whether a particular work belongs to the world of literary works or to the world of works of art. By using this term from the whole range of examples of art or non-art, literature and non-literature we can distinguish works in which text and picture have been so integrated that as a result of this artistic process a new aesthetic quality has been evoked. In the case of these works words are not a decoration of the picture, and images are not an ornamentation to add variety to the text. The term intermedia shows what relations are present between particular fields of art in specific artistic currents. By using the category of hybrid work we can show that a work from the borderline between literature and visual arts constitutes a kind of organic whole, like mythical hybrids, however, we can demonstrate in the whole that one element comes from one field of art, and the other one – from a different artistic field, and at the same time we can search for tools to

---

[1] The followers of Aristotle did not acknowledge a hybrid as a compound of two different natures. According to Aristotle these beings fail to come into existence because they appear without a purpose. Due to the nature's functionality the only beings which can exist are adequate and in conformity with nature. It is worth emphasizing that we will not find the term "hybrid" in the works by Aristotle. In the works *Generation of Animals* and *Problems* the philosopher discusses some anomalies about monsters. A monster is born when "[...] the movements (originating from the male) cease and the material (provided by the female) is not under their control, then what remains is the most general in being, and that is <<animal>>. The new born, as we used to say, has a head of a ram or an ox" (Aristotle 1979: 181). Similar anomalies can be observed among animals. The representative of one genus can have the head of another one. According to Aristotle monsters are scarcely similar to creatures they are said to be similar to. Therefore, the philosopher believes that they do not exist. Moreover, he claims that the being which is born must be the same as the being which provides the semen. From the horse's semen only a horse can be born, from a man only a man, in other cases we cannot call the being which is born an offspring. "For that reason our offspring is not something which comes from a different part of our body, or something that is corrupted or distorted" (Aristotle 1980: 62).

describe a particular hybrid. However, there is lesser risk that one of the languages will become more appreciated. The term hybrid emphasizes that in the case of concrete poetry, an artistic book, liberature, and new media works we face as unusual forms, a being for which the substantial dimension is essential, working on the assumption that it is ephemeral and frequently for use once only, and relations existing inside of the being are hard to grasp and analyze.

When we say form, what we have in mind is form understood as an organic whole in which it is impossible to display the insides and outsides of a work. In the case of hybrid works we can recognizemeaningful aspects of both the language's and the material's structure. That is why from this article's perspective the idea of Luigi Pareyson is significant since he acknowledges the work of art to be the form in which there is no division into form and content. According to Luigi Pareyson's theory of formativity the formation process of the work of art comprises of all its elements, including the matter which becomes essential.

The centre of Pareyson's theory constitutes formativity[2] which is a merge of formation i.e. production, and invention i.e. the way something is produced. The scholar believe that every human activity has a formative character, in other words, it is both production and invention at the same time (Kasia 2008: 19). In reference to art, the scholar determines formativity as content, matter, law. The content of the work of art (*il contenuo*) is the artist's whole life, his or her operating personality, not only the energy behind the formation but also the manner of formation, that is "style" (Kasia 2008: 19). If the content of the work of art is identified with the style, there is no longer a need to have a dispute concerning the primacy of form over content, or of content over form because the spiritual element of the work from this perspective is style precisely. We cannot talk of other modes of expressing, saying and conveying but production. For the researcher the matter of the work of art can be only and exclusively the physical substance because when we talk about formation in art, we have in mind the formation of matter (Kasia 2008: 19), that is to say, the work of art is formed matter.

---

[2] *Formatività* is a key term in the aesthetics of Pareyson, it is a neologism in Italian. By using the neologism Pareyson draws attention to one of the most important aspects of form to him, which is its active nature. That is why the Polish translator also provides a neologism – formativity. She believes that none of the previously used terms "formation" and "form-creation" renders the Italian *formatività*. However, by having this frequently appear in the text the Italian term could disturb the reading. Cf. Kasia 2008:19.

Particular works of art are permeated with the precise understanding and the morality of particular artists, their individual way of thinking and acting, the specific interpretation of reality and attitude towards life. "What we are discussing here is the person's whole life, his or her specific and complete spirituality, his or her individual and impossible to replace experience, which, by relying on the rule of concentrating all activities in an exact operation, must in a way enter into art" (Kasia 2008: 37). It is important for the artist to focus on producing the form, and not on the formation of thoughts, activities, virtues, character traits or objects meant for a specific aim. In favour of focusing on the form production is finding the right matter to form. Otherwise the pure formativity could turn out to be an abstraction, not set in the matter and deprived of "body". Once formed matter in the shape of pure form guarantees the autonomy of the work of art[3].

While following the line of thought of Pareyson, we cannot talk about spirit and body in reference to the work of art because the work of art has a meaning due to its sensual existence and physicality. In the work of art there is nothing spiritual that would not be physical as well.

---

[3] In Pareyson's terms we talk about the autonomy of the work of art when the philosopher writes about the completeness of the work of art (*Compiutezza dell' opera d'arte*): "The artistic perfection is not motionless and fixed but it is dynamic in its definite character, and its definite nature is the completion of formation process" (Kasia 2008: 112). The completion of the formation process happens when *lo spunto* matures, when the work of art becomes independent, that is to say there are no more author's changes, it becomes complete, closed, total and ready for interpretations (Cf. Kasia 2008: 81). *Lo spunto* is a moment in which the formative intentionality turns into an act of clearly defined purpose. At the time when an artist finds *lo spunto*, an impulse of some kind, he or she feels that a given work is going to be born, a specific form. We can assume that the artist narrows his or her vision of the world to one point, he or she yields to the transcendent power, which becomes real through the artist. The formation process would never take place if it were not for the artist. *Lo spunto* is motionless, it is the semen which is set free and gives direction to creative energy, it must mature to become a work of art (Kasia 2008: 67). Kasia compares Pareyson's idea of *lo spunto* to Martin Heidegger's interpretation of the source of the work of art: "The source is used here in the meaning of something from which and through which a thing is, what it is and how it is" (Heidegger 1997: 7). Nevertheless, the category of *lo spunto* remains mysterious, since we cannot point out its sources of origin, what we know is how it operates. Pareyson does not conclude if it is the manifestation of transcendent power or if it is of an inherent quality in the world. Surely this category is meant to explain the details of the formation process, which is to say, a widely understood artistic activity. It is the semen, and then the embryo of the work of art, the right to independent organization. The formation cannot be improvised because it relies on the information included in *lo spunto*.

The physical and spiritual elements of the work are identical because formation of the work is not formation of the content but rather formation of the matter. The meaning of the work should be acknowledged as its physical existence and unity which causes the aesthetic experience that is interpretation.

The importance of the material aspect of the artistic work is also emphasized by Wolfgang Welsch: "Thus we are today learning to value anew the resistibility and unchangeability of the natural as opposed to the universal mobility and changeability of media-worlds, and in the same way the persistence of the concrete as opposed to the free play of information, the massivity of matter as opposed to the levitation of imagery" (Welsch 2005: 128). The unceasing presence of electronic media bears in people the longing for individuality, as well as for physicality. However, Welsch emphasizes that he does not have in mind the thirst for returning to the sensual experience from before the age of electronics, the revalidation of the electronic experience in some measure results from the electronic one, and between both experiences there are numerous relations. In this context a good example is liberature which originates from some type of opposition against the omnipresent remediation which, at the same time, does not restrain Zenon Fajfer from using electronic media in his works.

Form, experience, cognition

Thus we are dealing with a triad of terms which are linked with each other in a hybrid work: the experience, the form originating from the experience, and the process of cognition which accompanies both the work's creator, who interprets his or her experience, and the recipient, who strives to perceive the work's form.

The relation between experience and form seems to have some features of circularity. It can be proven after we reflect on the forms of works. The recipients give their attention to the work's form, meant to present the man-subject and his or her experiences, and they discover that the relation between the form and the experience of the subject, if we apply the traditional categories of poetics, is circular[4]. Namely, the experience finds its form of expression and the work's form shapes the experience in

---

[4] The problem of the circular character of the relation between form and experience has been widely discussed by Antonina Lubaszewska in her book *The Poetics of Spiritual Experience: In the Direction of the Anthropology of Literary Forms*, Cracow 2009.

question, helps to recognize it. Antonina Lubaszewska in her book on the poetics of spiritual experience raises a question how the circularity manifests itself in literature (cf. Lubaszewska 2009: 9). Are we able, thanks to the form, the work's poetics, to recognize the experiences in search for their form, and what forms impose a structure on the experience? (cf. Lubaszewska 2009: 9). The author reflects on the notion of anthropological experience. However, in her research she refers to the biographies and works of St. Francis of Assisi, the Four Senses of the Bible, and the Desert Fathers; and she analyzes the widely understood spiritual experience, not necessarily in the religious sense. At this point, the article's reader could ask how the problem of experience and providing the hybrid work with the term of experience are typical of such artistic works. The modern art expresses the artist's experiences as well, it takes advantage of various carriers of meaning (e.g. conceptualism, text-art, or performance). What characterizes the relation between the form and the experience in the case of a hybrid work?

Generally, the experience is a relation as compared to what is outside, it is a result of the contrast with an alien element inside of us. What one must experience is not what he or she can conclude (cf. Droit 2006: 107). The recipient of a hybrid work (of other works as well) experiences it simultaneously as his or her own experience, and, at the same time, as a record of someone else's experience, since the form is the expression of spiritual experience, and also it is used to shape the experience. It needs emphasizing that we cannot indicate the works that would not constitute the form because the form as a manner of experiencing becomes attainable when it applies the measures enabling the recipient to experience something in a particular way. Even the creator who strives to free himself or herself from the forms does so through the form viewed as a result of the process of formation (if we apply the Pareyson's category).

The formation process of a hybrid work seems to differ in the sense that these works are formed as individual works in which the relation between the picture, word and sound is not in any way established. Hybrids do not create genres of clearly determined features. Surely they refer to numerous genological distinctions, in some works we can observe the contamination of different genres, and however, this process has no clearly distinguished frames, like in the case of opera or comic books which can hardly be recognized as hybrids. The attempt to interpret a hybrid every time resembles a case study in which it is difficult to find the clear rules of the reception process. Some readers could surely question the following argument and admit that in fact in art in the majority of cases we deal with hybrid works. It is worth taking into consideration that generic frames in art are not as essential as in literature, which has already been discussed by, among others, Jerzy Ludwiński:

> (...) particular genres of art, related to the purity of their own methods, floated to the separated destinations at different depths of reality. It was difficult to compare them, though from time to time their routes seemed parallel, and particular stages were astonishingly similar. As the movement was becoming faster and faster, and the artistic genres swelled with the new contents, the whole background – nobody's space between them – was slowly getting filled up. Here, where different fields were joined, the most fascinating things were happening; methods were crossing, conventions were losing sense, new tendencies and genres were being born such as concrete poetry, land-art, environment, happening, conceptual art, open theatre. Can anyone say today what we can still call music, art or theatre? Is it possible to determine correctly the border between the art and the rest of reality? Some say that everything can be music, poetry, theatre, everything can be art (Ludwiński 2009: 138–139).

Hybrid works are individual works of art, in the case of which the form of a specific work is typical of a single copy or of a series of copies, if we take into consideration artistic and liberatic books published in greater number of copies. If we compared *Spoglądając przez ozonową dziurę (But Eyeing Like Ozone Layer)* and *Oka-lecznie (Mute-I-Late)* by Zenon Fajfer and Katarzyna Bazarnik, we could easily notice that these two examples of hybrid works have been formed in a different way. Firstly, the book has taken the shape of a bottle in which on a transparent foil they have written a poem, and it has been placed in cardboard, and has been provided with a title and ISBN. Meanwhile, *Mute-I-Late* has taken the form of a triptych where we can find three different stories. For the listed works in the formation process a particular form has been chosen, its unique form. Therefore, what characterizes a hybrid work is its unique form. Thus it is of utmost significance to pay attention to every one of the works individually. Ryszard Nycz calls this process a "multidimensional case study" and recognizes it as the poetics of experience:

> The poetics of experience (...) which in practice assumes the form of a multidimensional case study does not refer to the assumed individual features, separate objects, "native" methods and theories; it declares its own non-paradigmatic and transdisciplinary character, and the "weak" interpretation as a fundamental strategy of research approach (Nycz 2007: 47).

Surely the type of interpretation suggested by Ryszard Nycz enables us to treat particular works as individuals, and we cannot say anything about them until the recipient starts to perceive it. In the case of hybrids it is impossible to pass judgments a priori on the work on the basis of its genre affiliation. We could paraphrase the statement of Roger-Pol Droit that a hybrid work is such an experience which cannot be concluded if we do not stay in touch with it. However, is it possible to perceive a hybrid work in such a non-paradigmatic and transdisciplinary manner? Finally, experience is possible if we perceive something according to the established, imposed, chosen categories. No subject is able to grasp "the flowing current of life".

To confirm this statement we can look into Herbert Read's book *The Origins of Form in Art* in which the author examines the essential sense of the form. Read believes that the art's task is not only to present but also to reach the deepest sources of cognition, which he puts in the following words: "art is an ability given to humans to distinguish the form from the chaotic whirl of its impressions, as well as to contemplate the form in its uniqueness"(Read 1973: 13). The scholar further notices: "if the form goes ahead of the human experience, we are entitled to expect that the awareness of the form has been received by people from their natural environment, and then they have spontaneously imitated it in the creations of their own hands. However, what has been imitated is the form, not the phenomenon, and the form has been symbolic" (Read 1973: 86). From Read's deliberations we can conclude that one can constitute his or her identity thanks to the artistic process of creation, and he or she can provide a frame to their own experiences.

We can notice that Georg Simmel speaks in a similar tone in his highly popular work *Bridge and Door*, where in one of the essays on fashion he introduces a term "basic forms of life". These basic forms of life, as defined by Simmel, are produced by a subject when he or she forms the specific matter, and at the same time he or she builds through the process the world of contents which are significant for this individual work. The subject touches the world, which moves constantly, and to whom the subject gives meaning. Then, as Simmel believes, the process of experiencing the world has contents, it produces internal objects: images, terms, knowledge; whereas they have their own meaning and substance, importance and order – different from the purely monotonous order of events. These contents, spiritual shapes assumed by existence, appear in some order: above all, in the mind of the subject who presents them to himself or herself. Therefore, the world is seen from the perspective of a centre which causes distances, accents, perspective shifts and cuts of the sensual and spiritual nature, without counterparts in the objective dimension of being.

Irena Chawrilska

Concrete Poetry as Experience

How can we relate the category of experience to concrete poetry?[5] In fact as readers of traditional poetry, we are used to reading in a poem which conveys content through metaphors, comparisons, and other various poetical measures. The lyrical I describes the world, his or her own experiences, informs about his or her adventures which in diverse ways are included in the poem. In the case of concrete poetry we cannot acknowledge that it conveys information on emotions, lyrical It's experiences, it does not describe the world in which the subject exists and which it experiences.

---

[5] The statement that concrete poetry belongs to the universe of hybrid works is thought to be controversial. It seems that the solution of the dispute over the affiliation of concrete poetry has already been provided by Stefania Skwarczyńska who derives it from the sources of a phenomenon which obtains things from the synthesis of arts viewed as a tradition. At the same time she emphasizes that discussion over and interpretation of concrete poetry goes beyond the language in the linguistic sense, in this case the language of art must be used, which in my opinion serves as an argument to place concrete poems among hybrid works ("If we intend to define the poetics of concrete poetry, hence its language as well, the scholarly poetics will have to shift contrary to its practice with <<traditional poetry>> – from the sphere of semantics to the orbit of semiotics. It means that it is going to deal not only with the language in the linguistic sense, but also with non-linguistic languages, and to be more exact and *ad rem:* with the language of art, that is to say with linguistic signs and iconic signs. The characteristics of concrete poetry would be problematic enough to overcome the understandable tendencies of semiology to put languages in order on the basis of their signs' homogeneity" Skwarczyńska 1977: 27). Even if we consider concrete poems to be physical objects in which it is impossible to separate word and picture, we should remember that in the reception process the recipient immediately separates one from the other and does not perceive concrete poetry as text and picture at the same time. Concrete poetry constitutes a hybrid because it is an expression of realizing by artists which are mechanisms of the language – its semantic and spatial nature. Thanks to the combination of poetry, visual art and music a new being is evoked which realizes the nature of language. Because of that concrete poets think that they have created a new language, and concrete poetry originates from the yearning for a new universal language in the face of its contemporary crisis. The language of concrete poetry is a turn towards visual text, the language turns out to be a hybrid, if we reduce it to a single word, and we notice in it "possibilities of the intrinsic orientation of the word to its own existence, to its own sign nature, structure and sense at the same time. The word with its clear meaning, sound and shape, thus the clearly impossible to notice self-definition has begun to serve as a base of a poem, its foundation, concrete", as written by Małgorzata Dawidek Gryglicka (Dawidek-Gryglicka 2012: 68). Małgorzata Dawidek-Gryglicka also refers to the above mentioned article of Stefania Skwarczyńska in her work on the visual text that made me draw my attention to the text, and I would like to express my gratitude for that reason.

Tadeusz Sławek notices that this type of poetry ignores "the Ptolemaic system of literature, concentrated around the author who in the work conveys his or her experiences" (Sławek 1989: 58). However, it does not mean that concrete poets do not refer to reality. They do so, but they refer to the language reality which is based on the elements of the real world. In concrete poetry the ties between the reality and the medium, which is a concrete poem in this case, are torn apart. The important part is played by the tension between linguistic elements, their meaning, picture and sound. All these elements joined together become an individual object, and, at the same time, a new universal language. Thanks to becoming independent from particular elements of the real world concrete poetry can penetrate various contexts of reality, which depends on who perceives the given work. It can become a way of experiencing reality.

In this context I would like to refer to a poem by Paula Claire[6] entitled ES-SENSE which is one (No 9) of the eighteen typographical poems produced on the basis of words: sense, nonsense, essence, quintessence, sensation, sensuous, sensual, sensitive[7]. The poems have been produced on a typewriter by writing the basic texts, and then by means of copying they have been put one on the other to obtain complex images. They are both visual and sound poems which are used by Paula Claire in her performances.

If we look carefully at the poem in question, we will surely notice the words sense and essence, vibrating and concentrating in some places, depending on the world-view we prefer.

Therefore, as I have already mentioned, concrete poetry penetrates the various contexts of reality, and as recipients in the perception process we are able to experience the universal, lingual and visual performance which enables us to focus on our experiences and reflections.

None of the elements of a concrete poem needs to be omitted: recipients can focus on the words, their visual form or meaning, they can refer to their own reflections and experiences, possibly to metaphysical ones as well.

It needs emphasizing that in the case of hybrids of this kind we can talk of contemplation as if it was the culmination of the process of perceiving a work, considering we do not deal here with a riddle, a puzzle needed

---

[6] Paula Claire is a British poet, artist, performer; she produces visual poetry, concrete poetry, sound poetry, artistic books, and performances. She has worked with Bob Cobbing. She lives in Oxford. She has established the archive of concrete poetry in Oxford – The Paula Claire Archive of Sound and Visual Poetry. We can find more information on the artist and her works on the website www.paulaclaire.com.
[7] Published as International Concrete Poetry Archive No 31, 1992.

to be solved in order to get through to the visual perception of a work or the other way around – to examine it from the visual perspective, and then to provide its meaning.

What can lead to contemplation are only the relentless interpretative actions: making inquiries, questioning, finding solutions, reaching as deep as possible.

The contemplation itself is seeing form as if it was form, obtaining a new way of seeing, it is a state of aesthetic pleasure (*il piacere estetico*) the source of which is beauty. Pareyson writes:

> Contemplation is not disturbed, it is entirely enclosed within its own gentleness, it is deprived of emotions and passions. Contemplation is *catharsis* because within its immobility life stops and there is a break, the tumult of feelings and affections gets quieter, even though its climax is the capture and ecstasy, and the one who contemplates, by gaining the view of a clairvoyant, forgers about himself, he is wholly included in the object, the subject almost gets out of himself. (Pareyson 2009: 225).

Another work by Paula Claire can possibly acquaint readers with the nature of relation between form and experience in case of hybrids, as well as, with the way such a work can be contemplated. What I have in mind is *Hymns to Isis* which are a couple of concrete poems produced by Paula Claire in 1992. The artist hung them on both sides of the mirror in her living room in her house in Oxford.

When we face the mirror, which has the poems on both sides, we can see the reflection of the River Thames. The river can be seen through the windows in Paula Claire's house which is separated from the river by the park. This is the view we can see the reflection of in the mirror – the park with the Thames flowing through it.

The artist tried to investigate where the name of the River Thames originates from. In ancient times the river was called Tamesis, and it is sometimes called Isis in Oxford. The name has inspired Paula Claire to reflect on the term of Isis. Obviously, the first association is the Egyptian goddess Isis who is believed to be the sister and wife of Osiris and the mother of Horus in the Egyptian mythology. In Roman times she was thought to be one of the incarnations of the Mother goddess. In art Isis is often portrayed as a sitting figure with a little Horus on her lap or next to her breast. Many researchers consider this type of goddedd's presentation to be the prefiguration of the picture of the Madonna and the Child Jesus in Christian iconography.

According to Paula Claire gods and goddesses represent our human need to grasp with our mind and imagination the mysterious forces (which she says *expressis verbis*: „For me, the idea of gods and goddesses shows our human desire to comprehend huge and mysterious forces"[8]). Isis is the goddess which represents the sun and moon, the male and female energy, like yang and yin in Chinese philosophy.

The artist has been inspired by the view of the river resembling melted gold at dawn on a January morning, when waves could be observed on the river. That is why the poem representing the yang energy has been written in gold on a white background, and the letters are vibrating because they have been placed alternately and therefore they give a dynamic feeling to the work's recipients.

The poem is called *Isis in Sunshine* by Paula Claire. The second poem, which reflects the yin energy, has been written in silver on a black background, and the letters have been put in separate lines and there is no interaction between them which gives the recipients a feeling of calmness and creates a reflective mood. The poem is called *Isis in Moonlight* and it has been inspired by the view of the Thames in the moonlight.

The ability to contemplate the work by Paula Claire is doubtless. When a recipient finds himself or herself in front of the mirror in the artist's living room which is the most convenient and the only place to perceive the work, he or she experiences the lingual form and also makes use of the colour and movement.

The recipient enters into relation with the reflection in the mirror which sets in motion another chain of events rooted in culture. The meaning of the two poems is the constant arising and multiplying of meanings depending on who stands in front of the mirror.

Despite the fact that the poems by Paula Claire are deeply rooted in reality and culture, thanks to their form they come, to some extent, to be independent from the River Thames, they become separate things and they can penetrate other contexts of reality, as well as shape the recipient's experience in their act of contemplation.

Tactile experience of experience

More and more frequently it is emphasized by scholars that the process of contemplation is impossible in case of the most recent works. In the times of *aisthesis* reconfiguration, term coined by Wolfgang Welsch, we cannot

---

[8] The quote comes from my talk with Paula Claire which took place on September 2, 2013 at her house in Oxford.

talk of contemplating works because they require the multisensory perception. The contemplation model in its traditional meaning assumed that the eye was privileged, it had been highest in the hierarchy of senses for centuries. In modern culture eyesight is no longer favoured in any way. Welsch remarks that eyesight "is no longer – neither in the world of modern physics, which is not based on what we can see with our own eyes, nor in the media – the reliable sense applied to keep in touch with the reality, as it was believed in the past" (Welsch 2005: 127).

Modern art requires multisensory perception as well. It will be certainly useful for the recipients of A.M.D.G. by Jim Butler[9]. The purpose of the artist was to produce a work which would enable him to express his reflection on growing up in the 1970s and 1980s, his friends from that time, and on attending a catholic school.

Butler has been wondering what kind of form would be the most appropriate to bear such experiences. He has decided that the form of a book would provide recipients with an intimate experience when they hold the work in their hands, and at the same time what they hold in their hands is not an insignificant wrapping of the text written inside.

The artist quotes the opinion of Ulisses Carrión and he considers the form of the book to be a sequence of spaces, and if each of these spaces is viewed at a different moment, a book is also a sequence of moments (which he recalls explicitly: "A book is a sequence of spaces. Each of these spaces is perceived at a different moment – a book is also a sequence of moments" (U. Carrión, *The New Art of Making Books*).

For that reason every page of A.M.D.G. is structured in a particular way, in order to „read" it recipients must understand all the elements of its structure. The tactile experience of the book is of utmost importance, the experience is not only an additional aspect of the perception apart from the eyesight perception, but it is as important as experiencing it through eyes.

The following pages of the book are structured in such a way that recipients can feel what they can see. The author plays with recipients and the game is the tactile experience of the book's space. The tactile experience of particular pages gives recipients the impression as if they were touching reality as "told" by Butler.

---

[9] Jim Butler – born in Dublin, lives in Cambridge, he has produced artistic books and other forms in which we can observe words integrated with the picture; he lectures in the Cambridge School of Art in Anglia Ruskin University. More infomation on the artist and his works can be found on the website http://www.jimbutlerartist.com

Jim Butler's book sets in motion many receptors, both – "mental" and "physical". The experience of A.M.D.G. begins at the moment when we touch the texture of the paper, we get familiar with the shape, and even with the weight of the book. Similarly as in the case of concrete poetry it has been the recipient who has filled up a concrete poem with his or her experience, who has completed the work in front of them with their own context, who has given the work a unique meaning through their experience. The same situation appears in the case of Jim Butler's A.M.D.G.

It's a risky statement to make but in the case of liberatic books we deal with similar processes of struggling with the form. In other words, the recipient in a way produces A.M.D.G., and in the perception process he or she again and again sets the rules of the work's perception.

For that reason the experience of Butler's book is different every time, the context of perceiving the book changes which is typical of every aesthetic experience. It needs to be emphasized that experiencing such works as A.M.D.G. is characterized by the fact that the multi-material structure requires to be experienced differently every single time: to change the order, the perspective of what to focus on, to experience more tactily and less perceptively with the eyesight or the other way around. Works of this kind can be determined by experience because the recipient actually produces them in the reception process.

Conclusion

It seems that hybrids are not the reproduction of experiencing reality, its representation or secondary determination. They may be acknowledged to be representatives of the phenomenon of "literature as experience", the term for these artistic works introduced by Ryszard Nycz (cf. Nycz 2007: 22).

In this sense art is the actual and specific experience of reality, art is, as described by the scholar, "the figure without which <<the silent masses of the unformulated inside of us>> (to use the term coined by Schulz) would never reach the threshold of consciousness and the conceptual and lingual formation of one's own identity" (Nycz 2007: 22).

At the same taking experience into consideration in the discourse does not mean that its sensual, deprived of reflection and meaning dimensions cannot still function in a work. Some aspects of the work, possible or impossible to express/show, are encoded in the work, in its "not fully explored theme of the semantic potential of its semiotic material", as written by Nycz (Nycz 2007: 22), and cannot be restored in the recipient's experience.

Bibliography

Aristotle 1979, *Generation of Animals*, Warsaw: PWN.

Aristotle 1980, *Problems*, Warsaw: PWN.

Carrión Ulisses 1975, *The New Art of Making Books*, http://www.arts.ucsb.edu/faculty/reese/classes/artistsbooks/Ulises%20Carrion,%20The%20New%20Art%20of%20Making%20Books.pdf.

Dawidek Gryglicka Małgorzata 2012, *The History of Visual Text. Poland after 1967*, Cracow–Wroclaw: Ha!art Corporation.

Dewey John 1975, *Art as Experience*, Wroclaw: Ossolineum.

Droit Roger-Pol 2006,"The Magnitude of Experience", *Second Texts*, No. 3.

Heidegger Martin 1997,*The Origin of the Work of Art*, [in:] *Off the Beaten Track*, trans. J. Miziera, Warsaw: Aletheia Foundation.

Kasia Katarzyna 2008, *The Art of Formation. Luigi Pareyson's Aesthetics of Formativity*, Cracow: Universitas.

Lubaszewska Antonina 2009, *The Poetics of Spiritual Experience. Towards the Anthropology of Literary Forms*, Cracow: Jagiellonian University Press.

Ludwiński Jerzy 2009, *The Art in the Post-Artistic Era and Other Texts*, Poznan: University of Arts in Poznan.

Nycz Ryszard 2007, "The Anthropology of Literature – the Cultural Theory of Literature – the Poetics of Experience", *Second Texts* No. 6.

Pareyson Luigi 2009, *The Aesthetics. Theory of Formativity*, trans. K. Kasia, Cracow: Universitas.

Read Herbert 1973, *The Origins of Form in Art*, trans. E. Życieńska, Warsaw: PIW.

Simmel Georg 2006, *The Bridge and the Door. Selected Essays.* trans. M. Łukasiewicz, Warsaw: Oficyna Naukowa.

Skwarczyńska Stefania 1977, *On the Place of Concrete Poetry and Similar Phenomena in the Research Interests of Scholarly Poetics*, [in:] *The Structure of Semantics of the Literary Text*, ed. Mihály Péter, Budapest: Akadémiai Kiadó.

Sławek Tadeusz 1989, *The Philosophy of Conjunction and the Poetry of Negativity*, [in:] *Between Letters. Sketches on Concrete Poetry*, Wroclaw: Dolnośląskie Publishing House.

Welsch Wolfgang 2005, *Aesthetics beyond Aesthetics. The New Nature of Aesthetics*, trans. K. Guczalska, Cracow: Universitas.

Agnieszka Karpowicz*
University of Warsaw

REINCARNATIONS OF THE WORD: MEDIA, GENRES, PRACTICES

Abstract
The text presents the project of study of the multimedia, contemporary verbal environment. It proposes the use of the category of speech genres (Bakhtin). Focusing on the secondary genres (genres of verbal creativity) it justifies the argument that "The word is not dead. It is merely changing its skin" (Dick Higgins), and therefore in the living verbal environment we deal with changing, heterogeneous media of verbal expression that determine, in part, the modes of functioning of particular genres and how they should be described. This paper presents performance, text and hypertext as basic means of functioning of the verbal forms in contemporary culture; means which demand adequate categories of description and research tools in order to avoid textualization of multimedia genres and not to treat them as literature.

Key words: media, speech genres, multimedia genres, practices, performance, text and hypertext

The Word and the snake

"The word is not dead, it is merely changing its skin" (Higgins 1979: 66) – there is probably no better or more accurate response to all kinds of literary discourses of crisis than this one aphorism by Dick Higgins.

Defining modern culture in terms of death of narratives, of the ever approaching waning of stories and books, of the agony of verbal forms, or of painful, fatal convulsions of the verbal art which is being forced out

---

* Faculty of Polish Studies, Univeristy of Warsaw, ul. Krakowskie Przedmieście 26/28, 00-927 Warsaw, e-mail: a.karpowicz@uw.edu.pl

by the havoc wrought by visual culture, audiovisual communication and other forms produced by the domination of the new media, resembles attempts to describe a living communicative environment and a dynamic, flexible and changeable media context with its emerging forms undertaken by someone, who has never taken the risk of actually immersing themselves in this sphere.

Meanwhile merely looking up from the book – in a manner quite different from what Roland Barthes proposed when trying to "star" the text and split its meanings from the inside, and from Umberto Eco who suggested readers should now go to libraries and study encyclopedias – is enough to hear the rumbling modernity, which hardly ever has its mouth shut, and to see the plethora of words that weave into both the everyday and the extraordinary. It is easy to notice then that the contemporary culture is shaped by, among other things, the verbal forms born from individuals' functioning in all kinds of spheres of linguistic activity. Moreover, most of these spheres are impossible without words: without recounting, saying or writing something.

We will then see a vision of a multimedia culture which is changeable, but in which we do not constantly stumble over cadavers of forms that have been exhausted, and over tomb portraits of void, if once noble genres, but rather we will be stunned, dazed and clamored down by the ever emerging new forms: personal webpages go out of fashion immediately and are replaced by social media profiles; slams compete not only with books of poetry but with competitive freestyle; the new media give rise to tweets and hypertextual novels; instead of daily aphorisms we have memes; stories on art of cooking and food history are listened to with bated breath and recipes published in album form cookbooks are page-turners comparable with best novels; advertisement becomes art and its creators play with words just as the most sophisticated linguistic poets did; RPG and MUD players not only read novels that are the basis for their games, but they also tell and write their own stories, while film adaptations of the classic youth literature lead to publishing booms, which are easy to spot in any contemporary bookstore.

All these creative verbal activities of those participating in culture most certainly prove that the word and linguistic expression do not disappear with the growth of the audiovisual and the multimedia, but they are displaced, they find new areas and nest in new media. Consequently, they also change status and aesthetic form. Therefore they require description and judgment, which are different than the ones worked out for effects, artifacts, frozen works. Accidentally, the same applies to contemporary visual art, which can hardly by properly understood from the perspective of the traditionally sanctioned art history.

In other words: the modes of description, categories and tools for analyzing verbal expression, which have been formed within the perimeter of the print culture, well adapted to study the products and phenomena typical of a typographic culture, will not necessarily apply when surveying and describing a post-typographic culture. Categories such as "text" and "literariness" are not objective, eternal, innocent and ahistorical, but are in fact modes of understanding a linguistic reality closely bound with the typographic culture. At a certain point it led to the emergence of the structuralist textualization of language, within which language is treated as a set of arbitrary linguistic signs. Another consequence was the semiotic textualization of almost the entire human cultural space, through, among other things, the significant and enduring tendency to apply the word "text" to phenomena such as image, gesture, body or space, which after all are not texts in any strict sense.

It seems that the light, effective metaphor employed in Higgins's aphorism is filled by contemporary, multimedia, heterogeneous communicative environment with a particularly concrete and consequential meaning. The phrase "changing its skin" presents the word as a living being, as a nourishing body covered with skin, and thus produces an association with an organism occupying a certain environment, and benefitting from its exterior through a double osmosis of sorts. The metaphor links the word with a snake, which constantly reemerges in a new form, after a period of molting which might seem to be a painful and degrading decay.

The word does indeed – as a flexible, fast, supple and cunning snake – squeeze in everywhere, and in the moments that we tend to perceive as its death all too eagerly, it is in fact shedding its skin, only to be reborn in a new form. As in a snake dance, the word reacts seamlessly to the snake charmer's music, that is to external impulses, movements and trembles of the cultural and media reality, it takes up various forms while interacting with its living, active tissue. If we do not treat the word as referring to reality, but as a form of doing something in it, as communicative being and being together (Godlewski 2003; Karpowicz 2003), we will see that the verbal forms are irremovable and inalienable products of acting in the world, being in it, while the world itself changes.

If there were no urban space with its walls, subway stations, commuter rail and advertising columns, why would anyone create graffiti or sticker art – and what would it look like? If there were no city club culture, for whom, where and what for would slams be organized and created?

Similarly, if there were no Internet, there would be no blogs, just as back in a day there would not have emerged anything like the novel and its legions of readers, if not for the printing press (Watt 1959). That is not to say that the new media and their materiality determine human verbal expression, but that they produce new space, they give rise to varying fields which – as the example of the Internet shows – we immediately want to take over, use in a creative manner, discuss, sometimes talk even them down, either with the forms and uses of language which we are already familiar with, or by transgressing them and producing new forms which sneak in, in a snake's manner, into fissures and empty spaces offered by the new media.

While immersing in the contemporary communicative environment, it is easy to move from one extreme to another and be overwhelmed by the richness of "literature", by the "textual" activity of those participating in culture; and to see – in this plethora of heterogeneous verbal forms – merely texts, a little different, but still texts, slightly deviating from the literary norm. Enough to announce, against critics and grumblers, that "literature is not yet dead!"

One can take precautions against falling into this trap by noticing, for example, that blogs, co-functioning in the net with commentaries and forum posts, only resemble traditional diaries very superficially, that popular novels listened to as audiobooks can hardly be called page-turners anymore, and that slams which please the enthusiastic crowds and the freestyle battles which keep up the tradition of masterly improvisations cannot really be identified with books of poetry. Hyper-textual novel can only be seamlessly turned into a printed book in its most limited versions, and its structure is not identical even with the postmodernist literary "model kits" created by authors who only had a vague dream of a hyper-textual utopia. The very textual, even literate character of these forms seems very problematic, or at least unobvious, not to mention their "literary" qualities.

If one looks closely at these practices, it turns out each of these products of expression can, if the need be, be recorded as a text. Is this, however, the same as saying the participants of culture produce texts and deal with them, and so do the audiences of freestyle battles or those who habitually visit their favorite logovisual blogs every day? Is their experience really analogous to communication based on text? Does a printed blog immediately become a diary, or does a hypertextual novel turn into a novel then? Does writing down the rhymes of freestyle produce simply textual verses and poems? The answer to all these questions is inevitably negative, so perhaps this means also that reducing living signs of contemporary verbal art to the category of writing, creating literature and texts is not entirely justified.

The word's skin and the text

The skin that the word is changing is then a cover, a shape it takes in order to continue functioning in the living, changeable communicative environment. This metaphor allows us to imagine all the media in which historically and synchronically various verbal forms have emerged, all connected with the members of a culture's creative expressions present in any medium: from orality, through writing and print, to the audiovisual and multimedia (Mencwel 2006: 57–58).

It seems that in order to describe and understand such a dense and varied communicative environment it will be essential to give up applying the category of "literariness" as it is tantamount in fact to textualization. Otherwise we take away the cultural specificity of these new genres. The aim is then to adapt the analytic tool and the language of description to the mode of being represented by verbal expression in contemporary culture, so that it is studied through the emerging forms as a creative, active environment, far from being in crisis or exhausted.

Some of these verbal forms – such as forum posts or urban poetry written on walls – can only take up the textual form as secondary, while they are primarily "literacy events" (Frankel 2010) or chirographic actions rather than autonomous, closed, static texts as defined by Walter J. Ong (Ong 2013). Other forms – such as slam and freestyle – are characterized by performance, which is defined by Richard Bauman as a form of verbal art which exist in fact only in doing, and is a way of speaking irreducible to text or even to a verbal enunciation because they are verbomotor, spectacular, immersed in situational context and emerging in interaction (Bauman 1975). It is not simply a speech act, more or less performative or fortuitous, however understood; it is not a communicative "enactment" of something prepared in advance, but a very particular type of enunciation closely knit with the particular medium of the word that is orality – primary orality, or the one taken up by the media based on some form of record (analogue or digital). Therefore the individual mode of being rooted in the inextricable medium context is crucial when defining the verbal forms we encounter in the contemporary media environment.

Performance is bound with oral expression, manuscript is a form typical of chirography, text is inextricably bound with the typographic culture, and hypertext, projects of which were being prepared already in the typographic culture, only reached its full development and gave rise to new forms in the new media environment. All these modes of being dependent on the media cannot be ignored when describing audiovisual forms. The last mode of being I have listed is the situation in which there is no coherent founding medium. This is the case of the audiovisual genres which are close to orality (the audio component), typography (visuality and textuality), or they remain very specific in their audiovisuality combining both elements. Even a manuscript cannot be completely innocently translated into a textual form; a diary, written for personal purposes – even if the author considers the option of future publication (Rodak 2011) – is different from a clear, transparent and sterile printed text. Moreover, the type of writing is important here, which, for examples, makes a genre such as haiku possible only in a culture using ideographic writing. Every effort to translate such works into a different environment requires splitting word and image or leaving the original form next to the one written in the alphabet. Of course, this is an extreme case, but it brings to the fore the importance of something as seemingly trivial as the types of medium: ideographic and alphabetic writing. It shows that such translation is never innocent. To use an example closer to our cultural context, we can understand this difference by realizing how it is impossible to translate urban tags into a text – and how this means they cannot be conceptualized through this category, even though they remain verbal enunciations.

The emergence of the new media and the ensuing category of hypertext requires redefining the very notion of text, which the term "hypertext" contains and thus forces us to notice not so much the analogies, but the differences, which are so important and meaningful for the analysis:

> Hypertext is [...] an intertext not only in its content and genre (as it is in case of relations described by Barthes and Bakhtin), but also in its construction. Hypertext's intertextuality is not potential, it is inextricable from it. Hypertextuality is also connected with interactivity, which assumes that the reader is an active subject, whose actions shape the reading (Rogozińska, Szewczyk 2014).

Text on the other hand is a closed message, decontextualized, linear, and independent from the author who is a potential reader of his or her own enunciation. It detaches verbal expression from do living, interactive "here and now" in which the message is born:

> Printed texts look machine-made, as they are. Chirographic control of space tends to be ornamental, ornate, as in calligraphy. Typographic control typically impresses more by its tidiness and its inevitability: the lines perfectly regular, all justified on the right side, everything coming out even visually, and without the aid of the guidelines or ruled borders that often occur in manuscripts. This is an insistent world of cold, non-human, facts (Ong 2013: 120).

Such view of the specificity of print as a medium of the word corresponds only to a limited section of linguistic reality of the typographic environment. Mechanicalness and desubjectification of a printed message, detached from human voice, and even of human hand, is unquestionable, but this is merely a model, ideal or dominating mode of typography, which best describes literature closed in a book. It seems that even in the case of typography, seen as one of the constantly changing snake incarnations of the word, looking in between the covers of a book is not a good starting point to understand cultural functioning of any form of verbal expression, and certainly not of the entire communicative environment of contemporary culture.

A linear text is merely one of the possible models here, and precision of definition is crucial, if we do not want to drown the specificity of blogs, forum posts, all kinds of urban "scribbles" and tweets in the textual universe which allegedly takes over the participants of culture: those who act, speak, write and type; if we do not want to trap them in a semiotic net of abstract signs. Seeing the specificity of the medium, in which a given content functions, is necessary, if we do not want to flatten the live performances and online activities, which achieve a similar level of immediacy, performativity and directness as the one characteristic of oral communication – even if it is mediated through writing – and if we do not want reduce it to dead letters of a text. Ultimately, and perhaps paradoxically, such approach will allow us to save the literature itself – the unique and original expression of the print culture and one of utmost achievements of a social formation identical with typographic formation – in the discursive universe, in the stream of chatter, twaddle and everyday communication which is necessary to act effectively in the world and simply to be in it; if it is important to us that we see in this undifferentiated linguistic world the difference between the novels of Dostoyevsky or Kafka and blog posts, the products of e-poetry generators, or even writing love poems in emails – and this is not a matter of difference in quality or artistic merit. These simply are not identical forms of expressions, and threating them all as "texts" or literary forms inevitably implies such identical character.

Even within the typographic culture textuality of some enunciations is troublesome, if we are willing to accept Ong's very narrow understanding of text. Sometimes they cannot be reduced to invisible, ephemeral particles, which serve merely (and solely) as carriers of content. The font is a visual phenomenon, it is visible and seen, even though its ideal type, belonging to Ong's concept of printed text, seems so transparent that it is almost invisible. However, logovisual genres, which are typical of the print medium, transgress this ideal type and hence undermine its textual character. Hence typographic forms go beyond such textuality, which is sometimes done on purpose, as in avant-garde experiments, and sometimes through taking over or mocking official writings and regular lines of majestic letters on city plaques and billboards, as is the case with graffiti and stickers. Text is related to the cultural function of legibility and lucidity of the typographic message, in which the visual is not brought to the fore. This type of visuality is characteristic of texts in the strict sense (meaning closed wholes, usually in form of books), and of textual variants of official writings, announcements, bills, printed law, as well as all sorts of signs prohibiting or enforcing something. This transparency has a cultural function too, for example it brings out the arbitrariness and the authoritative qualities of a message; its being machine-made and its mechanicalness contribute to the power, gravity and strength of what is being communicated through desubjectification: it emphasizes objectivity, universality, inviolability and indisputability. A second type of text's visuality includes signboards, posters, comic books, ads, postcards, magazines, but also visual poetry (with its transmedia and historical forms, among which lettrism and concrete poetry are purely typographic). Clearly, even printed words do not necessarily fulfill the potential of text in its full.

Moreover, as Marshall McLuhan strived to show, reading and seeing are not two separate functions of our minds: "The interiorization of the technology of phonetic alphabet translates man from the magical world of the ear to the neutral visual world" (McLuhan 2011: 21). McLuhan claimed that it is the invention of print that contributed to the hegemony of eye-centeredness and the visual perception throughout the 20th century. From that point of view reading is the beginning of a process of visual conquest, and of copying and popularizing knowledge and it leads to the domination of seeing the word rather than hearing it:

> When words are written, they become, of course, parts of the visual world. Like most of the elements of the visual world, they become static things

and loose, as such, the dynamism which is so characteristic of the auditory world in general, and of the spoken word in particular. [...] Thus, in general, words, by becoming visible, join a world of relative indifference to the viewer – a world from which the magic "power" of the word has been abstracted (McLuhan 2011: 23).

McLuhan shows the knot that ties the written word with image, referring to the mental level of perception, which means it is print that gives rise to the contemporary visual culture and it contributes to the shift from the auditory to the visual (and still verbal) mode of being in the world. From that perspective, it is difficult to understand why the growing importance of videocentrism should in any way pose a threat to the print culture and typographic cultural formation, rather than is simply its consequence.

Robert Bringhurst tried to convince his students who designed typography that printed letters should be a visual response to invisible ideas and thus chirography – "the dance of the living hand" (Bringhurst 2004: 11) – always remains the heartwood of typography. In doing so he compared the new devices, technologies and media of the written word to new leaves growing out of the branches every year. There can be new media and new technologies almost every year. A snake changes its skin cyclically, too. In both cases, however, these are situations not of waning, dying, but of changing shape and of verbally inhabiting ever-new areas, media and fields of social, communicative and creative action.

Of course, old forms are not immediately pushed out, they do not disappear. They are simply subjected to rules of remediation (Bolter, Grusin 1999; Bolter 2001), they can receive a secondary textual form, as was the case with myths, songs, epics in the typographic culture, to use the more archaic examples, which show that the process discussed here is not a unique, contemporary phenomenon of pressure from the new media. In the typographic and posttypographic cultures there are still niches of orality, constituted by various genres, which cannot be fully described apart from their roots in the oral medium, which is best illustrated today by phenomena such as freestyle, slam or a concert. There are also genres which would never have appeared or would never have acquired their current shape if it was not for the processes of change in the media. Other genres receive their second – and longer – life due to the new media (e.g. novel). If the word did not change its skin, it could certainly die out, because the skin needs to be thin, sensitive and flexible enough to allow for communication and interpersonal exchange.

Agnieszka Karpowicz

A snake with hands and genres of verbal creativity

In the Chinese tradition there is a parable about painting a snake with hands. A rich man decided once to offer one bottle of alcohol to his guests. It would go the person who would paint a snake on the floor the fastest and the best. When the first of the contenders finished, he saw he still had enough time and decided to add hands to his snake. And so he did. As can be imagined, he did not win the competition and never had the chance to enjoy the bottle.

Painting snakes with hands resembles operations such as analyzing freestyle or blogs in textual categories, and describing rhyme, rhythm and language games as if live performance was nothing but a meaningless bonus to the words and their content. The very act of classification, when we call a comic book or a blog "literature", endows these forms with qualities and functions they do not have in our culture at all. It is similarly misguided to claim that, let us say, oral cultures have their "literature" in form of myths or songs, except it is "oral literature". This retroactive textualization has its counterpart in the tendency to call hip hop or comic books "popular literature", or to call freestyling producing "an oral text", or to say that webpages are full of "texts" and "literature" only because what we see on the computer screen are letters.

The parable about painting a snake with hands warns against such attitude and it also shows that while trying to achieve a goal and be first, one must still be sensible and take into consideration the goal itself. Therefore the first condition is to diversify the language of description, to go beyond the textual limitations, so that finding orientation in this dense media environment does not imply reducing everything to a text, which is only one of the forms verbal creativity can take.

All these phenomena – which I have so far called forms or verbal expressions – can actually be named genres of verbal creativity (Karpowicz 2013), alluding – and not accidentally at all – to the thought of Mikhail Bakhtin, or at least to its part which is particularly concerned with "verbal creativity" and the notions of primary and secondary "speech genres" (Bakhtin 1986). Most broadly speaking, the idea is to use the redefined and elaborated Bakhtinian category to study genres of linguistic forms which function in the multimedia environment of contemporary culture. Without going into detail and contexts of the concept here, the choice can be justified by recalling that the speech genres have already been used for analogous goals on numerous occasions by linguistic anthropologists, ethnographers and other scholars trying to analyze the social environments through their verbal productions. However, their research was conducted not in their own cultures but on territories distant in time and space. One of such scholars, William F. Hanks, studies the Maya culture, combining the speech genres with Pierre Bourdieu's *habitus*. He writes:

> [...] speech genres are seen as both the outcome of historically specific acts, and themselves among the constituting dimensions in terms of which action is possible. Genres then, as kinds of discourse, derive their thematic organization from the interplay between systems of social value, linguistic convention, and the world portrayed. They derive their practical reality from their relation to particular linguistic acts, of which they are both the products and the primary resources (Hanks 1987: 671).

Other scholars pointed to a similar possibility of operationalizing this category, including Richard Bauman and Charles L. Briggs, who showed how it can be applied to oral cultures and folklore, which can be an additional valuable suggestion, when we want to describe genres related to urban folklore or the ones we are dealing with on the internet (Rogozińska, Szewczyk 2014):

> [...] the concept of genre (with or without the label) has played a role in linguistic anthropology since at least the time of Boas. Generic classifications helped set the agenda for research on Native American languages. The study of genre was later boosted by ethnoscience, structuralism, the ethnography of speaking, and the performance-centered approach to verbal art. The recent popularity of Bakhtin's translinguistics and new perspectives on emotion and gender have similarly accorded new cachet to generic investigation (Bauman, Briggs 2009: 214).

It is a matter of just such anthropologically oriented understanding of speech genres. These scholars have also been inspired by Bakhtin's distinction between two basic types of speech genres: primary genres and secondary genres, which, too, can be operationalized for the sake of studying contemporary communicative environment and the emerging specific, heterogeneous forms rooted in the media.

It seems that listing all speech genres in all media known to the contemporary culture would have been an impossible task and it would be in vain. Their changeability, the fact that new forms emerge incredibly fast, could lead either to a failure of research and a conclusion that the environment is limitless and indescribable, or – which would almost constitute a failure too – to describing them all, despite their diversity and the heterogeneous character of contemporary media, as "literature-like", or as varieties of text, or simply as normal, democratized, common and less institutionalized continuations of existing genres. However, there is a solution to this double deadlock.

Accepting that it is impossible to list all genres, so that each of them separately fulfills the criteria and categories of description, and admitting from the start to a failure in trying to keep the description up to date with the everyday growth and overgrowth of new forms of communication, it is in fact enough to focus on secondary genres, the definition of which, however, ought to be transformed from the original Bakhtinian inspiration. A primary (simple, originary) genre can be seen as one that does not absorb other primary genres and does not modify them. It is usually reduced to one function; its role is limited to a functional situational context, because its sole task is doing something in the social reality. Genres with a direct communicative function serve as examples here: their aim is to communicate something or to make one remember something, and they can be found both in oral communication and in the medium of writing, e.g. shopping list made before heading to a grocery store or a prescription given by a doctor which is a means of fulfilling a certain type of action. Such forms do not require any transgression of algorithm, even if it might happen due to individual intentions. However, breaking the convention can make fulfilling the action difficult or impossible, thus neutralizing its fortuitousness in the particular area. It is enough to imagine a prescription written in verse or in a form of concrete poetry, or as an elaborate first person narrative.

Secondary genres, to which the category of genres of verbal creativity applies, are rooted in the cultural context too and cannot be separated from it, especially as they are made of primary genres, directly linked to social situations of communication. Secondary genre is a complex form, absorbing at least one primary (simple) genre, transforming and modifying it. In that sense a genre of verbal creativity is a multifunctional whole which cannot be reduced to one role played in the functional context of a given situation. For example, a shopping list is not a secondary genre, even if it can be written in verse, because the individual intentions behind the use of a given genre of verbal creativity do not qualify as generic features. It would be a simple written genre, which can be absorbed by a different verbal form and hence constitute a multifunctional, complex whole, which becomes a secondary genre and transforms its aims and functioning, as is the case of one of the poems by Stanisław Barańczak. Similarly, phone text messaging has been absorbed, producing the complex form of tweets, which perform multiple functions (from self-promotion and self-presentation to spreading gossip or commenting on events to produce a positive image of oneself, or even to serving as aphorisms) and cannot be reduced to the primary function of conveying a message or simply informing.

Looking for genres of verbal creativity in media other than print is never simply about finding equivalents of literature or genres that have similar features or functions. The important reformulation of literary and theoretical text-centered perspectives lies in renouncing the tendency to treat literature as the model of all verbal creativity and replacing it with the approach that sees literature as only one of the possibilities, rooted in the particular medium. A literary work does not have any necessary features (such as language patterns, or narration), which would be an argument for treating all other genres of verbal creativity, rooted in other media, as secondary to it. It is also not about searching for secondary genres that can be described as literary or artistic. The notion of secondary genres as genres of creativity is an alternative to the categories mentioned above, as they are too closely bound with the definition of literature and literariness based on formal criteria, on criteria related to the interior organization of text, or on distinction (sometimes undermined in literature) between fiction and fact. All these categories are products of the humanities focused on texts and having sources in them.

Any attempts to distinguish and clearly classify genres of verbal creativity in this dense environment require reflection on how they are related to literature and text. The aim is not to find marginal genres, which could be labeled as "literature" – such approach only superficially ennobles other genres (which thus receive the status of verbal art), while in fact it degrades them, depriving them of their media or cultural specificity, as is the case when we call a song or a comic book "popular literature". In the first case it is an act of textualization, which reduces the genre to the text of the lyrics, which can very well be of minor importance or in fact have no meaning, as the sang words themselves have none. In the second case it is all too easy to ignore the logovisual character of the genre, while focusing on its narrative, treating it merely as a "story"; not to mention that the word "popular" carries a pejorative meaning, despite years of efforts to show the value this area of creativity. It is clear that such approach – and such a net of categories serving as a tool to grasp and describe various forms of creative verbal activity – would disfigure the research and the collected facts, would impoverish them, blurring their specificity and depriving them of it. Genres' mode of functioning is dependent on their medium. Particular works fulfill certain potential of the medium, to which the genre belongs, even though ultimately the medium does not determine their form and the limitations of the medium can be overcome. Attempts at designing a hypertextual novel before the real hypertext came to being, undertaken by, among others, authors of postmodern and experimental prose, are a point in case. In any media environment – due in part to the creative acts and practices of those participating in culture – there are both standardized primary genres serving the purposes of direct communication, and secondary genres, rooted in the media context, usually not simply fulfilling its potential, but actually transgressing it, going beyond the features and limitations of a particular medium of the word. Moreover, literature has a special place in this process, as it is often one of the most accurate and alert detectors of changes in the communicative environment, frequently the first to detect shifting thresholds of the logosphere (Rutkowski 1987), and it has a special social position as an independent, autonomous (artistic) sphere, which produces utopias and projects of future media environments, as was the case with the avant-garde and postmodern literature, bored to death with text and the abstraction of the word reduced to letters.

Apart from everything else, the media-centered perspective makes it clear that what is usually treated as literature, was not always literature (myth, epic), and is not always literature today (song, lullaby, radio play, blog). It also allows us to understand that such alleged deaths and crises of the word, narrative, text or language, that one hears about nowadays in context of the new media, have occurred in abundance throughout the history of culture, but none of them turned out to be a real agony: neither when writing "killed" the spoken word, nor when the printing press "wrought havoc" in the high art of the noble word and the lithography democratized both words and art, nor when TV soap-operas were giving the "fatal blow" to novels and stories. All these cyclical "deaths", "falls" and "wanings" do is they are a testimony to the fact, that the snake does indeed regularly change its media skin for a new one; that even today the repetitive process of remediation-reincarnation is underway; that: "the word is not dead, it is merely changing its skin".

Translated by Olga Kaczmarek

Bibliography

Bakhtin Mikhail 1986, *Speech Genres*, [in:] *Speech Genres and Other Late Essays*, trans. V. W. McGee, Austin: University of Texas Press.

Bauman Richard 1975, "Verbal Art as Performance", *American Anthropologist*, No. 2.

Bauman Richard, Briggs Charles L. 2009, *Genre, Intertextuality and Social Power*, [in:] *Linguistic Anthropology: A Reader*, ed. A. Duranti, Malden, MA: Blackwell-Wiley.

Bringhurst Robert 2004, *The Elements of Typographic Style. Version 3.0*, Point Roberts-Vancouver: Hartley & Marks Publishers

Bolter Jay D. 2001, *Writing Space: Computers, Hypertext, and the Remediation of Print, Second Edition*, Mahwah: Lawrence Erlbaum Associates.

Bolter Jay D., Grusin Richard 1999, *Remediation: Understanding New Media*, Cambridge: MIT Press.

Frankel Beatrice 2010, *Pojęcie wydarzenia piśmiennego*, trans. N. Dołowy, [in:] *Antropologia pisma. Od teorii do praktyki*, eds. Ph. Artières, P. Rodak, Warsaw: Wydawnictwa Uniwersytetu Warszawskiego.

Godlewski Grzegorz 2003, *Słowo o antropologii słowa*, [in:] *Antropologia słowa. Zagadnienia i wybór tekstów*, eds. G. Godlewski, A. Mencwel, R. Sulima, Warsaw: Wydawnictwa Uniwersytetu Warszawskiego.

Hanks William F. 1987, "Discourse Genres in a Theory of Practice", *American Ethnologist*, No. 4.

Higgins Dick 1979, *The Strategy of Visual Poetry*, [in:] *Visual Literary Critcism. A New Collection*, ed. Richard Kostelanetz, Carbondale IL: Southern Illinois University Press.

Karpowicz Agnieszka 2012, *Słowo – twórczość słowna – literatura*, *Antropologia twórczości słownej. Zagadnienia i wybór tekstów*, ed. K. Hagmajer-Kwiatek, A. Karpowicz, J. Kowalska-Leder, Warsaw: Wydawnictwa Uniwersytetu Warszawskiego.

Karpowicz Agnieszka 2013, *Poławianie gatunków. Twórczość słowna w antropologicznej sieci*, [in:] *Od aforyzmu do zina. Gatunki twórczości słownej*, eds. G. Godlewski, A. Karpowicz, M. Rakoczy, P. Rodak, Warsaw: Wydawnictwa Uniwersytetu Warszawskiego.

Mencwel Andrzej 2006, *Wiedza o kulturze a wiedza o literaturze*, [in:] *Wyobraźnia antropologiczna*, Warsaw: Wydawnictwa Uniwersytetu Warszawskiego.

McLuhan Marshall 2011, *The Gutenberg Galaxy*, Toronto: University of Toronto Press.

Ong Walter J. 2013, *Orality and literacy*, 30th Anniversary Edition, with additional chapters by John Hartley, New York: Routledge.

Rodak Paweł 2011, *Między zapisem a literaturą. Dziennik polskiego pisarza w XX wieku*, Warsaw: Wydawnictwa Uniwersytetu Warszawskiego.

Rogozińska Anna, Szewczyk Matylda 2014, *Internet jako medium i jako przestrzeń społeczna: wstęp do dyskusji o internetowych gatunkach twórczości słownej*, [in:] *Almanach antropologiczny IV. Twórczość Słowna/Literatura*, eds. G. Godlewski, A. Karpowicz, M. Rakoczy, P. Rodak, Warsaw: Wydawnictwa Uniwersytetu Warszawskiego.

Rutkowski Krzysztof 1987, *Przeciw (w) literaturze. Esej o poezji czynnej Mirona Białoszewskiego i Edwarda Stachury*, Bydgoszcz: Pomorze.

Rypson Piotr 1989, *Obraz słowa. Historia poezji wizualnej*, Warsaw: Akademia Ruchu.

Watt Ian 1957, *The Rise of the Novel: Studies in Defoe, Richardson, and Fielding*, Berkeley: The University of California Press.

Literature and Convergence

Ewa Szczęsna*
University of Warsaw

POETICS IN THE AGE OF CONVERGENCE[1]

Abstract
The aim of the study is to present changes in the structure of text (its structure and ways of creation, figures in particular) in digital discourse. The identity of digital communication is supported by existing signs, texts, and discourses; and how it develops in the process of their adaptation and reinterpretation. The Internet seems to be a really good space in which different discourses become alike. This process results in the creation of new poetics of text and discourse. Digital media modifies rhetorical figures (especially the ontology and functions of those figures), it cancel figures existing in traditional texts (for example, inversion is invalidated because no determined way of reading the text exists), and it creates new ones.

In digital discourse words and icons have a multifunctional nature (meaning-making, linking, acting, marking, and signalling the sender's emotions). Traditional textual forms, which differ semiotically and medially, are combined and transformed, so that the boundaries between forms of expression are blurred.

Key words: digital poetics, convergence, interactive figures, hypertext, link

New, yet old, or the term in the context of modernity

The term *convergence* in the field of literary studies is applied to phenomena which have long been discussed within other categories in the humanities, such as hybridisation or homogenisation, especially in reference to the mass media (Horkheimer, Adorno 1969; Macdonald 1959; Eco 1968;

---

* Faculty of Polish Studies, Univeristy of Warsaw, ul. Krakowskie Przedmieście 26/28, 00-927 Warsaw, e-mail: e.k.szczesna@uw.edu.pl
[1] This publication was created as part of a research project NN 103 398340, and financed by the National Science Centre in Cracow.

Kłoskowska 1983). The very term is not new, either, as convergence has been well established in the realm of biology, medicine, linguistics, historiography, anthropology, political science, and media studies.

As a matter of fact, the emergence of convergence within humanistic discourse and, more specifically, in literary studies, defines and actualises the phenomenon covered by the term: assimilation, or the occurrence of analogous processes in diverse fields and at times distant domains. The assimilation of texts, their structures, and genres, results in the similarity of terminology.

The wandering of categories and the application of terms from certain disciplines to others are phenomena discussed by theoreticians coming from diverse schools and fields of cultural studies, such as Roman Jakobson[2] (Jakobson 1971; 1989), Mieke Bal (Bal 2002), or Clifford Geertz (Geertz 1983). These phenomena reflect what is happening in textuality itself and in the space of cultural discourses, which organise social life and – as Michel Foucault would have said – exercise power over it (Foucault 2002). After Geertzian blurred genres and mixed ways of speaking, come blurred discourses. The democratisation of social life and thinking about texts, processes of globalisation, and the development of digital technologies lead to the obliteration of boundaries between political, scientific, religious, or artistic discourses, or rather – informative, persuasive, aesthetic, or ideological ones. This in turn leads to their convergence. Art is taking part in politics (Cerny), provocation (Kozyra, Libera); it is metatextual (Susid, the Spatialists, ready-mades), and metacritical. Messages which in their generic principle should be informative (TV news, history textbooks) are persuasive and evidently filtered through and biased by a certain ideology. Moreover, these filters and influences increasingly often apply not to the thematic layer of what is being directly stated, but to the semiotic layer of how it is declared. The usage of a particular composition, hierarchisation, shooting angle, tonality of colours, sounds, the choice of represented elements – in short, a certain cognitive perspective – modifies the subject, constitutes its sense, and initiates a specific understanding.

---

[2] Jakobson, while determining the place of linguistics among other branches of science, pointed to the analogy of processes, and the similarity of phenomena which were studied by distinct domains. According to the scholar, those analogies allow mutual borrowings of categories, e.g, the cooperation of linguists and biologists created an interest in the biological notion of mimetism on the linguists' part, and an interest on the biologists' part in the linguistic communication acts; the notion of redundancy was borrowed by information theory from linguistic research. (Jakobson 1989: 437, 460).

Texts almost exclusively refer to texts themselves. They are metatexts, whereas culture becomes metaculture (even Umberto Eco many years ago wrote in his *Postscript to The Name of the Rose* about the self-recognition of culture). The concept of reality as autonomous from text is fading away, which means that determining the relation of text to reality loses its *raison d'etre*. Such notions as the city, or human and social behaviour, are considered to be texts, which results in our living entirely in the world of text, or rather, of discourse, since our status of recipients of culture changes into users of culture, individuals who actively co-produce it.

Convergence, spoiling (ascribing different meanings to messages), sampling, meta-connectionism (associating everything with everything else), immersion, recombinant culture, flow, recycling, subversion[3], hybridisation – these are the terms used to describe contemporary culture. Their multiplicity and accumulation make an impression of acceleration within cultural changes. However, it is necessary to examine the range of meanings and terms more closely in order to see the name changes which are inscribed in permanent cultural processes. It is possible that such a plurality of descriptive categories is a form of dramatizing the scientific discourse. If so, it would reflect contemporary media practice, in which dramatisation prevails over the progress of action and which – as Eriksen commented in reference to contemporary TV series – is a drama standing in one place with a dizzy speed (Eriksen 2001).

The aforementioned categories name the textual operations and strategies, which are inscribed in the process of establishing the identity of text (and, as a consequence, the identity of culture). They illustrate that this identity is determined not by processes of creating something new, but by **processes of using something already existent**, in the process of content

---

[3] According to Łukasz Ronduda, subversion is a form of artistic appropriation, "(…) physical (technical) operations on a subject; the operations of criticism, reversal, transformation, the destruction of appropriated and ready-made material, (…) the strategy of constructing the artistic work based on the decontextualising and recontextualising operations of montage of "ready-made" visual materials (images), taken from the sphere of art and other forms of visual culture (Ronduda 2006: 9). According to Grzegorz Dziamski, on the other hand, subversion is strictly connected with imitation, and it is based on identification with the object of criticism and on shifts in meanings. As such, subversion refers to "the secret understanding with the viewers", who should continue constructing the meaning of work by themselves (Dziamski 2001). It is worth mentioning that the artistic avant-garde relied heavily on the use of subversion in techniques such as collage, decalcomania, assemblage, ready-made, photomontage, video scratch, and montage.

circulation and form replication, as well as the effects of those processes. Kazimierz Krzysztofek, in reference to Greg Urban's concept of metaculture[4], writes that this culture of repetition, cyclicity, seriality, "circulation within a closed circuit" (Krzysztofek 2012; 23), might be also called a, postfabricated product of culture, ready-made for consumption (Krzysztofek 2010: 22).

At present, the **interpretative** processes are responsible for determining this identity. Everything that already exists is later joined, reworked, recontextualised, and in effect reinterpreted. An element of differentiation can be achieved as a side effect of these processes. Assembling, locating in different environments, and permeating bring about an assimilation of elements, which lies at the basis of differentiation. In consequence culture, by reusing itself, is engaged in continuous self-reinterpretation. Culture, therefore, is metacultural in its essence.

The new is achieved in the process of using the old; in transferring structures and terms characteristic of one discourse to the space of another; or from one discipline to the terrain of others. This results in the creation of texts for which other texts are the frame of reference. Conversions of discourses are often based on the content of one discourse being filtered through structures of another discourse. An adequate example is provided by contemporary scientific or educational discourse at the academic level. To both of them the structure of economic (business) discourse is applied, as quality is measured in terms of quantity – points are given for the place of publication, or for the number of subjects taught (ECTS points). Ordering everything in charts with numbers and expected results, so typical of business planning, replaces the idea of truth in science or ideas of freedom, openness, and dialogicity of Academia, which illustrates the rule of convergence at the level of discourse.

The development of **digital technologies** is of fundamental importance for the processes of convergence. The common immaterial matter of a digital sign enables it to assemble various textual information (regardless of their semiotic or medial organization); whereas hyperlinks enable us to shift from one text to another, regardless of their adherence to a certain discipline or discourse. As such, they create a fertile ground for convergence, which then modifies the sphere of the poetics of a text.

---

[4] Kaziemierz Krzysztofek writes that according to what Greg Urban claims in his book *Metaculture: How Culture Moves through the* World (Urban 2002), metaculture is the commenting of consecutive levels of its own expansion. It is a self-copying creation, but also a deformation of already created products (Krzysztofek 2010: 21).

Digital culture (signs, texts, and discourses) has a recombined character. It is constituted as the result of reinterpretation of already existing signs, texts, and discourses, upon which new structures are built. In reference to Barthes' words, who defined myth as language-robbery, one could say that digital content robs the already existing text. The word "robbery", however, has a pejorative character – it refers to the appropriation of something belonging to someone else, without the owner's consent or awareness. Digital culture, which is being constituted at the moment, is both a component and a stage in the development of culture (in its total existence and all emanations). It is created in the process of continual metamorphoses and associations. If culture "robs", it robs itself, thus initialising its own development. Hence, a better word then "a robbery", would be "the usage". Anyhow, a certain type of textual and discursive strategy is meant here. It is based on using that which is already existent and inscribing it into one's own structures of meaning within an interpretative position. Such an inscription is always and inevitably tied to some alteration or deformation. Barthes characterises this process in reference to myth, perceived as a structure which does not cause a loss of meaning, but its transformation (Barthes 1957).

On the other hand, however, these migrations of terms, which occur together with migrations of the characteristics of genres and discourses, are not simple, neutral borrowings or repetitions dressed up in a new mask. It is also not the case that these new categories, whose meaning ranges hitherto functioned under other names; do not bring about anything new. There is no place in culture for an absolute void, omnipresent stagnation, or a perfect copy. An analogy can never be an identity; recurring elements take on a new form and reappear in a changed context, different conditionings, with a new hierarchy of constituent elements.

Convergence in the textual world is especially likely to occur wherever boundaries are being obliterated – not only genre boundaries, but semiotic and medial ones as well. To such spaces belong the Internet and, in a broader perspective, the space of digital communication, where the same immaterial matter of a sign facilitates affiliations, influences, inspirations, migrations, permeations, and the overlapping of textual forms.

Digital technologies are tools of transmuting textual forms and structures thus far implemented in separate discourses or media. They provide both a tool and a space for the **restructuring** of text and discourse – creating recombined textual, generic, and discursive forms. Computer Role Playing Games, which adapt literary and film narrative structures, might serve as a good example here. The assimilation of texts and digital discourses to already existing ones (e.g. a website which implies the continuation of a traditional paper book, the introduction of animation which imitates turning pages, the website design of digital libraries which iconically alludes to traditional libraries) function as a familiarisation of the new medium, an attenuation of conversion from one technology to another – from the technology of print to digital technology. Above all, however, they semanticise the message, they take part in creating meanings. As such, they are an example of the new approach to text organisation, in which meanings are co-created not only in a polisemiotic or interactive way, but most importantly, in a multi-discursive manner, where a textualisation of media tools takes place, as was the case with the text-creating function of the interface.

These modifications prove that Heidegger's stance. That technology is not only a means, but also a manner of experiencing and extracting, and as such has a creative character (Heidegger 1994) which is true and somehow prophetic.

Shifts in the sphere of figures: interactive figures, the atrophy of certain figures, and the creation of others

Poetics in the age of convergence (and in the age of digital media development, in whose space convergence is especially visible) is announcing its triumph, as it is interested in the universal and the common. Poetics (particularly in its theoretic branch) is concerned with constructing models (Markowski 2001: 54), with establishing what is the principle of a text. As such, it determines and assigns the logic of meaning, and it is directly connected with the text as a construct, in which it finds the rules of structurisation. One might risk a claim that convergence lies at the basis of poetics and is understood in such a way that it enables it to exist. Without the iteration of assimilated forms, it would be impossible to differentiate between genres, textual forms, and structures, as well as figures.

The assimilation of various textual forms and discursive orders, so characteristic of the age of convergence, results in the generation of polisemiotic, multimedial and **interactive** figures. The prevalence of polisemiotic textual structures shows that polisemiotic figures are not an aberration of verbal figurativeness, they are not something exceptional, something created aside, but rather, they are a broadly understood principle of textuality. It also displays that figurativeness is first and foremost **a product**

of thinking, whereas its sign constitution is not limited to *verbum*, but can be freely making use of various systems of signs, their connections, relations they enter in the process of meaning formation and communication. For instance, computer icons are a representation of specific actions performed on the text, which can be described with words, but they also are those very actions. As such, they create intersemiotic and at the same time interactive metonymies, synecdoches, or more broadly – metaphors. It has to be emphasised that the relations between an icon, a meaning, and an action fit into the framework of catachresis, or a metaphor that has become lexicalised, as opposed to the metaphor that is living and open for interpretation. The unambiguity of an assigned meaning and performed function quickly endows this relation with a quality of a lexeme. The figure in such a case is not a tool of the stylistics of a text, nor its rhetoric. It is a technical operation, or rather, it is similar to what Yuri Lotman has called empirical modelling, as opposed to rhetoric modelling (Lotman 2007). Digital communication does not clash together with various semiotic languages or mutually untranslatable codes within the frame of one structure, but rather, it coordinates them.

Thus, a question emerges: how is it that in Internet discourse it is so easy to coordinate messages which are not only stylistically and semiotically diverse, but also differ in terms of discourse. What was considered to be a deviation from a norm, which professed a separation of domains or stylistic levels and considered linking, or worse, mixing them as a sign of incompetence (repeated questioning of the credibility of bordering and interdisciplinary research) or a violation of the ancient *decorum* in the pre-digital culture, becomes a rule in digital communication. The technological aspect – the possibility of joining and processing all kinds of information by digital technologies – is not the only answer to this question, although undoubtedly it is a stimulating factor, as it fosters interactions between semiotic and medial systems.

Another very important factor is basing linking on figurative actions. Rhizomes and links actualize the rule of zeugma – a figure which Ziomek defines as "(...) subordinating many syntactic parts to the main part, most often a verbal phrase, which is not repeated" (Ziomek 2000: 216). As an example of zeugma the researcher recalls the first two verses of Jan Kochanowski's Song XXV "What wishest Thou for all the lavish gifts of Thine?

What for Thy benefactions boundless and divine?" in which the word "wishest" is omitted in the second verse. However, the ellipsis here seems to be natural and obvious (on the contrary, not to apply the ellipsis would result in a feeling of excess and redundancy. Syllepsis is a kind of zeugma, which Ziomek describes with the following words:

> When zeugma joins with one word two separate parts, to which the word indeed refers, but does so in a tricky way, because the word is in fact a homonym which covers two meanings, then we can call this figure syllepsis. (...) Due to the interplay between grammatical correctness and semantic inaccuracy, syllepsis can very easily become a domain of humour, as it either equates and approaches the parts which refer to the superior part, or uncovers and emphasizes the ambiguity of the main part through an incoherent reference. (Ziomek 2000: 217–218).

A clear and humorous example of syllepsis can be found in a saying about a certain femme fatale: "She aroused suspicion and men".

The structure of the Internet continuously uses zeugma, or rather, syllepsis. They are activated when the user performs some action – they have an interactive character. Rhizomes are the superior parts, which are joined by links with many parallel elements. They function here as homonyms, which bind different elements from various, often distant domains of social life. At the same time, however, they suggest some kind of correspondence, resemblance, since the superior part is always the same and each of the linked elements stays in a logical relation with the rhizome. The common rhizome for many elements, a justified linking of the rhizome with each separate element, has the effect of the propinquity of linked elements. Consequently, it makes the recipient accept the coexistence of relations which are, in fact, distinct, unrelated, coming from remote domains, and which create diverse senses. For example, the user quickly consents to parallel relations between the word "pearl," which functions as a rhizome (superior part), and other links (elements): references to a mineral product of a shelled mollusc; images representing various types of pearls; a female name and all famous people who had it, addresses to guesthouses and boarding houses which have the word "pearl" in their names; the title of Janis Joplin's fourth album, information about the symbol of innocence and the material of the gates to Heaven according to the New Testament, the programming language PEARL, or information about the novel *Girl with a Pearl Earring* by Tracey Chavelier, and many others.

The syllepsis here does not have the effect of a pun or word play, because it is deprived of the rhetoric aspect. Its function is not a stylistic or rhetoric modelling, but an empirical one – the syllepsis is subordinated to a superior goal, i.e., the maximisation of the range of information, which enables the user to reach some specific information in the easiest possible way without having to know about it in detail (the website address or the ability to assign it to a specific domain). In predigital communication, in order to reach certain information, it was necessary to know to which domain it belongs in order to search for it. It was crucial to be acquainted with the way in which information was organised, with the net of connections it formed with other information, as well as with the means of its distribution. Digital communication, thanks to the empirical usage of syllepsis, does not require this kind of knowledge. However, it makes the user accustomed to free associations on the basis of homonymy of information belonging to separate domains, which in turn fosters the dissolution of boundaries between disciplines.

Shifts in the sphere of figures refer to the way in which the figures are handled, or rather, used. Their usage is subordinated to the pragmatic function of digital discourse. The functionalisation of the way in which figures are used leads to seemingly contradictory actions (seemingly, as in fact they are teleologically justified). It happens so, because on the one hand, digital discourse uses shortenings and refers to the economy of elliptic thinking (or wider detraction), examples of which were the abovementioned sylleptic constructions. On the other hand, however, it makes free use of adjunction, as it is visible in intersemiotic repetitions or versions of the same information in various codes. Digital communication is characterized as having multiple code doublets, which function as palimpsests, where the existence of various versions of representations is revealed only after selecting a given element. One action (e.g. changing the font size, underlining, or using subscript and superscript in Microsoft Word editor) may be attributed with a choice of forms – versions of a sign (icon, alphanumeric symbols, verbal description).

Using multiple code doublets, syllepsis, or ellipsis is not directed rhetorically or stylistically, but it is driven by communication pragmatics (a user who is acquainted with the program will automatically use the iconic sign, as opposed to a beginner, who will direct the arrow pointer to the sign in order to reveal a full description of possible actions).

Using zeugma (which employs the figure of ellipsis), syllepsis (which employs homonymy), or metonymy in linking construction of the digital discourse is inscribed in widely understood metaphorical thinking. In *Media Poetics* (Szczęsna 2007: 103–104 a division of metaphors was proposed with respect to their dominating function. Cognitive metaphors (nominal, directed at naming the unnameable), aesthetic metaphors (which model the text stylistically), and persuasive metaphors (or broader rhetoric metaphors, directed at manipulating the recipient) were distinguished. Metaphoric actions with which we deal while linking, would be a pragmatic action, directed at functionality and usefulness of discourse (and of communication).

Similarly, a pragmatic character is to be found in questions which refer to actions undertaken by the user. They belong to the qualities which characterise digital communication. Repeated questions about confirming or cancelling a given action, questions about running an operation beneficial for the system (e.g. updating antivirus software) now or later; they are all not a part of the text, but of digital discourse. They have a technical character – they are generated automatically. The choice of an option, i.e., the action undertaken by the user, enables the flow of discourse to continue. As such, these questions also have a pragmatic character. At the same time, however, since they are technical elements, they contain an element of *poesis* – they take part in creating the poetics of digital discourse, they co-organise its structure. What is more, they also have a rhetorical function (or even a persuasive one). Questions which appear on the screen give the effect of initialising a dialogue, they play an apostrophic function. The act of responding (choosing one of the suggested answers or even closing the pop-up window with a question) engages the user in the discourse, it makes him a side of the dialogue.

The user is indeed aware that such questions and commands come from the system and that they have been previously programmed. However, when taking part in digital discourse, this consciousness is very often veiled by the suspension of disbelief. The structure of questions and commands is similar in characteristics to interpersonal relations. This in turn conduces the antropomorphisation of the system – and reacting to the system as if it were a living creature (Reeves, Nass 1996).

In hypertext, **inversion** becomes a problematic issue. Traditionally the term is used to name a violation of a prescribed (according to certain rules and established norms) order of elements in a text, a disturbance of hierarchy of elements (grammatical inversion, temporal inversion, axiological inversion). The presence of links prevents inversion at the level of discourse (but it can still be preserved at the level of a singular text). Since the user can shape the discourse freely by choosing links without any restraints and by returning to previous websites, and since it is the rule of digital communication, it means that there is no single order which could be violated. Each order is equally justifiable, as linking establishes many potential discourses.

It has to be emphasised here that cancelling inversion is equal to undermining the act of accepting one order of discourse as obligatory, as setting the norm. What is more, the category of inversion does not apply to our perception. This is possible because we always perceive the elements of each message as a sequence – in a linear way (it is also true for visual representations, whose elements are perceived by the eye in a sequence, not simultaneously). This aspect was pointed out by Wojciech Jerzy Burszta, who accentuated a specific conservatism of a book and the consistency of the reading practice. As the scholar writes, the book "is unchangeable; it is impossible to modernise it, as it is impossible to modernise the very practice of reading. Thus, it is a conservative action, which goes against the tide of mainstream consumerism" (Burszta 2007: 139).

Cancelling inversion in digital discourse also means that categories of proper composition, abiding to certain rules, are nullified. It is worth mentioning that rhetoric theory distinguishes two kinds of discursive orders: the natural order of discourse (lat. *ordo naturalis*) and the artificial order of discourse (lat. *ordo artificialis*). The latter was used in artistic works, which modified the natural order (ascribed to the rhetoric composition) by shifting, reshaping or omitting strictly defined components of the natural composition. An introduction, a presentation of the topic, argumentation, a rebuttal of the counter arguments, and a conclusion are still elements which organise many utterances. In digital discourse, however, the natural order is in fact characterised by the lack of established composition. The arrangement of discursive elements is set each time by users and by the goal they want to achieve.

Definitions of hypertext mostly highlight the non-linearity of reading. According to them, hypertext disturbs the linear order of the text and privileges the associating mode. Since the possibility of passing from one text to another had been designed and inscribed in the structure of hypertext, it seems that this passing by means of links does not disturb the pre-established order, but it actualises it. By clicking a link, the user does not break into another text, but uses the predesigned possibility of opening it. The solution to this apparent aporia is to perceive the discrepancy between text and discourse. In traditional communication, discourse somehow respected the order of reading determined by the text. For example, in journalistic discourse, the order of reception was determined by the order of the text. The situation is different in digital discourse, which adapts the text by subordinating it to its own specificity. And this specificity means that it is possible to pass from one text to another via links. In digital journalistic discourse, therefore, the order of reading is determined by digital discourse, which enables both the reception of the text according to the textual order and according to the order determined by discourse (possibility of passing to another text via links). Thus, it is possible for **the order of text and the order of discourse to split**. It is also possible for discourse not to respect the order determined by text. The split between the two orders emphasises in turn the difference between text and discourse.

Linking, which determines the specificity of the digital discourse, does not only cancel inversion, but also takes over the function of textual figures and strategies responsible for supplementation, extension, explanation, citation, or reference. What I mean here are first and foremost strategies present in the sphere of discourse, such as digression or allusion, which are introduced into the text by parenthetical utterances (in brackets), interpolations, subnections (complementation of the main thought with an aside thought), endnotes, or annexes. Linking might also take over the function of suspense, retardation, or even rhetorical comparison. This happens because linking enables a specific lag or even a stop of the action (discontinuation of the thematic line) in order to introduce additional content, which perform various functions: supplementary, explanatory, or persuasive. On the one hand, this multi-functionality and specific linking capacity in terms of performed functions in the discourse organisation points to the economisation of discourse. On the other hand, however, it implies a simplification and homogenisation, obliterating variety and diversification of forms (e.g. the difference between a digression and an allusion), or even impoverishment of digital discourse.

In effect with linking, another figure (textual form) is formed. A suitable term could be accumulation. It is based on ascribing a variety of functions to one sign, word, or expression. A linked fragment of a text might be a hybrid of two various functions. On one hand it performs a semantic function within the linear text which it co-creates (lexeme function). On the other hand, it has a function of a sign which marks access to another text – it is a specific transporter (or a medium), which creates a passage to another site, when activated. The accumulation here refers to functions, which the textual item performs (accumulation of functions); it is, however, possible to have accumulation in the sphere of meaning (**semantic accumulation**) or representation (**semiotic accumulation**). In predigital culture, the figure of semantic accumulation could have been found, for example, in the poetry of Stanisław Barańczak. His poem "Co jest grane" ("What's going on?") is based on it. The verses of the poem accumulate literal and metaphorical meanings of the phrase in the title, activating mutual reinterpretations. Thus, a style full of allusions, irony, and understatements, so characteristic of the prison poetry, is initialised.[5]

Accumulation is different from lexical polysemy (as a linguistic phenomenon which is accounted for in dictionaries) in the fact that the first

---

[5] The ambiguity of the phrase is associated with allusive references to the experience of Polish society living under the communist system.

one is a deliberate textual procedure, an intentional use of polysemy, an intended play with meanings. It is not a collection, but a choice of meanings, which provide a new stylistic and semantic quality when confronted against each other. In accumulation the importance is put on the simultaneity or coexistence of meanings and functions assigned to a textual item. This last characteristic (but also the intentionality of textual strategy) is what differentiates accumulation from homonymy.

Semantic accumulation – similarly to other rhetorical figures – can be also present in non-verbal texts. An example can be provided by Salvador Dali's "The Image Vanishes", where one representation evokes two different images – meanings (semiotic-semantic accumulation).

Semiotic accumulation is visible in polymorphic textual structures in computer communication. The best example is provided by icons in toolbars – selecting one with the arrow pointer reveals a multiplicity of representational forms which refer to one action (a kind of semiotic **redundancy**), e.g. the scissors icon, the word "cut", the periphrases, and the "Ctrl+X" combination of keys. (In language we encounter the phenomenon of doublet, names in various languages for the same object.) It is worth emphasising that the meaning of words / icons is subordinated to the function of generating actions within a text (the function of action is superior to the meaning, which only facilitates the action). The relation between iconic representation and meaning is a task for the new semiotics, which pursues connections between the means of representation (signs) and the associative processes, which play a fundamental role in the case of textual space organisation in computer communication.

The abovementioned examples of various types of accumulation present convergence in its second dimension – the same or analogous textual processes can take place in various media environments, in traditionally separate fields. Digital culture and globalisation undoubtedly promote convergence in the textual world. Nevertheless, they are not a condition sine qua non.

The new onticity (tissue) of text and discourse

A new recognition is needed for determinants of onticity, or of the formal status of text – especially **the role of the interface** to determine and also create genres has to be discussed here. The text is simultaneously a sign and a super-sign (because of its complexity) of meaningful entity with a specified ontic status. Both the meaning and the status of the text are constituted (actualised) in a communicative situation, in the usage, and therefore in discourse, whose essence is to mediate (White 1978: 1–25). Thus, this means that discourse has an interpretative character, and all changes within its existence bear an effect on the understanding and the ontic status of text.

In the case of digital messages, the method of representation is very important; it has a contentual (textual) or generic character. The elements of representation, the tools for text organisation (e.g. interface) **determine the form of the utterance**. They all play a decisive part in the meanings, genres, discursive possibilities (possible ways of dealing with the text). The site's organisation (before we even reach the content) is a carrier of information for the user: whether it is a portal, an internet service, a browser, an e-mail account, a text file. It establishes genre characteristics of discourse and text. Text undergoes a restructuring. Links play the function of **suspense**, which can lead the user into additional suspense by shattering and cancelling out the normative order (the freedom to choose an order by the user is the norm here). Links render it impossible to talk about the main discourse (or text).

The structure of websites, which are an access point to many parallel discourses, is governed by the rule of **hierarchisation**. It applies both to the position in which a given site is located (website positioning – SEO – is governed usually by the rules of commerce) and to every element on the webpage. The size and colour of an icon or of the font, the place it uses on the screen (quick visibility of the upper left corner and the middle of the webpage), and the movement of elements are all ways of graphic hierarchisation of the content, but also they are means of controlling the recipient's attention.

The relations between text and **context** are modified, too, as well as the onticity of those relations. Questions of text and context and analogically questions of representation plans: the foreground and the background are inscribed in the general problem of **composition**, which defines the arrangement of elements and the relations between them. Traditionally, when composition is discussed, one would talk about the compositional dominant, which organises the whole, or about the hierarchy of elements. Hypertext abolishes the stability of roles: text – context, foreground – background. In turn, hypertext substitutes it with relations and freedom of exchange due to the changing moment of reference. Linked texts which in a given moment constitute the context, a second later can become the main text. In the process of reading, the main tread or the central character in a hypertext novel can give way to other threads or a different character simply because of the reader's choice. The relations between text and context are determined by the recipient and the assumed order of reading. The interchangeability of these relations is, however, intentionally designed; it is inscribed in the onticity of hypertext.

Linking is also connected with shifts in the sphere of categories such as the beginning and the end. Linear texts which are placed in digital discourse retain their traditional, conventional and culture-specific marks for beginnings and endings of words, sentences, or longer passages of text. In our cultural sphere those would be: the direction of reading from left to right, which determines the beginnings and the endings of words and sentences; the use of spaces between words, the use of dots, capital letters, and paragraphs. However, linking used in words or longer units of linear text leads to disturbances of this order. Linking activates the **digressive** mode – linked words become a pretext (they encourage) to abandon the **actual (present) order of discourse**. When talking about abandoning the order of discourse, I use the word "actual" and not e.g. "main" on purpose. In digital discourse, which is based on the choice of links, passing from one part of the webpage to another, or from one website to another, it does not make any sense to talk about the main discourse.

On a webpage which we accessed through a link, other links can be found, which "invite" us to find new information (open successive pages). It is easy, therefore, to replace the linear order of so far dominating discourse with the associative one, which becomes a dominating discourse and which determines the specificity of digital communication. This last characteristic differentiates it from the way in which it is actualised in a linear text, where, if it appears, it is determined by the linear order which defines its limits.

A link as a constant element of discourse changes the characteristics of communication's limits. The beginning and the end of discourse are not determined once and for all by the sender's intentions, but they are moveable – each time they are different, defined by the user.

The openness of discourse range at the level of usage can be juxtaposed to the rigorous use of delimitation tags in a text on the level of programming. In a HTML document the greatest part of elements which define the content, the composition, the outline of the webpage (headline, main text, images) has some tags of opening and closing, e.g. <u> </u> (the beginning and the end of underline), <li> </li> (the beginning and the end of a position in an ordered list); <ul> </ul> (the beginning and the end of an ordered list). In the language of HTML 4.01, however, there exist tags which do not have their closing counterpart (e.g. the tag which marks the end of a paragraph <br>)[6]. Such tagging is visible at the user's level in a layout to which the user is culturally accustomed to. A script at the level of programming is a condition of receiving a desired form of text at the user's level. The obviousness and the transparency of signs which delimit texts, sanctioned by cultural recurrence (e.g. signs for the beginning and end of a sentence, locating the beginning of a text in the upper left corner of a page) are blurred at the level of programming. The lack of tagging, e.g. an unclosed tag, would result in the disintegration of the text, even when the capital letter and the full stop are preserved.

A start tag and an end tag at the level of programming are components of many commands. They do not mark the end of a fragment or of a whole text, as a full stop marks the end on a sentence. Rather, they guarantee that texts and images have a definite visual form.

Hypertext is intentionally open text, devoid of **confines**. Of course, one can and should talk about the confines of separate textual units (e.g. a press article on the Internet). However, locating a link within a textual unit blurs the confines of the text. It enables the user to create text outside of the traditional framework and to designate a new framework, which in turn leads to their multiplication. Setting the confines of text and appointing methods of meaning creation is in fact establishing the sense of text. In other words, the usage is the dominant factor of meaning creation. Thus, a question emerges – what happens to the text and what is the text here. Is it the initial text created by the author, or is the text generated by the user in the process of linking? Does it still make sense to talk about authorial intent in view of the ontically linked structure of hypertext? And finally, what is **the relation between text and discourse, and what form of activity (textual or discursive) are the user's operations**? If we consider text in the communicative situation as discourse, then those operations would be participation in discourse. Recognising those operations as the realisation of a pre-designed discursive activity undoubtedly protects the identity and integrity of text.

Hypertext proves that text which at a given moment is outside of our perception is a potentiality, a collection of data whose sense is being constituted only in the process of reading. As such, it is a product of participation in discourse. A pre-designed freedom (variantivity) to choose elements of content is inscribed in hypertext. This possibility of choice signifies that e.g. in a hypertext novel, the same units of content may have

---

[6] In HTML 1.0 all tags are closed, so the tag for the end of a paragraph is written as </br>.

various functions: a narrative one (the element of plot), or a descriptive one (the element of background), depending on the way in which text is read. This stands in opposition to traditional texts, in which only one intentional arrangement of units and one order of reception exist. Whereas in traditional text **"the usage" is present only at the level of interpretation**, in hypertext it functions on two levels: the primary level of perception and the expanded level of interpretation.

The possibility to pass freely from one text to another and to connect semantic units of diverse complexity and semiotic organisation by links, leads to textual convergence in the sphere of expressiveness and the functionality of text. Texts become a mixture of already existent forms. They join narrative elements with non-narrative ones (Ryan 2005), textual forms hitherto reserved for other genres of texts and discourses. As Markku Eskelinen writes, "It is hard to deny that texts are both thematically and formally heterogeneous" (Eskelinen 2012: 109).

Assimilation focuses here on the multifunctionality of signs and of textual elements. The hitherto prevailing functions of text: informative (cognitive), expressive, impressive (persuasive), poetic (aesthetic), communicative, phatic, performative, magical, and metatextual, are being joined by the **functions of activity and mediation.** Hyperlinks employ icons, but they also employ words. Linked words gain an ontically different status. While retaining their previous function of meaning creation (cognitive, expressive or other function), they acquire the function of **mediators** – transporters to other texts. Usually, a linked word (or expression) is connected with the text it leads to on a basis of synecdochic and/or metonymic relation.

Two issues are important here: what is specific about the function of activity as opposed to the previous functions and what happens with the initial text (what changes occur in the structure of text).

The function of activity joins aspects of functions that a word or an expression already had and, without duplicating them, creates a new quality. A common element with the expressive function is the indication to the sender and their preferences, ideas, and inclinations visible in the choice of linked elements. The influence on the user (encouragement to click on a link, information about the possibility of finding more about a given semantic unit) is an element common to the persuasive and the informative functions. However, while traditionally these functions are realised by the semantics of the word, here they are realised also by graphic organisation. The element of the cognitive function is always the same – information that we can find out more by clicking on a given word. Analogically, the persuasive element is the same – an invitation to click on a link. Thus, these functions are realised in a minimal and ephemeral way. Moreover, whereas the cognitive and the persuasive functions refer to context and go beyond text itself, the function of activity refers to the very text. This last point is a common element with the metatextual function, which positions the function of activity among the aforementioned tendencies to create discourse of culture from the elements already existent in culture in the processes of recycling, meta-connectionism, subversion, and in effect – in the process of convergence.

Poetics, and in a broader perspective, literary theory, are challenged by specific research issues when faced with convergence and its consequences in the space of digital communication. Questions to solve by literary theory might include the new functions of text in the process of communication, but also relations between hypertext and linking in comparison with allusion, digression, parenthesis, suspense, and retardation. Links might be described within the categories of extensions, or additions to the main text; whereas divergence from the main text to the linked parts can by analysed within the categories of suspension, or delay of the main argument. What is happening in the sphere of the semiotic tissue of texts, figures, or personal (and non-personal) relations in digital communication (reinterpretation of the sender-recipient roles) is of equal importance. The reconciliation of contradictions in contemporary medial text is another significant issue. It is so, because on the one hand we encounter redundancy – an excess of texts in relation to data (information) – a multiplication of texts which give the same information, recycling, converting, which produces a plethora of texts. On the other hand, a diminution of language is pointed to. It can be observed in the context of the growing importance of images in meaning creation and in influencing the recipient, or in view of abbreviations such as 'OMG' ('oh my God'), 'IMO' ('in my opinion'), 'BRB' ('be right back'), or emoticons which replace verbalisation to express emotions.

***

Undoubtedly, the aforementioned issues and processes, which take place in contemporary culture, especially convergence, are tempting literary scholars (and especially theoreticians of literature) to broaden their scope of interest, to go beyond literary texts in the direction of broadly understood textuality of various media and various discourses, but also to confront the way of thinking characteristically about literary studies as compared with that of media studies, psychology, and sociology. Perhaps it is not only a temptation, but also a methodological necessity, without which literary studies might be in peril of stagnation.

Bibliography

Bal Mieke 2002, *Travelling Concepts in the Humanities*, London: University of Toronto Press.

Barthes Roland 1957, *Mythologies*, Paris: Seuil.

Burszta Wojciech Jerzy 2007, *Książka i czytanie w popkulturowym reżimie symultaniczności*, [in:] *Gadżety popkultury. Społeczne życie przedmiotów*, eds. W. Godzic, M. Żakowski, Warsaw: Wydawnictwa Akademickie i Profesjonalne.

Dziamski Grzegorz 2001, „Wartością sztuki krytycznej jest to, że wywołuje dyskusje", *Gazeta Malarzy i Poetów*, No. 2-3.

Eco Umberto 1968, *La struttura assente. Introduzione alla ricerca semiologica*, Milano: Bompiani.

Eriksen Thomas Hylland 2001, *Tyranny of the Moment. Fast and Slow Time in the Information Age*, London: Pluto Press.

Eskelinen Markku 2012, *Cybertext poetics. The Critical Landscape of New Media Literary Theory*, London–New York: Continuum.

Foucault Michel 2002, *L'ordre du discours: Leçon inaugurale au Collège de France, prononcée le 2 décembre 1970*, Paris: Gallimard.

Geertz Clifford 1983, *Blurred Genres*, [in:] C. Geertz, *Local Knowledge: Essays in Interpretive Anthropology*, New York: Harper Collins Publishers.

Heidegger Martin 1994, *Vorträge und Aufsätze*, Stuttgart: Clett-Cotta.

Horkheimer Max, Adorno Theodor W. 1969, *Dialektik der Aufklärung. Philosophische Fragmente*, Frankfurt am Main: S. Fischer Verlag GmbH.

Jakobson Roman 1989, *W poszukiwaniu istoty języka*, vol. 1., ed. Mayenowa Maria Renata, Warsaw: Państwowy Instytut Wydawniczy.

Jakobson Roman 1971, *An Example of Migratory Terms and Institutional Models*, [in:] R. Jakobson, *Selected Writings: Word and Language*, vol. 2, Netherlands: Mouton & Co. Printers.

Kłoskowska Antonina 1983, *Kultura masowa: Krytyka i obrona*, Warsaw: PWN.

Krzysztofek Kaziemierz 2010, *Paratekst jako postfabrykat kultury*, [in:] *Pogranicza audiowizualności*, ed. A. Gwóźdź, Cracow: Universitas.

Лотман Юрий 2007, Внутри мыслящих миров. Человек – текст – семиосфера – история.

Macdonald Dwight 1953, "A Theory of Mass Culture", *Diogenes*, No. 3.

Markowski Michał Paweł 2001, „Interpretacja i literatura", [in:] *Teksty Drugie*, No. 5.

Ryan Marie-Laure 2005, *Narrative*, [in:] *Routledge Encyclopedia of Narrative Theory*, eds. D. Herman, M. Jahn, M.L. Ryan, London and New York: Routledge.

Reeves Byron, Nass Clifford 1996, *The Media Equation. How People Treat Computers, Television, and New Media Like Real People and Places*, Cambridge: Cambridge University Press.

Ronduda Łukasz 2006, *Strategie subwersywne w sztukach medialnych*, Cracow: Wydawnictwo Rabid.

Szczęsna Ewa 2007, *Poetyka mediów*, Warsaw: Wydawnictwo Wydziału Polonistyki Uniwersytetu Warszawskiego.

White Hayden 1978, *Tropics of Discourse. Essays in Cultural Criticism*, Baltimore and London: The Johns Hopkins University Press.

Ziomek Jerzy 2000, *Retoryka opisowa*, Wroclaw: Wydawnictwo Ossolineum.

Maciej Maryl*
IBL PAN

CONVERGENCE AND COMMUNICATION: GENRE ANALYSIS OF THE WEBSITES OF POLISH WRITERS

Abstract
This article categorizes new forms of expressions on writers' websites as means of maintaining communication with readers. The first part is dedicated to inter- and trans-medial analysis of various multimedia materials published on such websites (e.g. biographical notes, photographs, trailers). In the second part the website is analyzed as a hybrid text in which various types of expression are submitted to the main communicative purpose. On both levels of analysis the material is categorized in terms of the communicative function, for, as the author claims, the genre analysis of electronic discourse requires an approach which takes into consideration not only authorial intent and textual features but also the context of online utterance and the role of other partners of communication.

Key words: convergence and communication, writers' websites genre analysis, new media, hybrid texts

"Beata Pawlikowska: a writer, a traveller, a hunter" (A32)[1] – a short description posted on this writer's website gives us an idea about the variety of topics we are just about to encounter here. The author presents herself in diverse social roles, as a travel writer, teacher of foreign languages, and a TV and radio personality. On this website one finds a variety of materials: reportages, notes, travel plans, cooking recipes, information about books and TV shows, picture gallery, aphorisms, interviews... More-

---

* IBL PAN, ul. Nowy Świat 72, 00-330 Warsaw, e-mail: maciej.maryl@ibl.waw.pl
[1] The codes referring to individual websites (e.g. A9), and the addresses of quoted sub-sites (e.g. A9-1) are listed in the bibliography. All quotations from Polish websites were translated by the author.

over, readers can post their own letters, texts or ads ("ISO travel mate"). Those different types of materials (from literature through functional texts to promotional materials and conversations) require a new conceptual framework, capable of accounting for this variety.

The works published in a volume *Polska genologia literacka* [*Polish literary genre theory*] (2007) reflect some crucial problems of contemporary genre studies, which struggle to find new categories for texts created in a multimedia culture. Stanisław Balbus writes about the "extinction of genres", understood as a crisis of theory, whose taxonomies and typologies are not sufficient for new kinds of texts (Balbus 2007). Especially problematic are those texts, which draw from different media or semiotic systems. As Seweryna Wysłouch points out, the use of multimedia broke the monopoly of verbal culture and challenged the linguistic definition of a text (Wysłouch 2007: 300). The novelty concerns not only texts but also the entire communication scene, which results in a new array of possible problems and research questions: Edward Balcerzan (2007) investigates a "multimedia genre theory", and Włodzimierz Bolecki proposes a "different genre theory", based on features dismissed by traditional theory, such as media, or communication patterns (Bolecki 2007: 217).

This article does not aim at answering all those questions or proposing a new genre theory. Instead, I am going to discuss a communicational approach towards multimedia writings. I am going to analyze the way in which writers use new, digital media on their websites, along with the change of traditional genres brought about by the Internet. Hence, I will examine those texts not only in the light of literary tradition but also in the context of electronic communication. Although the texts described in this paper are usually considered "functional" or "paraliterary", I leave such classifications aside and concentrate on the forms and functions that those materials bring to a webpage. The main problems with electronic texts are: (1) their double, techno-semiotic nature; (2) the context of utterance which influences the genre status; (3) different levels of analysis.

Firstly, a webpage clearly exposes the double nature of every text, which – according to Stefan Żółkiewski (1980) – should be considered in both semiotic (meaning) and material (technology) aspects. For instance, if we consider a website as a text, we can distinguish between the communicative purpose of the web page (semiotic aspect), and its format (material aspect), which determines the shape of this document. Secondly, one should carefully examine both the communicational status of the utterance and the audience to which it is directed. The very same genre may serve different roles when published online or in print media. Thirdly, if we take another look on Beata Pawlikowska's website, we may notice two possible levels of analysis. On the one hand we may investigate various utterances (e.g. reportages, letters, interviews…) as separate texts, on the other we may consider the entire website as a hybrid of texts, which blends the texts from the lower level. We may analyze those materials from two perspectives – either using the tools of intermedial poetics, which deals with various media configurations in singular texts, or apply the transmedial poetics, which focuses on similarities of cultural texts created in different semiotic systems. The former approach highlights the differences between textual types; the latter seems to blur them (cf. Maryl 2009 b).

Those strategies are applied to the materials found on the websites of Polish writers. In the first part of this paper the focus is on the lower level of analysis (i.e. individual types of texts from websites), employing an intermedial perspective. In the second part the higher level (webpages as hybrid texts) is analyzed in the transmedial framework. The analyses were performed on a group of 85 websites of Polish writers.[2]

Texts on writers' websites

The format, or the material aspect of texts in an intermedial perspective

It is crucial that a survey of media employed by writers on their websites is defined. I understand 'medium' as a technological means of transmitting semiotic content, agreeing with Grzegorz Godlewski's distinction between 'basic' (word, image, performance) and 'detailed' media (e.g. print, oil painting) (Godlewski 2008: 277–278). The word, for instance, is perceived by Goldewski as a transmitter of the secondary modeling system (semiotic system) of literature (or – in a broader sense – art), whereas its 'detailed media' are "oral utterance, writing, print, electronic audiovisual effects, digital computer and network media" (ibid.: 279). Let us examine, how diverse detailed media serves as carriers of the word on writers' websites.

The electronic word depends on the context of utterance, formed by both the implied role of the reader and the choice of means of communication. Davis and Brewer define electronic discourse as:

---

[2] The bibliography contains only those texts which were explicitly quoted in this article.

> ... the two-directional texts in which one person using a keyboard writes language that appears on the sender's monitor and is transmitted to the monitor of a recipient, who responds by keyboard. The recipient may actually be a single individual or a group, large or small, of receivers. (Davis and Brewer 1997: 1).

Electronic discourse differs from "printed" texts (i.e. those which are available either in print, or as digital facsimile, see. Maryl 2009a) insofar that it is deeply rooted in the immediate context and aimed at the reaction of the reader. Let us consider this question on the example of two poems posted by Miłosz Biedrzycki (A4) and Ernest Bryll (A6). On the former's website we find verses bound in collections, just as they appear in print. Thus the reader can navigate the page as if she was walking through a library – choosing the collections and individual poems they contain. Bryll, on the contrary, publishes (or "reprints") his poetry in blog posts, usually with reference to current events or holidays. In this situation, the poem obtains double contextualization: chronological (e.g. it is posted on Easter) and situational (it appears on writers' blogs as a poem directed to blog readers who may comment on it).

Apart from the 'printed' and electronic word, writers' websites also contain audio and visual materials. Some authors post the excerpts of their works as audiobooks or, rarely, short movie clips. Usually there are not original productions, but rather adaptations of previous works, such as in the case of Antoni Hukałowicz's poem "Choroszczańskie błonia I" ['Choroszcza common I']. Students from his hometown shot a movie clip which shows the places described in the poem, read by a slightly affected young man (A6-2). Thus, the basic medium of the word is supplemented by the audiovisual sphere.

Literary trailers, short promotional movies, have somewhat different status. It is a fairly new phenomenon, which appeared on the Polish Internet in the middle of the previous decade (see Niemczyńska 2008). The adjective 'literary' is not a genre indication but rather a description of the field of its reference – a literary trailer, like a movie trailer, is an advertisement of a book.

Literary trailers draw from movie aesthetics. Jarosław Klejnocki's crime novel *Południk 21* [*Longitude 21*] is promoted by a short clip, which could be mistaken for a cinema-noir movie trailer: black and white pictures, a corpse in the woods, the writer interrogated in a prison cell.[3] Literary trailers of *Wroniec* by Jacek Dukaj employ the style of cartoons

---

[3] Literary trailers are listed in the bibliography.

(Wroniec 1) and documentaries (Wronice 2). Other stylistic references include experimental cinema (Robert Król), thrillers (Żulczyk, Orbitowski), music clips (Michalak), or amateur videos (Witkowski).

In one of the first conceptualizations of literary trailers phenomenon, Urszula Pawlicka describes multimedia features of this genre: word (subtitles, voice of the narrator, author or an actor), image (pictures, moving pictures), and music (Pawlicka 2008). Although Pawlicka points out to potential threats such trailers may pose to literary works as they – in her opinion – trivialize the books content, one should probably consider this form as simply an audiovisual version of such traditional genres as a note about a book, an excerpt, an interview, a blurb or a cover. A literary trailer comprises of word (information about the work) and image, which transmits a certain message in the same way as a bookcover does: trailers give a visual impression about the genre and the mood of a book. For instance, trailers of thrillers (Żulczyk, Orbitowski) are dark and full of tension highlighted by the music, whereas in presentations of women fiction (Fox, Michalak) the colors are warm and the music is peaceful.

Other visual materials, like writers' pictures, serve similar functions – on the one hand they seem to make the person more 'realistic' (one can see what the author looks like), but on the other they could be compared to short biographical notes. There are close links between the aesthetics of an author's picture and the genre of her or his output. This similarity is especially visible amongst the authors writing crime fiction, thrillers and women's fiction. For instance, the homepage of Krzysztof Kotowski (A19), crime and action stories writer, is entirely black and in its center we see the writer with a burning book in his hand. His name is surrounded by a frame covered in blood…Authors' portraits are usually less obvious, and mostly seem to imitate certain visual stylistics (e.g. Klejnocki's A18 and Krajewski's A21 black & white pictures) or employ clearly symbolic props like a raincoat (Krajewski A22), black glasses (Niemirski), burning candles (Darda A9), leather jacket and a hoodie (Orbitowski A31). Children fiction writers present themselves in warm colors: Paweł Beręsewicz is pictured on a bike, holding a book (A2), and Michał Daniel Mordarski smiles to us from behind a pile of books (A29). Smiles and pastel colors are also to be found in the pictures of female fiction writers – Marlena de Blasi (A10) and Katarzyna Michalak (A28). Other visual materials on authors' websites serve similar functions: background colors, pictures, and book covers… They all convey certain information about the authors, their writings or biographies.

Writers' websites should be then understood as new, multimedia utterances in which medium-specific genres (e.g. crime movies) are freely mingled into a multimedia text, subdue to a certain communication function. The information about writers is then conveyed through written, visual (bookcovers, pictures) and audiovisual (trailers) materials, which should be considered as one larger utterance, expressed through diverse media systems.

Henry Jenkins uses the term 'convergence' to describe the content flow between various media platforms (cf. Jenkins 2006). Convergence is a really broad term, which mostly refers to the media industry and the ability to transfer media content from one device to another. In this case I use this term to describe the utterances, whose elements, expressed through different media) complement each other. The best example of convergence on the Polish literary scene would be Jacek Dukaj's *Wroniec* with its promotional materials: trailers, pictures, wallpapers, animations, book excerpts read by Jan Peszek, songs performed by Kazik and an educational game. Supplementary materials are adapted to the new media reality – users may now choose among different forms of the story, or rather: different gates to the textual world. Quite similarly we may treat links to multimedia materials in electronic discourse, such as posting YouTube or Vimeo videos in blog posts. For instance, a poet Grzegorz Kwiatkowski recommended in his blog a song by Schubert (by posting a link), in order to convey the mood of his own poems in an extra-linguistic way (A25-1). Audiovisual material was used to complement and develop the verbal text.

In a multimedia culture different forms of expression create together one message, becoming a carrier of an utterance. Although those remarks concern mostly functional genres, it is obvious that such an electronic and multimedia "writing" is a dominant characteristic of the Internet environment and perhaps here – not in the complicated hypertextual constructs – lies the future of literary works.

Genres of webpage texts in a transmedial perspective

Let us take a look at texts from webpages in a transmedial perspective, i.e. genres are considered independently from the media used to convey them. I have already mentioned that the context of utterance is crucial for electronic discourse. Carolyn N. Miller in her programmatic piece "Genre as Social Action" suggests that in order to understand a genre we should understand it in a functional way. A genre analysis should include situational context and the motivation of social actors.

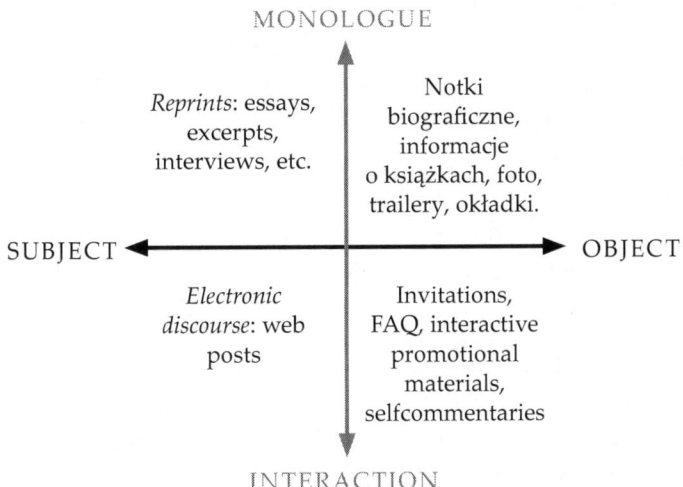

Figure 1. Classification of materials from writers' websites

Approaching those texts from the communicational perspective I am focusing on the form of communication. A similar approach was proposed in Krishnamurthy's study of blogs, which were categorized according to two dimensions: personal vs. topical, and individual vs. community (qtd. in Herrring et al. 2005: 145–146). Since the material analyzed in this paper is different and concentrated on writers, I came out with different dimensions, namely monologue vs. interaction and subject vs. object. Hence, I differentiate the 'monologue' forms (i.e. utterances whose receipent is not clearly defined) from 'dialogic' or 'interactional' utterances (i.e. those targeted at readers). The analysis allows us to distinguish the second level of analysis, which concerns the topic of utterance. Some texts express a writer's social status (the author and his work as the subject), whereas the others concentrate around writer's subjectivity (writer as a speaker) (see. Figure 1). This double dichotomy allows us to understand and classify various texts (expressed through different media) on writers' websites. The very same text can serve different communication functions depending on the context.

Subject/monologue

The first group of utterances is not immediately connected with the situational context. The main kind of material are reprints, i.e. excerpts from previously published literary works, essays or interviews. Non-literary texts are usually of informational matter and they are loosely connected with each other. For instance, on Olga Tokarczuk's website we may find a couple of short stories and a speech the author delivered after being awarded a literary prize. Some writers publish full volumes of poetry (A4, A25), but usually we encounter short excerpts which should encourage readers to buy the entire book.

Subject / interaction

Far more interestingly, from our perspective are those texts which aim at interaction, i.e. those utterances which were discussed above as electronic discourse. The main textual form in this group could be called a 'web post'. By this I mean all possible texts which employ one or more media and are created in the web environment, being directed to the networked audience. The best example of such an utterance is a blog post, in case of which both forms and the communicational context influence the content and style. A single utterance is usually a part of a series of dated entries, usually commented on by other users (cf. Gumkowska, Maryl i Toczyski 2009, p. 295;. Gumkowska 2009). The category of a 'web post' also consists of other textual forms like comments or welcoming notes on writers' websites. Due to the high subjectivity of the electronic discourse, most of the blog entries are based on traditional, biographical or intimate genres such as a diary, a letter, or autobiography.

Object/ monologue

This group consists of monological utterances about the writer, i.e. notes about authors and books, pictures, literary trailers, bookcovers. Some writers, e.g. Mariusz Sieniewicz (A34), provide press kits with short notes and high-resolution pictures. The main function of such materials is to promote writers and their output.

Object/ interaction

The last group consists of the utterances aimed at triggering readers' reaction and cooperation. Writers invite readers to book-readings or events somewhat connected to their writings (e.g. city walks dedicated to the places described in a book). Such utterances serve as an invitation to interaction along with such promotional materials as abovementioned wallpapers or quizzes about the novel (Beręsewicz A2, Mordarski A29).

One also has to distinguish a group of utterances dedicated to writers which mock the interaction like self-presentation in the form of "questions-and-answers". Katarzyna Leżeńska, a female-fiction writer describes herself in a fake interview about the writing process ("Where do you get the ideas? ... How long does it take you to write a book? ... Have you ever worked on two books simultaneously?" A26). Marta Fox describes what she likes and dislikes (A12) and Marek Krajewski interviews himself and answers questions "he had already answered multiple times" (e.g. Why do you write crime fiction? Do you work on a series of short stories? Do you miss the academic career?). A similar strategy is applied by such authors as Jacek Dukaj or Beata Pawlikowska, who publish the answers to frequently asked questions, and therefore avoid direct contact with readers.

Website as text

At the begining of this article reference was paid to Beata Pawlikowska's website. As we may recall, it contained various multimedia materials created by readers or the author herself, which were later categorized in terms of communication. But what if we want to analyze this website as a whole?

When we adopt the intermedial perspective we pay attention to the characteristics of singular media employed in the utterance. On the other hand, when we choose the transmedial approach, we focus not on the differences between those media but rather on the utterance as a whole. The former approach draws attention to the hybrid nature of electronic utterances, whereas the latter focuses on the message itself. Now, when analyzing websites as texts, I adopt the second approach, treating web pages as hybrid forms.

Concentrating mainly on the communication I will analyze websites in a perspective similar to rhetorical hybrids analysis, as proposed by Kathleen Hall Jamieson i Karlyn Kohrs Campbell (1982). In this perspective genres are understood as "dynamic fusions of substantive, stylistic and situational elements and constellations that are strategic responses to the demands of the situation and the purposes of the rhetor" (ibid.: 146). On the example of eulogies Jamieson and Campbell argue that every genre is "a potential fusion of elements that may be energized or actualized as a strategic response to a situation" (ibid.). In other words, a eulogy consists of various genres which are subdued to the main communicative intent (i.e. to praise the deceased person).

Although websites as rhetorical structures are less coherent than eulogies one may venture to point out a main communicative intent, which would dominate over various elements of the website. One should also take into consideration the previously mentioned duplicity of electronic texts, which consist of material and semiotic aspects, i.e. communication technologies and the meaning. This problem was elaborated by Askehave and Nielsen in their analysis of "web-mediated genres" (2004). They propose to analyze internet texts in three dimensions: communicative purpose, functional units and rhetorical strategies (ibid. 22–44). Yet, the authors claim, all those dimensions have both reading (semiotic) and navigational (technical) aspects. For instance, the main communicative purpose of a homepage (Askehave and Nielsen's main example) in the reading mode is to introduce "the user to general content of the site" (ibid. 9). However, in the navigation mode, the homepage functions "as the official gateway of the website as it enables the reader to access and navigate the site by providing navigational tools or links that branch off into the website as a whole." (ibid.)

This part of the article analyses the website as a whole in two aspects: its semiotic (or reading) aspect which is considered a genre, whereas its material (or navigational) aspect is understood as a format. A webpage's format is its entire technological side (programming), which shapes the communication and influences a genre by allowing certain forms of publication. A webpage's genre would be understood as its primal communicative purpose, which is visible in the way technological capacities are used. For instance, a blog should be conceived of as a format, i.e. a frequently updated webpage, usually allowing for comments. Yet, this very format can be employed by various genres ranging from travel blogs to simple personal webpages.

The formats of writers' websites

When assessing a website's format we consider such features as visual aspect (e.g. layout, colors, media) and the content structure (e.g. the list of entries or separate subpages). Among formats used by writers we can distinguish three main types: a simple webpage, blog and vortal.

Simple webpage

Although blogs and portals are technically also webpages, we will apply this name to simple websites (e.g. home pages). Such websites are usually quite straightforward, rather static and simple in programming. They usually consist of a homepage and several subpages, which sometimes can serve as categories for content. Dynamic elements, such as a news section or social-network plugins (e.g. Twitter) appear rarely.

A website's structure is usually hierarchical, taking a form of the tree: the homepage (1st level) gives users the access to the list of categories (2nd level), which are usually divided into subcategories or indexes (3rd level), which in turn direct users to individual pages (4th level). The number of categories and subcategories varies from a couple to a dozen or so. This structure is rooted in the files-and-folders metaphor: all elements of the website are arranged and categorized, so that browsing the webpage is similar to the act of leafing through a book.

Blog

A blog is a type of a webpage, based on a template, which allows a non-professional user to setup and maintain the service their own. Blogs are usually defined as "frequently modified web pages in which dated entries are listed in reverse chronological sequence" (Herring et al. 2005: 142). The form of a blog resembles a newspaper: entries are usually located in the central part of the website and indexes are located on the edges, along with the author's bio and a *blogroll*, i.e. list of links to interesting websites or blogging-friends. This format's dynamics is further highlighted by chronological indexes, and dates of entries or comments. A blogger may allow users to post comments under the entries.

Vortal

The last format type is vortal, i.e. vertical portal. Portals usually contain a large amount of diverse materials, and types of writing, and they usually focus on news (e.g. yahoo.com). Vortals, on the other hand, are less general and more topical. Users may not only comment on posted entries but they can also interact with each other and usually post their own content online. Hence, such websites allow not only for communication between writers and reader but they also create a platform for interaction between readers themselves (e.g. such is the case on Beata Pawlikowska's website (A32).

The genres of writers' websites

Let us now consider writers' websites as genres which are distinguished through the analysis of the content and communicative purpose (i.e. declared and visible goal for running a website). The genres which are distunguished (shopping window, bulletin, filter, blog) could be placed on a spectrum from static, print-like forms serving rather informative functions, which allow a limited feedback from the users, to dynamic, interactive forms, rooted in the electronic discourse. One should also point out that those genres are ideal types and may coexist on individual websites.

Shopping window

This genre is an occasionally updated, static webpage which main purpose is to provide information about the writer and her or his output. The term was coined by a poet, Miłosz Biedrzycki, who calls his website 'wystawka' ('a small shopping window'). This name depicts well both the shape and goals of such webpages, as well as the static way of presenting the content. Most of the shopping windows are based on a simple webpage format, however some writers, like Antoni Hukałowicz (A17), employ a blog format too.

A shopping window is deeply rooted in print culture – the homepage is an index of content and all categories are organized in a hierarchal way. For instance, on Olga Tokarczuk's website the category "Texts" leads us to an index of articles (A38). Shopping windows are rarely updated, mostly only when an author's new book comes out. They do not serve to function as a news medium, but rather provide basic information about the writer. The communication channels are limited – usually we find the writer's e-mail address or a contact form.

Analyzed websites representing this genre do not contain much current news about the author or upcoming events. The material posted on the shopping window, such as a bio note, book synopsis, photos or excerpts are 'timeless', i.e. they do not require frequent updates. Let us consider Olga Tokarczuk's website (A38): the cover of the newest book visually dominates the website. On the top we find the list of categories (bio, books, texts, reviews, various, audio, gallery, contact). Once we compare this website with other shopping windows prepared by the same publisher, Wydawnictwo Literackie (e.g. Ewa Lipska A27, Katarzyna Grochola A13), we see that they are virtually identical. Communication with readers is far less important than providing the information. Although some authors copy the communication patterns of the print culture and publish short 'forewords' (e.g. Rylski A33, Kotowski A19, Wrocławski A40), we may consider such notes as purely expressive, since they do not count on the readers reaction at any rate. Users are usually unable to post comments on shopping windows.

In certain cases the communication with readers is conducted through dedicated subparts of a website, such as visitor log or a discussion board. The former type usually functions as a 'letter to the writer', in which readers frequently express their gratitude and describe their amazing reading experiences. A discussion board, on the other hand, is a platform almost entirely dedicated to readers. Yet, this form of communication is quite scarce among writers' websites and does not attract many readers. For instance, Grażyna Bąkiewicz's forum had only 12 posts in 2 years (A1).

Bulletin

Krzysztof Beśka's homepage (A3) has a lot in common with a shopping window – the author is the main subject of the site, and the homepage contains basic biographical information and bookcovers. We do not find any direct references to readers, who cannot comment on posts. The main difference lies in the dynamics – the webpage is built on the blog format, so consecutive posts are displayed on the homepage. In other words, static and dynamic elements coexist within one website.

Posts' subjects vary, however it is usually concentrated around the writer and his output. Consecutive information give readers a chance to follow the creative process, learn about writer's inspirations, read the latest reviews of his books and obtain information about upcoming events. Yet, besides these dynamics and the blog form itself, Beśka's website (and many others) is closer to print culture than to electronic discourse. The website functions as a peculiar 'Writer's newspaper', or a bulletin published for unspecified readers. Bulletins provide information about inspirations, reviews and current events, such as author's meetings, media appearances or a book launch (c.f. websites of Julia Hartwig A16 and Błażej

Dzikowski A11). Hence, this genre is specifically tied to a writer's professional life – if there's no new book, no event or a prize coming, the bulletin goes on standby.

The bulletin usually consists of news, biographical notes and picture galleries. Their main function is to provide the latest news, so there is rarely any community-making involved and commenting is usually disabled (readers can write e-mails instead). Authors interested in interaction with their readers setup a different channel of communication: Marcin Wroński runs both an official bulletin (A41) and a less formal blog (A42) aimed at discussions with readers.

Filter

Max Cegielski's Blog (A7) is dedicated to a wide range of topics, reflecting the writer's interests: culture of the Far- and Middle-East (reporter), Indian music (musician), and contemporary Polish culture (journalist). Unlike in two previously discussed cases, Cegielski's website is not entirely dedicated to his self-presentation as a writer but rather to external topics. In this sense it serves as an appendix to Cegielski's writings, reflecting the themes his readers are interested in.

The term filter is used in weblogs classification, and describes those websites, which primarily contain "observations and evaluations of external, typically public events" (Herring et al. 2005: 147). In other words, they are topical websites dedicated to certain, quite well defined subjects (e.g. new technologies, crime fiction, home affairs). They play the role of 'live' RSS channels, i.e. they transmit certain news which is relevant from the writer's viewpoint. In a way, filters work like Twitter, a microblogging platform dedicated to "following" short messages sent by authors one wants to follow. The choice of the followed person entails the range of topics one wants to have the access to. Readers interested in certain topics find relevant information on such blogs. Hence, filters consist largely of links to external materials, which are commented on by the author.

The community created around such a website is a topical group – they are not so much interested in a writer than in the topics s/he writes about (or in the way s/he describes them). So, on Piotr Kowalczyk's filter (A20) dedicated to electronic literature, topical news is more important than his own writings. Beata Pawlikowska (A32) creates a vortal about travelling, Mariusz Szczygieł (A36) predominantly writes about Czech culture and society and Sylwia Chutnik discusses social issues (A8). This 'filtering' can be also understood more subjectively – as an emanation of writer's subjectivity. In a way every website is a filter of everyday life, containing material which the author finds relevant, which brings us to blogs.

Blog

The blog format is not a genre, since technological capacities may be applied in various ways. When we talk about the blog genre we have in mind a rhetorical hybrid, a platform for other genres subdued to the main communicative intent. Blogs are usually defined in communication categories. Herring et al. considers blogs as a "bridging genre", "intermediate between standard web pages and asynchronous CMC" (2005: 161). It should be noted that this statement does not refer to any stylistic features, but rather to the way the communication on the website is organized.

Jakub Żulczyk's blog (A43) is a good example of this genre. The author appears in diverse roles: as a writer, critic, or a private person. A blogger's subjectivity influences the way of writing – the author often makes strong statements and enters into arguments with readers. Apart from criticism and discussions we find here autobiographical narratives, announcements, invitations, or cultural news. The layout and structure are typical for a blog format, strongly underlining the "here-and-now" of communication (newest posts are displayed on the homepage). Moreover, there are no tags, no categories or links to older posts: chronology is the only ordering principle. This "here-and-now" aspect is also visible in the comments, since they mostly refer to actual entries rather than to other sources or the writers' output.

Although blog as a genre is closely linked to a filter (especially in the context of 'filtering' the external world through writer's subjectivity), it is also a very subjective, multifaced genre whichfocuses on a writers' personality. Blog's dynamics make it similar to a bulletin (as described earlier in this paper), however it is not concerned predominantly with a writers social role and self-promotion. The attitude towards readers is also different: Żulczuk often debates with other users, creating conditions for symmetrical communication. This symmetry of communication with readers, together with subjectivity makes up crucial characteristics of this genre.

Maria Cywińska-Milonas (2002) proposes a categorization of blogs according to their communicative characteristics. She distinguishes three kinds: monologic, dialogic and blog-community ("blogowspólnota").

Monologic blogs are those where comments are disabled (e.g. Remigiusz Grzela A14). The dialogic type is characterized by limited activity of the readers: comments are rare and mostly directed towards the author (e.g. Jakub Żulczyk A43, Łukasz Orbitowski A31). A blog-community, according to Cywińska-Milonas, is constituted through interactions between the readers. Yet, it must be noted that there are different kinds of such communities. For instance, blogs by Sylwia Chutnik (A8) or Maria Kryńska Szostak (A24) are created within blog-publishing services (iwoman and blogspot), whic encourage other bloggers to contribute and to hold discussions with each other. Somewhat different communities are constituted on individual websites, in the case of which the writer (or publisher) is solely responsible for the interaction (e.g. Jarosław Klejnocki A18, Jerzy Sosnowski A35). Those communities resemble literary salons, where frequent readers discuss various topics dedicated to culture, literature or society.

To conclude, if we consider the entire communicative spectrum of blogs we may distinguish the following instances: monologue, potential dialogue (no comments, although enabled), dialogue, salon, blog-community. Each of these forms is an outcome of both writer's intentions and the actual communication on the website, which largely depends on the readers' interest. Blog as a hybridic genre is predominantly aimed at communication with readers, which makes it a model example of electronic discourse.

Conclusion

This article aimed at describing diverse texts from writers' websites in a communicational perspective. New electronic means of communication reshape traditional forms of contact between writers and readers and this change leads to three conclusions.

Firstly, the transfer of literary life into the internet environment changes the way in which literary communication functions. Writers are more responsible for connecting with the audience and providing various non-literary materials.

Secondly, the internet context makes communicational approaches towards new genres more important. Taking into consideration both the communicational and communal character of texts from webpages allow us to understand better the functions of such materials and websites as wholes (treated as texts).

Thirdly, the electronic medium allows us to incorporate into one utterance materials from different media systems. However, we ought to analyze those texts in the context of other genres available on the website.

This is just a snapshot of a fairly dynamic situation. On the one hand, we may observe how one writer after another sets up a webpage and how the online self-presentation strategies are being established. On the other hand, the evolution of electronic communication shows clearly that fairly new forms (e.g. static websites) slowly become obsolete and the writers are going to look for new communication solutions in the nearest future. The internet is now an indispensable part of literary life, which is not limited to self-presentation and commercial moves. The web allows readers to reestablish a symmetric communication with readers.

Bibliography

Askehave Inger Anne, Ellerup Nielsen 2004, *Web-Mediated Genres – A Challenge to Traditional Genre Theory*, [in:] *Working paper 6*, Aarhus: Center for Virksomhedkommunikation.

Balbus Stanisław 2007, *Zagłada gatunków*, [in:] *Polska genologia literacka*, eds. D. Ostaszewska i R. Cudak, Warsaw: PWN.

Balcerzan Edward 2007, *Nowe formy w pisarstwie i wynikające stąd porozumienia*, [in:] *Polska genologia literacka*, eds. D. Ostaszewska i R. Cudak, Warsaw: PWN.

Bolecki Włodzimierz 2007, *O gatunkach to i owo*, [in:] *Polska genologia literacka*, eds. D. Ostaszewska i R. Cudak, Warsaw: PWN.

Cywińska-Milonas Maria 2002, *Blogi (ujęcie psychologiczne)*, [in:] *Liternet. Literatura i internet*, ed. Piotr Marecki, Cracow: Wydawnictwo RABID.

Davis Boyd H., Jeutonne P. Brewer 1997, *Electronic Discourse: Linguistic Individuals in Virtual Space*, Albany: State University of New York Press.

Godlewski Grzegorz 2008, *Słowo – pismo – sztuka słowa. Perspektywy antropologiczne*, Warsaw: Wydawnictwa Uniwersytetu Warszawskiego.

Gumkowska Anna, Maciej Maryl i Piotr Toczyski 2009, *Blog to...blog. Blogi oczyma blogerów. Raport z badania jakościowego zrealizowanego przez Instytut Badań Literackich PAN i Gazeta.pl*, [in:] *Tekst (w) sieci, t. 2. Literatura. Społeczeństwo. Komunikacja*, ed. A. Gumkowska, Warsaw: Wydawnictwa Akademickie i Profesjonalne.

Gumkowska Anna 2009, *Blogi wobec tradycji diarystycznej. Nowe gatunki w nowych mediach*, [in:] *Tekst (w) sieci, t. 1 Tekst, język, gatunki*, ed. D. Ulicka, Warsaw: Wydawnictwa Akademickie i Profesjonalne.

Herring Susan, Lois Ann Shedit, Elijah Writh i Sabrina Bonus 2005, "Weblogs as a Bridging Genre", *Information, Technology & People*, No. 18.

Jamieson Kathleen Hall, Karlyn Kohrs Campbell 1982, "Rhetorical Hybrids: Fusions of Generic Elements", *Quarterly Journal of Speech*, No. 69.

Jenkins Henry 2006, *Convergence Culture: Where Old and New Media Collide.* New York: New York University Press.

Maryl Maciej 2009a, *Reprint i hipermedialność – dwa kierunki rozwoju literatury ucyfrowionej,* [in:] *Tekst (w) sieci,* t. 2. *Literatura. Społeczeństwo. Komunikacja,* ed. A. Gumkowska, Warsaw: Wydawnictwa Akademickie i Profesjonalne.

Maryl Maciej 2009b, „Poetyka tekstu kultury – niedokończony projekt", *Teksty Drugie,* No 6.

Miller Carolyn R. 1994, *Genre as Social Action,* [in:] *Genre and the New Rhetoric,* ed. A. Freedman, P. Medway, London: Taylor & Francis.

Niemczyńska Małgorzata I. 2008, *Książkowe teledyski w internecie,* [in:] *Gazeta Wyborcza,* No. 59, 10 III.

Pawlicka Urszula 2010, „Trailery literackie – o reklamie literatury pisanej «żywą kamerą»" *Niedoczytania,* 6 IV, http://niedoczytania.pl/trailery-literackie-o-reklamie-literatury--pisanej-zywa-kamera [10 V 2011].

Wysłouch Seweryna 2007 *Nowa genologia – rewizje i interpretacje,* [in:] *Polska genologia literacka,* eds. D. Ostaszewska i R. Cudak, Warsaw: PWN.

Literary trailers

Dukaj Jacek, *Wroniec* (1), http://www.youtube.com/watch?v=b-1PVW3po1k (11 V 2011).

Dukaj Jacek, *Wroniec* (2), http://www.youtube.com/watch?v=S7eTCfrcOws (11 V 2011).

Fox Marta, *Kobieta zaklęta w kamień czyli Marta Fox dla dorosłych,* http://www.youtube.com/profile?user=WLchannel#p/u/4/46j61P-hqFU (11 V 2010).

Klejnocki Jarosław, *Południk 21,* http://klejnocki.wydawnictwoliterackie.pl/strona/14/ (11 V 2011).

Król Robert, *Pamięć podręczna,* http://www.youtube.com/watch?v=ElLZN36z6NE (11 V 2011).

Michalak Katarzyna, *Poczekajka,* http://katarzynamichalak.pl/poczekajka/teledysk (11 V 2011).

Orbitowski Łukasz, *Nadchodzi,* http://www.youtube.com/watch?v=3UJj9g7Ch1k (11 V 2010).

Żulczyk Jakub, *Instytut* (1), http://jakubzulczyk.ownlog.com/2114705,link.html (11 V 2011).

Żulczyk Jakub, *Instytut* (2), http://jakubzulczyk.ownlog.com/2125505,link.html (11 V 2011).

Writers' websites

A1 – Bąkiewicz Grażyna, http://www.grazynabakiewicz.pl/ (26.01.2011).

A2 – Beręsewicz Paweł, http://www.pawelberesewicz.neostrada.pl/ (12.01.2010).

A3 – Beśka Krzysztof, http://krzysztofbeska.blogspot.com (12.01.2010).

A4 – Biedrzycki Miłosz, http://free.art.pl/mlb/index.html (29.12.2010).

A5 – Bocheński Jacek, http://jacekbochenski.blox.pl (19.01.2011).

A6 – Bryll Ernest, http://www.bryll.pl (19.01.2011).

A7 – Cegielski Max Maksymilian, http://maxmasala.blox.pl (11.01.2011).

A8 – Chutnik Sylwia, http://sylwiachutnik.blog.iwoman.pl/ (14.02.2011).

A9 – Darda Stefan, http://www.stefandarda.pl/ (26.01.2011).

A10 – de Blasi Marlena, http://www.marlenadeblasi.pl/ (26.01.2011).

A11 – Dzikowski Błażej, http://blazejdzikowski.wordpress.com (26.01.2011).

A12 – Fox Marta, http://martafox.pl/ (20.01.2010).
A13 – Grochola Katarzyna, http://grochola.wydawnictwoliterackie.pl/ (26.11.2011).
A14 – Grzela Remigiusz, http://remigiusz-grzela.bloog.pl/ (26.12.2011).
A15 – Harny Marek, http://www.harny.pl/ (26.01.2011).
A16 – Hartwig Julia, http://juliahartwig.blogspot.com/ (27.01.2011).
A17 – Hukałowicz Antoni, http://www.antonihukalowicz.blogspot.com/ (28.12.2010).
A18 – Klejnocki Jarosław, http://klejnocki.wydawnictwoliterackie.pl/ (29.12.2010).
A19 – Kotowski Krzysztof, http://www.krzysztofkotowski.pl/ (26.01.2011).
A20 – Kowalczyk Piotr, http://www.passwordincorrect.com/ (15.02.2011).
A21 – Krajewski Marek, http://www.marekkrajewski.pl/ (22.12.2010).
A22 – Krajewski Marek, http://www.marek-krajewski.pl/ (26.01.2011).
A23 – Król Robert, http://www.robertkrol.art.pl/ (30.12.2010).
A24 – Kryńska-Szostak Maria, http://studiumczasoprzestrzeni.blogspot.com/ (10.02.2011).
A25 – Kwiatkowski Grzegorz, http://grzegorzkwiatkowski.com/ (12.01.2011).
A26 – Leżeńska Katarzyna, http://www.lezenska.pl/ (27.01.2011).
A27 – Lipska Ewa, http://lipska.wydawnictwoliterackie.pl/ (26.01.2011).
A28 – Michalak Katarzyna, http://katarzynamichalak.pl/ (26.01.2011).
A29 – Mordarski Michał Daniel, http://www.mordarski.pl/ (26.01.2011).
A30 – Niemirski Arkadiusz, http://www.niemirski.com/ (27.01.2011).
A31 – Orbitowski Łukasz, http://orbitowski.pl/ (26.01.2011).
A32 – Pawlikowska Beata, http://www.beatapawlikowska.com/ (9.02.2011).
A33 – Rylski Eustachy, http://www.rylski.pl/ (12.01.2011).
A34 – Sieniewicz Mariusz, http://www.sieniewicz.art.pl/ (12.01.2011).
A35 – Sosnowski Jerzy, http://www.jerzysosnowski.pl/ (11.02.2011).
A36 – Szczygieł Mariusz, http://www.mariuszszczygiel.com.pl/ (27.01.2011).
A37 – Tochman Wojciech, http://www.tochman.eu/ (27.01.2011).
A38 – Tokarczuk Olga, http://tokarczuk.wydawnictwoliterackie.pl/ (29.12.2010).
A39 – Wencel Wojciech, http://wojciechwencel.blogspot.com/ (28.12.2010).
A40 – Wrocławski Bohdan, http://www.pisarz.eu/ (10.02.2011).
A41 – Wroński Marcin, http://marcinwronski.art.pl/ (30.12.2009).
A42 – Wroński Marcin, http://wronski.wordpress.com/ (30.12.2010).
A43 – Żulczyk Jakub, http://jakubzulczyk.ownlog.com/ (01.10.2011).

Quotations from writers' websites

A25-1 – "Eine Kleine Todesmusik, czyli pośmiertne przyjemności", http://grzegorzkwiatkowski.com/?p=254 (12.1.2011).
A6-2 – "Film „Choroszczańskie błonia", http://antonihukalowicz.blogspot.com/2009/03/film-choroszczanskie-bonia.html (5.1.2011).

Katarzyna Sitkowska*
University of Lodz

> I would have written a shorter letter,
> but I did not have the time.
>
> *Blaise Pascal*

TOWARDS A GENERIC ANALYSIS OF THE MICROBLOG (BASED ON A STUDY OF TWITTER)

Abstract
This article is an attempt to determine the place of microblogs, posted on Twitter, on the Internet or, more broadly in the multimedia genealogy.
First, the service itself is presented and mechanisms of its functioning are described. Then its importance for society is mentioned. Furthermore, some crucial issues related to the theory of genres are presented and they constitute an essential introduction to the research methodology. The "guides" on the path of reflection and on the characteristics of microblogs are the "older siblings" of this form of expression: the Internet, journalistic and other genres, whose determinants have already been described. Such an order is matched against another one – the tradition of genres' description in four aspects: structural, pragmatic, cognitive and stylistic.

Key words: microblog, new genres, multimedia genealogy, theory of genres, Twitter

Introduction

The goal of this article is to establish a preliminary definition of the place of microblogs, published on the Twitter website, in the Internet – or more broadly, multimedia – genealogy. It will be accompanied by reflection on

---
* Philology Department, Univeristy of Lodz, al. Kościuszki 65, 90-514 Lodz, e-mail: k_sitkowska@uni.lodz.pl

genealogy itself, since–making this goal an especially interesting research challenge–the current state of research on the genres of all linguistic texts does not give any ready answers to the questions concerning them that are asked by linguists and literary critics, as well as by media studies scholars and scholars of culture in general. The analysis presented below is not a synthesis of long-term studies on the issues connected with Internet communication and its genealogy, but an "exploratory" record of contact with them. Thus it is also not motivated by the idea of presenting a definitive solution, but of showing the points that give rise to further questions. Such an approach allows one to look at a relatively new[1] phenomenon with the curiosity of an "explorer".

First of all the service itself and the way it works will be presented, and next its meaning in society. After as brief a presentation as possible of Twitter, I will go on to the core issues tied to the theory of genres, which are an essential introduction to the study's methodology. As "guides" on the path of reflection about the genealogical description of microblogs I have chosen the "older siblings" of this form of expression: Internet genres, press genres and other speech genres whose characteristics have already been described. This line of thought intersects with another – the tradition of generic description based on four aspects: structural, pragmatic, cognitive and stylistic (Witosz 2001: 84; Wojtak 2004: 16). Thanks to this manner of presenting the issues, the summary will be a straightforward (but not necessarily easy) drawing of conclusions on the subject of the generic indicators of the studied communications observed in the four aspects mentioned above.

What is Twitter?

"Welcome to Twitter. Find out what's happening, right now, with the people and organizations you care about."[2] Three fundamental aspects of Twitter's operation can be gleaned from this greeting which initiates contact with the recipient: it is a source of information about *people*, it is a source of information about *organizations* and, finally, a source of infor-

---

[1] Twitter was founded in 2006, other sites offering microblogging services appeared mainly in the wake of its popularity (http://pl.wikipedia.org/wiki/Mikroblog Accessed: 23.08.2012).

[2] http://twitter.com/ Accessed: 23.08.2012. All quotations found in the text maintain the original spelling and punctuation.

mation concerning them *"right now."* Twitter thus calls itself an "information network."³ The information transmitted through the service takes the form of messages, able to contain links, whose total length cannot exceed 140 characters. These messages are called *tweets*. A user of the service can be a recipient only, can also send out messages, and can combine these functions at will at any desired frequency. The user can see the tweets sent by any given person or organization, provided that they are not restricted. He can do this in an orderly manner, choosing feeds which he will "follow": "Build your timeline. Follow people to get their Tweets."⁴ A "timeline" is a list of tweets published by profiles followed by a given user, ordered from newest to oldest (such ordering is also used when viewing individual profiles)

Fig. 1. Twitter: Example "timeline"

---

³ http://twitter.com/about Accessed: 23.08.2012.
⁴ https://twitter.com/#!/welcome/recommendations Accessed: 23.08.2012.

Fig. 2. Twitter: Example user profile (summary)

Twitter is a social network: by making lists of "following" and "followers" groups of Internet users are built; use of it is free, and requires only registering and then logging in.

The limit on the length of messages allows tweets to be counted among microblogs. Wikipedia[5] defines a microblog as:

> (...) a kind of Internet diary in which the main bearers of information are short entries that usually are one sentence long. Like conventional blogs, a microblog can also contain pictures, audio clips or films; it can be available to all or to a narrow group selected of readers chosen by the author. The idea behind microblogs is the transmission of information on actions happening at a given moment, small thoughts or plans which are to be carried out in the near future. It is also possible for conversations to take place between users through the use of entries.[6]

The remaining traits of the service will be described in the parts of the article dealing with the issues connected with them.

---

[5] The *Słownik terminologii medialnej* [Dictionary of Media Terminology] (2006) does not contain an entry for the word "mikroblog".

[6] http://pl.wikipedia.org/wiki/Mikroblog Accessed: 23.08.2012.

Why Twitter?

In order to answer this question, I mention several responses taken from the media:

> Social media are already not only popular, but also opinion-shapers. Here they beat out television and magazines. These are the results of the latest (from June) report of the Instytut Monitorowania Mediów [Media Monitoring Institute]. It finds that in a ranking of the ten most often cited medias one finds both Facebook and Twitter, and in fifth and sixth place at that.[7]

"Mariusz Błaszczak's entry from two years ago is the hit of the weekend on Polish Twitter"[8]. "Radosław Sikorski has again caused an uproar on Twitter. This time the Polish diplomatic head's update describing the Warsaw Uprising as a 'national catastrophe' provoked a reaction from opposition members of the Warsaw city council."[9] "This tragic death [of a teenage boy who purchased a bag of Skittles moments before his death – K.S.], however, became a pretext for a discussion of racially-motivated violence and prompted heated protests. The actor and director Spike Lee, known for his activism against racism, sent out a call on Twitter for people to send bags of Skittles to the Stanford chief of police. Thus the candies became a symbol of a protest across the entire nation."[10]

> "The reaction to Wojewódzki and Figurski's critiques had just begun to fade when the next, although this time short-lived, wave of outrage was provoked by the Euro-MP Marek Migalski, who published an update on Twitter comparing the athletic (and black!) tennis player Serena Williams to [Polish MP Anna] Grodzka. What was Migalski counting on? Provoking a scandal, of course. And as noisy a one as possible, as that."[11]

Tweets of a racist nature sent out after England lost in the quarterfinals of the Euro 2012 Football Championship provoked a response from the

---

[7] http://www.rp.pl/artykul/10,921585-Facebook-i-Twitter-w-pierwszej-dziesiatce.html Accessed: 24.08.2012.

[8] http://wyborcza.pl/1,75478,12296224,Wpis_Mariusza_Blaszczaka_sprzed_dwoch_lat_weekendowym.html Accessed: 24.08.2012.

[9] http://polska.newsweek.pl/sikorski-zhanbil-pamiec-powstania-radni-pis-przed-1-sierpnia,80291,1,1.html Accessed: 24.08.2012.

[10] http://wyborcza.biz/biznes/1,100896,11447920,Wyslij_Skittles_policji__ktora_kryje_zabojce.html Accessed: 24.08.2012.

[11] http://spoleczenstwo.newsweek.pl/miedzy-slowami--chamstwo-iii-rp,94030,1,1.html Accessed: 24.08.2012.

police, as was noted on television by the BBC immediately following the match.[12]

The above collection is not the result of exhaustive research, but instead was gathered somewhat "in passing"; one could cite a significantly larger number of anecdotes about Twitter. When observing the place of Twitter in the media system, one can recognize that Twitter is not only worthy of attention, including from the linguistic point of view, but quite simply cannot be ignored. It appears that Twitter is not only a place for commenting on reality – it can also shape it.

The statements cited above show that, as a place for the exchange of information, Twitter not only influences the world of the media (for example by giving rise to political scandals), but can also play a large role in the creation of social views or in the operations of candy companies. While not a subject for linguistic analysis, the significance of the creation of Twitter on the functioning of the Internet should be noted as well. As one programmer and expert on the service states, "Twitter has revolutionized five different areas of the web: communication in real-time, mobile access to the Internet, 'non-reciprocal' social networks, short form communication, the use of APIs."[13]

Twitter is thus not mere "tweeting", but an influential media outlet. Thus the question of its genealogical status is non-trivial.

Why genre?

Given the general human tendency towards organizing, sorting, cataloging, and even at times pigeonholing, the concept of genre seems very useful. It allows one to place different types of works in their network of mutual relations. Assigning a genre is also a visible sign of recognition for a given phenomenon, and what has been recognized has been, to a certain degree, mastered, or at least domesticated. This gives one a feeling of control, and, furthermore, of safety as well.

Verbal formulations are also subject to categorization. When a certain human creation (not necessarily an artistic one) falls outside of man's ability to define it in terms of genealogy, this means that man has lost power over the products of his own hands and mind. Such a situation can be

---

[12] http://www.bbc.co.uk/news/uk-england-london-18582171 Accessed: 24.08.2012.
[13] http://www.orianmarx.com/2012/07/12/what-twitter-wants/ Accessed: 24.08.2012. Translated into Polish by K.S; English article citation based on original site.

extremely dangerous to the human race, as has been explored in numerous works of science fiction. Leaving groups of verbal utterances uncategorized will not drive mankind into extinction, but does, however, cause a certain discomfort. Hope for regaining academic comfort can be found in the view of Bakhtin, who stated that there are no texts which do not make use of "concrete, relatively long-lasting and typical forms of constructing the whole" (1986: 373) and thus are not genres of speech. Accepting this assumption requires, in the opinion of B. Witosz, developing an "appropriately elastic conception of genre," that is to say, one from which we do not expect a "finite catalog of necessary and sufficient traits" (2001: 70).

The problem for genealogy is that it enters into a higher level of complexity, however, when we take into consideration texts found on the Internet, which, due to its discursive character, is at times seen as "genealogically amorphous" (Kawka 2010: 67). One exit from this line of thought, which threatens to exclude the Internet from genealogical consideration, is to adopt a static research perspective (Wojtak 2004: 16), while of course maintaining full awareness of the fact that the described texts belong to a wider discourse. Texts found on the Internet are characterized by an enormous diversity resulting from their essential characteristics (see: Grzenia 2006), from the hypertextuality of communications that make use of it.[14] Due to this diversity, as well as the enormous size of the production and the shockingly quick evolution of texts on the Internet, their classification is made more difficult. These phenomena, in the opinion of A. Gumkowska in her analysis of blogs, are a factor "which inclines some researchers to a definitive rejection of theory about their generic status" (2009: 241). In turn M. Kawka, also in a description of blogs, ascribes the cause of the lack of a delineated, canonical generic model to this their very "Internet-ness": changeability, hybridity, multicodality, etc. (2010: 67). The literature on genres indicates a potential solution to the problems involved with placing Internet texts in a genealogically sorted world. First of all, the above-mentioned elastic definition of genre would have to be drawn up. Helping to meet this need is a theory which discusses the identification of genres on the basis of prototypes (Witosz 2001: 74 et seq.), which also creates space for the discursive character of the Internet, indicating the relativity involved in determining genre and the dynamic nature of categorization itself as a result of the "(inter)subjective selection of criteria". Fully in agreement with this is the view that the "author" of a hypertext is the "receiver" surfing the web (Wilk 2000: 39 et seq.) and that genre

---

[14] The indicators of hypertextuality are discussed by U. Żydek-Bednarczuk (2003: 8).

is recognized by navigating in the scope of the global text (Żydek-Bednarczuk 2004: 432). Second, while the specific nature of Internet texts make it impossible to a significant extent that the indication of their mutual and permanent structural traits, generic indicators can be sought in the "communicative message" of texts which are united by genre while lacking canonical variants of a model (Wojtak 2010: 14). Thirdly, it is clear that "the majority of texts simultaneously enact the traits of several models" (Witosz 2001: 80. Cp. Żydek-Bednarczuk 2004: 432), it seems fitting to steer research towards secondary and complex genres whose models have an alternative or adaptive character.

Many researchers, however, do not agree with this last proposition to a greater or lesser degree (eg. Kawka 201, Gumkowska 2009: 232[15]), raising among others the argument that the specific nature of the Internet means that there is no way to relate texts found on the Web to man's traditional verbal activities, for example:

> (...) the attempt to find in blogs the *remnants* of other known genres, and thanks to this a simple redefinition of their affiliation, is from the methodological point of the view doomed to failure from the outset, since this type of networked writing was born in completely different communicative circumstances, fills different needs of both sender and recipient, and above all is not a sum, selection or compilation of other traditional genres. (Kawka 2010: 62)

And here again the classic conception of the problem of genre proposed by Bakhtin comes to the rescue in resolving the problem of "un-generic" texts. When defining genres, he pointed out the fact that "[they – K.S.] take shape depending on their function (...) and the special, innate to each domain, circumstances of linguistic intercourse" (1986: 354). In my understanding the Internet is a separate sphere of linguistic intercourse. Its circumstances are different from those of face-to-face communication and mediated communication via other media, but remaining unchanged is the fact that man is the user of the Internet and along with the appearance of new transmission media he began to apply known methods of "linguistic intercourse" to the new possibilities and limitations.

We learn that speech genres, by gathering up communicative competencies, are the legacy of all generations (Balcerzan 2000:89); it is thus impossible to hold that the Internet created new genres or rather new utterances outside of any genealogical belonging. New genres are the effect of the eternal evolution of communication, requiring only modernized

---

[15] More on this subject in the research methodology section.

and/or new tools which allow them to be recognized and described. For obvious reasons, these tools only arise in response to the growth of the genres themselves, and so, due to the fact that Internet genres are forming at a rapid pace, researchers are repeatedly forced to pause in their excitement and decide if, when and in what way to change the manner of their analysis. They are thus not always able to keep up with the production of tools, and perhaps one should not expect them to be.[16]

In summary: one can state that the Internet is a domain in which texts escape generic categorization. It is, however, too vast a forum for the exchange of human thought to allow research to be content with only pointing out the difficulties in the creation of an Internet genealogy. With the present state of knowledge of Internet communication, still after all in its early stages, even those researchers who try to point out its un-genericity are helpless, to a certain degree and at least in regards to traditional terminology, and willing or not are describing *genres*.

Can a new Internet *genre* be described? (Analysis methodology)

The goal of this work is to outline a preliminary answer to the question of whether a microblog is a new, distinct genre or else if it is a variant of an already-described and established by tradition genre (or genres). The method that seems the most simple for answering this is the comparison of the microblog with other genres operating both on the Internet and outside of it.

Adopting a comparative perspective might be controversial to some. Voices were raised against this method in the context of the study of blogs. A. Gumkowska cites the views of D. Boyd, according to whom the description of blogs as "Internet journals", that is, using a known term that makes reference to a genre already entrenched in society, is the use of a metaphor – "exploratory schematics" – with whose help "researchers build stiff frameworks that force the acceptance of a determined point of view and limit the ability for sensible analysis" (op. cit: Gumkowska 2009: 242). While calling blogs Internet journals does indeed seem a bit too narrow of a conception, nevertheless the use of exploratory schematics can be fully justified by the novelty of the genres, with the key being to

---

[16] More on this subject in the research methodology section.

go beyond these frameworks on the path to expanding the new genres. The described practice is presented by D. Boyd as a treatment helping new "readers unfamiliar with Internet realities" "to come to terms with the new form and the new technical possibilities" (op. cit: Gumkowska 2009: 241). Here one must ask about the role of the users (including those who read only) of the Internet in the formation of genres.[17] I cite one other opinion, which was raised as a side note to the critique of comparative methods in genealogical research on blogs by M. Kawka: "Many times it happens that remnants, traces of traditional genres can be found in blogs, but this results only from the writing habits and customs of the blogger or their lack of ability in this field" (2010: 64). One can make the conclusion from this that the idea of the blog is an innate, natural one, which the users of the Internet should, in fact must, come to terms with. It is not clear to me in what way, in the opinion of D. Boyd, researchers, who themselves are necessarily always a step behind the participants of communication about which they write, are supposed to help "untrained" users of the Internet in coming to terms with it, and on what basis M. Kawka assesses the competence of bloggers. A genre is, after all, and in terms of multimedia, a changeable communication perhaps above all else, "a collection of conventions which guide the members of a certain community as to what shape to give certain interactions" (Wojtak 2004: 16), and their crystallization is a process that unfolds over time. Which communication strategies become conventional for a given genre is decided by the "configuration of goals or cultural conventions" (Balcerzan 2000: 91). Accepting such a supposition, one can be freed from an overly authoritarian judgment of Internet users' competence, leaving their evaluation to the specifics of that kind of communication, since "within the realm of non-aesthetic communication, failure to respect the rules of the genre is interpreted as the result of insufficient communicative competence, which interferes with interaction" (Witosz 2001: 82). Therefore the participants in the communication themselves reject those transmissions which do not meet their expectations, those regarding genre included.

One can thus state that texts created on the Internet have a form resulting from the generic models previously mastered by their creators, and only on the terrain of this new medium are they subject to often far-reaching transformations, adapted to the goals of participants in communication acts which are achievable thanks to the particular qualities of this medium.

---

[17] Taking blogs into consideration is very essential in an attempt to analyze microblogs. They are both concerned with an approach to a new phenomena.

New users develop their Internet fluency by absorbing its rules in a manner close to that of the process of becoming acquainted with traditional speech genres, and moreover the democratic and anonymous nature of Internet communication allows for the introduction of innovations to a significantly greater degree than in other "spheres of linguistic intercourse."

In the dispute over the legitimacy of using the comparative method in research on new media genres, one can place on the other side of the barricades those researchers who see such a method as the result of the "complicated nature" of the texts and the condition of modern "genealogical awareness" (Krzempek 2006: 369), those who are convinced that "research on concrete linguistic interactions must (…) place emphasis on uncovering their *genealogical complexity* (…)", but cannot be content with only this (Witosz 2001: 80), and also those who consider the secondary character of new genres in relation to traditional ones to be axiomatic.[18]

In light of the above-mentioned arguments, in my opinion, adopting the comparative method in research on the generic indicators of the microblog is justified. This analysis will be conducted, in accordance with the earlier justification, from a static perspective in terms of four aspects: structural, pragmatic, cognitive and stylistic (Wojtak 2004:16, cp. Witosz 2001: 84), with greatest significance being ascribed to pragmatic indicators (cp. Żydek-Bednarczuk 2004: 434). After all, they constitute the "life context" of the genre, "that is the model circumstances of use and institutional ties" (Dobrzyńska 1992: 79). Her observation allows insight into the way in which mediation via the Internet influences particular communicative acts. In addition, as B. Witosz holds, "the transformations which come into play in the framework of genres transported from another context to new surroundings" are, next to "the transformations taking place as a result of the mutual interaction of the constitutive genres" and the discovery of the secondary character of genres, the phenomena which "must be emphasized (…) by research on concrete linguistic interactions" (2001: 80). The figures from the field of pragmatic communications – sender and receiver – determine the essence of the genre according to the respective "creation models" and "horizons of expectations" they adopt (T. Todorov, via Wojtak 2004: 17)[19] Likewise, coming at it from the other side – that of the subject of research – concentrating

---

[18] "Already a preliminary examination of the Web allows one to see that it makes full use of traditional genres" Woźniak 2010: 55.
[19] The communicative functions of the genealogy of literary works are discussed by K. Bartoszyński (2000: 15).

on the pragmatic aspect of generic models seems to be the optimal route, since, as A. Gumkowska observed, changes in the nature of communication brought by the Internet "concern above all the structure of transmissions and the *arrangement of sender-receiver roles* [emphasis – K.S.]" (2009: 231).

Therefore the similarity to other genres, resulting from the secondary genealogical nature and differences between genres, which are the result of the "Internet" character of microblogs, mainly in terms of the life context of the genre and relations between sender and receiver, will be the backbone of the analyses conducted of texts published on Twitter.

Twitter or tweet?
(The subject of research and research materials)

One more controversy must be added to those that come up in connection with the genericity of Internet texts: what should be considered to be the "text" that is said to represent one genre or another. In light of the hypertextuality of the Internet, which, for example, makes the final shape of a communication dependent on the user-receiver, the question of the subject of research can quickly reach the limits of the recognizable, since there are as many hypertexts as there are individual states of web users' activity. Thus yet again we must, in order to say anything at all about linguistic communications found on the Internet, or in this case on Twitter, choose artificially separated, "laboratory" selections of hypertexts. While bearing in mind their fragmentary nature and the context in which they operate, they allow for the drawing of conclusions in regards to the greater whole. While these will not be the real networks of connections between these fragments, as the researcher does not have access to these, they will be potential hypertexts, or even more importantly, information about the *possibilities* latent in this kind of communication. The decision still remains, however, as to what to take as the fundamental unit – the subject of research.

In the case of the Twitter, the options are numerous. The first option, which I have already rejected to a certain extent, was to consider examining Twitter as a whole. It requires a few additional remarks, however, mainly in light of the interesting proposal by M. Wilkowski (2009):

If we begin to analyze the various forms of content publication on the Internet, we will see that perhaps what matters is not genres as publication tools (blogs, wikis, homepages, microblogs) but genres as the form of contents (literary genres, the form of a literary work, characterized by its own construction and style). A great variety of genres can be made available on a blog within the framework of one publication infrastructure. On a blog one can publish an academic article with footnotes, a story, a poem, a film or an audio recording. A wiki page can contain not only an Internet encyclopedia (possessing a defined, permanent form of entries) but also, for example, free-form notes connected with hyperlinks or a collection of biographical information. On Twitter, one can use 140 characters to publish dry information, biting commentary or a haiku. One can even ask the question: does the Internet appropriate literary genre?

Perhaps in discussions on blogs and microblogs instead of the concept of *genre* it would be better to use the term cultural interface, as proposed by Lev Manovich based on HCI (...) it is impossible not to agree with the above remarks. As in other forms of mediated communication, on the Internet and beyond (text messages, blogs), one can see their dual mode of function – they are interdependent channels and also communications transmitted by means of these channels (Wolańska 20012: 22; Gumkowska 2009: 240). Concentrating only on the content, as M. Wilkowski suggests, while allowing one to avoid ill-fitting generic characterizations and attempts at separating hybrid forms, can however lead us to throw out the baby with the bathwater by depriving our description of a perspective that would seem to be purely formal, but also has a significant influence on the pragmatic contours of microblogs. The attention paid in this proposal to the role of the interface in the description of Internet genres is, however, important. J. Grzenia has already discussed this. He remarks that technical conditions literally create the textual framework that places boundaries on hypertext, to which otherwise delimitation would seem to be foreign. In addition, that framework demarcates the length of the text (quite clearly in the case of Twitter) and also decides on the hierarchy of verbal and non-verbal elements (Grzenia 2006: 151).

The next possible way of designating a research subject would be to single out texts by one author. Such a solution would place central emphasis on the individual characteristics of certain texts as "marked" by the idiolect of certain senders, bringing the analysis of generic indicators closer to stylistic analysis. While this should also be considered in the genealogical characterization of text (Witosz 2001: 81), choosing the category of author as the criterion for designating the subject of research can lead to an incomplete analysis. First, the perspective of the sender is the furthest from the real functional form of Internet texts, which places the main burden of communication on the recipient. Second, the tweets of a single author can display either a great deal of formal and functional variation or exactly the opposite – complete homogeneity; and furthermore the individual traits of units understood as a stream of entries by one author can to a large degree make the synthesis of knowledge on the subject of genre impossible. After all, each author's entries can be brought into dialog by himself or by other users.[20] Considering these replies as part of the context automatically brings texts by other authors into the field of analysis.

The third eventuality that takes into consideration the possibility of interacting within Twitter is the adoption of the "profile perspective" – recognizing the entries visible under a given profile as the subject of research, and thus in doing so considering alongside the entries of one author citation-tweets and reply-tweets. This solution, like the previous ones, can significantly hinder the indication of commonalities, and in addition unduly complicate the process of analysis. Establishing boundaries on which links to follow, even when only considering those within Twitter (links can also lead to any given Internet location), would require making arbitrary decisions each time on the place of their designation.

Given this situation, the most fitting, although certainly not perfect, solution to the problem delimiting the subject of research can be considered to be the analysis of individual tweets. One of the merits of such a solution is the ability to carry out a typology in which a larger role will be played by traits resulting from the nature of Twitter, and a lesser role by the individual influences of specific authors. This will also allow us to analyze individual tweets in the context of the interactions of which they are a part, but of only these interactions – without becoming entangled in broader dependencies (authorship, location on one profile). In addition, in situations where messages placed on Twitter leave the service, the tweet is treated as a relatively autonomous unit, which is also regulated by the rules concerning the citation of Twitter put in place by the service's owners (for example, the rule that tweets be cited in their entirety). Finally, during such a preliminary stage of research the simpler (less complicated) the objects of analysis, the more precise the conclusions drawn.

The research material recorded for this study consists of 300 tweets found on 18 profiles, whose authors are 48 users.[21] Among them are public and private individuals, governmental and non-governmental institutions, members of the media, both personal and institutional, commercial enterprises and representatives of non-commercial initiatives, promoting, for ex-

---

[20] I return to this in later portions of the study.
[21] The study also includes some exceptionally chosen examples.

ample, a style of life. The only source of information on each user was the user's profile page. Some of them were marked to indicate their identity had been verified – mainly in the case of profiles for public persons. The recorded material was gathered from April to September of 2012, during which the 10 most recent, sequential tweets by a given author, along with all the tweets by other authors related to it, were recorded, and so the time span of the entries depends on the activity of the individual users, and in some cases (less active users, breaks in activity) spans back as far as July 2011.

Is a microblog a blog?

The fundamental question that arises during the genealogical analysis of tweets is: is a microblog a variant of the genre "blog" or is it also a separate genre? M. Kawka calls the microblog a variety of blog (of the diary, political/journalistic sort), but places it in the same category as audioblogs, videoblogs, and moblogs (blogs written via a mobile phone) (2010: 65), which could mean that the difference between a blog and a microblog is purely a technical one, and in fact the microblog is technologically the closest to the blog of all the above mentioned types. What is more, both blogs and microblogs can contain additional graphical and audio elements, whereas tweets can only contain links to multimedia files.

The subject of links raised above requires historical examination of the interdependencies between blogs and microblogs. At the time of their origin blogs were lists of hyperlinks to other websites (Gumkowska 2009: 233). Twitter, in the opinion of S. Rosenberg, an expert on this issue, took over this area of blog functionality (Wilkowski 2009). Tweets are indeed to a large degree simply links, while they differ from the early blogs in that they also contain commentary, for example:

> @grzywaczewski: *Historia jednej z najsłynniejszych fotografii stanu wojennego [History of one of the most famous photographs of Martial Law [in 1981 in Poland – trans.]]:* http://www.polskieradio.pl/101/1564/video/489031 ...

> @rozathun: *Pieniadze Nagrody ktorą w Asconie otrzymal #DonaldTusk poszly w calosci do polskich organizacji charytatywnych [Money from the Prize that #DonaldTusk received in Ascona went entirely to Polish charities]* http://m.onet.pl/kraj/5210212,detal.html ...

> @android_polska: *Podcast http://Android.com.pl #27 [14.08.12]* http://android.com.pl/podcast/4795-podcast-androidcompl-27-140812.html ...

Such a characterization does not, however, convey the idea of the microblog, since many tweets do not contain any links at all, for example:

@bromancestory: *HEJ BYSTRA WOODA BYSTRA WODZICKA, PYTAŁO DZIEWCE O JANICKA XD [YO, FAST CARS, FAST MONEY, ALL DA LADIES WANT MY HONEY XD]*

@Ostojanews: *Zapraszamy na środowe nabożeństwo – temat: „Jak usługiwać mocą chrztu w Duchu Świętym?". [Come to our Wednesday church service – this week's topic: "How to use the power of baptism in the Holy Ghost?"]*

Before beginning to define the unique elements of tweets, it is worthwhile to indicate the traits held in common by blogs[22] and microblogs. Among them are:
- a diary-like character,
- the previously-mentioned multimediality,
- the domination of use function over aesthetics,
- the ability to carry out an analysis of similar types (for example, one can discern: practical advice; information and promotions; editorials; half-public, half-private; personal diaries),
- a hierarchy of presentation beginning from the newest entries,
- a framework imposed by the interface,
- a subject category aiming towards self-presentation.

The fundamental differences, however, can be described in terms of two aspects: structural and pragmatic. In both of these aspects the difference is tied to the length of the text. The limitation of tweets to 140 characters forces adaptation to formal techniques allowing for the condensation of the content, something which also influences their stylistic aspects. In turn, from the point of view of functionality, the short form has as its task to make the communication near-instantaneous; it is meant to occur in real-time; therefore, the discursive power of tweets can differ significantly from that of blogs. The brevity of tweets also has an immediate impact on their mass reception. As confirmation of this hypothesis, consider the previously-mentioned citations speaking of Twitter's influence on the public life of the societies in which it operates.

Despite their numerous and important similarities, the differences outlined above between Twitter updates and blog entries do not allow the unqualified recognition of the tweet as a variety of blog. The seemingly only difference – regarding the length – incites a process in which the microblog recedes from the peripheries of the blog's generic field, since

---

[22] I refer here to the article by A. Gumkowska (2009).

its consequences can be seen in all the other aspects of the description of genre. A. Wilkoń has pointed out the interdependency of the length of texts and the style, pragmatic usefulness (which in tweets is tied with the recognizability function) and their expressive function, building a definition of the genre of text (2002: 199). In this he made it clear that it is not a matter of the literal length of the text in terms of the number of words. One can then conclude that if the interdependencies described arise when the span of the text is limited only compared to other genres (for example, short story – novel), then the physical limitation, not even in words, but in characters, is a very strong "genre-forming factor."

What is the difference between 140 characters and 160 characters? (tweets and text messages)

If we consider the limitation to the length of tweets as one of their most essential generic traits, then the question automatically arises of their similarity to text messages, whose length is limited to 160 characters. A genealogical analysis of text messages has been conducted by E. Wolańska (2002) and M. Krzempek (2006), and the generic indicators of text messages mentioned in these works were used as a point of reference for the description of tweets.

On the structural level, both types of texts are strictly tied to length. In connection with this, they are characterized by a condensation of contents and brevity on all levels – from notation to phrasal syntax and the construction of the message as a whole. The similarities are not, however, exact.[23] First, the length limit in the case of text messages has less significance, since the programs used to write text messages allow one to write longer texts, separating them only on the technical level into fragments 160 characters in length. The consequences for the communication are minor; the sender only has to bear proportionally increased costs. On Twitter messages clearly spread out over more than one tweet occur rarely. There are, it is true, markers, for example "1/2" at the end of the beginning tweet and "2/2" at the beginning of the next, but despite these the sender constructing his message in this way risks their separation by various reply-tweets, and also that his message will begin to function, for example

---

[23] The analysis of tweets carried out for the purposes of this study did not allow for an unambiguous indication of the differences in the manner of content condensation. This issue will be the subject of further research by myself.

as a citation, only in its fragments. In addition, the later-created fragment will appear higher in the tweet hierarchy, for example:

Fig. 3. Example of a communication spread out over two tweets

In the case of text messages, such disruptions in communication have little chance of occurring.

In stylistic and cognitive terms these two kinds of communication do not differ by much. The greatest divergence in the traits of tweets and text messages can be seen, as in the relation of tweets to blogs, in the pragmatic aspect. First, the category of receiver differs – text messages are for the most part communications directed at an individual and concrete recipient. Mass communications via text message are most often institutionalized. The idea behind Twitter, however, is that of "one-to-all" communication, even if the tweets have the character of a dialogue between two users, which is indicated by joining the tweets into a "conversation" and indicating the addressee beginning with the @ character, for example:

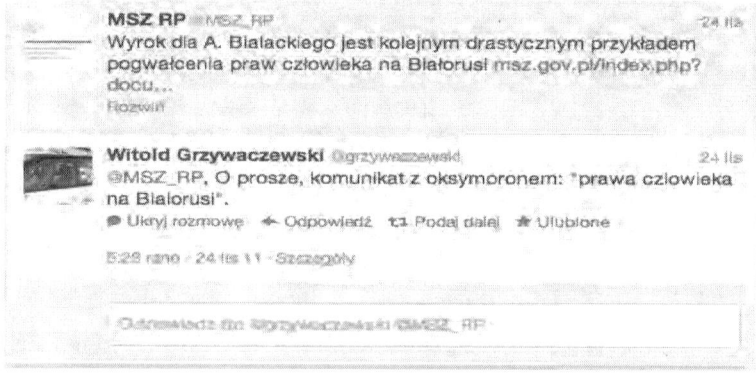

Fig. 4. Twitter: Example conversation

This communication then takes place on two levels: the micro – between specific users – and the macro – in view of all the users of the service. During this, with regards to the fact that in addition to the mass nature of its recipients another constitutive trait of Twitter is the lack of required reciprocity (the non-reciprocity of communication), one can establish that not infrequently the mass communication scale is very important for Twitter's users. It is worthwhile mentioning here that almost the complete democratization of communication is arising in this way. "Almost", since users can hide their profiles from unwanted observers; however, such behavior is not in line with the main idea of the service.

From the mass nature of the recipients come the further traits distinguishing tweets from text messages. The latter above all serve a "practical-life and phatic" function (Krzempek 2006: 367). Tweets usually are not used for practical purposes, and their dominant function could be seen to be expressive, cognitive and phatic. Here again the mass nature of communication via tweets influences the specific understanding of the goal, which is to make and maintain contact, since in a situation where the immediate recipient is not indicated, tweets can be seen as a cry into the void, in hopes of making contact with "anyone at all", for example:

> @_catheeee: *wszyscy już śpią? [everyone asleep already?]*
> and the subsequent responses:
> @jackmalecki: *@_catheeee nie [no] ;-)*
> @iKvS: *@_catheeee nieee! Panda Smietanka nie spi! [noooo! Panda Cream is not asleep!] Xd.*
> @Kasia_Jot: *@_catheeee nie.* [no]
> @pryses: *@_catheeee bicz pliz, nie ja [bitch please I aint sleepin] ;)*

The unspecified nature of the addressee is tied to the fact that it is hard to indicate the common life wisdom of communication partners. The sender decides to create tweets concerning only a narrow, often professional topic, or with strong stylistic markings, limiting in this way the circle of potential recipients, for example:

> @android_polska: *Doom 3 na Androida? Rozmowa z deweloperem portującym grę [exclusive!] [Doom 3 for Android? Conversation with developer porting the game] http://android.com.pl/artykuly/artykuy/4801-doom-3-na-androida-rozmowa-z-deweloperem-portujcym-gr.html ...*

> @bromancestory: *nie no. dobry trend [well no. thats a good trend] XD 1D xD*

> @EndiPL: *@_catheeee jak ja uwielbiam takie gimbusowe określenia [oh how I love these kinds of junior-high expressions] -.-'*

Text messages that operate as mass communications have a neutral, generalized character due to their institutional senders.

The pragmatic traits of tweets also result in a specific etiquette. Insofar as greeting and parting formulas and terms of address often appear in text messages, despite their limited length, due to the simultaneous nature of communication via tweet (and again: their mass nature), such niceties are very rare. If they do occur, this is usually at the beginning of one's activity on Twitter or after a break in this activity (cp. the previously-cited article on the entry by Mariusz Błaszczak). The function of terms of address, however, is taken over in a large part by the above-mentioned signals for contacting a user or referencing his entry, that is, the name of the user. In their context, these terms of address seem "uneconomical", but they surely bear witness to a respect to the receiver and a transfer of the center of communication difficulty to the scale of the microcontact, eg:

> @psington: @rozathun Pani Rozo, bardzo ciekawa rozmowa o jezykach obcych w Trojce – dziekuje [Ms. Roza, that was a very interesting discussion of foreign languages today on Radio 3 – thanks] :)

User names cannot, however, be seen as equivalent to terms of address. This is confirmed by the above example (the seeming doubling of address), and also the situation in which the name of the user serves the function not only of identifying the recipient, but also a vocative function (signalized with punctuation marks), whose fulfillment is not systematically predetermined, for example:

> @rozathun: @DziadekWaldemar ?!? Czemu tak mowisz? Czy slyszales/czytales przemowienie PDT kiedy odbieral nagrode Karola w Akwizgranie? Br polecam! [Why do you say that? Have you heard/read PDT's [Premier Donald Tusk's] speech when he accepted the Charlemagne Prize in Aachen? Highly recommended!]

Text messages and tweets are made similar by traits resulting from limiting their lengths to a concrete number of characters. Their differences in pragmatic terms are, however, important enough that in placing these two types of communication together, one can only speak of a similarity (and not of a kinship) of genres represented by the short forms, which are secondary genres next to the equivalent longer forms – letters and blogs – that have undergone transformation due to the technical demands of the medium by whose means they are transmitted.

What's all the tweeting about?
(Tweets in the context of press genres)

The cognitive function, one of the dominate ones, that tweets serve, allows them to be observed through the prism of their "elder relatives" – the factual journalism genres characterized by their short form. These are the news brief, the classified advertisement, and the teaser. For the purposes of the present work I will treat these generic indicators in fairly general terms; I am however well aware that these are forms with their own rich identities (cp. Wojtak 2004; Chomik 2008; Wiśniewska 1998).

One can consider the chief generic traits of the news brief to be the ability to answer the questions: Who? What? Where? in regards to the given fact (*wzmianka* [news brief], *Słownik terminologii medialnej* [Dictionary of Media Terminology]). In the gathered material, one can find tweets on various topics that are indeed similar to news briefs for example:

> @Radio_TOK_FM: *Chaos w Warszawie: woda wdarła się na budowę stacji II linii metra* [Chaos in Warsaw: water has flooded the building site of a station for the second subway line] http://dlvr.it/20RGYb

> @AdamWajrak: *Odszedł Wiktor Wołkow, który fotografią malował Podlasie* [Wiktor Wołkow, who painted Podlasie in photographs, has died] http://wyborcza.pl/1,96585,5641818,Wiktor_Wolkow___Wiegolud_z_amparatami.html ...

> @android_polska: *Czarny Galaxy S III pojawił się na stronie amerykańskiego T-Mobile* [Black Galaxy S III appears on the US T-Mobile homepage] http://android.com.pl/news/sprzet/4812-czarny-galaxy-s-iii-pojawi-si-na-stronie-amerykaskiego-t-mobile.html ...

Seeing as how links appear in the majority of tweets associated with the news brief, we could skip this step of the comparison and go right to the convention of the teaser as performed in tweets. Yet indicating the traits that link a large group of tweets with the news brief has as its goal shedding light on two phenomena. First, the teaser is a secondary genre, in relation to the news brief among others, which makes it a "genealogical oddity" (Wojtak 2004: 118). A tweet built on the convention of the teaser, enacting in part the generic model of the news brief, is thus secondary by several degrees. Second, one can distinguish two kinds (at least) of tweets referring back to other texts (here texts are understood very broadly, as multimedia communications found on the Internet). Next to the already mentioned tweets-news briefs, one can distinguish a group of tweets-teasers, which are characterized by a clearly persuasive character, for example:

> @grzywaczewski: *Mocny tekst: http://www.tomaszgabis.pl/?p=631 Az sobie wydrukowalem ;) [Powerful text:* http://www.tomaszgabis.pl/?p=631 *I even printed it out ;)]*

> @MarekKaminski: *Foto i video relacja cz 1 z Madagaskaru na profilu na Facebooku:) Zapraszam! [Photo and video report part 1 from Madagascar on my Facebook profile. Check it out!]* https://www.facebook.com/Marek.Kaminski.polarnik ...

> @nowymbank: *Słyszeliście zapowiedzi, że w weekend będzie gorąco? To dlatego, że w Katowicach trwa OFF Festiwal. Zapraszamy :-) [You heard the news that this weekend is going to be off the hook? That's because the OFF festival is going down in Katowice. Come check it out :-)]* http://fb.me/1RoKKBkqr

M. Wojtak distinguishes a frequently appearing type of adaptation of the teaser's generic model based on the "printing of a news fragment and referring to the whole published within the issue" (2004: 114). Twitter users have adopted this kind of adaptive model from the teaser, bringing it to the creation of tweets which contain a fragment of the target text that fits in 140 characters. These are references to texts found on another social network – Facebook. The unusualness of this kind of communication results from the fact that the text can break off at any given point without affecting its informative value, for example:

> @nowymbank: Nie oglądałeś spotkania z Brettem Kingiem na żywo? Możesz nadrobić zaległości – zapraszamy do obejrzenia filmów z... [Didn't watch the meeting with Brett King live? You can catch up – come watch the films from...] http://fb.me/1jyEXre1Z

> @mwojciechowska: Kochani! Właśnie wylądowałam w USA i od jutra przez kilka kolejnych dni jestem w Centrali National Geographic w... [Dear friends! I just landed in the US and for the next few days starting from tomorrow I will be at the National Geographic Headquarters in ...] http://fb.me/1IMNKR7s5

> @OnetWiadomosci: PILNE: CBA skierowało do Prokuratury Generalnej zawiadomienie o podejrzeniu popełnienia przestępstwa w jednej z... [BREAKING: the Central Anticorruption Office has passed on to the Prosecutor General information about suspected criminal activity in one of ...] http://fb.me/20AkoaJHm

The above examples are evidence of the way in which the transfer of one kind of text to another medium (press – Internet) can influence every aspect of the description of genre:

- structural – enclosed within the imposed form of 140 characters,
- cognitive – decrease in the importance of the completeness of communication,
- stylistic – when communication can be broken off without damage to its communication value (one need only click the link), the short form of the teaser, which determines its style, paradoxically ceases to be a requirement; however, its persuasive qualities (in the press achieved by means of appropriately chosen stylistic methods) are replaced by the effect of *suspense* that is achieved by this very informational incompleteness of the communication,
- pragmatic – thanks to the fact that on the Internet the user can navigate to texts across the web, going from reading an announcement to reading the text to which it refers is significantly easier and quicker, requiring a smaller set of actions. The teaser is simultaneously the "route" – the link.

The contents of tweets can also be identical to the contents of a classified ad, for example:

> @Ostojanews: *Nabożeństwo „środowe" odbędzie się we wtorek (6.IX) – godz. 18:30!Gościć będziemy pastora Kamila Hałambca oraz min. dr. Francois Carr'a...* ["Wednesday" church services will be held on Tuesday (6.IX) – at 6:30 PM! Our guests will be Pastor Kamil Hałambiec and Minister Dr. Francois Carr...]

> @praca_medycyna: *Zatrudnimy lekarzy specjalistów ZOZ – Głogów* [Now hiring specialist doctors at the area health service administration – Głogów] http://www.pracamedycyna.pl/zatrudnimy-lekarzy-specjalistow-zoz-glogow/ ...

In the case of this genre, filling the tweet with the contents of a classified ad (in informative, stylistic, structural terms) again results in changes mainly in the pragmatic aspect. Firstly, the availability of small classified ads increases; secondly, again, despite appearances, their contents can be richer thanks to the links placed alongside them.

Already even this abbreviated (in comparison to the expansive issues tied to the generic indicators of teasers, news briefs and classified ads) comparative characterization of tweets allows one to state that the placement on Twitter of texts fulfilling the conventions of the above-mentioned genres is not only an automatic transfer of well-worn forms to a new environment, but in fact this transfer provokes deep changes in the field of the traditional genres.

Katarzyna Sitkowska

Is the tweet a genre?
(Summary)

The presented analysis does not exhaust the subject of the genealogical characterization of communications found on Twitter. Its development depends on further research on many of its aspects: linguistic, semantic, and a deepened analysis of the pragmatic. Nevertheless the comparative method adopted in this study allows one to mark out the trails which might lead to a definition of the generic indicators of the tweet. In addition, it has shown that, under the influence of the Internet as a new sphere of linguistic intercourse, traditional genres are subject to profound transformations. That is why the work has made use several times of a family metaphor in which certain traits are inherited in a straight line, others appear in later generations or in side branches of the family, and still other appear as a result of kinship – as one can describe the relation between tweets and text messages. On the basis of the observations presented above one can recognize the inherent traits of tweets to be:

– "unfolding" brevity – resulting from the formal boundaries on the one hand, but on the other from the placement of links for the nearly limitless expansion of their possibilities in the realm of fulfilling informative functions;

– multimediality – tweets are characterized by a curious combination of linguistic elements with other (visual, audio) elements – these elements are not given simultaneously, but are available through words, and thanks to verbal communications the user makes the decision to continue on to other elements. (In the treatment of language as a medium, here one should mention that it is not uncommon to find tweets created in various languages within the context of one profile);

– micro- and macrosituatedness of the communications, with a marked domination of macrocommunications;

– dialogic potential;

– characteristic sender-receiver relationship

– broadly conceived intertextuality, one the one hand tied to hypertextuality, on the other enacted as citing tweets from other profiles

M. Wojtak identifies mutual structural traits in genres that develop a canonical version of a model, a common communicative message, yet recognize as a bond alternative variants to the generic model (2010: 14). Tweets seem to contain traits in common with both of these fields – they have a form narrowly defined by the interface, within which the users create a wide variety of texts, but their diversity has its center within the completed communicative goals. These also immediately result from Twitter's character – the influence of the service, in whose context even the most banal tweet takes on the potential of the whole. Thus despite the great diversity of tweets, concentrating mainly on the structural and pragmatic aspect of the model allows one to sketch out their generic fields. Further research will supplement and verify it.

Translated by Travis Currit

Bibliography

Bachtin Michaił 1986, *Estetyka twórczości słownej [Aesthetics of verbal creation]*, trans. D. Ulicka, Warsaw: Państwowy Instytut Wydawniczy.

Balbus Stanisław 2000, *Zagłada gatunków [The Extinction of genres]*, [in:] *Genologia dzisiaj [Genealogy today]*, eds. W. Bolecki, I. Opacki, Warsaw: Instytut Badań Literackich.

Balcerzan Edward 2000, *W stronę genologii multimedialnej [Towards a multimedia genealogy]*, [in:] *Genologia dzisiaj [Genealogy Today]*, eds. W. Bolecki, I. Opacki, Warsaw: Instytut Badań Literackich.

Bartoszyński Kazimierz 2000, *Wobec genologii [On genealogy]*, [in:] *Genologia dzisiaj [Geneaology today]*, eds. W. Bolecki, I. Opacki, Warsaw: Instytut Badań Literackich.

Chomik Dominik 2008, *Kilka uwag na temat perswazyjności ogłoszeń drobnych [A few remarks about the persuasiveness of small classified ads]*, [in]: *Język w marketingu [Language in Marketing]*, ed. K. Michalewski, Lodz: Wydawnictwo Uniwersytetu Łódzkiego.

Dobrzyńska Teresa 1992, *Gatunki pierwotne i wtórne (czytając Bachtina) [Primary and secondary genres (reading Bakhtin)]*, [in:] *Typy tekstów [Types of texts]*, ed. T. Dobrzyńska, Warsaw: Instytut Badań Literackich.

Grzenia Jan 2006, *Komunikacja językowa w Internecie [Linguistic communication on the Internet]*, Warsaw: PWN.

Gumkowska Anna 2009, *Blogi wobec tradycji diarystycznej. Nowe gatunki w nowych mediach [Blogs and the diaristic tradition. New genres in new media]*, [in:] *Tekst (w) sieci [Web texts / texts on the web]*, vol. 1. *Tekst, język, gatunki [Text, language, genres]*, ed. D. Ulicka, Warsaw: Wydawnictwa Akademickie i Profesjonalne.

Kawka Maciej 2010, *Blog jako gatunek dziennikarski – ewolucja i transgresja [Blogs as a journalistic genre – evolution and transgression]*, [in:] *Internetowe gatunki dziennikarskie [Internet journalistic genres]*, eds. K. Wolny-Zmorzyński, W. Furman, Warsaw: Wydawnictwa Akademickie i Profesjonalne.

Krzempek Monika 2006, "SMS jako genologiczne 'signum temporis'" [Text messages as genealogical 'signum temporis'], *Stylistyka* XV.

Słownik terminologii medialnej [Media terminology dictionary] 2006, ed. W. Pisarek, Cracow: Universitas.

Wilk Eugeniusz 2000, *Nawigacje słowa. Strategie werbalne w przekazach audiowizualnych [Word navigations. Verbal strategies in audiovisual messages]*, Cracow: Rabid.

Wilkoń Aleksander (2002), *Spójność i struktura tekstu [Text structure and cohesion]*, Cracow: Universitas.

Wilkowski Marcin 2009, *Blogi i mikroblogi: ewolucja interfejsu a nie gatunków treści [Blogs and microblogs: the evolution of the interface and not content genres]*, http://historiaimedia.org/2009/09/22/blogi-i-mikroblogi-ewolucja-interfejsu-a-nie-gatunkow-tresci/, accessed: 2012.11.07.

Wiśniewska Agnieszka 1998, „Genologiczna charakterystyka ogłoszenia prasowego" *[Genealogical characterization of newspaper classifieds]*, Rozprawy Komisji Językowej Wrocławskiego Towarzystwa Naukowego.

Witosz Bożena 2001, „Gatunek – sporny (?) problem współczesnej refleksji tekstologicznej" *[Genre – a controversial (?) problem in contemporary textological thought]*, Teksty Drugie, No. 5.

Wojtak Maria 2010, *Analiza gatunków prasowych [Analysis of journalistic genres]*, Lublin: Wydawnictwo Uniwersytetu Marii Curie-Skłodowskiej.

Wojtak Maria 2004, *Gatunki prasowe [Journalistic genres]*, Lublin: Wydawnictwo Uniwersytetu Marii Curie-Skłodowskiej.

Wolańska Ewa 2002, „Właściwości komunikacyjne, genologiczne i językowe krótkiej wiadomości tekstowej (SMS).Wybrane zagadnienia" *[Communicative, genealogical and linguistic characteristics of short text messages (SMS)]*, Poradnik Językowy, z. 10.

Woźniak Wiesława 2010, *Gatunek w sieci [Genre on the web]*, [in:] *Internetowe gatunki dziennikarskie [Internet journalistic genres]*, eds. K. Wolny-Zmorzyński, W. Furman, Warsaw: Wydawnictwa Akademickie i Profesjonalne.

Żydek-Bednarczuk Urszula 2003, *Tekst w Internecie i jego wyznaczniki [Text on the internet and its characteristic traits]*, http://uranos.cto.us.edu.pl/~dialog/archiwum/zydek-bednarczuk.pdf, accessed: 12.11.2012.

Żydek-Bednarczuk Urszula 2004, *Od rozmowy do talk show. Uwagi o telewizyjnych gatunkach mowy [From conversation to talk show. Remarks on television speech genres]*, [in:] *Gatunki mowy i ich ewolucja [Speech genres and their evolution]*. Vol. 2 *Gatunek a tekst [Genre and Text]*, ed. D. Ostaszewska, Katowice: Wydawnictwo Uniwersytetu Śląskiego.

Webpages:

http://pl.wikipedia.org/wiki/Mikroblog Accessed: 23.08.2012.

https://twitter.com/ Accessed: 23.08.2012.

https://twitter.com/about Accessed: 23.08.2012.

https://twitter.com/#!/welcome/recommendations Accessed: 23.08.2012.

http://www.rp.pl/artykul/10,921585-Facebook-i-Twitter-w-pierwszej-dziesiatce.html Accessed: 24.08.2012.

http://wyborcza.pl/1,75478,12296224,Wpis_Mariusza_Blaszczaka_sprzed_dwoch_lat_weekendowym.html Accessed: 24.08.2012.

http://polska.newsweek.pl/sikorski-zhanbil-pamiec-powstania-radni-pis-przed-1-sierpnia,80291,1,1.html Accessed: 24.08.2012.

http://wyborcza.biz/biznes/1,100896,11447920,Wyslij_Skittles_policji__ktora_kryje_zabojce.html Accessed: 24.08.2012.

http://spoleczenstwo.newsweek.pl/miedzy-slowami--chamstwo-iii-rp,94030,1,1.html Accessed: 24.08.2012.

http://www.bbc.co.uk/news/uk-england-london-18582171 Accessed: 24.08.2012.

http://www.orianmarx.com/2012/07/12/what-twitter-wants/ Accessed: 24.08.2012.

Irena Chawrilska*
University of Gdansk

HOW DOES A HYBRID WORK OF ART EXIST?

Abstract
The aim of this article is to analyze the relation between hybrid works of art in the background of philosophical texts by Luigi Pareyson, Jurij Łotman, Wolfgang Welsch. The questions which are taken into consist of – What is the definition of a hybrid work of art? What is the impact of contemporary culture on the way of being a hybrid work of art? Do the hybrid works of art reflect the experience of contemporary reality? My considerations are based on concrete poetry, book works, book objects and liberature.

Key words: hybrid work of art, theory of formativity, liberature, concrete poetry, artistic book, contemporary culture

Deconstruction has led to the dethronement of sound in favor of writing and it is said that *pictorial turn* has happened in culture. W.J.T. Mitchell writes about it in his famous book *Picture Theory*. In parallel, the *linguistic turn*, related to the question of language as a communication tool – which apart from links with the *linguistic turn* in philosophy, is linked with influences coming from structuralism and poststructuralism – is being discussed in art[1].

The main issue of this article is the mode of existence of the hybrid work of art. Reflection on this problem will be possible if we will define what kind of works of art will be discussed in this paper.

---

* Philology Department, University of Gdansk, ul. Wita Stwosza 55, 80-952 Gdansk, e:mail: i.chawrilska@gmail.com

[1] "(...) subsumption of linguistic processes into art. Since Marcel Duchamp's readymades", D. Beech, *Turning the Whole Thing Around: Text Art Today*, in: *Art and Text*, ed. D. Beech, Ch. Harrison, W. Hill, Black Dog Publishing, London 2009, p. 26. I have omitted the problem of interest in language which is also significant in the works of the First Great Avant-garde, and has a different character.

I will focus on the attempt to describe the works in which the integration of visual and verbal signs occurred (on selected examples), which in effect changes the perception of such works. Language in this type of work (located on the border between literature and visual arts), and in fact the writing with its visual aspects, is the material that serves as the foundation of the process of forming an artwork. At the core of hybrid works lies the ontological heterogeneity, because the carrier of sense is not homogeneous in their case. An important role is played by the materiality of the work, which also fulfills the semantic role. From the perspective of literary studies and the "baggage" of Ingarden's category, the situation is worrying. The elements of language have been appearing in art for a long time. Suffice it to recall that cubist experiments with language elements in the early twentieth century. It is worth asking whether poetry, an artistic book, or a variety of projects relating to placing text in a public space should be considered as literature or art? Is the phenomenon of hybridity only the integration of different carriers of sense? Certainly this phenomenon is a process deeply rooted in culture. To this end, it is worth to look at how the ancients defined and understood the category of "hybrid".

Ancient appeal

The term "hybrid" is associated with variability, lack of consistency, strangeness, heterogeneity, and even anomalies. Hybridity in ancient times also does not necessarily mean a monster, but heterogeneity. They are known in many ancient cultures – even the Sumerian, Egyptian, and Greek. Hybrids are creatures of Chaos, Pre-ocean, not fully formed before the emergence of the world, which can express unity before individualization of beings. They are composed of pre-material, and exist as potential beings. Hybrids can also be interpreted as a visual way to present the relation of all the spheres of the universe: earth and sky-.of the universe. Animal hybrids are cosmic symbols, but also those of characteristic human concern in the *anthropos* sphere.

The ancient philosophers dealt with hybrids in the biological sense. Empedocles in his work *On Nature* describes the oxen with human heads. However, Aristotle in *Physics* writes: "[...] whereas those which grew otherwise perished and continue to perish, as Empedocles says his 'man-faced ox-progeny' did" (Aristotle 1994c: 276) Aristotelians did not accept the hybrid as the composition of two different natures. It seems that, for Aristotle, the formation of such beings actually does not take effect, because they do not arise in a purposeful way. Accordingly the purposefulness of nature is to arise only if relevant and compatible with nature. It is worth noting that in the works of Aristotle, there is no concept of "hybrid". In *On the Generation of Animals* the philosopher deals with the problem of anomalies and monsters. A monster arises: "If the movements imparted by the semen are resolved and the material contributed by the mother is not controlled by them, at last there remains the most general substratum, that is to say the animal. Then people say that the child has the head of a ram or a bull [...]" (Aristotle 1994a: 311). Similar anomalies occur in animals. The representative of one species can have, for example, the head of another animal. According to Stagirite monsters are just like creatures for which they are considered. Therefore, the philosopher denies hybrids the right to exist. Moreover Aristotle believes that a being who is born must be the same as a being, from which the seed came. Of the seed of the horse can be born only a horse, of human only a man, and in another case it cannot be called the offspring of a being who is born: "For these reasons we do not regard as our offspring that which is produced either from anything else in us except the semen, or from the semen when it is corrupted or fails to achieve perfection" (Aristotle 1927: 878a) Aristotle is also interested in the hybrid political system, as he writes in *Policy*.

It can be considered that *On Poetics* refers to the literary hybrids, when Aristotle compares the Epic with the Tragedy. The Epic seems to be a kind of a hybrid consisting of the tragic and comic actions:

> That there is less unity in the imitation if the epic poets, as is proved by the fact that any one work of theirs supplies matter for several tragedies; the result being that, if they take what is really a single story, it seems curt when briefly told, and thin and waterish when on the scale of length usual with their verse. In saying that there is less unity in an epic, I mean an epic made up of a plurality of actions [...] (Aristotle 1994b: 699).

The plurality of actions, in this context, is the work with many plots. *The Iliad* and *The Odyssey* consist of various elements, which are "each one of them in itself of some magnitude" (Aristotle 1994b: 699). These considerations Stagirite included in the *On Poetic* in which he compares the Epic and the Tragedy. Aristotle demonstrates the superiority of the Tragedy over The Epic, even though it is a kind of epic art designed for a more educated audience. Although the Tragedy requires the presentation on the stage, and therefore the use of different materials, which is acting, according to Aristotle, yet that does not mean that it is the lower form of art. The tragedy just like The Epic achieves its aim; already in the process of reading we can experience purification. Perhaps Stagirite estimated the Tragedy higher than the Epic because of its hybridity. He writes that tragedy: "[...] Tragedy has everything that the Epic has (even the epic metre being admissible), together with a not inconsiderable addition in the shape of the music (a very real factor in the pleasure of the drama) and the Spectacle. That its reality of presentation is felt in the play as read, as well as in the play as acted" (Aristotle 1994b: 698–699).

In ancient thought we are dealing with phenomena of hybridity which is variously understood. Certainly the ancient philosophers were mostly focused on the hybrid in the biological sense, but they were familiar with thinking about art in such a way that shows these fragments from *On Poetic* by Aristotle. Finally *ut pictura poesis* formula also comes from ancient times and shows the affinity of painting and poetry, which is also a form of hybrid. It is worth reflecting on how contemporary culture understands and defines hybrid.

Hybrid as a form of culture

However trivial it may sound, this argument must begin with the following observation: as users of contemporary culture, we operate in a multicultural reality or even transcultural – in a world of globalization, digitization, virtuality, new media. Various researchers are trying to describe the processes occurring in the culture, creating for this purpose a variety of categories and theories which aim is to adequately describe the processes taking place in the area of culture. An example in this context can be the theory of semiosphere by Jurij Łotman. He defines semiosphere as "a continuum of a specific organization" (trans. I. Ch.) (Łotman 1984: 7). This organization is primarily that the semiosphere is separated from non-semiotic reality. The limit is "a kind of filter, the device selectively permeable texts from other cultural areas and non-texts. [...] It has a function of a bottleneck through which messages have to squeeze from the outside to become a reality of semiosphere" (trans. I. Ch.) (Żyłko 1998: 15).

Inside the semiosphere there is no established order or rule:

> The hierarchy of languages and texts is constantly violated: they collide with each other, as if they were on the same level. Texts are immersed in inadequate languages, while codes which decode them may be absent at all. Imagine a room in the museum, where exhibits from various ages, subtitles in familiar and unfamil-

iar languages, decoding instruction, explanatory text for the exhibition composed by methodologists, tour route patterns and rules for visitors are placed in various showcases. If you locate here the visitors with their semiotic world, we get something that will resemble the image of semiosphere (trans. I. Ch.) (Łotman 1984: 12).

It should be noted that the semiosphere is characterized by heterogeneity. In the periphery the semiosphere is less organized. There are flexible structures there, so that within the semiosphere changes occur. Periphery is in fact the source of all dynamic processes within its borders (Żyłko 1998: 15). Besides, the semiosphere develops at different speeds at different levels. Changes occur more rapidly in the periphery than in the core area which is structured, marked by its own grammar and meta-description. It is impossible to talk about the synchronicity of processes' development that take place in the semiosphere (because different languages develop at different speed, natural languages evolve more slowly than other cultural phenomena) (Żyłko 1998: 16).

It is interesting that Łotman considers dialogue as a mode of semiosphere's existence. This dialogue includes a variety of elements: from the cerebral hemispheres of the individual to cross-cultural contacts. It follows that within the semiosphere it is possible to distinguish levels: from the semiosphere of individuals to the semiosphere of the world – "the global village, which is constantly expanding throughout the ages, has taken the comprehensive character, including signals of artificial satellites, and poems, and the cries of animals. The mutual relationship of all elements in the semiotic space is not a metaphor, but a reality" (trans. I. Ch.) (Łotman 1984: 16–17)

Another example is the theory of transversal reason invented by Wolfgang Welsch (Welsch 1998: 405–440). The feature of the reason is the ability to move from one rational configuration to another, demonstrating differences, disputing and innovating. It has nothing to do with substantial, principled, total interpretations of the reason which would even it out with intellect. The activity of transversal reason consists in crossing from one system to another, its synthesis remains partial. The holistic interpretation of any issues can never be talked about by transversal reason. It does not overcome pluralism, whereas it tries to justify it as a form of reason.

Welsch, just as Lotman in the case of the semiosphere, shows, how transfers between rationalities occur, reffering to ethics, economics and aesthetics, which, in his opinion, the distinction is necessary. Types of rationality are divided into sectors, although this distinction is sometimes confusing, because different autonomous rationalities are set free, and they can themselves determine its meaning and boundaries. How rationalities are linked with each other and how the transversal reason moves from one to the other? Welsch gives, in this context, an example from a field of art. It was like this that art was recognized as an autonomous area according to the motto *l'art pour l'art,* at other times its sense was constituted in crossing aesthetic barriers and passing on to life. Here we see the two concepts of aesthetic rationality, which areas vary widely, both cross each other and connect. Therefore, the sectors are not stand-alone beings and speaking with one type of rationality always refers to the second. Of course, there is the problem of individual rationality distinction. Between particular paradigms occur the various processes, such as the reinterpretation or rejection. The differences between the types of rationality, which are in sectors, define these sectors and thanks to this they distinguish them from others. It should be noted that particular rationalities are derived from a common cultural root, so rationalities refer to each other in various ways by negation and reinterpretation. Therefore we can talk about transculturalism in the sense: obliterating differences between our culture and foreign, constructing cultural networks, that extend beyond the boundaries of a culture, media networks that create the culture of technology and hybridity, which, according to Welsch, is a feature of contemporary culture. Its effect is transculturalism. I invoke here the theories of Lotman and Welsch to show how hybridity is written in contemporary culture and theories that attempt to describe it. Emmanuel Molinet shows how the category of "hybridity" is used in modern technology, politics which in effect is a change in perception of reality, or the formation of its various elements. In the contemporary world the concept of hybridity is rooted in science, where its meaning is limited to the composition of an object with a few items or materials. Molinet emphasizes that the current use of the term "hybridity" assumes human intervention, human activity, which is changing the nature of some things through different methods: cloning, molecular biology, genetic testing, and artificial intelligence.

In the art language category of "hybrid", "hybridity", "hybridization" is primarily associated with works, in which new technologies and new media are used: "Technologie numerique favorise d'une estetique de l'hybridation" (Molinet, http://leportique.revues.org/index851.html). It can be said that contemporary art, in which an important role play such forms as installation and performance, creates the hybrid model (*modele hybride, discipline hybride*). Besides, it is impossible to distinguish one model of hybridization and to describe what exactly the hybridization process is, because various processes can be referred to as this. First of all, it is unclear whether a hybrid as a form is, from an aesthetic point of view, even a work of art, an artistic phenomenon, or a cultural creation. Would you say that hybrids are created when there are new forms in art? Then it must be considered that the synthesis of romantic art, unexpected juxtaposition of various forms is also a hybrid. Similarly, it would be with a number of works which are referring simultaneously, for example, to surrealism and abstraction. The question is whether it can be considered a hybrid work of art from the past, whether the concept in language of art should remain reserved for recent works. It is worth noting that interdisciplinarity, and as probably Welsch would suggest, transdisciplinarity is associated with the emergence of new technologies, multimedia and virtual reality. In this case, hybrids could be considered as a form of cultural expression in the age of globalization, the form that expresses various interpretations and meanings, transcends genre boarders and combines a variety of art. Such an understanding of hybrid could be considered a form of culture, not only in the category of adequately describing contemporary art.

The hybrid from a literary point of view

If the process of hybridization is not only limited to technology, politics and science will not stop in interpreting this process as only related to the visual arts. As we consider it a form of culture, it can be interesting – in the context of this argument – to refer to it in literature. The most important are considered to be hybrids that are at the interface between literature and the visual arts, which include: concrete poetry, artistic books, liberature and literature related to new media. It seems that it is impossible to create a separate category of hybrid works that would not have anything to do with a sound and broadly understood spectacle, and would be only a group of works in which the integration of visual and verbal signs occurred, although it may certainly be possible to find examples of this kind even among concrete poetry.

Returning to an attempt to define the phenomenon of hybridity, this time from a literary perspective, simply speaking, researchers of works of this kind think that language in this type of work, and in fact the writing with its visual aspects, is the material that serves as the foundation of the process of forming an artwork. The meaning of the work is constituted by the recipient as much as on the basis of the semantics of the language and semiotics of matter, the shape and configuration of print, paper physicality, spatiality and architecture of the volume, the iconic potentiality of the page (Kalaga 2010: 75). Externality of the text is cancelled, all elements are equally important; they are integral aspects of the work. The works are hybrids at the core of which lies the ontological heterogeneity, because the carrier of sense in this type of works is also the physical shape and material basis. In the hybrid text there is a fusion of two ontological orders, that is the material sphere of the work and his intentionality in Ingarden's categories. The theory of Ingarden is recalled here because in his theory it is particularly evident as to how the role of matter is reduced to writing functions, which does not play any significant role. The sphere of literary material only allows, according to Ingarden, to reach its intentionality in the process of concretization. In the case of hybrid text, the materiality of the work does not depreciate its intentional layers. If we wish to use the terminology of Ingarden then the process of concretization also includes non-linguistic aspects. An important role is played by the physical space of the artwork, because the material itself also has semantic function.

There is formed a structure which can be described as literary space-time, which seems to be the reverse process to the theory originating from Lessing's *Laocoon*. According to Lessing, both painting and poetry are mimetic arts, however, they use different signs. The researcher believes that in the case of painting there are figures and colors in space, and in the case of poetry – articulated sounds in time. It is important that signs of painting are natural, whereas signs of poetry are free. Lessing also determines which objects can be represented by each art discipline, to make them compatible with the nature of the signs. The painter shows the objects existing side by side in space, poetry – objects consecutive in time. So painters focus on bodies and their parts, whereas poets concentrate on activities (Lessing 1962: 63–65). The radical separation of the two pieces, arising somehow form the cultural context and time in which Lessing lived, is negated in liberature, concrete poetry and artistic books.

These works are hybrids in which it is negated by the division of interior and exterior making it appear to be an organic whole – a form. This type of work in which significant aspects are cooperating semantics of language and material structure, I propose define, following Luigi Pareyson, as a form. The theory of formativity by Luigi Pareyson is interesting from the perspective of this article because the researcher considers a work of art as a form, in which there is no division between form and content. This does not mean that the content is not relevant for this type of artwork. Already the Russian formalists in the second decade of the twentieth century recognized literary work as a "contenting form" (Eichenbaum 1986: 174), and it would seem that the formalists should estimate positively only formal aspects of the work of art. They do not, however, renounce the other aspects. According to Pareyson the process of forming a work of art covers all its aspects, including the matter, which becomes significant. The content of the work of art (*il contenuo*) is "an artist all his life, his acting personality, but not only the forming energy, but also a method of forming, that is the style" (trans. I. Ch.) (Pareyson 2009: 19). If the content of work of art is identified with the style, there is no reason to carry on an argument about the primacy of from over content, and content over form, because the spiritual element of the work of art in this approach is the style. One cannot talk about the other expression, speaking, communicating the content but making. The matter of the work of art, for the researcher, can be only a physical matter, because "in the art forming means forming a matter" (trans. I. Ch.) (Pareyson 2009: 19), that is the work of art is a formed matter. The work of art is simultaneously the law and the result of the process of forming; it acts as a forming factor before it is completely formed. The recipient can see the artistic value of the work if he looks at it as an inseparable whole – both a forming and formative form, such as "the right of process which is the result" (trans. I. Ch.)(Pareyson 2009: 20).

Hybrid in terms of genology

It seems, however, that just being a complex of two or more types of materials is not enough to talk about the phenomenon of hybridity. But before I will try to clarify what specific form of existence this type of work of art consists of, let us look at genological distinctions, from which emerges a kind of ontology outline of a hybrid work of art.

In the literature, quite traditionally understood, or at least one that remains at the level of the text and is not a hybrid consisting of a variety of media and materials, it is said about genre syncretism or the so-called "kind syncretism"[2]. These types of terms should be used with caution, however, because it is often associated with combining together different literary forms primarily for romantic masterpieces (Grochowski 2000: 16). In a sense, Ryszard Nycz refers to this sphere of problems in his hugely popular work "Sylwy współczesne. Problem konstrukcji tekstu"

---

[2] Polish theory follows the tradition which distinguishes three main literary genres (the so-called "kinds"): poetry, prose and drama, other genres being subordinated to this division.

(Wrocław 1984). It should be noted, however, that "sylwy współczesne" are primarily of a historical category, which refers to a particular historical field of art. Hybrid is a typology which is deprived of specific references to the philosophical. Therefore "hybrid" is poorer in content than *sylwa*, but having a wider range (Grochowski 2000: 17). There are works in which heterogeneity is analyzed as a combination of literary elements and elements of other discourses, such as: scientific, journalistic, philosophical etc. within a literary text. It is also worth noting that the concept of genre syncretism or so called "kind syncretism" rather connects with some solid trans-generic fusions, such as ballad, poetic novel and romantic drama. The concept of hybridity, however, refers to the connections of a more ephemeral and unexpected nature.

The hybrid work of art is also something different form the so called "bordering genres". To talk about them, one should indicate a kind of cultural center with a clearly structured repertoire of genres in a particular historical situation, in relation to which the bordering genres could be distinguished. Besides, these bordering genres being situated in the periphery would have to refer to an invariant pattern, to be able to justify their position on this and not elsewhere of cultural phenomena. We are all aware that in today's culture, we see a strong tendency to go beyond the explicit genological allocations. We associate easily recognizable genres with popular culture and class B films as: romance, western and horror. In the case of "bowl of strategies" and *blurred genres*, as Clifford Geertz appropriately described it (Geertz, http://hypergeertz.jku.at/GeertzTexts/Blurred_Genres.htm), it does not come to the formation of new and constant "genological individuals". There are new and unique configurations. Therefore, I think that the term "hybrid" is much more appropriate than the syncretic genre or bordering genre. This concept is also less evaluative, it merely implies a distinction between more crystalized forms and ambivalent and indefinite forms.

In the case of hybrids which are at the interface between literature and the visual arts, it is still an issue of two type carriers of sense. Why, therefore, do I remain with the definition of a hybrid work of art and not, for example, *intermedia*?

The term *intermedia* Dick Higgins borrowed from the writings of Samuel Taylor Coleridge of 1812 and referred it to works "which fall conceptually between media that are already known" (Higgins 2001: 52). As intermedia Higgins defines works, in which the visual element is conceptually fused with words. This concept is not, however, the category having roots in the history of art and literature. It is purely typological, and, according to Higgins, does not evaluate this type of work in any way. In addition, Higgins points out that the category of intermedia sometimes facilitates the allocation of a work of uncertain origin. But it is not important for him, what is the formal status of a work, but rather the importance of a work for the recipient (Higgins 2001: 53) He even considers that the term "intermedia" is characterized by an inner contradiction. This concept allows:

> [...] for an ingress to a work which otherwise seems opaque and impenetrable, but once that ingress has been made it is no longer useful to harp upon the intermediality of a work. No reputable artist could be an intermedial artist for long--it would seem like an impediment, holding the artist back from fulfilling the needs of the work at hand, of creating horizons in the new era for the next generation of listeners and readers and beholders to match their own horizons too. What was helpful as a beginning would, if maintained, become an obsession which braked the flow into the work and its needs and potentials. (Higgins 2001: 53)

This kind of approach leads to a poor ontology of contemporary works of art. According to the typology of Jens Schröter intermedia which are the fusion of various media, are described as ontological intermediality (Ontomedialität)[3], which is associated with the materiality of different media. It should be noted that various components of the media in a single work normally are the result of intentional double coding strategy, which also leads to the fact that this type of hybrid should be interpreted not only in terms of aesthetic connectivity of arts. An important issue turns out the results of interaction effects of media which are independent to each other. Hence intermediality understood – as a future of the latest art – becomes one of the phenomena which enable the diagnosis of contemporary culture. According to Andrzej Hejmej, contemporary intermedia art is based on the effect of directness and immediacy, which reveals the contingency of being in the world (Hejmej 2010: 284). These works impose a multisensory form of communication, at the same time braking the "spectator theory" or neutrality of the recipient. It is worth noting that the intermedia works are the result of the modern experience of being in the situation of media and mediated. Also the current literature belongs to this kind of artistic practice. It is formed intermedia literature realizations which do not have any norm. In this approach, each intermedial text is, in the genological sense, a unique hybrid. And yet, in some way, works which are on

---

[3] Apart from the ontological intermediality, the researcher enumerates also the intermediality: synthetic, formal and transformational. The division is given for: A. Hejmej, *Intermedialność I literatura intermedialn*, in: *Kulturowe wizualizacje...* (Cultural visualisations...), p. 279–280.

the border between literature and visual arts are classified by certain genological categories. There are concrete poetry, liberature, artistic books, and different varieties of hypertext and cyberspace poetry.

One of the controversial and at the same time interesting genological decisions is a category of "liberature" by Zenon Fajfer in 1999 to define the literary work in which both the word and the spatial, material and graphic shape of works are equally important. Let us skip the Fajfer's programme statements, in which he wanted to make liberature a fourth literary genre. He ultimately retired from this idea[4]. It is worth nothing that the artist regards liberature as a total literature in which the author saw not only to the individual words, a represented world, the characters, but also the space in which these words are – "representing world" – a graphical representation of the text.

In a similar tone Wojciech Kalaga voices his view when he recognizes liberature as a trans-genre, which transgresses the boundaries of literary typologies (Kalaga 2010: 10). The researcher points out that the hybridity of liberature is by no means an invention of the contemporary avant-garde. Kalaga refers to the beginnings of visual poetry which go as far as the third century BC – to the works of Simias of Rhodes and Theocritus. Then Kalaga refers to the visual poetry of the twentieth century underlining the difference between it and traditional visual poetry by stating that in twentieth century poetic experiments: "It is not merely the matter of synchronizing the shape or contour of the poem with its content but of the exploration of the visual-semantic potentiality of the linguistic sign" (Kalaga 2010: 10). The matter of the text are equally important in the literary work of both the represented world and the representing world. The essence of the literature seems to be the totality of the work, which integrates semantic aspects of the text and its fabric into a semiotic unity (Kalaga 2010: 11).

And what is the difference between the artistic book and liberature? According to Z. Fajfer liberature is a spatial literature, but it is still the

---

[4] In 2010 in the text "Liberature – 496 Words of Conclusion" Fajfer expresses doubt about attempts to distinguish the fourth literary genre: "But I would be more cautious now. Perhaps I wouldn't pose liberature as some *fourth literary mode*, as I don't see much sense in such three-coloured divisions now. A genre? Even if I mention this, I remember a cautionary tale about the African elephant, resembling its Indian cousin, and geneticists' claim that its actual cousin is the mouse. Indeed, genetics sexes life up. So perhaps good old Croce was right when he questioned generic divisions? Perhaps there are only specific works that constitute universes in their own right? If we agree with that, I will happily abandon liberature" Z. Fajfer (2010:149).

literature. In the case of an artistic book text is subordinated to the book, in liberature it is the book that is subordinated to text (Fajfer 2010: 61). The artistic book as a book-object is a work closer to sculpture in which the text is but one of several, equally important components, sometimes it is absent in the work at all. Liberature but annexes into its territory the physical space of the book. Therefore, according to the researchers one can talk about liberature as a new literary genre and not a new form of art.

Is it possible when the same work once placed in the gallery and another time on a shelf in the library or the bookstore will be recognized by the recipient in the first case as the artistic book, and the second – as liberature?

It seems that Fajfer gives an affirmative answer to this question when he underlines the importance of the context in which the work is installed, and the function of the recipient. Perhaps putting *But Eyeing Like Ozone Whole* by Zenon Fajfer in the gallery space could be considered as the artistic book. According to the creator of this work, it should be regarded as a poetic text, which required another form of materialization and he found it through a bottle. Apart from the text printed on a transparent plastic, there are no other graphic or artistic elements in this work. This poem cannot be seen from the perspective of Duchamp's ready-mades, as Duchamp did works of art with everyday objects, while Fajfer annexed the glass bottle in the sphere of literature and made him a book instead of the traditional paper-made codex. As a further argument the artist gives the uniqueness of the artistic book. Fajfer's poem is a piece addressed to readers, available in bookshops, priced as an average book, having an ISBN and published in a relatively large print run. Reviews and notes on the book are addressed to the literary audience (Fajfer 2010: 138). Fajfer's argument, however, is based on a kind of external aspects of the work of art, so that we can classify the artist's poem as a literary work. If we saw the poem in the gallery space and knew nothing about its literary origin, we would have recognized that the work before us is a book-object, in which the text can also play an important role. In this context, there is also a problem of the "artist's book" – a notion invented by Leszek Brogowski. According to the researcher, the artistic book, which is published in several copies and is available for the few, due to the price, is a unique work and at the same time it excludes the majority of the population from the opportunities of watching it. Whereas the artist's book is a form of expression and social communication tool, as it is published in a large edition (Brogowski 2010: 123–137).

Irena Chawrilska

The mode of existence of a hybrid work of art

According to Wojciech Kalaga the hybrid work of art as a symbiosis of textual semiosis with the semiosis of the material vehicle is an artistic creation of a different ontological status than the artistic book, which is, according to the researcher, just a beautiful, material artifact (Kalaga 2010: 11). This vehicle of the hybrid may be constituted by an appropriately shaped volume, card, but also, as in the case of hypertext or so-called e-liberature, a computer interface. Liberary books direct our attention primarily to their physical "bookishness" and, like metafiction relates to the qualities of its plot and narration, the liberary book becomes a meta-book that comments upon its own bodily subjectivity. Kalaga uses the term, a "hybrid text". In my opinion the more appropriate term is a "hybrid work of art", because it does not evaluate, which of the substances is more important. This is particularly important when we take into consideration that contemporary works of art very often use not only semantic aspects of language and visuals, but they extend also to other types of materials. In this way artistic books can also be considered as hybrid works of art, which very often constitute meanings emerging from the interaction between semantics of the language and structure of the material. For example, artistic books which I name for Piotr Rypson "conceptual books", just like concrete poetry, do not involve the senses of the recipient (Rypson 2000: 7). They often provoke reflection on the value of the language. They are a kind of "puzzle" with elusive sense. There are also books which arouse the aesthetic experience in recipients. "Books-Stories" use the traditional narration, and in the case of their interpretation it is necessary to know the various elements of culture.

Whereas concrete poetry draws the recipient's attention to the language, to its apparent transparency, materiality and physical shape. The task of the recipient is made difficult; reading requires more concentration, because it is impossible to determine the meaning, which would be obligatory in a certain group of recipients or on some level, in the perspective of selected methodology. First of all, it depends on a recipient and what meaning will be given to the work. Each choice of the order and method of perceiving leads to the creation of a new aesthetic object. The recipient is not able to reach the *signifié*. This does not mean, however, that the content gives up the seat to form. The semiotic model which reduces a concrete poem to content and form, or *significant* and *signifié* is not suited in this type of poetry. Concrete poets do not aim to establish one artistic code, one perspective, which would integrate the variety of formal solutions. Artists very often use only letters, which, before it creates a word with the other characters, becomes independent and makes its own meaning, it becomes a material of the visual text. The symbolic signs become at that time the iconic sign, liberated from the language, its grammar and syntax, it becomes the object of the game between linearity and simultaneity. That is why the hybrid works of art should be regarded as polyphonic. We are dealing with polyphony semiotic: "Word-images are isomorphic – visual and literary, but both of these characters (letter and picture) appear in the superposition intensifying the transmission (not a tautology) (trans. I. Ch.)" (Gryglicka 2005: 128). The letters, pages, text, image, text-image, volume create polyphonic, semantic and visual spectacle, which in literary texts is realized in various ways.

The artist functioning in the world, experiencing it, even via the "weird form" still "imitates" the surrounding reality. The hybrid works are one of many examples of the crisis of the mimesis classical concepts. This does not mean, however, that they are not mimetic at all. In a specific way, they are trying to interpret the specificity of the contemporary world. In the works of this type we are dealing with the destruction of the temporal and causal order of the represented world by introducing simultaneity (Kalaga 2010: 103). It is important to realize that these types of works in a way imitate the "multi-level complexity of simultaneity, hybridity, ambiguity of (post)modern reality" [trans. I. Ch.] (Kalaga 2010: 103). They are structured in such a way that each reading experience is aporetic. The recipient is assuming that it is impossible to reach an unambiguous sense, and even a few which are coexisting with each other. On the basis of the analysis of many works, which program the recipient's experience, it can be concluded that these types of works communicate that we are dealing with aporias and indefiniteness at a higher level – that is at the level of reality in which one cannot reach the unambiguous sense of any phenomenon. Just this aporia appears through visuals integrated with a word that is not able to show the complexity of the world, as in the traditional literature a clear world describing the various elements of the world. The inability to express the sense, which faces the literature, however, speaks to the contemporary audience, sometimes to the rationality of the mind, but as often as it is the extra-rational experience, which, like according to the Russian Formalists intensifies the way of seeing and makes the perception of the recipient non-automated. Through the experience of the hybrid work of art the recipient has a chance to reflect on the contemporary world, as these works are not only the experiments of artists seeking new forms of expression: "Mimesis is here designed for language-visual-(tactile) experience of aporia as a metaphysical quality present in the world around us: the experience of inherent inability to reach the meaning unambiguous or ambiguous and inherent incompatibility of these senses [trans. I. Ch.]" (Kalaga 2010: 104).

If, indeed, we agree that the art is the result of experience, from which it was born one interpretation of the things, as Aristotle thought, we can conclude that hybridization processes are part of media culture, transcultural, in which the inherent phenomena are heterogeneity and aporia. Hybrids are just more than heterogeneous works complex of various materials, which are characterized by weird form. They are hybrids not only at the level of structure, such as those which are originated from the period of First Great Avant-Garde – for example, volumes of poetry, which is the effect of collaboration between Julian Przyboś and Władysław Strzemiński ("Z ponad") or artistic books from the mainstream of beautiful editing. In the books of avant-garde the graphic rather creates the parallel aesthetic plan than performs a function as a traditional illustration. They are autonomous works, created as an independent work of art (for example the book of M. Szczuka) or in close cooperation with the artist and writer, as in the case of "Z ponad". In these works it has been overcome that the division of the text develops in time and the image is seen in space (Rypson 2000:11).

Hybrid works that were created after World War II and those which were created after 2000 differ strongly in their ontological status than ones from the period of The First Great Avant-Garde. The aim of this article was to show what is involved as concerns concrete poetry, artistic book, liberature, works being at the interface between literature and new media. They are a deep expression of the cultural experience, not only in its structure. Moreover, as I emphasized following Dick Higgins, just staying in creative activities on the level of intermedia is not enough to create a work of art, regardless at the interface of which arts and disciplines it is located. In this context, it is extremely current that the concept of Pareyson which adequately describes what is the content of the work of art – the spirituality of the artist, which is reflected in the style. Although the hermeneutic reading is often insufficient for hybrid works, the observation concerning the content of the work of art and its treatment as a form seems to be a universal aspect of Pareyson's theory.

Bibliography

Aristotle 1927, *Problemata IV*, [in:] *The Works of Aristotle*, ed. W. D. Ross, vol. VII *Problemata*, ed. E. S. Foster, Oxford: Clarendon Press 1927.

Aristotle 1994a, *On the Generation of Animals*, trans. A. Platt, [in:] *The Works of Aristotle*, vol. II, *Great Books of the Western World*, ed. M. J. Adler, Chicago: Encyclopaedia Britannica, INC.

Aristotle 1994b, *On Poetics*, trans. I. Bywater, [in:] *The Works of Aristotle*, Volume II, *Great Books of the Western World*, ed. M. J. Adler, Chicago: Encyclopaedia Britannica, INC.

Aristotle (1994c), *Physics*, [in:] *The Works of Aristotle*, Volume I, trans. R. P. Hardie and R. K. Gaye, *Great Books of the Western World*, ed. M. J. Adler, Chicago: Encyclopaedia Britannica, INC.

Beech Dave 2009, *Turning the Whole Thing Around: Text Art Today*, [in:] *Art and Text*, ed. D. Beech, Ch. Harrison, W. Hill, London: Black Dog Publishing Limited.

Brogowski Leszek 2010, *Éditer l'art. Le livre d'artiste et l'histoire du livre*, Rennes: Éditions Incertain Sens.

Dawidek-Gryglicka Małgorzata 2005, *Konstrukcja przez redukcję. Porządki przestrzenne w poezji konkretnej*, [in:] *Tekst-tura Wokół nowych form tekstu literackiego i tekstu jako dzieła sztuki*, ed. M. Dawidek-Gryglicka, Cracow: Ha!art.

Eichenbaum Boris 1986, *Teoria metody formalnej*, [in:] *Teoria badań literackich za granicą. Antologia*, ed. S. Skwarczyńska, vol. 2: *Od przełomu antypozytywistycznego do roku 1945*, part 3: *Od formalizmu do strukturalizmu*, Cracow: Wydawnictwo Literackie.

Fajfer Zenon 2010, *Liberatura – 496 słów podsumowania*, [in:] *Liberatura czyli literatura totalna. Teksty zebrane z lat 1999–2009*, ed. K. Bazarnik, Cracow: Ha!art.

Fajfer Zenon 2010, *Nie(o)pisanie liberatury*, [in:] *Liberatura czyli literatura totalna. Teksty zebrane z lat 1999–2009*, ed. K. Bazarnik, Cracow: Ha!art.

Fajfer Zenon 2010, *Jak liberatura redefiniuje książkę artystyczną. Uwagi na marginesie projektu „Kolekcja POLSKA KSIĄŻKA ARTYSTYCZNA Z PRZEŁOMU XX I XXI WIEKU"*, [in:] *Liberatura czyli literatura totalna. Teksty zebrane z lat 1999–2009*, ed. K. Bazarnik, Cracow: Ha!art.

Geertz Clifford 1980, *Blurred Genres, The Refiguration of Social Thought*, http://hypergeertz.jku.at/GeertzTexts/Blurred_Genres.html

Grochowski Grzegorz 2000, *Tekstowe hybrydy. Literackość i jej pogranicza*, Wroclaw: Wydawnictwo Uniwersytetu Wrocławskiego.

Hejmej Andrzej 2010, *Intermedialność i literatura intermedialna*, [in:] *Kulturowe wizualizacje doświadczenia*, eds. W. Bolecki, A. Dziadek, Warsaw: Instytut Badań Literackich PAN.

Higgins Dick 2001, „Intermedia", *Leonardo*, vol. 34, no. 1.

Kalaga Wojciech 2010, *Liberatura: słowo, ikona, przestrzeń*, [in:] *Liberatura czyli literatura totalna. Teksty zebrane z lat 1999-2009*, ed. K. Bazarnik, Cracow: Ha!art.

Kalaga Wojciech 2010, *Tekst hybrydyczny. Polifonie i aporie doświadczenia wizualnego*, [in:] *Kulturowe wizualizacje doświadczenia*, eds. W. Bolecki, A. Dziadek, Warsaw: Instytut Badań Literackich PAN.

Lessing Gotthold Efraim 1962, *Laokoon czyli o granicach malarstwa i poezji*, Wroclaw: Wydawnictwo PAN.

Łotman Jurij 1984, „O semiosfere", *Trudy po znakovym sistemam XVII*.

Mitchell William J. T. 1995, *Picture Theory. Essays on Verbal and Visual Representation*, Chicago–London: University of Chicago Press.

Molinet Emmanuel 2006, *L'hybridation: un processus décisif dans le champ des artes plastiques*, http://leportique.revues.org/index851.html

Pareyson Luigi 2009, *Estetyka. Teoria formatywności*, trans. K. Kasia, Cracow: Universitas.

Rypson Piotr 2000, *Książki i strony. Polska książka awangardowa i artystyczna w XX wieku*, Warsaw: Wydawnictwo Centrum Sztuki Współczesnej.

Welsch 1998, *Rozum Transwersalny*, [in:] *Nasza postmodernistyczna moderna*, Warsaw: Oficyna Naukowa.

Żyłko Bogusław 1998, „Uwagi o Łotmanowskiej koncepcji kultury", *Przegląd humanistyczny*, No. 4.

Irena Górska*

Adam Mickiewicz University

LIBERATURE IN RELATION TO THE RECONFIGURATION OF AISTHESIS

Abstract
This article proposes to inspect the phenomenon of liberature from the perspective of the reconfiguration of aisthesis, as described by Wolfgang Welsch. In the German researcher's approach, this consists in questioning the primacy of vision in favour of other senses, and is, first of all, an effect of the dominance of the media. However, in a broader approach towards the reasons of transformations, aisthesis must be looked for in phenomena that are summarised in the formula of "new aesthetics", as proposed by Arnold Berleant. One of the significant features of this concept is the constant expansion of the area of art and the appearance of forms that stimulate the audience's experience, requiring the activation of new sensory receptors. Without a doubt, liberature is one of those forms of art that requires interactivity and a special involvement. Being a unique example of the co-existence of various types of messages (verbal, iconic and material), liberature requires a polysensory perception. This, in turn, can be a source of aesthetic satisfaction, but also a reason for an impoverishment of the aesthetic experience spanning between aisthesis and anaisthesis.

Key words: liberature, aisthesis, aesthetic experience, polysensory perception

Every culture and every age has its favorite model of perception and knowledge that it is inclined to prescribe for everybody and everything. The mark of our time is its revulsion against imposed patterns. (McLuhan 1964: 6).

Even the distinctions among the arts have broken down, and we are often unable to decide where a new development belongs – whether, for example, environments are sculpture or architecture; assemblages are paintings or sculptures; Happenings are theater, painting (as an outgrowth of action painting), or an entirely new art form synthesizing elements of theater, sculpture, dance, painting, and music (Berleant 2004: 57).

---

* Polish Philology Department, Adam Mickiewicz University, A. Fredry 10, 61-701 Poznan, e-mail: irenaszandor@poczta.onet.pl

The doubts expressed by Arnold Berleant could, to some extent, also refer to the phenomenon of liberature. It is difficult to claim that liberature is simply literature, or even a fourth literary genre, as Zenon Fajfer postulated some time ago (Fajfer 2010 A)[1]. Liberature should rather be seen as a peculiar kind of art, which combines the verbal, the iconic, and the material. Liberature remains a specific combination of mutually determining contents and material form of a work, and constitutes a "combination of textual semiosis with the semiosis of the material medium" (Kalaga 2010: 11). Moreover, according to a checklist by Katarzyna Bazarnik, a work of liberature uses typographical means of expression, spatial organization of the text, self-reflexivity or metatextuality, hybridity, interactivity, and ergodicity (Bazarnik 2010: 160–161). It is even possible to say that liberature spans between literature and visual arts. Moreover, in a sense it refers even to architecture, and, at that, in two dimensions: the space of text on a page, as it "plays" with its own "texture" (cf. Tekst-tura, 2005), and the space of the material medium itself, as it often does not resemble the traditionally binded book. It is also important that the function of external form is not merely practical or ornamental, but above all the external form becomes a carrier of meanings that are inseparably linked with the content. There is, consequently, no exaggeration in the statement that liberature is the most literal embodiment of Marhall McLuhan's famous dictum that the medium is the message. This peculiar entangling of form and content is very consequential. It makes it almost impossible to inscribe a work of liberature into another medium. According to Katarzyna Bazarnik, the characteristic features of a work of liberature, especially the material and iconic ones, disappear or are distorted in the process. This is why the concept of e-liberature seems to be a little misguided (Bazarnik 2010: 161–163 A).

A separate, and highly important question is posed by the fact that technology distorts the intensity of the direct, sensual contacts with any work of art. Materiality which, according to Bazarnik, is the genre-defining feature of liberature (Bazarnik 2010 B), disappears in e-space. At best, it can be replaced by its own image. Each materialization of a work in the media is more like an archivization, as Grzegorz Dziamski observes. An archivization points out to what a work could look like, but not to what it indeed is (Dziamski 2007: 207). In this context, Rüdiger Bubner's words seem to be particularly appropriate, when he claims that "sensual directness cannot be transmitted by technical means" (Bubner 2005: 71).

---

[1] Unless otherwise indicated, all the quotations from non-English texts are translated by the author of the article.

It is noteworthy that liberature has an undoubted advantage not only over traditionally published books, but also over electronic publications, which is because liberature, by demanding a peculiar kind of perception, introduces more qualities into the experience of reception. This is because the electronic book, according to Tomasz Goban-Klas, usually preserves the significant qualities of the original publication, and is consequently read in a linear manner, just like a traditionally published paper book. The important change is the lack of physical contact with the material substance of the book, which is replaced by the monitor of an electronic reader (Goban-Klas 2001: 124–125). The content, thus, has been transferred onto another medium, which obviously changes the reader's interaction with a work, and demands, as Małgorzata Sopyło observes, skills in the use of electronic devices (Sopyło 2008). It must be emphasized that the e-book demands, above all, reading, whereas liberature asks for other kinds of reader's activity.

It seems, thus, that the specific peculiarity of liberature as a form of art is the fact that, in the age of popularity of audiobooks and e-books, it demands a direct, physical contact with its own material substance. This is because liberature is a graphic display of the conviction that the work of art is, as Mieczysław Wallis wrote some years ago, "part of its own physical medium" (Wallis 2004: 67), or more aptly: "It is nothing but its own material substance" (Pareyson 2009: 59)[2]. Thus, both the artistic and the aesthetic dimensions of the work are determined by its materiality. A change of one medium/transmitter into another would actually disintegrate the essence of a work of liberature, by destroying its multidimensionality.

As a context for the argument presented above, there is another important reference to McLuhan: "The printed book had encouraged artists to reduce all forms of expression as much as possible to the single descriptive and narrative plane of the printed word. The advent of electric media released art from this straitjacket at once" (McLuhan 1964: 54). Bearing in mind the words of the Canadian philosopher, it can be assumed that liberature is a compromise between the traditional book, which limit forms of expression, and electronic media, which overcome the limitations.

Undoubtedly, liberature is inscribed in the milieu of contemporary art, which encourages reflection about the ways of perceiving the world, not from the position of an external, usually passive observer, but as an active

---

[2] Pareyson writes: "there is no art that would not realize itself through adopting some physical matter, such as words (which are sounds, regardless of their meaning), colors, marble and stones, or the human body, as in mime and dancing" (Pareyson 2009: 54).

participant, or even a co-creator of a work. This attitude means "a departure from the attitude of observation [...] to the attitude of immersion in the world [...] from noesis to aisthesis" (Wilkoszewska 1999: 21).

Towards a new aisthesis

It is precisely in the Greek word aisthesis that describes "perception through senses." Thus, in fact, the equivalent of aisthesis is, as Katya Mondoki remarks, the word "to perceive," and in this sense every experience remains, by definition, an aesthetic one (Mandoki 2007: 35). The author of Aesthetics beyond Aesthetics also emphasizes the fact that our refrence to reality and our cognition have an essentially aesthetic nature (Welsch 1997: 87). Whereas, following the argument by Rudiger Bubner, it is possible to say that aesthetic experience is simply a special case of ordinary human experience (Bubner 2005: 181). An analogous reflection is voiced by Berleant. The critic claims that although the phrase "sensory perception" remains by itself neutral, the fact that it is always additionally determined various, biological, historical, and cultural factors, and by our own personal experiences, which all gives our experience an aesthetic dimension. The aesthetic experience is, thus, not only culturally mediated, but is cultural by its nature (Berleant 2004: 45, 54). It remains in close relation with all human experiences, and encompasses not only art, but all other areas of reality, and requires by no means any particular attitude, distance, or detachment. Thus, the human sensory perception always has an aesthetic nature.

Aisthesis, meaning a broadly understood sensory perception, refers us both to distance receptors (vision and sound), and to contact receptors (touch, taste, smell). However, the category has been, in fact, always associated mostly with the senses of vision and sound, as the "higher ones." Physical perception, on the other hand, was given a lower status. The division into the sensual and the un-sensual was for a long time a consequence of the accepted duality of body and soul. As Arnold Berleant notices, the distinction, which is rooted in ancient Greece, was perhaps consequent of the fact that aisthesis was usually associated with the experience of fine arts (painting, sculpture, architecture, music, and poetry). In the traditional approach, thus, the discipline called "aesthetics" was concerned with arts, not with perception. This sprung from the conviction that artistic objects need a detached contemplation, and that the senses appropriate for contemplation are the distant receptors. The consequence was a peculiar denigration of contact receptors (Berleant 2004: 68–76).

Today, however, the division between distant and contact receptors cannot be maintained, as it is claimed by Arnold Berleant, Wolfgang Welsch, or Richard Schusterman. The dualistic division of the human being into the carnal and the mental is defied by the very phenomenon of sensory perception, which is, after all, simultaneously psychic and somatic, as the author of Body Consciousness observes (Shusterman 2008: 186). The inventor of somaesthetics points out to the fact that the body is ever-present in human experience, even when we interact with advanced media technologies, and adds that "we cannot get away from the experienced body, its pleasures, pains and emotions" (Shusterman 1997: 47). Berleant, too, claims that "the sensual enters with the sensuous and, in a vast area of art and aesthetic experience; the sensual becomes a major if not predominant feature of its sensuous appeal. Indeed, the two are often indistinguishable" (Berleant 2004: 78). The division between distance and contact receptors becomes invalid, according to Berleant, also in confrontation with modern science and the knowledge that every sensory perception is simply a neurobiological activity (Berleant 2010: 57). Berleant also claims that "the aesthetic never loses touch with its origins in body activity and receptivity" (Berleant 2010: 44).

Moreover, in the context of contemporary art forms, the distinction between "mental" and "bodily" sense also seems invalid. The senses of vision and hearing, valued as "higher" ones, lose their privileged position in favor of an integrated complex of five senses. The five-sense human being experiences the world, as Katarzyna Otulakowska claims, "not only through vision/invision, but also through the touch, hearing, smell, and taste" (Otulakowska, 2010: 489). Wolfgang Welsch observes that "The field of aesthetic perception is polymorphous" (Welsch 1997: 96), and Berlant directly observes that definition of an art by the sense through which it was perceived leads to a distortion of aesthetic experience (Berleant 2004: 75). The author of Aesthetics beyond Aesthetics is close to this position, when he claims that overemphasis on one of the sense results in anesthesia or dormancy of the others. In this approach, the experience, apart from the aesthetic dimension, would also have an anesthetic one (Welsch 1998: 537). Thus, overemphasis on one sense at the expense of others cannot have good consequences for the human experience, as the experience would become impoverished and limited.

At present, thus, the somatic dimension of aesthetic experience, a dimension that was ignored by Kant, has been assuming more importance. The experience can no longer be reduced to disinterested liking or not liking that is to a mental state, an intellectual pleasure. Following Shusterman, aisthesis can be defined as the use of the body as a medium of sensory-aesthetic consciousness (Shusterman 1997: 34). The aesthetic experience, as the philosopher claims, never exists solely in a human subject's head (Shusterman 2003: 306).

For the above mentioned critics (Berleant, Welsh, Shusterman), aisthesis has changed entirely the character it had before. It seems to be not only an aesthetic experience as such (which refers to art and all other fields of human activity), but the terms also, importantly, describes a mental and somatic dimension of every human perception. The terms rejects the divisions into "higher" and "lower" senses, treating all senses as equals, and referring simultaneously to psyche and soma. This is because, an aesthetic experience only reaches its synesthetic fullness when, as Berleant observes, all senses are activated to some degree (Berleant 2010: 86). Only in this framework, the multi-sensory and somatically experienced perception could overcome the understanding of aesthetic experience as a mental state of consciousness (Berleant 2010: 87).

This highly significant change in the understanding of the aisthesis was aptly described by Wolfgang Welsch, when he proposed the term reconfiguration of aisthesis. Welsch's phrase summarizes the polisensory, bodily and mental experience. The phrase also points out to the fact that the primary role of vision has been questioned in favor of other senses. The German critic claims that "The cards of sensibility are being reshuffled and instead of a firmly established hierarchy one tends either to an equitable assessment of all senses, or (which I would prefer) to different, purpose-specific hierarchies" (Welsch 1997: 87). Welsch identifies the roots of this change in the understanding of aisthesis, particularly in the dominance of media and development of new technologies. He also relates the change to constantly transforming patterns and demands of culture. In a broader perspective, however, the reconfiguration of aisthesis is not only the effect of various cultural changes (including the developments in media technology), but also of the transformations in art itself. New forms of art demand a new aisthesis, in which no sense will be able to dominate the others.

The above conviction is part of the category of "new aesthetic," proposed by Berleant. The category rejects the qualities of traditional aesthetics, and turns to, among other things, to new currents in art and to new artistic forms[3], which, in turn, demands adequate work of perception. Listing

---

[3] Among the many new forms of art, which demand new kinds of perceptive work, Berleant enumerates the happening, environment, film, functional architecture, and mobile sculpture (Berleant 2004: 85).

the positive effects of the new aesthetic, the philosopher cites broadening of the art domain, as well as the perceptive integration of all elements of the aesthetic field[4]: the creative, the objective, the appreciative, and the performative (Berleant 2004: 8). Berleant writes: "Not only have the distinctions between the creator of art, the aesthetic perceiver, the art object, and the performer have been obscured; their functions have tended to overlap and merge as well, becoming continuous in the course of aesthetic experience" (Berleant 2004: 67). He emphasizes the fact that expansion of the art domain results with appearance of such forms of art that provide a more dynamic experience for recipients, frequently demanding an inclusion of new sensory receptors, including the senses of touch and kinesthesis (Berleant 2004: 65–83). The demand for an increased activity by the audience also means that the boundary between the audience and the artist is blurred. Liberature, as it seems, is precisely one of these new forms of art, which embody the "new aesthetic," and consequently demand a new, reconfigured aisthesis.

Liberature and the aesthetic experience

Although Zenon Fajfer is right, when he writes "there is no book so all-ecompassing, no work so total that it would engage all the senses" (Fajfer 2010: 82 A), liberature, as an object of aesthetic experience, demands a particular engagement by the reader. Being a peculiar combination of qualities typical for various arts (literature, visual arts, and even sculpture or architecture), it simultaneously transforms our mode of perception. This is because it demands simultaneous reception of the material, the iconic, and the verbal. As every work of art, it activates particular forms of perception, and by itself, to quote the author of Aesthetics beyond Aesthetics, it becomes a nexus where different forms of perception are combined. By referring to various senses, liberature activates numerous modes of perception and each time integrates them into a unique system (Welsch 1997: 91–96). This multiplicity and diversity of activated modes of perception of a work of liberature is inscribed in its very structure. This is because a work of liberature can assume practically any shape, appearance, and be made of practically any material, which is important for the sense of touch. When a conventional book form is modified, e.g. by closing a traditionally bound volume in covers made of concrete (as in Świątynia kamienia [The Temple

---

[4] The idea of "aesthetic field" was already proposed by Berleant in 1970, in The Aesthetic Field. A Phenomenology of Aesthetic Experience.

of Stone] by Andrzej Bednarczyk) or replaced by a glass bottle (as in Zenon Fajfer's Spoglądając przez ozonową dziurę [Looking through the Ozone Hole]), the traditional experience of reading must be entirely transformed.

Thus, it can be claimed that liberature, by promoting interactivity and necessity of multi-sensory perception, negates the traditional model of contemplation and the time-honored hierarchy of the senses, which mostly favored the vision. The vision, as Welsh observes, "is in fact no longer the reliable sense for contact with reality that it was once held to be – this no longer holds in a world in which physics has become indemonstrable, and just as little in the world of media" (Welsch 1997: 87). The vision is not privileged by modern forms of art either, including liberature.

In the case of works of liberature, thus, it is difficult to say that they refer to only one of the senses. Inasmuch as traditional painting is the art of vision, and traditional music is the art of hearing, liberature demands the activation of many receptors, including both "mental" and "somatic" ones. Quoting from Fajfer, it is possible to describe liberature as "a body for reading [...] with the eyes, ears, and hands; for seeing, hearing and touching". We begin to know a work of liberature as soon as we experience its weight, shape, or the texture of the paper (Fajfer 2010 A: 81).

Consequently, it demands simultaneous activation of both vision and touch. It can be even claimed that liberature activates the sense of kinesthesis, when a work demands physical manipulation of the volume, which is in fact a physical activity, an engagement of the body, to read a text written vertically or upside down, or to face a challenging shape or spatial dimensions of the work. Undoubtedly, thus, liberature demands polysensory reception. This is because, for an experience of a work of art, "only when complex does it succeed" (Welsch 1997: 96).

In the context of critical inquiry into the nature of liberature, the recipient remains the key category. As opposed to the reader of traditional literature, the recipient of liberature must be an unusually active discoverer of meanings, willing to face the challenges posed by liberature. As Agnieszka Przybyszewska observes, most works of liberature demand a recipient of the Dionysian type, whose activity helps to fulfill the meanings and complete the structure of the text (Przybyszewska 2005: 45). On the one hand, thus, the reader "creates" a works of liberature, when, in the act of perception, her or she determines its shape and rules of perception. Thus, the reader experiences the work in a different way each time, not only because of varying contexts of interaction with the artistic object (this aspect would be true for every aesthetic experience, regardless of whether it is of art or of an un-artistic object), but also since a work of liberature, because of its alinear quality and use of various specific materials, always demands new forms of reception. Quite often, for instance, liberature encourages endless changes in the sequence of reading/watching; it constantly forces the reader to make new choices.

On the other hand, as in Oka-leczenie, which remains a model example of the work of liberature, the freedom given to the reader is opposed by the demand for meticulous reading with the precision of "one-thusandth of a letter" (Fajfer 2010: 113 A). This does not change the fact that the reading of the three-volume work can be started from every volume, which is because Oka-leczenie combines three volumes into one. The three volumes correspond to three texts, referring to three different events, which, as Katarzyna Bazarnik writes, are connected on a hidden level, and mutually determined. The structure of Oka-leczenie, thus, points out to both the autonomy of each volume, and to the circularity of their narration (Bazarnik 2010: 155 A). In fact, the three combined volumed forces the reader to "the circularity of tactile experience: opening of a book, in fact, has no ending, because when we close one part, we open up another one" (Kalaga 2010: 15). In other words, closing and opening, the beginning and end of the act of reading, assume a common identity. The book, thus, ceases to be a transparent medium, but becomes a structural element of the work. Everything is meaningful: the specific binding of the volume covers, the color of the grid and font, the shape and size of letters, their arrangement on the page, as well as the transformation of words into images.

All such elements are, for the reader, specific tasks to be performed. The experience of art, thus, becomes an act of creation, of an unceasing reconstruction of the order of experience. The performative act seems to be an indispensable factor in the experience of liberature. Following Pareyson, it is possible to say that performance seems to be the only possibility of access to the work (Pareyson 2009: 244).

Among the significant qualities of liberature, of particular importance are undoubtedly "interactivity and ergodicity, that is engagement of the reader into determination of the course of narration, and the reader's active participation in giving the work a final shape through the process of reading" (Bazarnik 2010: 160 A). Importantly, the ultimate shape is structured time and again, during each interaction with a work. The recipient's experience, in the words of Rüdiger Bubner, seems to be always new and inexhaustible. The aim of an aesthetic experience is the discovery of the unity of a work. This unity, in turn, remains the effect of reflection, oscillating between details and the whole work, in an attempt to capture mutual relations between them. Thus, the unity of a work is always unstable, and never allows us to capture the entirety of a work, which is unceasingly transformed in each act of perception. It is precisely in the unity of a work, as it was conceived of by Bubner, where the infinite repetitiveness of experience rests, so that the experience never wears out (Bubner 2005: 69, 74). It would be right to observe that each experience of a work gives it, as Luigi Pareyson wrote, "a new edition" (Pareyson 63).

To put it provokingly, the ultimate shape of a work in general, and a work of liberature in particular, is never ultimate. Contingency and alinearity as qualities of liberature create, as Tadeusz Miczka puts it, "a state of permanent aesthetic contingency" (Miczka 1999: 61). This is because a work is constituted "for a while" during reception. It exists, time and again, in performative gestures of sense-creation, which are forever changing in their versions. Materiality, verbality, and iconicity of a work of liberature always occur in new configurations during the process of experiencing. As Fajfer claims, sometimes the architectural aspect of a work can be dominating, at another time it can be the visual aspect, then the material one, or all of them combined (Fajfer 2010 A: 5)[5] The whole remains elusive, however, The totality of a work cannot be captured, because, as Bubner puts it, the access to the totality is never full and ultimate.[6] "In place of a logocentric model, there enters the principle of the aleatoric and spatial rhizome" (Kalaga 2010: 18). It is contingency and multiplicity that give the special quality to the experience of a recipient. Liberature would be a very suggestive example of it, because liberature demands particular enegagement, which Berleant describes as "aesthetic engagement."

This attitude, as the author of Sensibility and Sense presents it, radically refutes the Kantian proposition of dividing the aesthetic experience from the practice of life and from the sphere of cognition, and thus refutes the model of disinterested contemplation, which the critic calls "academic anachro-

---

[5] Fajfer writes that there are various types of liberature: the first kind is dominated by the architectural factor (so that the texts demand a particular structure of a book or its fragment), another kind is more visual (so that the graphical layer, e.g. photographs and drawings, is somehow integrated in the text or the text itself forms an image). Another type of liberature is represented by works whose material aspect is brought to the foreground (the paper and other materials constitute a sort of installation art) (cf. Fajfer 2010 A: 62).

[6] Bubner argues that every interpretation is given with the work, and he describes this "freedom from the interpretation requirement" as the total aspect of art. In the notion of totality, thus, there is a conviction that everything that is necessary for the understanding of a work is already present in it. However, it is only in the meeting of totality with sensuality, in the process of aesthetic experiencing, that creates a specific tension between them. "It oscillates between sensual perception of austerity and lack of conceptual demand. [...] Witholding of this tension decides about the aesthetic experience in its entirety" (R. Bubner 2005, 73).

nism" (Berleant 2004: 34). Engagement, in Berleant's terms, assumes a new meaning, which, as Krystyna Wilkoszewska observes, was eliminated from aesthetic and which should be associated with practical attitude (Wilkoszewska 2008: 219). This is because engagement demands an embodied subject to be introduced into aesthetic experience, a subject equipped with all senses, both contact and distance ones. It is precisely the category of embodiment[7] that is employed to neutralize the traditional division into body and soul. This is because embodiment reaches its fullness through "active presence of the human body in appreciative experience" (Berleant 2004: 85), and demands inclusion, into an aesthetic activity, of not only of consciousness, but also of the bodily presence of the recipient. In this context, it is worthwhile recalling a pertinent observation by Teresa Pękala, who writes: "Interactive artistic activities, which demand cooperation of many senses, refer to cognitivity, especially to intellectual cognitivity. Its advantage is, undoubtedly, directness and striving for unity, resulting from the quality of emotions and polysensory quality of cognition" (Pękala 2008: 158). This kind of aesthetic interaction with a work is well described by the term engagement, which, being highly perceptive, demands more of somatic sensitivity, experiencing meanings rather than perceiving them intellectually (Berleant 2004: 84). It is possible to say, quoting from Maurice Merleau-Ponty, that the body knows more, because it records all previous perceptions and experiences, even the unconscious ones (Merleau-Ponty 2002: 231).

Berleant argues that engagement corresponds "far better than disinterestedness the perceptual, cognitive, and somatic involvement that responsive appreciation joins to powerful art" (Berleant 2004: 9). Intimate participation would be an indispensable quality of engagement, since it allows us to "overcome the sense of separateness that divides us from things" (Berleant 2010: 30)[8]. According to the critic, engagement thus points out to two very important qualities of aesthetic experience: its active character, and participation as its indispensable quality (Berleant 2004: 35).

Precisely this kind of activeness and participation is demanded by works of liberature. Interaction with liberature is certainly of a different quality than

---

[7] Berleant writes about embodiment in two fundamental meanings. In the first meaning, the "aura of physical presence is embedded in the art work," whereas in the second it "occurs in the aesthetic response to art when the somatic participation of the appreciator is involved" (Berleant 2004: 84).

[8] Importantly, the category of aesthetic engagement is also used by Berleant for emphasizing the continuity of art. It is a specific bridge between traditional art and its modern forms (Berleant 2004: 18)
Aesthetic engagement was already discussed by Berleant in his pioneering work, Art and Engagement, Temple University Press, Philadelphia 1991.

in the case of traditional books, but undoubtedly in liberature, too, the touch of the book, as well as "the look, feel and smell of its pages present a special axis of experience" (Shusterman 1997: 45). In a work of liberature, the recipient faces the challenge of synthesizing, in the experience of reception, the material, verbal, and iconic dimensions of a work. Remembering about the attitude of engagement, it must be emphasized that in works of liberature, unlike in traditional books, even the script itself can be challenging for the recipient. This is because in liberature the script is not only a "prosthetic" for the spoken language. It does not merely constitute a physical foundation for the spoken language, as Roman Ingarden would put it (Ingarden 1973: xxv–xxvii), but is simultaneously a text and an image, and by expressing meanings, the script also, as it were, embodies them. This is because liberature has turned the qualities of the printed script into one of its most important subject-matters, and for this reason liberature does not allow "to make for a transient perception of print or handwriting, and to facilitate the progress towards perception of a typical sound of a word and of its meaning" (Ingarden 1981: 278). On the contrary, it is possible to say that in a work of liberature, as in, for instance, in concrete poetry, the script "plays" with its own graphics, or, to put it in a different way, that we interact with the sceno-graphics of script. The play with script can be, of course, dismissed as a peculiar form of barrier to "access" to the meanings hidden in the text, but it can also be seen as a challenge for a patient and inquisitive reader.

The emanative text is certainly a special case of liberature[9]. The creator of emanative text admits that this peculiar novelistic experiment was conceived of as an expression of perfect iconicity. By remaining invisible, it still can be seen (Fajfer 2010: 97 A). It demands an increased activity and a specific kind of perception in order to realize itself. It must be emphasized that in an emanative text there is inscribed a necessity for an

---

[9] The emanative text, at least to a degree, can be treated as a peculiar reference to the anagrammatic concept of literature, as proposed by Ferdinand de Saussure. This is because anagrams, as well as emanative texts, create "secondary meanings and secondary texts, which are [...] hidden, but which are at the same time obvious" (Dziadek 2006: 50). Both projects, referring to the book by Jean Starobinski, Les mots sous les mots. Les anagrammes de Ferdinand de Saussure, Paris, Gallimard, 1971, can be described as "words under words." It must be emphasized, however, that inasmuch as the script and single letters as being important for an "embodiment" of an emanative text, de Saussure's anagrams were primarily phonetic. Their meaning, thus, diverges from the traditional literary and theoretical approach. In the analyses of the Swiss linguist, the primary goal was to read and record various combinations of sounds, not letters (cf. Dziadek, 2006: 34). Importantly, in an emanative text all layers of text are given to the reader, even if not directly, whereas the method of anagrammatic reading never gives certainty that the word found is the only one, that there are no other theme-words (cf. Dziadek, 2006: 38–39).

unusually strong engagement by the reader, who literally brings the text into existence. This is because the reader cannot, as in the reading of a traditional script, give the text a cursory glance, because the text becomes visible through attentive effort. By following the instructions given by the author, the participatory reader must remove several layers of the text to discover the camouflaged meanings and to give an incarnation to, as Zenon Fajfer put it, "the incorporeality of a higher order" (Fajfer 2010: 113 A).

The idea of an emanative text involves the need to read the initial letters of each word, as a new layer text surfaces from under the initials, and then another and another, until the journey's end, where the reader finds the source-word[10] (Fajfer 2010 A: 126 B). On the one hand, it is possible to ascribe a particular importance, or consistence, to this expression, because all the previously eliminated layers of meaning are summarized. On the other hand, it seems to be important that the discovery of the source-word simultaneously forces the reader to remove, or in fact negate, all the "bypassed" layers of text. Emanative text, thus, is not played out between what is visible and invisible, but also between presence and destruction, between words, but also without them. Its essence can be aptly described in John Dewey's words: "The visible is set in the invisible; and in the end what is unseen decides what happens in the seen; the tangible rests precariously upon the untouched and ungrasped" (Dewey 1958: 43–44).

The recipient, by reconstructing the invisible, and discovering several layers of meaning, becomes, as Agnieszka Przybyszewska observes, a guarantor of coherence of a work (Przybyszewska 2005: 57). Thus, a work of liberature, and particularly an emanative text, exists thanks to the interactive work of a perceiver. The necessity for active interaction, which, as Anna Łebkowska observes, is similar to reading an interactive hypertext novel (Łebkowska 2008), is simply inscribed in the text. It would not be an exaggeration to say that, in a sense, liberature is similar to multimedia art, with its characteristics, as Maria Popczyk argues, interactivity, creation of a work during reception, and unpredictable versions of the final results (Popczyk 1999: 133–134). To quote from McLuhan's terminology, it is possible to define liberature as a cold medium, which, as opposed to hot media, forces the reader to cooperate and fill in (McLuhan 1964: 201 ff).

The engagement of the recipient in the experience of liberature has, thus, an unquestionable sensual and conscious dimension. It poses challenges

---

[10] "Source-word" can be associated with the "theme-word," which was an important element of the anagrammatic concept of reading by de Saussure. The linguist even claimed that the writing of texts based on anagrams was, in fact, a decomposition of the theme-word by a creative writer (cf. Dziadek 2006: 38).

and intensifies the spaces of interpretation, it forces the recipient to be inquisitive, to decipher meanings, and even to set up the structure of a text. The effort of facing all these requirements can be, of course, a source of aesthetic satisfaction, but at the same time, it must be admitted that an excess of stimuli can cause a dispersal and erasure of meanings, or even discourage the recipient. "Whoever is constantly exposed to optical and acoustic provocations, eventually ceases to see and hear" (Bubner 2005: 182). Similarly, Richard Schusterman observes that the media that engage in most sensory modalities can actually impoverish our experience (Shusterman 1997: 45).

In the case of liberature, too, the iconic layer of work and the material dimension of a work, can be, as it seems, a diversion and an addition to the verbal layer, but might just as well be received as an obstacle on the way to the meanings of a text. This is because it is difficult to discard the traditional habits of linear reading. Independence given to the recipient, which can be seen as an invitation for the co-creation of a work, which often leads to uncertainty and helplessness. Wojciech Kalaga is right, when he writes that the two ontological orders combined in liberature, the intentional and the material-visual, can cooperate to provide a different experience of reading, but they can also do the reverse, and lead to a dispersal of meanings in the recipient's experience (Kalaga 2010: 19).

The deliberations presented above lead to the conclusion that liberature as a "total art" in which "the matter of the statement belongs to the space of the book, and the space of the book to the material of the statement" (Fajfer 2010: 125 A), demands also a total aisthesis. Paradoxically, however, the totality can turn out to be a trap set against the recipient who desires more sensations. This is because, on the one hand, liberature can certainly be a pleasing surprise and question our received habits of perception, bringing freshness and novelty. On the other hand, however, liberature can be simply irritating and confusing. As it seems, the necessity of giving the same importance to all senses, which liberature demands, can actually eliminate the effect of increasing the aesthetic satisfaction, instead of bringing it about. Thus, ironically, the excess of sensations, which activate various sensory receptors, can lead us to disappointment, instead of an aesthetic fulfillment; it can lead from aesthesis to anaisthesis (Welsch: 1998)[11]. As it seems, one must be "careful with liberature!"[12]

---

[11] Cf. also Odo Marquard's Aesthetica i anaesthetica. Rozważania filozoficzne, transl. K. Krzemieniowa, Warszawa 2007.

[12] The expression "Careful with liberature" is a paraphrase of the title of the book Ostrożnie z literaturą! (przykłady, wykłady raz inne rady), [Careful with literature! (Translations, lectures and other pieces of advice)], ed. S. Balbus, W. Bolecki, Warszawa 2000.

Bibliography

Bazarnik Katarzyna 2010a, *Liberature or on the Origin of Literary Species*, [in:] Zenon Fajfer, *Liberatura czyli literatura totalna. Teksty zebrane z lat 1999–2009 / Liberature Or Total Literature. Collected Essays 1999–2009*, trans. and ed. K. Bazarnik, Cracow: Korporacja Ha!art.

Bazarnik Katarzyna 2010b, *Materialność jako wyznacznik gatunkowy liberatury* [in:] *Materia sztuki* ed. M. Ostrowicki, Cracow: Universitas.

Berleant Arnold 2004, *Re-thinking aesthetics: Rogue Essays on Aesthetics and the Arts*, Aldershot: Ashgate Publishing.

Berleant Arnold 2010, *Sensibility and Sense: The Aesthetic Transformation of the Human World*, Exeter, Imprint Academic.

Bubner Rüdiger (2005), *Doświadczenie estetyczne*, Warszawa, Oficyna Naukowa.

Dewey John (1958), *Experience and Nature*, wyd. 2, Dover Publications, New York.

Dziadek Adam (2006), *Na marginesach lektury. Szkice teoretyczne*, Katowice: Wydawnictwo Uniwersytetu Śląskiego.

Dziamski Grzegorz 2007, *Wizje i re-wizje. Wielka księga estetyki w Polsce*, ed. K. Wilkoszewska, Cracow: Universitas.

Fajfer Zenon 2010a, *Liberatura czyli literatura totalna. Teksty zebrane z lat 1999–2009*, red. K. Bazarnik, Cracow: Korporacja Ha!art.

Fajfer Zenon 2010b, *Od liberatury do tekstu niewidzialnego (autoportret z Ingardenem w tle)*, [in:] *Materia sztuki*, ed. M. Ostrowicki, Cracow: Universitas.

Goban-Klas Tomasz 2011, *Wartki nurt mediów. Ku nowym formom społecznego życia informacji. Pisma z lat 2000–2011*, Cracow: Universitas.

Ingarden Roman 1973, *The Literary Work of Art. Evanston*, Evanstone, IL: Northwestern University Press.

Ingarden Roman 1981, *Wykłady i dyskusje z estetyki*, ed. A. Szczepańska, introduction W. Stróżewski, Warsaw: PWN.

Kalaga Wojciech 2010, *Liberature: Word, Icon, Space. Introduction*, [in:] Zenon Fajfer, *Liberatura czyli literatura totalna. Teksty zebrane z lat 1999–2009 / Liberature Or Total Literature. Collected Essays 1999–2009*, trans. and ed. Katarzyna Bazarnik, Cracow: Korporacja Ha!art.

Kant Immanuel 1986, *Krytyka władzy sądzenia*, trans. J. Gałecki, Warsaw: PIW.

Łebkowska Anna 2008, *Doświadczenie interakcji i identyfikacji (Hipertekstowa powieść interaktywna)*, [in:] *Nowoczesność jako doświadczenie. Analizy kulturoznawcze*, ed. A. Zeidler-Janiszewska, R. Nycz, B. Giza, Warsaw: Wydawnictwo SWPS Academica.

Mandoki Katya 2007, *Everyday Aesthetics: Prosaics, the Play of Culture and Social Identities*, Aldershott: Ashgate.

Marquard Odo 2007, *Aesthetica i anaesthetica. Rozważania filozoficzne*, trans. K. Krzemieniowa, Warsaw: Oficyna Naukowa.

Merleau-Ponty Maurice 2002, *Phenomenology of Perception*, trans. C. Smith. London: Routlege Classics.

McLuhan Herbert Marshall 1964, *Understanding Media*, New York: McGraw-Hill.

Miczka Tadeusz 1999, *Multimedia – oczywistości i domysły. Szkic o estetycznej przygodności nowych mediów*, [in:] *Piękno w sieci. Estetyka i nowe media*, ed. K. Wilkoszewska, Cracow: Universitas.

Otulakowska Katarzyna 2010, *Zero jedynkowa zmysłowość człowieka*, [in:] *Materia sztuki*, ed. M. Ostrowicki, Cracow: Universitas.

Pareyson Luigi 2009, *Estetyka. Teoria formatywności*, trans. K. Kasia, Cracow: Universitas.

Pękala Teresa 2008, *Estetyczne doświadczenie przeszłości*, [in:] *Nowoczesność jako doświadczenie. Dyscypliny, paradygmaty, dyskursy*, eds. A. Zeidler-Janiszewska, R. Nycz, Warsaw: Wydawnictwo SWPS Academica,.

Popczyk Maria 1999, *Dzieło sztuki jako medium*, [in:] *Piękno w sieci. Estetyka i nowe media*, ed. K. Wilkoszewska, Cracow: Universitas.

Przybyszewska Agnieszka 2005, *Niszczyć, aby budować. O nowych jakościach liberatury i hipertekstu*, [in:] *Tekst-tura. Wokół nowych form tekstu literackiego i tekstu jako dzieła sztuki*, ed. M. Dawidek Gryglicka, Cracow: Korporacja Ha!art.

Magdalena Lachman*

University of Lodz

LITERATURE IN/OF THE CITY
– INTRODUCTORY COMMENTS

Abstract
The article attempts to describe a variety of possible ways in which literature makes itself present within the space of the city. It assumes two basic perspectives to investigate the issue. First of all, the article analyses how the city and its multiple institutions support the literature's circulation and availability for the readers. The city offers a number of venues for writers to present their works and promote them through precisely targeted events and literary festivals. The city is seen as a stage or background on which literary works and events can become fully available. Secondly, the article analyses how literary critics or more broadly philosophers and sociologists interested in urban studies use literature to understand and describe the city in its artistic and everyday dimensions. The fruitful collaboration between city as an active factor shaping artistic imagination and writers leads to developing new forms of expression as well as formulating new ideas about art. It also offers a possibility to communicate with readers in ways which are better accommodated to modern visual imagination and different forms of everyday activity.

Key words: literature, space of the city, literature's circulation, urban studies, new forms of expression

The city – an area of literary explorations

Long present in literary studies, urban research is now approached from novel angles (e.g. Rybicka 2003; Rewers 2005 and 2010; *Miasto w sztuce...* 2010). Despite the fact that considerable attention is still devoted to traditional analyses of the motif of the city in literature (confer, for instance:

---

* Institute of Polish Philology, University of Lodz, Pomorska 171/173, 90-236 Lodz, e-mail: magdam@uni.lodz.pl

Miasto, kultura literatura... 1993; *Obraz stolic europejskich...* 2010; *Literackie i nieliterackie obrazy miasta...* 2011), many scholars examine the identity-shaping, social, historical, political and cultural aspects of urban spaces depicted in literary works (e.g. Suchojad 2010, Adamczewska 2011) and investigate the ways in which urban aesthetics contributes to the development of new artistic solutions. Although the city is not always placed at the centre of consideration, it often accidentally becomes the subject of attention, as in the case of a review of Steve Sem-Sandberg's novel *The Emperor of Lies* (2011): "The novel has many narrators, who gradually fall silent [...] What remains in the end is the city – an empty artifact observed through the eyes of one of the few dwellers who hide in it" (Krzymianowski 2011; emphasis added). Another telling remark in this respect concerns Piotr Paziński's literary debut and can be found in an interview with the writer: "One could expect that an admirer of Joyce and Dublin would write an urban novel rather than a story set in a manor in the midst of woods", to which the interviewee responds: "Citiness is indeed very crucial to me. Outside the city I go insane. I feel bad in the countryside. I could live in Manhattan or in Paris. I've never enjoyed visiting my friends' summer houses. You never know how to get out of such places" (Paźniewski 2010: 48)[1].

It is symptomatic that literature and literary studies nowadays uncover the ways in which the image of the city encoded in various texts tends to be conditioned, for instance, by post-dependence (e.g. *Narracje migracyjne...* 2012), postcolonial, gender, or ecocritical discourses. In an attempt to decide whether and what changes taking place in the structure of cities find a reflection in literature, literary scholars take part in various inter- and transdisciplinary projects inspired by the topographical turn in cultural studies (e.g. *Miasto między przestrzenią...* 2010). Besides, *spatial turn* and *place studies* or *urban studies* constitute crucial points of reference in geopoetics, geocriticism, literary geography and humanistic geography – dynamically developing theories that also constitute a methodological background for contemporary urban research in the field of literature (Rybicka 2008; 2011, 2012b). What seems equally crucial in this context is the problematics of literature in/of the city, which in Poland so far has not been comprehensively explored, although it has been introduced in dictionaries (Potrykus-Woźniak 2010: 126–136) and in popular magazines (e.g. Kazimierczyk 2010).

---

[1] These issues also echo in the final questions of the interview: "Do you already have any ideas for new novels? [...] Are you going to write anything about the city?" (Paźniewski 2010: 48).

It seems that the urban ways in which literature functions can be narrowed down to two aspects. These can be described by means of the following comprehensive formulas: "literature in the city" and "literature of the city". The former applies to a situation in which the city serves as a background for the literary and literature-related activity and as an arena for literary works and other forms of writing. The latter emerges when the city, its distinctive elements and its information layout are considered in terms of a (para)-literary message. The so defined subject matter covers very specific activities which consist in "reading/writing" or "textualizing" the city; various forms of "spatial narratives"; the case of *architecture parlante* ("speaking architecture"); potential literary determinants of urban epigraphy which serves both commercial and non-conformist purposes; as well as all events, campaigns, shows, happenings and other actions that evoke certain associations with various forms of writing. Still, what seems conspicuous about the above approaches is the vagueness of the very category of literature, which functions as a term open for interpretation, frequently used in an arbitrary way.

Literature in urban space

The existence of literature and literary facts in urban space can be to a certain degree described with terms, such as distribution, promotion, reception or the so-called "applied literature", which are well-known in literary studies. One aspect of such a broadly defined field of research is the exploration of the ways in which the city creates an institutional background for literature. The city can be perceived as an abode and a generator of the most important institutions of literary life, such as cafés (Fitch 2006), cabarets and literary museums, book institutes, writers' houses, artists' retreats, libraries, bookstores, publishing houses, community centres, artists' associations, foundations, clubs, festival centres (such as Biuro Literackie in Wrocław) or literary magazines. Their role is to stimulate and create rules that govern the circulation of art. Furthermore, they frequently search for new forms of literary activity in the city and aim at activating urban audiences. Therefore, these institutions are largely responsible for the development of typically urban ways of popularizing and promoting literature (also in an unintended fashion, since sometimes the very fact of the existence of institutions organizing literary life stimulates the development of grass-roots initiatives that challenge the official channels of culture). Contemporary initiatives promoting and popularizing specific authors and their oeuvres include: anniversaries (e.g. in Poland 2004 was announced the Year of Gombrowicz, while 2011 – the Year of Miłosz) and literary festivals (e.g. the Conrad Festival, the Czesław Miłosz Literary Festival in Cracow, Tyrmandiada – the Leopold Tyrmand Festival in Warsaw, or Mironalia organized in Warsaw to celebrate Miron Białoszewski's oeuvre), or Bloomsday and other such festivals of writers. Furthermore, there is a wide range of projects promoting books and readership (Kazimierczyk 2010), such as *bookcrossing* or the Bibliometro, the latter functioning in Chile and, since recently, in Spain (small library desks where books can be collected or retained by the underground users) various forms of happenings and flash mobs (like, for instance, the "Czytaj na Centralnym" flash-mob, which took place on 24 September 2011 at the Central Square in Nowa Huta, the actions in the Tri-City organized by Zjednoczenie Czytelnicze (Readers' Union), an informal group of people who once in a while gather at one place to read books in silence for a couple of minutes, e.g. on 18 September 2010 on the Sopot Pier as a part of the "Molo Książkowe – czytamy od deski do deski" project). Similar one-time or cyclic events in Cracow are organized under the auspices of such organizations as Strefa Wolnego Czytania (Free Reading Zone – www.strefawolnegoczytania.pl), which marks reader-friendly places with special labels and organizes books exchanges, family picnics with a book and events such as "Cała Kładka Czyta" (people reading books together in the middle of a day on the Footbridge of Father Bernatek), "wielkie leniuchowanie" (set in the fresh air, comfortable sofas with the organizer's logo invite to relax with a book), and "literary graffiti/typomural" workshops (as a part of the project, a mural depicting a shelf with recommended books was painted on the wall of a block of flats in Traugutta Street). What serves as an excellent example of a contemporary attempt to reorganize urban space in such a fashion is the contest announced in 2012 by the organizers of the Conrad Festival:

> Are you creative? Do you like designing? Do you have interesting and unconventional ideas? And above all – do you love books? If so, then the *Think: Literature!* competition is perfect for you! In connection with the 4th edition of the Conrad Festival (the 22nd–28th of October), we would like to encourage all artists: let's take books to the streets together, in order for them to be associated with something more than just libraries. We are waiting for designs of original installations inspired by books and feasible in the public space. We will present the most interesting ideas during the festival on the streets of Krakow and in the festival bookstores. (http://www.conradfestival.pl/en/4/1/338/think-literature-and-design-a-book-installation; accessed: 31.08.2012).

One should also mention here another example of this kind, namely reading literary works aloud in public space (e.g. reading Joyce's works during the Cracow Bloomsday or reading Adam Mickiewicz's epic poem *Sir Thaddeus* on 8 September 2012 in various cities in Poland as a part of the "Narodowe Czytanie *Pana Tadeusza*" project) or presenting them on murals and billboards or in various public means of transport (in trams, in the underground, in trains ...); for instance, during the fourth edition of the Conrad Festival in 2012, every day throughout the week at 8 p.m. poems by Piotr Sommer were displayed on the Town Hall Tower in Cracow. The *Rain of Poems* project, initiated in Chile by the CasaGrande artist collective, has gained an international dimension. It consists in dropping leaflets with poems from a helicopter over cities that have experienced aerial bombing in the past (such as Santiago de Chile, Dubrovnik, Guernica, Warsaw and, in 2012, London). Since 1986 London has been the site of the *Poems on the Underground* project, which involves displaying poems on advertising boards in the London Tube. The poems to be presented in this way are selected about three times a year by Judith Chernaik, Cicely Herbert and Gerard Benson. Chernaik, an American writer and the initiator of the project, explains that she wanted to bring poetry to a wider audience, who would encounter it in everyday, unexpected and accidental situations. While choosing poems, what matters is their relevance to contemporary events or to the general direction of civilization changes. The jury also considers whether they harmonize with the urban iconosphere and toponomastics. Liberated from the confines of book covers, poems lead a new life, entering unexpected interactions with the citizens of and visitors to London and the informational and commercial ornamentation of the city. The result of these undertakings is also anthologies published in a traditional, printed form, which collect the texts that have earlier been shown to the public. The initiators of similar projects all around the world (e.g. in Poland the *Wiersze w Metrze* project has been in operation since 2008 – see: www.wierszewmetrze.eu) use both canonical and more contemporary texts. It is also a common practice to present commissioned works which have been written specially for a non-standard distribution in urban space. What may serve as a Polish example of this tendency is Miejska Powieść Odcinkowa (The Urban Serial Novel), run by Nowy Teatr (New Theatre) in Warsaw in collaboration with the Ha!art Corporation and the Kultura Gniewu publishing house. In the first three months of 2009 a booklet containing a new episode of a novel was distributed free of charge at railway stations as well as in trams, busses and other public facilities in Warsaw, Cracow, Poznań, Wrocław and Bytom. Each subsequent episode of the novel was written by different authors and comic book creators (among those involved in the undertaking were, for instance: Sylwia Chutnik, Jacek Dehnel, Sławomir Shuty, Adam Wiedeman, Natasza Goerke, Wojciech Kuczok and Ignacy Karpowicz, and such comic writers as Krzysztof Ostrowski, Maciej Sieńczyk, Przemek Truściński, Agata "Endo" Nowicka, Tomek and Milena Leśniak, Michał "Śledź" Śledziński and Jakub Rebelka). The initiators of the project stress that "The Urban Serial Novel aims not only to add colour to the cultural landscape of Warsaw, but above all to bring the novel to random audience who do not read books on a daily basis" (http://www.ha.art.pl/prezentacje/29-projekty/128-miejska-powiesc-odcinkowa.html). Still, such actions, in fact, focus on the needs of a particular group of addressees who are willing to take up reading in unusual situations and who are familiar with contemporary conventions of artistic communication.

Another issue in this area is the specific, urban reception of literature, which covers a variety of actions initiated by cultural animators; these include, for instance: *urban gaming* (*Warszawskie gry...* 2009; Nowakowska 2011), *questing* (a form of sightseeing, during which a participant follows a new, unmarked trail and solves rhymed riddles), or different forms of literary tourism, such as literary tours in the footsteps of writers or tours into the fictional worlds they have created. One may, for instance, explore the city of Prague seen through the eyes of Franz Kafka, the Lisbon recommended in Fernando Pessoi's guidebook *Lisbon – What the Tourist Should See*, the Barcelona described in Carlos Ruiz Zafón's novels or the Dublin known from the biography and works of James Joyce. Such tours can also be inspired by popular bestsellers; one could mention, for instance, guided city walks based on fashionable crime novels and their film adaptations which have recently gained popularity (Reijnders 2010). At the same time, we observe a growing demand for books and travel guides depicting various places through the prism of literary references; for example, in Joanna Orzechowska's guidebook *Podwórka Piotrkowskiej* (*The Backyards of Piotrkowska Street*) the exploration of the immediate vicinity of the main street in Łódź is organized on the basis of quotations taken from literary works (Orzechowska [2011])[2].

There is yet another way to saturate urban space with literature-inspired activities. For instance, what contributed to the growing number of love inscriptions in Reggio di Calabria in Italy (Piastowska 2008) were

---

[2] Literary testimonies are also used by, for instance, the authors of the monograph on Chłodna Street in Warsaw (Piotrowski 2007; Nadolski 2008). Also confer guidebooks of Karpacz, Sosnówka, Jagniątków, Szklarska Poręba and Jelenia Góra addressed to children (*Bajkowa...* 2010; *Bajkowy przewodnik...* 2008, 2009, 2010).

two popular novels for teenagers authored by Federico Moccia. Both novels, *Tre metri sopra il cielo* (1992) and its sequel *Ho voglia di te* (2006; *I Want You*), were adapted to film, which only stimulated the desire of teenage audiences to imitate the characters and the way they confess love through texts inscribed on walls (using a secret code, Moccia's protagonist composes a short text which alludes to the intimate relationship with his lover; he writes it in black paint on a bridge so that his beloved can see it every day on her way to school). Furthermore, the novel *Tre metri sopra il cielo* has contributed to the popularity of love padlocks in Italian and other European cities, where one observes a revival of the custom of affixing locked padlocks with engraved initials or names of couples, their important dates and sometimes love confessions in public places, usually bridges (the key to the padlock is intentionally thrown away, which is supposed to seal the relationship and highlight is permanence)[3].

Furthermore, literature frequently serves as an incentive for visual artists, which is conspicuous in their proposals for the management of public space. A characteristic example of what may be referred to as the contemporary "well art" is Max Sauk's work of 1986 made in Hannover. It is an "interpretation of Kurt Schwitters's poem – *Anna Blume*. The text of the poem is engraved on a well. Anna Blume, depicted as hybrid of a woman and a flower, gushes water into a marble pool "(Wolting 2005: 203). In the 2011 Cracow "4P – Pisarz/Poezja/Proza/Przestrzeń Publiczna" ("4P – People of Letters/Poetry/Prose/Public Space") project, launched during the ArtBoom Festival of Visual Arts and as a part of the celebrations of the Year of Miłosz, the organizers presented works of art depicting various allusions to literature embedded in urban landscape that had won a special contest (e.g. at the windows of a tenement house curtains covered with Bohdan Zadura's poems were hanged, in St. Gertruda's Street excerpts from Jan Brzechwa's poems were displayed on illuminated coffers, while

---

[3] The custom of expressing one's love in this form has a long tradition. It has its source in a Florentine legend. However, its contemporary popularity is stimulated by the popular novel addressed to young readers. In Poland, love padlocks can be found, for example, on the Footbridge of Father Bernatek in Cracow, on the Tumski Bridge in Wrocław, on the Holy Cross Bridge in Warsaw or on Bishop Jordan's Bridge in Poznań. This social phenomenon and its literary connotations have recently become the subject of media reports and analyses in the press (cf. e.g. Rzepka, Bugaj 2011); love padlocks also have a separate entry in Wikipedia (cf. http://en.wikipedia.org/wiki/Love_padlocks; accessed: 15.12.2012; http://pl.wikipedia.org/wiki/K%C5%82%C3%B3dka_mi%C5%82o%C5%9Bci; accessed: 15.12.2012).

Miłosz's neighbours recited poems of the Nobel Prize winner through their intercoms at the given hour). Moreover, literature has frequently served as a source of inspiration for Jenny Holzer, an artist who interferes in the urban landscape by means of, for instance, electronic streams of text projected onto the walls of buildings. In her projections she used sonnets and other poems by Henri Cole and passages from Elfride Jelinek's prose works. In 2011 in Poland she projected Wisława Szymborska's poems on the facades of Stary Browar (the Old Brewery) and the City Hall in Poznań; she also ornamented Wawel and a part of the bank of the Vistula river in Cracow with quotations from Czesław Miłosz's poetry, displayed after dark (*For Krakow* project). Such a non-standard form of distributing traditional poems aims at their reinterpretation and actualization in new social and cultural contexts.

What may serve as a unique example of the urban reception of literature are works of architecture, such as those designed by Daniel Libeskind, who declares that his ZŁOTA 44 apartment tower in the centre of Warsaw (commonly referred to as the "glass sail") was largely inspired by the poetry of Wisława Szymborska, Czesław Miłosz and Adam Zagajewski. Working on a project entered for a contest organized by The Museum of the History of Polish Jews in Warsaw, he took inspiration from Bruno Schulz's works and, in particular, Schulz's concept of "the book" and his short story under the same title. Although without the author's commentary the sources of allusions remain in such cases rather difficult to trace, they deserve our attention as examples of the ongoing presence of the given writer's oeuvre in the contemporary artistic consciousness and as a non-standard expression of a search for the visual equivalents of words, especially that the phenomena of this kind are becoming increasingly popular and are not limited to architecture.

Cecylia Malik's performance *365 Trees* is a curious example of a project alluding to literature. It was inspired by Italo Calvino's novel *Il barone rampante (The Baron in the Trees)*. Its main character, a rebellious twelve-year-old boy, decides to climb a tree after a quarrel with his father and remain there for the rest of his life. Every day throughout a year Malik, each time dressed in a different fashion, climbed a carefully chosen tree in the city and documented her project on photographs (Malik 2011; also see: http://www.cecyliamalik.pl/?t=365). These photos evoke associations with Pippi Långstrump, another protagonist in children's literature. It is conspicuous that in such projects artists use concepts deeply rooted in the collective consciousness not so much through the agency of literature, but thanks to the unlimited recycling power of mass culture.

Another example of this phenomenon is the *Géant tombé du ciel* (*A Giant Fallen from the Sky*) show (a mobile art installation?) of the French Royal de Luxe company, which is a travesty of the story of Gulliver and the Lilliputians known from Jonathan Swift's *Gulliver's Travels*, much indebted to the depictions of this motif in popular culture (Féral 2012: 109–111). Furthermore, mass culture also develops and imposes its own standards on the urban reception of literature. In contemporary times one comes across various souvenir stalls and gift shops offering t-shirts, bags, pins, mugs, stickers and other gadgets, with, for instance, literary quotations or portraits of writers. Nowadays the function of a medium for literary or literature-inspired content is also performed by the human body, which is visible in the growing popularity of tattoos with excerpts from literary works, portraits of writers, or visual renderings of literary motifs[4]. This controlled form of the reception of literature aims, above all, at a commercial success and can be seen as an act of imposition rather than promotion of writers' achievement. Still, this shows that the dynamic perception of literary texts is deeply rooted in the contemporary consciousness. Such an active approach informs a number of activities whose goal is to popularize the art of letters. The need for experiencing literature in a non-traditional way is conspicuous in the actions performed as a part of the Miłosz Wyzwolony (Miłosz Liberated) project in Cracow in 2011; for instance, dressed in t-shirts with random excerpts from poems of the Nobel Prize winner, young people searched for each other in the streets and via the Internet, making acquaintances and trying to reassemble the fragments of the texts. The poems of Miłosz were also available in cafes and pubs on napkins, coasters, or even sweets.

Moreover, there is a wide variety of spontaneous, purely urban forms of literature. This refers both to the presentation of occasional and utilitarian texts to the public and all the unconventional forms of the literary activity of writers who use non-standard artistic media. The city has long been the natural domain of so-called "applied literature", which is accurately illustrated by the popular phenomenon known as "street literature". Leslie Shepard, one of specialists in the field, applies this term to such examples of applied art as broadside ballads, chapbooks, proclamations, news-sheets, election bills, tracts, pamphlets, cocks, catchpennies and other ephemera, in other words: to everything that can be observed

---

[4] See e.g. http://www.contrariwise.org/; http://pulowerek.pl/2010/10/literackie-tatuaze/; http://ksiazki.wp.pl/gid,14655106,tytul,15-najlepszych-tatuazy-literackich,galeria.html; http://reniferu.pl/59855/literackie-tatuaze/. Also confer: Drozdowski 2009: 141–171.

in the streets and that can be easily popularized (Shepard 1973). Scholars are also attracted to other unique forms of communication in urban space; for instance, in his monograph *Wiersze z cmentarza* (*Poems from the Cemetery*) Jacek Kolbuszewski investigates transformations of epitaphs. He considers the way they manifest themselves in the form of grave inscriptions or other public inscriptions, such as commemorative plaques, as their generic feature (Kolbuszewski 1985). Another example of this kind of occasional poetry are poems distributed in Manhattan in New York City after the September 11 attacks on the WTC in 2011 (Fraenkel 2010: 64–65, 74)[5], and in Poland after the 2010 Polish Air Force Tu-154 crash in Smoleńsk or, more recently, after the tragedy in Sosnowiec (the death of the six-month-old Madzia, whose story of alleged kidnapping was covered extensively in the media at the beginning of 2012). The immediate nature of such forms of expression is closely connected with the need for making them public, which illustrates a wider phenomenon of the engagement of local communities in topical events. These events tend to produce specific narratives, such as, for instance, *urban legends* (Barber 2007; Czubala 1993, 1995, 2005; Rok 2011; Potrykus-Woźniak 2010: 96–98). Treated as sociological and ethnographical phenomena, urban legends tend to be considered as "literature" rooted in the urban consciousness.

At the same time, numerous authors who consider themselves writers make use of the contemporary forms of presenting their achievement offered by the city; for instance, Juliusz Erazm Bolek designs posters put up at bus and train stops and in the streets. Already in the 1980s, Bolek distributed his poems on miniature stickers. He also presents them on table-cloths and napkins. Furthermore, Bolek takes pride in developing in 2004 a new poetic medium – the *bodybook*, a miniature book to be worn on one's neck on a specially designed lanyard (Dunin-Wąsowicz, Varga 1998: 17). Michał Zabłocki's *Multipoetry* project is realized in an equally consistent way, through writing poems on pavements or as a part of the *366 Poems in 365 Days* campaign (every day since 24 October 2002 a different poem by Zabłocki was displayed on the facade of a tenement house in Cracow and in Warsaw), advertised as the "Word Premiere of the First

---

[5] After the September 11 attacks, Adam Zagajewski's poem "Try to Praise the Mutilated World" gained popularity among the citizens of New York City. First it was published in *The New Yorker*, but later it was many times republished and spontaneously distributed in public places, stuck on car windows and passed from hand to hand. It was considered that the poem perfectly conveys the moods and emotions of the New Yorkers and that it can "endure the tension of mourning" (Zagajewski 2002: 1).

Poetic Book on the Wall!" (http://poemat.com.pl/?page_id=76; accessed: 12.09.2012). Zabłocki is also the initiator and coordinator of the *Poems on the Walls* project (every day after dark a poem written by a user of the poetic social networking service Emultipoetry.eu is projected on the facade of the tenement house located at 1 Bracka Street – until recently in two, Polish and English, language versions). The project has been permanently in progress since 1 November 2010. Yet another example is Gerard Jurgen Blum-Kwiatkowski, who in 1997 launched *Das Offene Buch* (*The Open Book*) project in the German town of Hünfeld. It consists in displaying works of various concrete and visual poets from all around the world on the walls of buildings (Dawidek Gryglicka 2005: 132–134).

Urban public space seems obligatory for the existence of numerous contemporary events that tend towards literary forms (events that show such aspirations or are perceived in this fashion by observers and commentators). These are, for instance, poetry slams, which combine elements of recitation, improvisation and performance and take place in pubs, clubs or other urban venues where young audiences meet (it is conspicuous that the first poetic slam in Jarosław in September 2012 was organized with the motto: "Poezja na ulice" ("Let's Bring Poetry to the Streets") – http://slam.art.pl/; accessed: 17.09.2012). The city is a medium not only of literature but also of literary gestures, which materialize in the urban landscape they match so well. This is perfectly illustrated by performances of avant-garde artists (who are frequently the patrons of literary projects performed in public space). In a similar way, one may perceive, for instance, literature-inspired dandyism, which can be successful only in the urban context. It seems conspicuous that Jacek Dehnel, who nowadays promotes such an attitude, presents himself to the public on photographs in which he is depicted in his elegant frock with a top hat and a cane, walking in a dignified manner along the streets, against the background of city walls, pavements, park benches and avenues.

Even such a brief overview of the most representative forms of the existence of literature in urban space gives the reader a general idea about the regularities of phenomena taking place in this sphere nowadays: on the one hand, we observe an increase in all kinds of activities that promote literature and facilitate its materialization in the city; on the other, it is visible that the sanctioned, traditional orders are overlapped by new/additional/more intense forms of the participation of literature and literariness in the urban landscape. This happens not only through the agency of artists themselves, but also thanks to the contribution of scholars who study various aspects of citiness.

Magdalena Lachman

Literature and the literariness of urban space

Evidently, nowadays it is not only literature that is becoming increasingly urban, but also the city seems to be more and more literary. In other words, its concrete characteristics can be perceived though the prism of features typical of the art of letters. Scholars have been long stressing the fact that literariness is one of the aspects of the city, and thus the city can be read and perceived like a work of literature or a literature-related genre. This is the source of such popular metaphors as the city as a text, the city as a book, the city as a palimpsest, or the city as a stage – a metaphor that has recently gained more recognition due to the performative turn (Rybicka 2012a: 29). These approaches have a long-standing tradition, since they derive from such classics of urban literature as the works of Charles Baudelaire, Walter Benjamin or Franz Hessel (Molisak 2004: 623–635). Already in the 1920s Hessel firmly stated: "a street is a unique kind of text. Read it" (Hessel 2001b: 161). Contemporary academic discourse frequently employs this concept[6] and advocates analyzing the city's information layout with tools developed by poetics and the theory of literature, for instance, using such figures of speech as palindromes, oxymorons, anagrams, anacoluthons, synecdoches, asyndetons, catachreses or onomatoids (pseudo-names) (Rykiel 2008: 142–143). "The city – by nature a wok in progress – is aimed to be de-re-constructed in its different plans and on a number of levels" (Zeidler-Janiszewska 1997: 8), at the same time encouraging us to decode the multiple meanings it contains in a literary fashion.

Advertising is nowadays often considered within the literary category of "the operating manuals of reality" (Krajewski 2005: 161). Tomasz Stępień, for instance, perceives the escalation of advertising as an ironic implementation of the postulates put forward by avant-garde artists, whose works were realized in and through the city and needed the city as a platform of communication:

> The dreams of the early 20th century avant-garde artists have been made true in an unexpected way. In the streets we are surrounded with a colourful hubbub of texts clashing with one another. Walking, driving or strolling leisurely, we pass by texts, we read texts and we are read by texts. Everything is a text; everything can be art;

---

[6] For instance, in the accounts of her walks around the city of Milan, Małgorzata Bogunia-Borowska acknowledges her indebtedness to Hessel (Bogunia-Borowska 2009: 71). Also confer: *Pisanie miasta – czytanie miasta* (1997); (Frydryczak 1998).

everyone can be an artist, though (s)he may not be aware of this – of post-modernism and the total commercial anesthetization of everyday life. The phantasmal hyperreality of the texts-simulacras around us constitutes a homogenic mass of people and objects, advertising, art, politics and religion (Stępień 2002: 106).

Writing about the labyrinthine space of Westin Bonaventure hotel in the centre of Los Angeles, a well-known construction designed by John Portman, which belongs to the architectural canon of postmodernity (Jameson 1991: 38–45), Wiesław Godzic mentions curious behaviour of his American friend, which he found even more fascinating then the building itself:

> A professor of literature told me that he often visits this place in order to lose himself in the chaos of contemporaneity. Tired of wandering, he finally finds Virgil (the ghost of Virgil – he corrected himself), who directs him to one of the exits. Till now I am not sure whether he was joking when he said that what helps him in this are advertisements of his favourite cigarettes (Godzic 1996: 212).

If "the contemporary reception of advertising is to be understood as an inalienable element of spatial imagination in the post-modern world" then advertisements can be considered, following, for instance, Jean Baudrillard's diagnosis, as "a new public space, imitating the theatre of social life" (Godzic 1996: 213), in which literary thinking plays a part.

Scholars also find a literary potential in the specifically urban phenomena associated with the nonconformist culture, such as *subvertising, adbusting, culture jamming, brandalism* or various forms of street-art such as stickers, graffiti or murals (Stępień 2002)[7]. These practices are often treated as a reflection of the need to saturate the urban tissue with literary gestures and the writing impetus: "Young people cover the walls of cities with a web of meanings, in this way creating a peculiar journal of reality. [...] Filled with writing, the walls of tenement houses turn into palimpsests" (Piastowska 2008: 21). Urban inscriptions are a reaction to topical events, a form of protest, a sign of resistance and negation, and, at the same time, a universal commentary on reality. Considering "the use of writing in public space as an act of non-conformism" (Araya 2010: 95), one should pay attention to its graphic, pragmatic and illocutionary power (Araya 2010: 98–99) as well as its literary subversiveness. A need for a literary translation of such phenomena is increased by the fact that they are easily decontextualized. These phenomena break away

---

[7] For a more detailed discussion of this subject, see: (Klein 2000); (Drozdowski 2009: 87–139); (Żakowska 2009: 117–123); (Bińczycki 2010: 14–18); (Lamireau 2010).

from their origins and the ideas that they were initially determined by, which indicate their considerable susceptibility to multiple readings and interpretations. This is, for instance, the case with the famous "Kilroy was here" inscriptions and in Poland the inscriptions referring to "Józef Tkaczuk". Disliked by the pupils, Tkaczuk was a caretaker in a grammar school in Warsaw. His name started functioning as a recognizable logo "a name-catchphrase, a magical formula »stolen« from the official structures and transformed into a secret code of the alternative world, into a peculiar »contemporary myth«" (Sulima 2000: 90). A similar role was played by the famous inscriptions on Parisian walls and banners in May 1968. Curiously, these inscriptions also invaded literary space, since they have been frequently catalogued in books, for instance, in the anthology *"Les murs ont la parole". Journal mural Mai 68, Sorbonne, Odéon, Nanterre etc...* (1968; 2nd edition: 2007). Referring to this type of urban "signs of opposition" and "eruptions of spontaneous writing", whose first large-scale manifestation were the Paris student riots (Petrucci 2010: 184), paleographers often use the term "graphic-literary »genre«" (Petrucci 2010: 181).

The possibility of shaping reality through "exposed writing [*écriture exposée*]" seems attractive to people of letters (Araya 2010: 95). Analyzing its role as a tool of opposition against Pinochet's dictatorship in Chile, Pedro Araya accentuates the fact that the Vanguard Scene (Escena de Avanzada), supported among others by writers, played a considerable role in the protests against censorship and the oppressive ideology. Through their projects, often performed in urban space, the members of the movement deconstructed "traditionally sanctioned literary and artistic ideologies, focusing mostly on revolutionizing the artistic language and its applications in the social context" (Araya 2010: 100). Writers (the novelist Diamela Eltita and the poet Raúl Zurita) were also members of the Colectivo Acciones De Arte (CADA), an activist group promoting "acting through art" and aiming at the transformation of the city into a metaphor" (Eltit 2000: 158; quoted in: Araya 2010: 100).

Of course, one should not consider all the spectacles of meaning performed in urban space (not only those that make use of the written word, but also dramaturgical and narrative intervention actions) in purely literary terms. Still, it is conspicuous that such (often metaphorical) categorizations are frequently employed by the interpreters of these phenomena. The term "visual poem" is, for instance, often applied to the strategies of resistance used by such activists as the participants in Occupy Wall Street (Ogrodzka 2012: 4). In 1991 the Polish Pegasus prize was awarded to a Łódź artist, Cezary Bodzianowski, whose "performances discover poetry in everyday prose". As further stated in the verdict,

> Cezary Bodzianowski moves gleefully through the world as if it were a story [...] Fragments of reality become cues for narratives of his own. [...] Narration is a way of exploring the world of fiction. Bodzianowski constructs his stories using various methods, most of them tested beforehand. He uses disguise and deception, shifting meanings between domains, employs elephantine associations based on semantic similarity and contiguity. Infrequent forays into parody [...] usually pale before his propensity for poetry. [...] Bodzianowski builds his statements around linguistic associations, restoring the figurative nature of language. Some actions illustrate figures of speech [...], showing the potential of semantic associations with breath-taking legerdemain (Mytkowska 2003: 183–185).

The case of the "speaking architecture" may also be treated as an attempt to create a different pattern of communication using the art of letters, which is best illustrated by the architectural concepts of Bernard Tschumi (Rewers 1998: 96–100; King 1996: 170–171; Hays 2010: 160). During Tschumi's seminar in the 1970s, his students designed projects of buildings inspired by the works of such writers as Edgar Allan Poe, Franz Kafka or Italo Calvino, while Tschumi himself suggested applying the narrative structure of Joyce's *Finnegans Wake* to the new spatial organization of the Covent Garden in London, so that the district would gain a specific "incidental" quality (the project was never put into practice, yet one may get insight into the ideas behind it, investigating Tschumi's documentation).

Such projects aim at "textualizing" the urban tissue (Gądecki 2005) and show a possibility of considering it from the rhetorical, persuasive, narrative and literary perspectives. Similar categorizations are not so much a result of a conviction that the above phenomena allude to the traditionally-understood literature (which is not always the case) or of the involvement of writers in them (which frequently takes place, yet not as a rule), but, above all, they are a consequence of the functions they perform, since literature is understood in this context as acting with and through words (Fraenkel 2010: 79). Therefore, what comes to the fore are the performative and pragmatic aspects of literariness, whose essence, in this context, resides in the ability to unveil the unsatisfactory order and in motivating the addressee to rearrange or even radically challenge the *status quo*. Such a perspective provides legitimate grounds for the use of the term "literary event", whose role is to communicate and influence reality.

The indispensability of (urban) literature

The proposed overview of literature in/of the city still seems far from exhaustive. Thus it is difficult to draw any unequivocal conclusions. Yet it is already noticeable that the discussed phenomena cannot be easily generalized in literary terms. Of course, the analysis of the above examples with the standard descriptive language can be useful if one aims at indicating the traditions of such forms of presentation and the basic social dimension of the functioning of literature. At the same time, however, if we attempt to capture the contemporary essence and semantics of these examples, our efforts appear to be bound to failure. The nexus between citiness and literariness leads to the production of new qualities or, at least, meanings unique to the discussed phenomena, which can only be activated in a concrete spatial configuration. Let us, for instance, consider how Bloomsday is described by one of Joyce's scholars, who assumes such a perspective:

> the contemporary commemoration of *Ulysses* allows Joyce's novel to recode the city, charging its everyday sites with esoteric significance, producing a surfeit of meaning that hovers just out of view, traceable only by the costumes going through the motions. Of course, the production of multiple, unsuspected levels of significance for the apparently quotidian also characterizes *Ulysses* itself, where everyday actions flip into Homeric counterparts. Doubling this effect, Bloomsday has transformed Joyce's book into an epic subtext for the real (Brooker 2004: 211–212).

As highlighted by the scholars diagnosing the changes that have been taking place: "Instead of questions […] about the meaning of space and the ways it produces meaning, what comes to the fore nowadays is the question who inscribes space with the given [in this case, literary – M.L.] meanings and what for" (Grochowski 2008: 9). From such a perspective, the urban tissue seems to be a result of various literary conceptualizations as well as a factor stimulating further literary explorations in the field of not only the (re)distribution of literature and the ways of preserving it, but also literary gestures and events. At the same time, the following questions remain open: does literature creatively absorb the city? Or does it adjust to the city (and in this process even loses its autonomous character)? Does literature gain a new identity in the light of these practices? Or perhaps these practices only legitimize ideas already present in literature, which were earlier less visible and less accentuated?

Instead of offering any conclusive answers to the above questions, one should postulate introducing a new discourse to describe these practices. In this respect, one may, for instance, take recourse to media studies and the idea of c o n v e r g e n c e they propose, with particular emphasis placed on assimilation, combining media, multimediality and the culture of participation (Jenkins 2006).

The specific codes of access to literature, also in its proliferating urban and spatial forms, show that what matters nowadays is not only the message, but more importantly its desired and programmed impact (what is important is not the aesthetics or the aestheticizing aura of the message but the possibility to memorize it). At the same time, this situation, associated with the redistribution of literature and literariness and their impact on urban space, shows that spectators, tourists and participants in communal cultural practices are nowadays becoming the typical addressees of art. Such an addressee as a participant, consumer, spectator or passer-by, an addressee shaped by the verbocentric models of communication is the target of the contemporary authors, who cherish the assumption that the addressee may not necessarily crave for books or reading experience, but he/she still needs some kind of literature. And let us conclude with this optimistic note.

Translated by Katarzyna Ojrzyńska

Bibliography

Adamczewska Izabella 2011, *Pomiędzy blokiem a wieżowcem. Przestrzenne kakotopie*, [in:] *"Krajobraz po Masłowskiej". Ewolucja powieści środowiskowej w najmłodszej polskiej literaturze*, Lodz: Primum Verbum.

Araya Pedro 2010, *NO+ (Chile 1983–2007). Uwagi o piśmie kontestacyjnym. W stronę pragmatycznej antropologii pisma*, trans. N. Dołowy, [in:] *Antropologia pisma. Od teorii do praktyki*, ed. Ph. Artières, P. Rodak, Warsaw: Wydawnictwo UW.

Bajkowa Jelenia Góra. Przewodnik dla dzieci (2010), ed. R. Chrześcijańska, Jelenia Góra: Wydawnictwo Ad Rem.

Bajkowy przewodnik dla dzieci. Szklarska Poręba. Magiczne miasto Ducha Gór 2010, ed. M. Nienartowicz, O. Danko, J. Rochnowska, Jelenia Góra: Wydawnictwo Ad Rem.

Bajkowy przewodnik dla dzieci. Jagniątków 2009, ed. M. Nienartowicz, M. Miszczuk, Jelenia Góra: Wydawnictwo Ad Rem.

Bajkowy przewodnik dla dzieci. Sosnówka 2009, ed. M. Nienartowicz, Jelenia Góra: Wydawnictwo Ad Rem.

Bajkowy przewodnik dla dzieci. Karpacz 2008, ed. R. Rzepczyński, M. Nienartowicz, Jelenia Góra: Wydawnictwo Ad Rem.

Barber Mark 2007, *Urban Legends Uncovered: An Investigation into the Truth Behind the Myths*, Chichester: Summersdale Publishers.

Bińczycki Jan 2010, *Nielegalne przestrzenie kultury*, [in:] *Kultura niezależna w Polsce 1989–2009*, Cracow: Korporacja Ha!art.

Bogunia-Borowska Małgorzata 2009, „Mediolan – subiektywny portret metropolii", *Kultura Popularna*, No. 2.

Brooker Joseph 2004, *When He's at Home. Joyce's Reception in Ireland*, [in:] *Joyce's Critics. Transitions in Reading and Culture*, Madison, Wisconsin: The University of Winsconsin Press.

Czubala Dionizjusz 2005, *Wokół legendy miejskiej*, Bielsko-Biała: Wydawnictwo ATH.

Czubala Dionizjusz 1996, *Nasze mity współczesnej*, Katowice: Fundacja dla Wspierania Śląskiej Humanistyki.

Czubala Dionizjusz 1993, *Współczesne legendy miejskie*, Katowice: Wydawnictwo UŚ.

Dawidek Gryglicka Małgorzata 2005, *Konstrukcja przez redukcję. Porządki przestrzenne poezji konkretnej*, [in:] *Tekst-tura. Wokół nowych form tekstu literackiego i tekstu jako dzieła sztuki*, ed. M. Dawidek Gryglicka, Cracow: Korporacja Ha!art.

Drozdowski Rafał 2009, *Obraza na obrazy. Strategie społecznego oporu wobec obrazów dominujących*, 2nd edition, Warsaw: Zysk i S-ka.

Dunin-Wąsowicz Paweł, Varga Krzysztof 1998, *Bolek Juliusz Erazm*, [in:] *Parnas bis. Słownik literatury polskiej urodzonej po 1960 roku*, 3rd edition, Warsaw: Lampa i Iskra Boża.

Eltit Diamela, *Emergencias. Escrotos sobre literatura, arte y política*, Santiago 2000 (quoted in: Araya 2010: 100).

Fajfer Zenon 2010, *Liberatura czyli literatura totalna. Teksty zebrane z lat 1999–2009*, ed. K. Bazarnik, Cracow: Korporacja Ha!art.

Féral Josette 2012, „Rzeczywistość wobec wyzwania teatru", trans. W. Prażuch, *Didaskalia*, no. 109/110.

Fitch Noël Riley 2006, *The Grand Literary Cafés of Europe*, London–Cape Town–Sydney–Auckland: New Holland Publishers.

Fraenkel Béatrice 2010, *Pojęcie wydarzenia piśmiennego*, trans. N. Dołowy, [in:] *Antropologia pisma. Od teorii do praktyki*, ed. Ph. Artières, P. Rodak, Warsaw: Wydawnictwa Uniwersytetu Warszawskiego.

Frydryczak Beata 1998, *Okiem przechodnia: ulica jako przestrzeń estetyczna*, [in:] *Formy estetyzacji przestrzeni publicznej*, ed. J. St. Wojciechowski, A. Zeidler-Janiszewska, Warsaw: Instytut Kultury.

Gądecki Jacek 2005, *Tekst czy kontekst, o czytaniu architektury*, [in:] *Tekst-tura. Wokół nowych form tekstu literackiego i tekstu jako dzieła sztuki*, ed. M. Dawidek Gryglicka, Cracow: Korporacja Ha!art.

Godzic Wiesław 1996, *Reklama, czyli kontekst kultury popularnej*, [in:] *Oglądanie i inne przyjemności kultury popularnej*, Cracow: Universitas.

Grochowski Grzegorz 2008, „(Nie)widzialne miasta", *Teksty Drugie*, No. 4.

Hays K. Michael 2010, *Architecture's Desire. Reading the Late Avant-Garde*, Cambridge, MA: Massachusetts Institute of Technology.

Hessel Franz 2001a, „Flâneur w Berlinie", trans. S. Lisiecka, *Literatura na Świecie*, No. 8–9.

Hessel Franz 2001b, „Sztuka spacerowania", trans. S. Lisiecka, *Literatura na Świecie*, No. 8–9.

Jameson Fredric 1991, *Postmodernism, or, Cultural Logic of Late Capitalism*, London: Verso.

Jenkins Charles 2006, *Convergence Culture. Where Old and New Media Collide*, New York–London: New York University Press.

Kazimierczyk Marta 2010, *W poszukiwaniu straconego czytelnika. Nowoczesna promocja czytelnictwa*, http://www.polityka.pl/kultura/aktualnoscikulturalne/1510614,1,nowoczesna-promocja-ksiazek.read, 4.12.2010.

King Ross 1996, *Emancipating Space. Geography, Architecture, and Urban Design*, New York: Guilford Press.

Klein Naomi 2000, *No Logo*, New York: Picador.

Kolbuszewski Jacek 1985, *Wiersze z cmentarza. O współczesnej epigrafice wierszowanej*, Wroclaw, Polskie Towarzystwo Ludoznawcze.

Krajewski Marek 2005, *Kultury kultury popularnej*, Poznan, Wydawnictwo Naukowe UAM.

Krzymianowski Grzegorz 2011, „Arbeit macht frei", *Kronika Miasta Łodzi*, No. 4. (http://literatki.com/5334/arbeit-macht-frei).

Lamireau Clara 2010, *"Bazgrzący" i czytelnik miejski. Graffiti antyreklamowe w przestrzeni publicznej Paryża*, trans. N. Dołowy, [in:] *Antropologia pisma. Od teorii do praktyki*, ed. Ph. Artières, P. Rodak, Warsaw: Wydawnictwa Uniwersytetu Warszawskiego.

"Les murs ont la parole". Journal mural Mai 68, Sorbonne, Odéon, Nanterre etc... (1968), ed. J. Besançon, Tchou, Paris.

Literackie i nieliterackie obrazy miasta. Łódź przełomu wieków oczami niemieckojęzycznego autora – Carla Heinricha Schultza (2011), ed. M. Kucner, W. Kessler, Lodz: Primum Verbum.

Malik Cecylia 2011, *365 drzew*, Warsaw: Fundacja Bęc Zmiana.

Miasto między przestrzenią a koncepcją przestrzeni 2010, ed. M. Banaszkiewicz, F. Czech, P. Winskowski, Cracow: Wydawnictwo UJ.

Miasto w sztuce – sztuka miasta 2010, ed. E. Rewers, Cracow: Universitas.

Miasto, kultura literatura. Wiek XIX 1993, ed. J. Data, Gdansk: Gdańskie Towarzystwo Naukowe & Wydawnictwo Gdańskie.

Molisak Alina 2004, *Miejska przestrzeń literatury dwudziestowiecznej – Berlin, Berlin...*, [in:] *Dwudziestowieczność*, ed. M. Dąbrowski, T. Wójcik, Warsaw: Wydział Polonistyki UW.

Mytkowska Joanna 2003, *Games of Rhetoric*, trans. A. Zapałowski, [in:] *Cezary Bodzianowski*, ed. J. Mytkowska, Warsaw–Frankfurt am Main: Fundacja Galerii Foksal & Revolver.

Nadolski Artur III 2008, *Pani Chłodna (opowieść o warszawskiej ulicy)*, Warsaw: Bellona.

Narracje migracyjne w literaturze polskiej XX i XXI wieku 2012, ed. H. Gosk, Cracow: Universitas

Nowakowska Olga 2011, „Wszystko gra! Gry miejskie w przestrzeni Warszawy", *Homo Ludens*, No. 3, on-line: http://ptbg.org.pl/dl/70/Olga%20NOWAKOWSKA%20-%20Wszystko%20gra!%20Gry%20miejskie%20w%20przestrzeni%20Warszawy%20.pdf.

Obraz stolic europejskich w piśmiennictwie polskim 2010, ed. A. Tyszka, Lodz: Wydawnictwo AHE.

Nowaczewski Artur 2011, *Szlifibruki i flâneurzy. Figura ulicy w literaturze polskiej po 1918 roku*, Gdansk: słowo/obraz terytoria.

Ogrodzka Dorota 2012, „Okupacja jako sztuka. Przestrzeń publiczna do tworzenia", *Didaskalia*, No. 109/110.

Orzechowska Joanna 2011, *Podwórka Piotrkowskiej. Przewodnik*, Lodz: Centrum Inicjatyw na Rzecz Rozwoju "Regio".

Paetzold Heinz 1997, *Architektura i urbanistyka. Zarys krytycznej filozofii miasta*, trans. J. Gilewicz, [in:] *Pisanie miasta – czytanie miasta*, ed. A. Zeidler-Janiszewska, Poznan: Wydawnictwo Fundacji Humaniora

Paziński Piotr 2010, „Już nie ma kogo zapytać", interviewed by J. Sobolewska, *Polityka*, no. 6.

Petrucci Armando 2010, *Pismo. Idea i przedstawienie*, trans. A. Osmólska-Mętrak, ed. J. Kujawiński, Warsaw: Wydawnictwa UW.

Piastowska Alicja 2008, *„Ti amo to znaczy kocham* – o wyznaniach miłosnych na włoskich murach. Analiza tekstów z Reggio di Calabria", *Kultura Miasta – Miasto w Kulturze*, No. 4.

Piotrowska Magdalena 2006, „Rocznicowe *czytanie* Mickiewicza", *Kronika Miasta Poznania*, No. 4.

Piotrowski Igor 2007, *Chłodna. Wielkość i zapomnienie warszawskiej ulicy w świetle literatury pieknej, wspomnień i fotografii*, Warsaw: Mazowieckie Centrum Kultury i Sztuki & Wydawnictwo Trio.

Pisanie miasta – czytanie miasta 1997, ed. A. Zeidler-Janiszewska, Poznan: Wydawnictwo Fundacji Humaniora.

Potrykus-Woźniak Paulina 2010, *Literatura w miejskiej przestrzeni*, [in:] *Słownik nowych gatunków i zjawisk literackich*, Warsaw–Bielsko-Biała: Wydawnictwo Szkolne PWN ParkEdukacja:

Reijnders Stijn 2010, "Places of the Imagination: an Etnography of the TV Detective Tour", *Cultural Geographies*, No. 17.

Rewers Ewa 2010, *Miasto-twórczość. Wykłady krakowskie*, Cracow: Akademia Sztuk Pięknych im. J. Matejki. Wydział Architektury Wnętrz.

Rewers Ewa 2005, *Post-polis. Wstęp do filozofii ponowoczesnego miasta*, Cracow: Universitas.

Rewers Ewa 1998, *Zdarzenie w przestrzeni miejskiej*, [in:] *Formy estetyzacji przestrzeni publicznej*, ed. J. St. Wojciechowski, A. Zeidler-Janiszewska, Warsaw: Instytut Kultury.

Rok Agata 2011, „Ewolucja memu "Czarnej Wdowy" w przestrzeni miejskiej, czyli o urban legends w Santa Cruz de la Sierra, Boliwia", *Teksty z Ulicy*, No. 13, (on-line: http://www.memetyka.us.edu.pl ISSN 2081 – 397 X).

Rumińska Anna 2009, *Teksty literackie w przestrzeni publicznej miasta. Studium przypadku: Wrocław*, [in:] *Kody kultury. Interakcja, transformacja, synergia*, ed. H. Kubicka, O. Taranek, Wroclaw: Wydawnictwo Sutoris.

Rybicka Elżbieta 2012a, „O możliwości performatyki miasta", *Didaskalia*, No. 109–110, pp. 28–35.

Rybicka Elżbieta 2012b, *Zwrot topograficzny w badaniach literackich. Od poetyki przestrzeni do polityki miejsca*, [in:] *Kulturowa teoria literatury 2. Poetyki, problematyki, interpretacje*, eds. T. Walas, R. Nycz, Cracow: Universitas [expanded edition (Rybicka 2008)].

Rybicka Elżbieta 2011, „Geografia, literatura, wyobraźnia: w stronę wspólnego słownika", *Tematy z Szewskiej*, No. 1.

Rybicka Elżbieta 2008, "Od poetyki przestrzeni do polityki miejsca. Zwrot topograficzny w badaniach literackich", *Teksty Drugie*, No. 4.

Rybicka Elżbieta 2006, *Geopoetyka (o mieście, przestrzeni i miejscu we współczesnych teoriach i praktykach kulturowych)*, [in:] *Kulturowa teoria literatury. Główne pojęcia i problemy*, ed. M.P. Markowski, R. Nycz, Cracow: Universitas.

Rybicka Elżbieta 2003, *Modernizowanie miasta. Zarys problematyki urbanistycznej w nowoczesnej literaturze polskiej*, Cracow: Universitas.

Rykiel Zbigniew 2008, *Szata deiznformacyjna miasta*, [in:] *Szata informacyjna miasta*, ed. B. Jałowiecki, W. Łukowski, Warsaw: Wydawnictwo Academica & Wydawnictwo Naukowe Scholar.

Rzepka Bartosz, Bugaj Anna 2011, "Zamknijcie swoja miłość na kłódkę", *Gazeta Wyborcza. Poznań*, No. 51. [on-line: http://poznan.gazeta.pl/poznan/1,36037,9192606,Zamknijcie_milosc_na_klodke.html].

Shepard Leslie 1973, *The History of Street Literature. The Story of Broadside Ballads, Chapbooks, Proclamations, News-Sheets, Election Bills, Tracts, Pamphlets, Cocks, Catchpennies, and Other Ephemera*, Newton Abbot (Devon): David & Charles.

Stępień Tomasz 2002, *Poezja ulicy*, [in:] *Dwudziestowieczna ikonosfera w literaturach europejskich. Wizualizacja w literaturze*, ed. B. Tokarz, Katowice: Śląsk.

Suchojad Izabela 2010, *Topografia żydowskiej pamięci. Obraz krakowskiego Kazimierza we współczesnej literaturze polskiej i polsko-żydowskiej*, Cracow: Universitas.

Sulima Roch 2000, *O imionach widywanych na murach*, [in:] *Antropologia codzienności*, Cracow: Wydawnictwo UJ.

Warszawskie gry literackie 2009, ed. A. Czetwertyńska, K. Grubek, Warsaw: Fundacja Centrum Edukacji Obywatelskiej (on-line: http://www.ceo.org.pl/sites/default/files/CEO/davBinary/Publikacje/gry_literackie1.pdf).

Wolting Monika 2005, *Przejęcie motywów literackich przez współczesną sztukę studzienną*, [in:] *Motyw studni w literaturze i sztuce niemieckiej. Studium kulturoznawcze*, Wroclaw: Oficyna Wydawnicza ATUT – Wrocławskie Wydawnictwo Oświatowe.

Zagajewski Adam 2002, "Ironia i ekstaza", interviewed by B. Gruszka-Zych, *Tygodnik Powszechny*, No. 12.

Zeidler-Janiszewska Anna 1997, *Słowo wstępne*, [in:] *Pisanie miasta – czytanie miasta*, ed. A. Zeidler-Janiszewska, Poznan: Wydawnictwo Fundacji Humaniora.

Żakowska Anna 2009, "Hegemonia porządku i utopia wiecznie żywa", *Kultura Popularna*, No. 2.

Natalia Lemann*

University of Lodz

LITERARY STUDIES, HISTORY AND POPULAR CULTURE – THE SPACES OF CONVERGENCE

Abstract

The aim of the article is to juxtapose literary studies, literature and history as neighboring branches of humanistic knowledge. The author compares the methodologies of history and literary studies in the field of narrativity, and, in accordance with Hayden White, comprehends history as a type of fiction, historio-graphia, and literary artifact. In this optics historiography and literary studies are diagnosed as forming a sisterhood relationship. When the opportunity arises it is shown that the idea of postmodern history is no novelty, since up until the decline of the XVIIIth century history and literary studies have not been opposite at all. Actually, the way of thinking about history as an (literary) art has a splendid tradition rooted in antiquity. In the scope of Braudel`s history of the "longue durée" it is the model of history as a (hard) science separated from literary studies as an art and ideographical science that constitutes a methodological aberration. Comparative analysis leads to the conclusion, that both these "scientific" branches developed almost simultaneously (cf. feminism, gender, postcolonialism, posthumanism, animal studies). Moreover literary genres, such as the (post)modern historical novels, alternate histories or historical fantasy, opened the space of convergence between history and the literary, because of mutual fluctuation and the "parasiting" of ideas, topics and poetics. The participation of popular culture makes the history and literary studies more transgressive, widely open for contemporary forms of communication and more hearable. In this scope, the author presents historical game books, facebook`s historical events, transmedia historical stories.

Key words: Literary studies, historio-graphia, popculture, (post)modern historical novels, alternate histories, historical fantasy, new forms of communication

---

* Institute of Contemporary Culture, University of Lodz, Pomorska 171/173, 90-236 Lodz, e-mail: natalialemann@uni.lodz.pl

Natalia Lemann

Introduction

Literary and historical studies, ones of the most important and at the same time, neighboring branches of humanistic knowledge, have stayed in close and multilevel contacts from their origins. Their relations could be described as a sisterhood; therefore, it is no wonder that they went through stormy quarrels, hysterical separations and affectionate reunions... Nowadays, when thanks to deep and various changes in humanistic, both literary and historical studies became not even an inter- but a transdisciplinary, holistic science about the human being, it has become obvious that they could be closer than ever before. The narrative turn made historians understand[1] that history as the rerum gestarum is subjected to the same creational and interpretational principles as literature stricto sensu. As a result of focusing attention on the historical narration, "only the text (discourse, narration) remains as the subject of analysis, separated from outside-the-text reality, which is from its ontological and epistemological context. History in this scope became not the study of past reality, but the result of a literary, rhetorical act" (Topolski 1996: 84). No wonder that, Dominic La Capra suggested that the academic study of history be relocated to literary or philosophy faculties (La Capra 1985; Topolski 1996: 85). Obviously such opinion is extreme and rare[2] among historians, but it depicts well the leaning of history towards literature, ongoing for a long time.

Beginning with Roland Barthes and his famous manifesto announcing the universalism of the narrative (1966) – "international, transhistorical, transcultural: it is simply there, like life itself" (Barthes 1977: 79) or "is it fully legitimate to see a constant opposition between the discourses of poetry and of the novel, the fictional narrative and the historical narrative?" (Barthes 1981: 7). Modifications in the paradigm of history led to a modification in thinking about history – the narrative history. Linda Orr in her work about Michelet claimed categorically that history and literature could not be defined separately in the sense that the former has to

---

[1] Methodologists of history stress the importance of raising historians` self-awareness. Meant are elementary points, such as the semantic range of basic historical concepts, which, according to Reinhart Koselleck`s observation (Koselleck 2001; 2009) are inconstant and change their meaning, affecting the rules of historical ratiocination.
[2] Most historians, among others Jerzy Topolski, protect the scientific, empirical status of history. Of course, this attitude does not question the narrative nor the rhetorical character of historical works.

be understood as relating to facts, and the former as relating to fiction (Orr 1976). In turn, Arthur Danto claimed that 'history tells stories" (Danto 1965), while for Hayden White history is historio-graphy, a verbal artifact, writing about history being "the kind of writing belonging to the class of artistic discourses" (White 2009: 80) because "the history is the land of fantasy" (White 2009: 37). Historical knowledge is constructed, thus belonging to the field of constructivism, and therefore it cannot be understood as totally alternative to literature and fiction. (White 2009: 12–13).

History and literature in the longue durée perspective – a perverse picture

Of course, the narrativist historians did not want to question totally either the scientific status of history or its ability to draw apposite conclusions. Their aim was to direct attention to the humanistic, ideographic, and not nomothetic character of history. Both historical sources and historical narratives (res gesta and rerum gestarum, or following another terminology primary and secondary historical sources) have a narrative and thus a rhetorical, persuasive and construable character. The crucial goal of narrativist historians was to make historians see clearly the constructiveness of history, as opposed to the widely accepted, derived from the XIXth century positivism idea of history as a science equal to natural sciences. But even in XIX$_{th}$ century historians were aware that history resembled literature in many ways.

Leopold von Ranke, an adherent of the "scientific" approach to history and author of the famous formula that "history has to tell how it really was" („er bloss will sagen, wie es eigentlich gewesen") (Ranke 1874, as cited in: Grabski 2003: 473, cf. Heintel 1979; Kosellecek 2001: 94) – wrote in 1831:

> History is different from science insofar that it is simultaneously art. History is a science because it collects, finds and penetrates; it is art because it re-forms, representing what was found and recognized. (…) As a science history is related to philosophy, and as art it is connected to poetry. (…) History blends them in something else entirely, something exclusively specific of history. (Ranke 2003: 82–83).

Since Ranke emphasized the importance of details in historical research, Hans Robert Jauss saw him as the precursor of the microhistorical approach (Ranke 2003: 84, cf. Jauss 2003: 406–412) or even of the ethical turn. The proof of Ranke`s ethical and empathic attitude are the following words:

> In the historical work not only the author's being and opinions are expressed; it is interesting for us rather because of the alien life contained therein. Many of what was described was lost, other things were not described at all – all this was touched by death; they did not die completely, their essence and being affect inasmuch as they are understood; the true death comes when memory dies. (Ranke 2003: 91–92).

The roots of the narrative turn in historiography apparently stick deeper in the historiographical soil than it is commonly believed. It is interesting that the famous formula "to tell how it really was" gets a slightly different meaning when quoted in its full context:

> History was designated to judge the past and advise the present-day, for the benefit of future generations; this essay is not worthy of such high authority; it only wants to tell how it really was. (Ranke 1874, as cited in: Grabski 2003: 473).

This is how the German historian protests against the historia magistra vitae topos, advocating the singularity of events and timing of the past (history understood as a singular event or a universal relationship of dependences: Kosellecek 2001: 87) as opposite to history (educational exemplum message: Kosellecek 2001: 87). It is important to remember the concept that history and the singularity of events are not completely synonymic is due to Reinhard Koselleck. This significant concept shifting, causing a new understanding of the term "history" took place in the XVIIIth century. Since that time history has been not only the sum of all stories (*rerum gestarum*), but has also included rules of its own functioning and generating, constituting an undisputable entity in its singularity (history as historical process, *res gestae*).Thanks to the convergence of hitherto different concepts history became its own subject (*res gestae*) and object (*rerum gestarum*) (Kosellecek 2001: 85–106; Kosellecek 2009: 71–77). Perceiving the non-classical, or even 'postmodern' elements in Ranke`s philosophy of history shed a new light on the essence of the narrative turn in history. It appears that the critique of Ranke by Hayden White or Franklin Ankersmit could be understood as a failed attempt to prevent unwanted methodological affiliations. It is based on hyperbolization and, according to Harold Bloom`s "the anxiety of influence" theory, on demonization (Bloom 2002) of thoughts of forerunners, in some ways even too similar to postmodern historian concepts, is made obvious by the intentional 'mis-reading' or 'un-reading' Ranke`s, fitting him totally into the paradigm of scientific and positivistic thinking about history, so as to make sure that there is no similarity to narrativist thought in the reception of his ideas (cf. Lemann 2008: 5–39). That in turn proves the importance of reading works of well-known historians individually and penetratingly, even if they seem to have a long established position in the academic world. In fact, postmodern historians recalled the old concept of perceiving history as connected with art, dating it back to antiquity. "Historia est proxima poetis est quaddammodo carmen solutum", said Kwintylian (Institutionis oratoriae, lib. X, 31).

The exploration of connections between history and literature leads us to Aristotle, who saw history and poetry as separate insofar that "it is not the role of the poet to relate what happened, but what may happen – what is possible according to the law of probability or necessity. (…) The true difference is that one relates what has happened, the other what may happen" (Aristotle: IX). His conclusion was that poetry was more philosophic and serious because "Poetry, therefore, is a more philosophical and a higher thing than history: for poetry tends to express the universal, history the particular." (Aristotle: IX). It`s tempting to think that the ensuing development of history as a science contradicted this distinction. When applying the Koselleck`s differentiation between history (rerum gestarum) and the historical process (res gestae) it becomes obvious that history was first focused on the general, exemplary, repetitive (history as a story, rerum gestarum) and afterwards on the undivided, integral and unrepeatable (history as the historical process, res gestae). The minuteness postulated in Ranke`s works was a way of making the chronicle description maximally scrupulous and detailed. The detail as such was not essential; its function consisted in concretization of political, factual history. It became an essential component of the historical narrative only with the upcoming of microhistory, one of the most important currents in unconventional historiography (Domańska 1996, 1999, 2006, Topolski 1996; 1998). A specific detail or a specific, unique, human being now became the subject of research and description thanks to its usefulness for re-construction of a specific culture, symbolizing this culture through micro-descriptions. Geertz`s 'thick description' is applied to the "small" object of observation, thus uncovering deep hidden culture patterns. Invisible in the scope of classical, political history, the ordinary man returns to the history. It is possible because of the extension or change of the definition of historical source, now encompassing private, commercial, judicial and ecclesiastical documents, hitherto skipped. Jerzy Topolski, a high-valued Polish methodologist of history stated that "It is worth to practice history just for simple fact of knowing that Béatrice de Planissoles really existed" (Topolski 1998: 155). Béatrice de Planissoles, a woman from the Middle Ages (the XII/XIII Centuries) was brought out from the darkness of oblivion by Emmanuel Le Roy Ladurie and became the heroine (sic!) of his book Montaillou, village occitan de 1294 à 1324 [1975]. Le Roy Ladurie belongs to the third generation of the French school of Annales, focused on social history and microhistory. From the Braudel`s perspective of longue durée the scientific, positivistic paradigm created by Ranke et al. could be described as a methodological perversion.

For precision's sake it has to be reminded that until the late XVIIIth century, history and literature were not divided. Until the XIXth century history was a part of literature (Culler 1998: 30) and "history was a type of oratorical discourse and the subject of rhetoric" (White 2009: 28). Even today the historical narrative is shown as a part of the literature of a specific period. It is obvious for instance in the prominent series History of European`s Literature published from 1977 by PWN (cf. Topolski 1996: 5–6). The first history chair was founded in 1504 at the University of Mainz. The aim of the „Lectura historiae" chair was reading writers of antiquity, because of their ability to give "moral lessons", and interpreting ethical ideas (history known as "vitae magistra"). Its head, Bernhard Schofferlin, in his translation of Titus Livy work (Ab Urbe condita libri CXLII) indicated profits from the study of the ancient writers and philosophers. The first chairs of history in the modern sense were founded in Germany at the decline of the Napoleon Bonaparte era, in Berlin in 1810 and later at the Sorbonne, in 1812. Sometime earlier, during the Enlightenment, (1737) the University of Göttingen was founded, which soon became famous as the "historical university", thanks to David Köhler, creator of „Academia Historica", the first ever historical institute (Grabski 2003: 354–355). In XIXth century historians attached equal importance to historic credibility and to literary quality of their works, knowing perfectly that literary values were not contrary to historical one. Moreover, literary values guaranteed popularity, which in turn increased the range of the "historical reality effect". Jacob Burchardt, Leopold von Ranke, Karol Szajnocha, Jules Michelet, Christian Matthias and Theodor Mommsen, the laureate of literary Nobel Prize in 1902 are still read with pleasure, since their works are not only works of history, but also ones of literature,

All the more surprising is the opinion of a famous Polish historian, Marcin Kula, who stated while researching historical reportage as a kind of contemporary historiography that "history ought to be either scientific (factual history) or interesting to read, Tertium non datur" (Kula 2011: 311), thus invalidating, at least to a certain extent, the great importance of the literary splendor of former historiography. It could be an effect of the progressing specialization of historians; as Kula himself said: "there are no historians any longer, there only exist specialists of specific periods" (Kula 2011: 311). Probably Kula is afraid that the scientific character of history would melt in the literary, belles-lettres elements. Fortunately there are historians more affirmatively perceiving the changes in their field. For instance, Andrzej Radomski, interpreting the works of Ryszard Kapuściński, sees the latter as a historian of contemporary times, although admitting of course that from the point of view of academic history his works "lack detailed analysis of sources, establishing facts, flicking trough archives or critical historical apparatus" (cf. Radomski 2010: 82). It is symptomatic that Kula in his article quoted above also refers to Kapusciński, uncovering his own "ambivalent attitude to the referred issue (N.L: to the domination of the literary element in the historical reportage)" (Kula 2011: 311).

However, Marcin Kula reluctantly admitted that:

> *The Szachinszach* and *The Emperor* contributed a lot to the understanding of the revolution phenomena even in the historians community. I`m afraid that the aforementioned reportages were more significant than our numerous works, often too monographic and scholarly to be suitable for reading or for generalization, a prerequisite of scientificity. (Kula 2011: 311)

It is however Andrzej Radomski, an adherent of opening of the university borders, who boldly asks the important question "On the other hand, why only the academic historiography is to have monopoly on historical knowledge?" (Radomski 2010: 82). The same issue was raised a few years earlier by Krzysztof Pomian: „It would be easy to don the academic robe and announce that only works of academic historians belong to history, whereas the other ones are mere journalism or literature, which allows to treat them indulgently or even contemptuously." (Pomian: 2006: 224).

The question of novelization of history, of the presence of literary elements in historical works and of a loss of monopoly on 'truth' is a subject of controversy among academic historians. Not for all of them it is easy to adapt to the dynamically changing rules of production/creation and distribution of knowledge. It shows that not everyone eagerly accepts either the necessity of negotiating their "vocabulary" with the world or the fact that that neither "dictionary" is the final one.

Natalia Lemann

"The third way" – history willing to be literature

Tertium est datur! Such historical bestsellers as Stalingrad by Anthony Beevor are an example of a third way, approaching the historical monograph to the poetic of reportage. This historian noticed that his popularity is the effect of: "the long tradition, whose father was Edward Gibbon. Afterwards, it had great heirs like Thomas Carlyle, Macaulay, Trevelyan. This is history understood as a story, a narrative. We, in England, have always believed that history is a part of literature. That there is a need for reconciling the academic lecture of history with a well told story allowing for good reading." (Beevor, Stasiński 2009). It should also be reminded that Theodor Mommsen was the laureate of the Noble prize for literature! For Anthony Beevor history is a bestseller, and exactly that is the title of his interview. Marcin Kula, whose opinion was quoted above, mentioning the surname of Stalingrad`s author, paraphrased his words significantly: "Beevor stated, that history is not [bold by N. L.] a science but a bestseller." (Kula 2010: 310). But those are not the exact words used by Beevor, and it is significant and to a certain degree alarming that for Kula the terms "science" and "bestseller", which is "literature" are totally disjunctive. In such optics there is no possibility for the historical to be literary at the same time.

Contrarily to this hermetic opinion, nowadays even the status of "celebrity historian" has emerged. This term, in my opinion, is useful for understanding the position of Norman Davies as an exquisite historian, famous for his precision and very popular thanks to the literary values of his publications, such as: *The God`s Playground. A History Of Poland*, II vol; *Europe: A History*; *Rising `44: The Battle for Warsaw*) or (for different reasons), the status of Jan Tomasz Gross. The latter is a controversial scholar/writer, who used scandal as a strategy of promotion and marketing (cf. Michałowski 2003: 80). It has to be honestly said that his works (*The Neighbors: The Destruction of the Jewish Community of Jedwabne*, Poland; *Fear: Anti-Semitism in Poland After Auschwitz*; *Golden Harvest*) are very well written and they are asking to be analyzed in the manner literary texts are. It seems that precisely the analysis of the narrative and persuasive strategy and of the rhetorical tools could be the best way of understanding and most of all neutralizing the Gross` writing phenomena. Contrasting strictly academic 'obese' and detailed monographs with Gross` works is not efficient in the discussion with an author of historical bestsellers. In the mediality era a historian who wants to be heard has to be (again) a good writer.

History and literary studies – methodological biographies, non-ideally parallel

The phenomenon of convergence between history and literary studies is older than the term convergence. According to Henry Jenkins, it describes a new era of transition, where new media collide "by convergence I mean the flow of content across the multiple media platforms, the cooperation between multiple media industries and the migratory behavior of media audiences who will go almost anywhere in search of the kind of entertainment experiences they want. Convergence is a word that ménages to describe technological, industrial, cultural and social changes depending on who`s speaking and what they think they are talking about." (Jenkins 2006: 2–3). Convergence is a permanent process, and therefore it seems that this term could be projected into the past so as to search its earlier forms and effects. Especially interesting is the relationship between history and literary studies and most of all phenomena which came into being or were intensified by functioning in the transmedia platform, i.e. in the reality of Web 2.0 and in the field of complicated fluctuations occurring throughout Internet and popular culture. The intention here is to indicate first the major points of convergence between history and literary studies as far as their methodological paradigms are concerned, happening basically without the participation of new media.

A lot of methodological paradigms developed parallel in history and literary studies. This in turn proves the necessity of a holistic view of humanistics irrespective of its particular branch. It seems that literary studies, and above all theory of literature are more 'elastic', adaptable to methodological changes than their more conservative 'sister' history. The reception of methodological innovations is parallel in history and in literary studies, but in the former it occurs more naturally, without strong resistance from the academic community.

Feminism and gender studies in literary studies developed parallel with the project of her-story in historical studies, both originating from the late sixties (cf. Ohrn 1995; Domańska 1994). It was the effect of the emancipation and of subversive objection to patriarchal historiography, therefore it was connected with social, political and academic changes. Women participating in this movement perceived classical historiography as the phallocentric weeding out of women from history. Paraphrasing the famous words of Gayatri Spivak it could be said that women asked the question "could the woman speak (in history)?" Indeed, in traditional historical sources, suitable for the political, factual history, women hardly ever appeared, thus proving the existence of "Great Silence", mentioned by Mary Daly (Daly 1973, cf. Gajewska 2008: 28). It is striking that second wave feminism does not attach any importance to the classification of and division between humanistic scholarly disciplines, and it even returned to the old meaning of the term "literary" (including rerum gestarum). Feminist publishing houses, like Virago Press (established by Carmen Callil in 1973) published belle-letters as well as scientific historical monographs alike.

It is worth observing that feminism as a methodology encountered some obstacles while penetrating the academic community. Basically, in several countries (including Poland) it remained an "insurrection" project connected with subaltern studies. It is only today, when in Western scholarship women studies are a kind of played-out paradigm in which they start to find their way into academic consciousness. In the nineties, professor Anna Żarnowska founded the Women`s History Comitte affiliated with PAN (Polish Academy of Sciences), and active till 2010. After the founder's death prof. Jadwiga Hoff became its chairwoman. The Committee`s work resulted in an VIII volume series of "Woman and….", presenting multiple aspects of women`s life in Poland in XIXth and XXth centuries (woman and society, politics, education, culture, work, marriage).

An example of interest in women`s history in contemporary scholarly life in Poland are scientific conferences organized by IPN (Institute of National Memory), such as "Women in the Social Resistance and Political Opposition in Poland (1944–1989) – comparative view and its second edition, taking place in September 2012: "Women at the crossroads: 1939–1989[3]. One should also mention the Internet project Historia Pol(s)ki (History of Poland(les)women),organized by Gender Studies, Warsaw Group and PAN (http://historiapolki.genderstudies.pl/). Each of those projects has a transdiciplinary character. Compared with the above, the achievements of feminist and gender researchers in literary studies are perfectly well known, and it is not necessary to quote their abundant bibliography.

Some methodological retardation could be also observed in the postcolonial reflection in historiography. The (Post)-colonial novel is notably earlier than the founding work of Edward Said (*Orientalism*, 1973), and similarly postcolonial research in literary studies is prior to the historiographical

---

[3] I had the pleasure to participate in this conference and I could observe that IPN community members were reluctant towards this problem. They suggest that there exist much more "grave" issues to be discussed, like political opposition. However, the extent of the discussed issues demonstrated that women`s history in the PRL history is an important scientific problem but unfortunately neglected by some academics.

reflection about colonialism. Subaltern Studies Group was founded at the beginning of the eighties, its basic aim being the re-writing of India's history, according to signals coming from (post)colonial novels and the theory of literature. Nowadays, the natural fluctuation between postcolonial historiography and literary studies could be named precisely convergence. This part of the subject is extremely interesting, but is unfortunately beyond the scope of this paper. Microhistory is another current of historical research developed in connection with literary studies and art. The shifting of gravity center in philosophy of history from historical representation (dominating in the 80-ties) to memory studies (cf. Ankersmit 2004: 367–401; Saryusz-Wolska 2009, LeGoff 2007) and historical experience took place in mid-nineties. Microhistorical writing is still the most popular kind/genre of the unconventional historiography. "History afresh leans over the man" (Domańska 1999: 20) said Ewa Domańska and indeed, such history is more humane, respecting the human experience. Microhistorians describe small events of common days, days without the hot breath of history. They concentrate on the research of "small worlds": villages, small towns, streets, backyards and families, the simple life of their existence, which are worth remembering because of their otherness and uniqueness. Books like *The Great Cat's Massacre* (1984) by Robert Darnton, *Cheese and Worms* (1976) by Carlo Ginzburg or Montaillou: *Village occitan de 1294 à 1324* (1975) by Emmanuel Le Roy Ladurie have action, protagonists, dialogues, and a non-discreet narrator (the historians of "I": cf. Domańska 1999). It is obvious that this kind of historical writing owes a lot to belles-lettres. Those books are bestsellers, read not only by historians. An extremely interesting one is Simon Schama's *Dead Certainties* (1991). This historical work has no footnotes and the leading character gen. Wolfe is fictional. Schama's book is factually valuable, but the truth being spoken is more essential than literal. Schama, according to Aristotle's distinction, reached (with excellent results) poetical abilities, depicting events "that may have happened". The microhistorians' works show that it is possible to stay faithful to the requirements of "scientific" history, being at the same time a writer. Moreover, it is also possible to be a historian while choosing the artistic modus of writing, instead of the strictly academic one.

Sometimes the distinction between science and art is so vague that the book is hard to classify. This is the case of Peter Englund's writing. Books such as *The Beauty and Sorrow: An Intimate History of First World War* constantly meanders between historiographical work and belle-lettres, which is actually hardly surprising in the array of Geertz' blurred genres. In the introduction Englund states:

> This is the book about First World War. This isn't a story about the War. You rather find the human not the facts, rather expressions, experiences and moods than war processes. My aim was reconstruction the worlds of feelings not the progress of fighting. (...) This is, in a sense a work of anti-history, an attempt to deconstruct this utterly epoch-making event into its smallest, most basic component – the individual, and his or her experiences. (Englund 2011: 7).

There is no doubt that Englund's book is much more easily readable than the monumental opus *The First World War* by Janusz Pajewski (1991). The former gives also a much deeper – because it is filtrated through specific humans existences – humanistic understanding of what happened during the four years of this total war.

Non-anthropocentric history (especially animal studies and post-humanism) is another current which has developed simultaneously in the field of historical research and theory of literature. Animal studies in history, among others the role of draught animals in the economic development of Europe; horses in the conquest of America; animal trials in the Middle Ages, have been undertaken since the second generation of Annales (cf. Darnton 1984). Nowadays the popularity of this kind of research is constantly growing, inter alia thanks to the mass-media and convergence era. The participation of animals in epoch-making events is discussed and their own 'history': horses (Bucephalus, the horse of Alexander the Great, the 'chestnut' mare own by Józef Piłsudski); birds (Capitoline gooses who saved Rome), famous elephants (the notorious elephants serving in Hannibal's army, but also Salomon, a character of the extraordinary fact-based novel *The Elephant's Journey* by Jose Saramago, a Nobel prize in literature winner. Salomon was a wedding gift for archduke Maksymilian Habsburg (XVIth century) and it made a long journey from Lisbon to Vienna.); dogs (sheepdog Blondi belonging to Adolf Hitler, Łajka, the dog-astronaut). It seems that the radical shifting of perspective proposed by animal studies is in its literary aspect the effect of the "points of view" strategy, perfectly known in literary studies and initiating the "bizarre" perspective (cf. W. Szkłowski). In literature the animal perspective has been known since antiquity, for instance in Apuleius of Madaura's Metamophoses or the Golden Ass. Using this bizarre, original focalization enables extraordinary literary effects, and results in a strong empathy of the reader/spectator and his immersion in the literary world. That in turn makes the voice of the Other clearly hearable and creates the opportunity to show human matters with desirable detachment. Nowadays probably everyone knows the story of "Wojtek, soldier bear", a Syrian brown bear, "corporal Wojtek", adopted by soldiers of the 22nd Artillery Supply Company of the Polish II Corps, commanded by Gen. Anders. Wojtek served during the battle of Monte Cassino. The person who brought Wojtek to public attention, allowing him to speak (it could be seen that animal studies belong to the insurrectional, subaltern studies current in historiography) was Major Wiesław Antoni Lasocki, who wrote 3 books dedicated to the brave bear[4]. The first one was published in London in 1968 (Wojtek spod Monte Cassino: opowieść o niezwykłym niedźwiedziu). Mjr Lasocki is the precursor of animal history, a fact which has been often forgotten; in 1966 he wrote a book titled *Żołnierze i zwierzęta* [*Soldiers and Animals*]. Nota bene it is a contribution to the discussion about the nature of the scientific revolution and the tempo at which methodological 'innovations' spread as well as of the transformation of those 'innovations' into scientific paradigms. It is no wonder that in the convergence era this process has become faster. Wojtek's story owes its popularity precisely to documentary movies, a Polish production *Piwko dla niedźwiedzia*, 2008 [*Beer for a Bear*] by Maria Dłużewska, and Wojtek, *The Bear Who Went to War* [*O niedźwiedziu co poszedł na wojnę*], from 2010, directed by Will Hood and Adam Lavis in cooperation between TVP and BBC. The history of Anders` army combat trail seen from the bear's point of view is simply much more interesting! It is also noteworthy that Wojtek`s brothers in arms, used to reaching for the heroic ethos in their war memoirs (and therefore to sad, melancholic tones, and according to White`s tropology to the tragedy topos) smile while talking about their recollections about Wojtek and the soldier bear's adventures. Thus denying the stereotypical opinion that in times of war people do not have a right to joy. The story of Wojtek, soldier bear already has a comic strip version, available in 4 languages. It was created by pupils of Zespoł Szkół Tekstylno-Handlowych in Żagań as part of the Etwinning projects [Jak niedźwiedź Wojtek został polskim żołnierzem, http://www.zsth.home.pl/etwinning/nasz_komiks.html]. The story of Wojtek is a typical example of a transmedia story (Jenkins 2007: 260). Similarly popular is the story of the rabbits who used to live in no-man`s land near the Berlin Wall, *Królik po Berlińsku*, directed by Bartosz Konopka and Piotr Rosołowski [*Rabbit à la Berlin*, 2009].

Post-humane historiography i.e. one based on the category of abiekt (J. Kristeva`s term) is another current developing slowly but consequently. This proposition is a part of non-classical, unconventional historiography, using "controversial scientific approaches, which are interesting because

---

[4] Incidently, in the English wikipedia site, dedicated to Wojtek [http://en.wikipedia.org/wiki/Wojtek_(soldier_bear)] mjr Lasocki`s books are not even mentioned.

they are inspiring proposals rather than prepared models" (Domańska 2006: 77). This non- anthropocentric historiography discusses for instance cannibalism in extreme situations or scatological issues, because "historiography aestheticizes things culturally threatening, (abominable)." (Domańska 2006: 101). It is worth emphasizing that aestheticization, a standard, elementary procedure in literature, gives the historiography the opportunity to include difficult problems into its field of research.

A awkward which needs to be asked is: is aestheticization of abominable allowed only in the field of historiography and forbidden in the belles-lettres?

For Domańska, post-humane issues are of interest such as: the status of shadows on the walls in Hiroshima and Nagasaki, resulting from nuclear explosions, which in fact are humans remains, imprinted into stones or pavements; or the moral value of commemorating human beings by means of implantation of human DNA into trees; or else production of LifeGems, artificial diamonds made of cremated human corpses; those diamonds are prêt-a-porter! (cf. Domańska 2005). All those problems open the wide field of philosophical and ethical questions, which have actually been brought up by the belles-lettres (especially SF) for a very long time already.

"The third way", second version
– literature willing to be history

It is the literature, or, more precisely, the historical novel and its latter invariants, that provide the widest space of convergence with history. It is easy to discover and describe the spreading of trends or the reciprocal fields of comparative inspirations. Lately Hayden White proposed the term "historical prose" arguing that "in the effect of long studies I'm sure that historical writing is itself a literary genre." (White 2009: 17; Introduction dated July 28th 2008). In his essays/articles published in this book White often refers not only to belle-lettres connected with history (Latin-American prose: Alejo Carpentier, Carlos Fuentes; *Austerlitz* by W. G. Sebald, alternative history genre, for example *The Plot Against America* by Philip Roth) but also to the movies, such as *JFK* by Oliver Stone. Stone`s movies are for White a proof of mixing up historical and fictional elements. White`s term "historical prose" could be juxtaposed with theoretical concepts like "historiographic meta-fiction" (Linda Hutcheon), palimpsest novel (Christine

Brooke-Rose) or "epic historiography" (Natalia Lemann). In the era of loss of monopoly on historic truth by academic historians and of democratization of the discourse about history, literature is able to be an art, speaking relevantly about historical facts, nature of historical process, epistemology, philosophy and methodology of history.

A few examples from my own research shall be pointed out[5]. Hanna Malewska, a writer and archivist working in Kórnik`s archive wrote *Listy staropolskeh z epoki Wazów* (1959) [*The Old-Polish Lettres from the Waza Epoch*] and *Panowie Leszczyńscy* [*The Leszczyński Gentlemen*] (cf. Lemann 2010: 217–233). The former is a historical work, a selection of epistolography with an afterword by Malewska, and the latter is a historical novel taking place during the Waza reign in Poland (1587–1668). The novel *Panowie Leszczyńscy* was widely commented upon by historians. Janusz Tazbir at first criticized the optimism in the evaluation of the political organization and state efficiency in the Waza era which in his opinion was immoderate. He also disapproved of Malewska's idealism in the assessment of her protagonists' motives, resulting in seeing many of them as political altruists. Later Tazbir changed his opinion and conceded that:

> After almost 40 years since the first review of Panowie Leszczyńscy the review author `s evaluation of the XVIIth century has changed and came close to the opinions expressed by Hanna Malewska in the commentary to Listy staropolskie and the novel [*Panowie Leszczyńscy*: N.L.]. Nowadays scholars evaluate the baroque era warmer and warmer, but no one wrote an anthology with a comparably discerning commentary. (Tazbir 2003)

Next in enumeration are the works of Jacek Bocheński (*Nazo the Poet*, 1970) and Christoph Ransmayr (*Die letzte Welt: The Last World*, 1988), who, although within different literary genres and independently of each other, both analyze the reasons of Ovid's exile. It is noteworthy, that both writers came to conclusions which escaped the attention of professional, academic historians. The latter, afraid of accusations of methodological mistakes, have omitted Ovid`s literary works as historical sources. Only recently have historians used in their inquiries Letters from Pontus and Regrets (Tristia) with the same results as the aforementioned writers (cf. Lemann

---

[5] In such juxtaposition one has to mention Tedor Parnicki, a key writer tracing the influences between history, literary studies and literature. The limited size of this paper prevents a full analysis of Parnicki`s novels, since it is simply impossible to speak briefly about them. The omission of Parnicki's works in this article is therefore a conscious academic choice. Therefore I refer anyone interested in my own studies about Parnicki to consider the following: (Lemann 2008: 39–71; Lemann 2012, Lemann 2012c).

2011: 129–148). Those examples prove that the contemporary historical novel, far from her Walter Scott- style cousin, has the power of outdistancing the research of professional historians. The major difference between such novels and academic historians' monographs consists in the choice of a different modus of writing; it has become obvious that the belles-lettres modus does not invalidate epistemological efficiency (cf. Lemann 2008). This is the right place to quote Aristotle's opinion that "The work of Herodotus[6] might be put into verse and it would still be a species of history, with metre no less than without it." (Aristotle: IX).

It is commonly known that writers eagerly use the works of academic historians, but nowadays it is also possible that literary bestsellers provoke or "re-fresh" interest in specific historical works. *Nasza Klasa [Our class]* a drama by Tadeusz Slobodzianek was inspired by books such as those by Jan Tomasz Gross (Gross 2004), *My z Jedwabnego (We, from Jedwabne*, Poland 2004) by Anna Bikont or documentaries like *Miejsce urodzenia [Place of Birth]* by Łoziński, *Shtetl* by Marzyński and *Sąsiedzi [The Neighbours]* by Arnold (2001). Słobodzianek`s drama "re-freshed" the interest in those texts of culture and made publicity for the work of IPN historians *Wokół Jedwabnego [Around Jedwabne,* 2002]. IPN historians notice that Słobodzianek in *Nasza klasa* omitted their research concerning the number of victims. The writer used Gross' statistics, instead of the IPN historians' ones. It is known that his drama provoked a public debate, which will probably be revived very soon, this time in connection with *Pokłosie [Aftermath]*, a movie by Władysław Pasikowski. The postmodernist strategy of parasitizing or, speaking more elegantly, the formula of alegacy (Giséle Mathieu-Castellani) is reciprocal. Słobodzianek exploits the results of scholarly research as a support of his creation and as a way of being 'trendy' while historians gain publicity.

"Historians did their job, the movie makers, politicians, journalists, attorneys, judges, moralists did their job. And the cadavers are still unburied." (Neuger 2009: 104). Whereas the public debate about Jedwabne bored the society, Słobodzianek`s drama was a new voice and gave the public discussion a new life. As Neauger sustains "the word once set free does not want to return to the sphere of silence." (Neuger 2009: 104). This observation provokes the question if obtaining the literary prize Nike by Słobodzianek, is not the effect of the effort of reviving this discussion again.

---

[6] Notabene, the Stagirite chose his example rather unhappily, since *The History* of Herodotus is not a model either of methodological self-consciousness or of proper procedure of source criticism. The authority of Herodotus as a historian was already undermined in ancient times.

The same situation might be observed in the case of W ciemności [In the Darkness], a movie by Agnieszka Holland, which brought a wave of interest in the memories of Krysia Chiger, Dziewczynka w zielonym sweterku [The Girl in the Green Sweater] (Chiger 2011) and of In the Sewers of Lvov: a Heroic Story of Survival from the Holocaust, a historical work by Robert Marshall (Marshall 2011). Also the widely commented, controversial novel The Kindly Ones [Les Bienveillantes, 2006], provoked a media storm in Poland and all over the world (cf. Izdebska 2011: 209–231; Koronkiewicz 2008; Chwin 2008; Pięciak 2008). The debate engaged journalists, historians and writers. According to Littell`s statement The Kindly Ones has had two major inspirations. The first one is a historical book by the aforementioned Antony Beevor, The Stalingrad – reading this book provoked an "irresistible vision of Maximilian Aue", the second one is a photograph of a hanged, cadaver of young Russian girl, half naked and gnawed by the dogs (fragment of interview with Little published in the "La Revue Littéraire", from maxaue.pl). The influence of this photograph should be interpreted in terms of semiofor (K. Pomian), that is to say a document mediating the past and constituting a specific prosthesis of memory, connecting the material and semiotic aspect (Pomian 2006: 143; cf. Ankersmit 2002: 55–83), whose ekphrasis may be found in the novel. Both Littell`s inspirations demand deeper analysis. The limitations of this paper allow only for the short observation that between the style and rhetoric of The Kindly Ones and Beevor`s Stalingrad numerous similarities adhering spaces might be observed, concerning the language and the way of analysing and depicting. The phenomenon of Little`s novel results in the fact that, as Pierre Nora`s said "On this level only a historian might understand such a phenomenon, not the publisher and not even the author." (this expression was quoted by Littell in an interview given to „Le Monde") [maxaue.pl]. Numerous historians took up the challenge of discussing Little`s novel, and expressed contradictory opinions: "The publication of The Kindly Ones by Littell ended the narrative crisis of contemporary prose (…) The suffering of people victimized by history is more true and credible in fiction than in historical academic discourse." (Michel Guénaire, quote for: maxaue.pl). The overwhelming majority of debaters accused Little`s novel of scatology and pornography of death. Here I would like to recall Domańska`s assertion that "historiography aesthetizised the abominable" (Domańska 2006: 101). The Kindly Ones cries for historical and literary analysis, as the very first sentence of the novel recalls not only Francois Villon`s The Great Testament – in English translation: "oh my human brothers let me tell you how it happened", in the French original "Frères humains, laissez-moi vous raconter comment ça s'est passé". (cf. Ètienne de Montety, "Le Figaro Littéraire", quote from maxaue.pl; Izdebska 2011: 209–231) but also the ironically paraphrased formula of scientific history by Ranke "to tell how it really was". Therefore, Littell's novel demands inspection in the aspect of ironical travesty of many historical methodological concepts, such as counter history (M. Foucault), of the danger of abusing the insurrection history project, of ironical "topsy turvy" tope of "epistemic privileges of the oppressed" (bell hooks) which is based on the assertion that executioners cannot have either their true history or the empathy of the reader. The last formulation sounds a little strange given the differences between classical historiography based on truth and the unconventional, non-classical one faithful to the category of sincerity. In the context of Aristotle`s distinction between poetry and history it is interesting that Littell was ready to write The Kindly Ones only when he understood that it had to be based on the structure of Oresteia by Aeschylus [interview with the writer made by Florent Georgesco, published in «La Revue Littéraire» n°28, autumn 2006, quote from maxaue.pl]. Thus in a new entourage the old questions return – if the structure of the tragedy can justify the aestheticization of Holocaust and death? Littell`s novel provokes questions fundamental for historical and literary studies, by the same token causing the raise of interest in the history of the Third Reich. The web site site, maxaue.pl, "encourages" the game. The reader, entering the site is obliged to choose one option: civilian or soldier. His next choice has to be answering a few basic questions ("breaking the code") about the Second World War's history. Now, how many persons give up the game and choose to enter the page as civilian? The exploitation of agon`s mechanism widens the space of empathy with the major character of The Kindly Ones.

Literature and history in the arms of popular culture – the issue of transgression and audibility

Nowadays it has become clear that even popular literary genres participate in the creation of historical consciousness. This phenomenon is evaluated in two ways, according to one's general approach to popular culture. There is a clash between the liberal attitude, represented among others by Richard Shusterman (Shusterman 1998), and the critical one. The "concern" (euphemistically speaking), or even fear is caused by the fact that alternate history and historical fantasy are important literary genres and have notable influences in the process of formation of historical knowledge and of the awakening of interest in history, not only for the young generation. It seems that skepticism towards those genres is the aftermath of a wider phenomenon – the approach to education. The historical fantasy 'label' should not be an instant act of anathema, particularly that this "odium" is connected with ignorance about principles of the genre. Historical fantasy novels might be and often are splendidly historically based. The proof could be Andrzej Sapkowski`s series about *Hussite wars* (Sapkowski 2002; 2004; 2006), utilized by Czech historian Martin Čapský in his biography of Przemek from Opawa (Čapský 2005). The Czech scholar not only enumerated Sapkowski`s novels in his bibliography (in the separate section next to historical sources and academic monographs) but also provided chapters of his monograph with quotations (mottos) therefrom. This "small historical realism" (Pietrasik 2007, Sapkowski, Bereś 2005: 131) is supported by the poetics of the fantasy genre. Pietrasik's term "small historical realism" is an allusion to a current in Polish prose from the first half of the sixties, depicting ordinary people's everyday life. In Pietrasik`s opinion Sapkowski comes close to this poetics, describing the filth of the streets, or the physiological side of human existence. However, in this aspect it seems more proper to use the neologism "the scatological realism". I therefore utilize Pietrasik's term, but in a different context. I suggest that this term is an excellent proposition for describing the endeavors of Sapkowski and other historical fantasy writers to create the "(historical) reality effect", as Roland Barthes put it (Barthes 1982). As a proposal the epithet "small" could be added as a form of distinction between the historical fantasy writers and historians. The fact that Sapkowski and other writers use historians' research was proven in the case study dedicated to *Hussite Wars* cycle by Sapkowski (cf. Lemann 2008: 141–177).

Fantasy writers are interested in basing their literary creation on professional historians statements because in this way the authority of history (alegacy: Giséle Mathieu-Castellani) supports the acting of the apocrypha strategy or, in other words, of the strategy of sub-creation (J. J. R. Tolkien) of magic into the flesh of commonly known historical events. It is very helpful to the process of the communication with the reader and of the strategy of lending credence. The reader acquainted with facts easier gives his approval for instance to the assertion that magic supported Wellington in winning the Waterloo battle (Clarke 2004) or that the participation of dragons was of great assistance to Napoleon Bonaparte`s adversaries (Temeraire series: Novik 2006). The readers are able to respect simultaneously principles of the game between factual history and fiction, because it is paradoxically encrypted in their "anticipation horizon" (W. Iser). Surprisingly for all skeptics the historical fantasy genre 'label' sharpens the vigilance and introduces the relational reading modus.

A very interesting example of the educational range of historical fantasy and of alternate history is the popularity of a novel by Seth Graham Green, *Abraham Lincoln: The Vampires Hunter* (2010). Recently also a movie directed by Timur Bekmambetow was released (2012). It is easy to guess that in the novel the young future president is occupied with hunting vampires who had killed his mother. Surprisingly, or horribly (it is a free choice depending on the attitude towards popular culture) the novel is strongly fact-based. It is significant that the public relations officer of Lincoln's library and museum Dave Blanchett said, that he was very happy with both the novel and the movie, because "thanks to the movie the history of the president became of interest for the young generation" (Blanchett). In this optics, it is totally irrelevant that this more than popular novel came to existence thanks to the vampire boom of last years. It is a fact that historical fantasy and alternate history novels simply awake the interest in history in the youngsters, referring them to the real historical text and contributing to a better historical knowledge. Interesting examples of convergence of history, literature and popular culture might be observed in the field of creating "a fashion" for some historical events. This type of action engaged literature, history and of course, popular culture and mass media. When Swedish heavy metal band Sabbaton recorded the song *Forty to One* dedicated to the Wizna Battle from September 1939, interest in this historical event, called "Polish Thermopiles", exploded in the mass media and popular culture. Curiously enough, it is said that information about the Wizna battle was given to Sabbaton by a Polish fan. As a result, the battle became a trans-media story. Rafał Rowiński created the comic book *Wizna 1939 40:1*, as part of the promotion strategy of Sabbaton's clip. This comic may be downloaded from www.wojskopolskie.pl. As could be observed, in a case like this the most important issue is the publicity submitted by the media, still commonly seen as belonging to very popular culture. The myth about "Polish Thermopiles" was sustained, because the conclusion is a paraphrase of a famous epigram by Simonides of Ceos' "Stranger, send the news home to the people of Sparta that here we/ Are laid to rest: the commands they gave us have been obeyed" This epigram in the 40:1 comic reads: "Passer-by, tell in the country that we fought till the end, doing our duty." (Roskowiński 2008: 12). Public television in Poland participated in the promotion, of the song's *40:1* and also in the promotion of another Sabbaton's song, *Uprising*, dedicated to the Warsaw Uprising of '44. Both songs were broadcast in the main edition of the news on TVP1. The story of captain Raginis immediately became a media story and finally, after almost 70 years, the grave of the courageous defender was found ... It is obvious that nowadays popular culture is of great support in the processes of building historical consciousness of society. The Wizna Battle and Capt. Raginis` story are very archetypical and heroic, and those are the reasons for the enormous interest therein. Public institutions eagerly use the popular culture media if they only see the opportunity of formation of the society`s historical consciousness in the way they wish. Popular culture could be a splendid educational medium and a part of history policy agency. History policy relies on – according to the words by Marek Cichocki, one of the term`s promoters – "strengthening the public discourse about history by various forms of its institutionalization." It is (using words of Dariusz Gawin), "the instrument of affirmation of collective consciousness (above all about common past)" (Cichocki 2006: 11; Gawin 2006; cf. Cichocka A., Panecka A. 2005; Gawin 2009).

At the occasion of Sabbaton`s song dedicated to the Wizna battle some popularity was gained by dr Tomasz Wesołowski, a historian researching the myth of Wizna for many years. Information went around that dr Wesołowski was working on a monograph dedicated to the Wizna battle (Wesłowski, Żmijewska 2009). Unfortunately, Wesołowski debunks the carefully cultivated myth and maybe this is the reason why his monograph has not been published yet.

The next literary genre of popular origin and with great educational potential is alternate history[7], forcing the reader into relational reading. The reader has to compare the literary creation of alternate history with the factual historical events. The educational potential of this genre was appreciated by NCK [National Cultural Centre, Warsaw] by initiating the series Zwrotnice Czasu [Switching Points of Time] including a novel series and a website game for the readers/Internauts. They are invited to propose their own ending for alternate scenarios published on the website. NCK intentionally utilized the Internet as a space of communication and interaction with the user for the purpose of building eligible visions of the past. The Internet might be an important support for public education. The Facebook medium was used for the project Henio on Facebook, an example of "commemoration in web society" (Solska 2011). The author of this project was Paweł Brożek, a history student, employee of the cultural centre Lublin "brama grodzka-teatr NN". On September, 18th 2009 he created a FB profile of the youngest Żytomirski family member, born in 1933, deceased in the Holocaust. The commemorative simulation of Henio`s profile was a great success. Henio was added to contact lists, he received

---

[7] I analyzed this genre in the following studies: Lemann 2011a; 2011b; 2012.

letters. It is a great example of positive utilization of Internet's educational potential in web society, relying on building bridges across generations and of a space of empathy allowed by micro historicity.

On the reverse of the official NCK's initiatives are grassroots initiatives democratizing the historical discourse. Such initiatives give the opportunity for undertaking debates about controversial historical issues, which in turn might lead to opening rooms for negotiations about history, and even for the restoration of deliberative democracy. A good example might be the www.powstanie.pl website, administrated by detractors of the Warsaw Uprising `44 myth whereit is possible to download monographs from (e.g. *Kulisy katastrofy powstania warszawskiego 1944. Wybrane publikacje i dokumenty, The Inside Story of the Disaster Warsaw Uprising `44 Selected Documents and Studies* 2009), presenting a different assessment of the Uprising. In order to ensure a dialogue, administrators of the website provided a full bibliography complete with links to apologetic studies.

Another extremely interesting idea concerning innovative historical education through the Internet are computer and board games. Also here convergence between history and literature may be observed. Unfortunately, it seems that history searching for innovative, unconventional media narration sometimes gets ambushed by "modernity". According to Jerzy Szeja, researcher and admirer of games, the games the great hope of Web 2.0 education (cf. Radomski 2010). As the game amateur, Szeja carefully avoids to mention such extravagances of too liberal an imagination as Dante's Inferno, a game condemned once by literature scholars and historians. In this game Dante departed on the third crusade (sic!), in the company of King Richard the Lion Heart, conquered Akka and moved on Jerusalem. All that, bagatelle, 200 years before *The Divine Comedy*! Colloquially speaking not every game which utilizes a historical or literary costume has educational potential...

The Museum of Warsaw Uprising also eagerly used games. Filip Małuński created the game *Mali Powstańcy* [*The Little Insurgents*], published by Egmont in cooperation with the Museum and Związek Harcerstwa Polskiego [Association of Polish Scouts]. The strategy of the game's promotion included a press conference in the Museum of Warsaw Uprising residence. The game's characters, little insurgents, had the task to transport dispatches across strategic points of the capital. The aim of game was to teach by way of entertaining, but unfortunately, it had disastrous reviews. It turned out that not only did it not teach about the Warsaw Uprising but it did not even encourage learning about the history of the Scouting Movement on one's own. Indeed, the game is playable and interactive, but suffers from lack of immersion into the created world and of opportunity for empathic identification with characters. After the failure of the game in the Internet a counter proposal game book Janek, historia małego powstańca, [Janek, the history of Little Insurgent] was created, written by dr Maciej Słomczyński and Beniamin Muszyński (www.masz-wybor.pl cf. Machocka 2009). Słomczyński noticed that "playing Little Insurgents [published by Museum of Warsaw Uprising: N.L.] willingly or unwillingly we infantilize the events of the Warsaw Uprising. If we attempt to understand, evaluate and form the attitudes and not only to remember, it has to be asked if a board game is the proper tool." (Słomczyński, Muszyński 2011: 5). The text of the game book *Janek, historia małego powstańca* is divided into numbered paragraphs and at the end of each paragraph the player makes a real choice, choosing alternate paths indicating the number of the following chapter. It is the player who decides how the story of Janek, little insurgent, develops – "you are at the same time reader, author and character". The game book offers navigation in alternate directions described by the metaphor of "tree of links" (Machocka 2009: 168). The identification with the characters is made possible by the dynamical narration. Out of concern for probability and educational values the game's creators provided a few "mines". Reckless bravado decisions result in death or serious injury of the player, and therefore in his return to the beginning of the game. This should induce the player to find a better, more careful path. "Remember also, that you are allowed the comfort of undoing the time, although in the combat field many little heroes and heroines did not have such a chance" (Słomczyński, Muszyński 2011: 11). The game book is encrypted in the comparative spaces together with the achievements of the OuLiPo Group or with literary masterpieces of Julio Cortazar`s *Rayuela* (*Hopscotch*) and Italo Calvino`s *Il castello dei destini incrociati* [*The Castle of Crossed Destinies*] and *Se una note d`inverno un viaggaiatore* [*If on a Winter`s Night a Traveler*] or the wrongly underestimated Die unendliche geschichte: Vor A biz Z [*The Neverending Story*] by Michael Ende.

Inthe example of the game book Janek, historia małego powstańca it can be very well seen that the widest spaces of convergence are across the history, literary studies and literature which are made possible by the phenomenon of narration. History and literary studies both speak about humans, and let it be reminded that narration is like life itself. In life, although there are tempests, breaking offs and happy reunions, still the important things are family bonds. And I hope that this study might be proof of a long existing sisterhood between history and the literary, the two of them similar and perfectly fitting together.

Bibliography

Ankersmit Frank 2004, *Postmodernistyczna „prywatyzacja" przeszłości*, trans. M. Zapędowska, [in:] Idem, *Narracja, reprezentacja, doświadczenie, Narracja, reprezentacja, doświadczenie. Studia z teorii historiografii*, ed. E. Domańska, Cracow: Universitas.

Ankersmit Frank 2002, *Pochwała subiektywności*, trans. T. Sikora [in:] *Pamięć. Etyka i historia. Anglo-amerykańska teoria historiografii lat dziewięćdziesiątych. Antologia przekładów*, ed. E. Domańska, trans. E. Domańska and others, Poznan: Wydawnictwo Poznańskie.

Aristotle, *Poetics*, trans. S. H. Butcher, A Penn State Electronic Classics Series Publication http://www2.hn.psu.edu/faculty/jmanis/aristotl/poetics.pdf.

Ashby Ruth, Ohrn Deborah (ed.) 1995, *Herstory: Women Who Changed the World*, New York: Viking Junevile Press.

Barthes Roland 1982, *The Reality Effect* [in:] *French Literary Theory Today. A Reader*, ed. Tzvetan Todorov, Cambridge: Cambridge University Press.

Barthes Roland 1981, *The Discourse of History*, trans. S. Bann, *Comparative Criticism*, 3 (1981): 7–20: http://www.clas.ufl.edu/users/pcraddoc/barthes.html.

Beevor Anthony 1999, *Stalingrad*, London: Viking Press.

Beevor Anthony, Stasiński Maciej 2009, „Historia to bestseller", *Gazeta Wyborcza* [19.03. 2009], cyt: http://wyborcza.pl/dziennikarze/1,84011,6399794,Historia_to_bestseller__a_-Brytyjczycy_wiedza__jak.html?as=1&startsz=x

Bereś Stanisław, Sapkowski Andrzej 2005, *Historia i fantastyka*, Warsaw: SuperNOWA.

Bikont Anna 2004, *My z Jedwabnego*, Wołowiec: Czarne.

Bloom Harold 2002, *Lęk przed wpływem. Teoria poezji*, trans. A. Bielik-Robson, M. Szuster, Cracow: Universitas.

Bocheński Jacek 1974, *Nazo poeta*, Warsaw: Czytelnik.

Čapský Martin 2005, *Vévoda Přemek Opavský (1366–1433). Ve službach posledních Lucemburků*, Brno-Opava: Knižnice Matice Moravské.

Chiger Krystyna 2011, *Dziewczynka w zielonym sweterku*, trans. D. Paisner, Warsaw: PWN.

Chwin Stefan 2008, „Erynie wybaczą każdemu", *Tygodnik Powszechny* No. 40/2008.

Cichocki Marek 2006, „Polityka historyczna za i przeciw", *Mówią wieki*, No. 8.

Clarke Susanne 2004, *Jonathan Strange & Mr Norrell*, New York and London: Bloomsbury.

Culler Jonathan 1998, *Teoria literatury. Bardzo krótkie wprowadzenie*, trans. M. Bassaj, Warsaw: Prószyński i S-ka.

Daly Mary 1973, *Beyond God the Father, toward a Philosophy of Women's Liberation*, Boston: Beacon Press.

Danto Arturo 1965, *Analytical Philosophy of History*, Cambridge: Cambridge University Press.

Darnton Robert 1984, *The Great Cat Massacre and Other Episodes in French Cultural History*, New York: Basic Books.

Domańska Ewa 2008, *O poznawczym uprzywilejowaniu ofiary. (Uwagi metodologiczne)*, [in:] *(Nie)obecność. Pominięcia i przemilczenia w narracjach XX wieku*, eds. Hanna Gosk and Bożena Karwowska, Warsaw: Elipsa.

Domańska Ewa 2006, *Historie niekonwencjonalne. Refleksja o przeszłości w nowej humanistyce*, Poznan: Wydawnictwo Poznańskie.

Domańska Ewa 2005, „Diatantaty. Prochy, diamenty i metafizyka obecności", *Czas Kultury* No. 3–4.

Domańska Ewa 1999, *Mikrohistorie. Spotkania w międzyświatach*, Poznan: Wydawnictwo Poznańskie.

Domańska Ewa 1996, *Montaillou – Arkadia „heretyckiego" historyka*, [in:] *Historia. Mity. Interpretacji*, ed. H. Barszczewska-Krupa, Lodz: Wydawnictwo Uniwersytetu Łódzkiego.

Domańska Ewa 1994, „Historia feminizmu i feministyczna historia", [in:] *Odra* No. 7–8.

Dziamski Grzegorz 1995, Co oznacza formuła „kryzys estetyki", *Kultura Współczesna*, No. 3–4, http://kulturawspolczesna.pl/sites/default/files/artykuly/662.pdf ds. 19.09.2012.

Englund Peter 2011, *Piękno i smutek wojny. Dwadzieścia niezwykłych losów z czasów światowej pożogi*, Cracow: Znak.

Gajewska Agnieszka 2008, *Hasło: Feminizm*, Poznan: Wydawnictwo Poznańskie.

Gawin Dariusz 2009, „Polityka historyczna – próba bilansu", *Arkana*, No. 6 (90), cited as in: http://www.teologiapolityczna.pl/dariusz-gawin-polityka-historyczna--proba-bilansu-arcana-nr-90-#p,1 [30.12.2011].

Gawin Dariusz 2006, „Wspólnota przeszłości", *Rzeczpospolita*, No. 07.10.2006. cited as in: http://www.teologiapolityczna.pl/gawin_06_10_wspolnota_przeszlosci, ds. 30.12.2011.

Ginzburg Carlo 1989, *Ser i robaki: wizja świata pewnego młynarza z XVI wieku*, trans. R. Kłos, Warsaw: PIW.

Goff Le Jacques 2007, *Historia i pamięć*, trans. A. Gronowska, J. Stryjczyk, introduction. P. Rodak, Warsaw: Czytelnik.

Grabski Andrzej Feliks 2003, *Dzieje historiografii*, introduction R. Stobiecki, Poznan: Wydawnictwo Poznańskie.

Green Seth Graham 2010, *Abraham Lincoln: Vampire Hunter*, New York: Grand Central Publishing.

Gross Jan Tomasz 2011, *Złote żniwa. Rzecz o tym, co się działo na obrzeżach zagłady Żydów*, Cracow: Znak.

Gross Jan Tomasz, 2008a, *Sąsiedzi. Historia zagłady żydowskiego miasteczka*, Cracow: Znak.

Gross Jan Tomasz 2008b, *Strach: Antysemityzm w Polsce, Historia moralnej zapaści*, Cracow: Znak.

Heintel Erich 1979, „*Jak to właściwie było?". Historiozoficzny przyczynek do problemu metody w historii*, [in:] *Perspektywy historiozoficzne*, ed. J. Litwin, Wroclaw–Warsaw: Ossolineum.

Izdebska Agnieszka 2011, „Opowieść dla „Braci śmiertelników", czyli „Łaskawe" Jonathana Littella", *Zagadnienia Rodzajów Literackich*, No. LIV, 54, issue. 1.

Jak niedźwiedź Wojtek został polskim żołnierzem. http://www.zsth.home.pl/etwinning/nasz_komiks.html

Jauss Hans Robert 2003, *Historia jest tekstem. O metamorfozach dyskursu historycznego*, [in:] *Opowiadanie historii w niemieckiej refleksji teoretycznohistorycznej i literaturoznawczej od oświecenia do współczesności*, ed. Jerzy Kałążny, Poznan: Wydawnictwo Poznańskie.

Jenkins Henry 2006, *Convergence Culture: Where Old and New Media Collide*, New York: New York University Press.

Koronkiewicz Marta 2008, *Kto się boi Littela?* http://ogrodynauk.pl/Czasopismo/Artykul/52

Koselleck Reinhart 2001, *Semantyka historyczna*, ed. H. Orłowski, trans. W. Kunicki, Poznan: Wydawnictwo Poznańskie.

Koselleck Reinhart 2009, *Dzieje pojęć. Studia z semantyki i pragmatyki języka społeczno-politycznego*, trans. J. Merecki, W. Kunicki, Warsaw: Oficyna Naukowa.

Królik po berlińsku (movie) 2009, director Bartek Konopka.

Krwawy Abraham Lincoln, http://kultura.gazeta.pl/kultura/2029020,114438,11799341.html

Kula Marcin 2011, *Reportaż historyczny jako rodzaj współczesnej historiografii*, [in:] *Historia w kulturze współczesnej. Niekonwencjonalne podejścia do przeszłości*, eds. P. Witek, M. Mazur, E. Solska, Lublin: Wydawnictwo UMCS.

Kulisy katastrofy powstania warszawskiego 1944. Wybrane publikacje i dokumenty 2009, http://powstanie.pl/ ds. 19.09. 2012.

Kwintylian 1951, *Kształcenie mówcy*, ed. M. Brożek, Wrocław.

La Capra Dominic 1985, *History and Criticism*, Ithaca–London.

Ladurie Le Roy Emmanuel 1998, *Montaillou: wioska heretyków. 1294–1324*, trans. E. Żółkiewska, Warsaw: PIW.

Lasocki Wiesław Anatoni 1966, *Zwierzęta i żołnierze*, London: Polska Fundacja Kulturalna.

Lasocki Wiesław Anatoni 1968, *Wojtek spod Monte Cassino: opowieść o niezwykłym niedźwiedziu*, Gryf Publications LTD, London: Stowarzyszenie Polskich Kombatantów.

Lasocki Wiesław Anatoni 1986, *Wojtek. Niedźwiedź-żołnierz*, London: Instytut Polski i Muzeum im. gen. Sikorskiego.

Lemann Natalia 2012a, *AntiPODes of History? "Muza dalekich podróży" by Teodor Parnicki and "Lód" by Jacek Dukaj as Two Diffrent Models od Approaching Alternative History*, [in:] *Re) Visions of History in Language and Fiction*, ed. D. Guttfeld, M. Linke and A. Sowińska, Cambridge 2012: Cambridge Scholar Publishing.

Lemann Natalia 2012b, *Czy historia może być skandalem? Rzecz o historiach alternatywnych i ich sporach z przeszłością/teraźniejszością*, [in:] *Skandal w kulturze*, ed. B. Płona-Syroka, Warsaw: DIG.

Lemann Natalia 2012c, *PODobni NiePODobni. „Muza dalekich podróży" Teodora Parnickiego i „Lód" Jacka Dukaja jako przykład dwóch sposobów relatywizacji historii, PORÓWNANIA* No. 10, 2012.

Lemann Natalia 2011a, *„Czy można uchronić się od przeszłości? – historie alternatywne i uchronie jako literackie aporie wiedzy historycznej i polityki"*, *Zagadnienia Rodzajów Literackich* 2011/2, vol. 54.

Lemann Natalia 2011b, *PODobna historia, czyli rzecz o historii alternatywnej i jej miejscu we współczesnej historiografii i literaturoznawstwie*, [in:] *Exploring the Benefits of the Alternate History Genre/W poszukiwaniu pożyteczności gatunku historii alternatywnych*, eds. Z. Wąsik, M. Oziewicz, J. Deszcz-Tryhubczak, Philologica Wratislaviensia: Acta et Studia. Vol. 5, Wroclaw: Wydawnictwo Wyższej Szkoły Filologicznej we Wrocławiu.

Lemann Natalia 2011c, *Literackie metamorfozy Owidiusza w cieniu wieży Babel. Powieści „Nazo poeta" Jacka Bocheńskiego i Ostatni świat Christopha Ransmayra – czyli pożytki płynące z rozplenienia dyskursów (historia–literatura–fantastyka)*, [in:] *My w wieży Babel. Między przekleństwem, a błogosławieństwem)*, eds. M. Cieszkowski, J. Szczepaniak, Bydgoszcz: Wydawnictwo Uniwersytetu Kazimierza Wielkiego.

Lemann Natalia 2010, *Fabularyzacja i re- narracja źródeł historycznych w powieści historycznej na przykładzie „Listów staropolskich z epoki Wazów" i „Panów Leszczyńskich" Hanny Malewskiej*, [in:] *Zapisywanie historii. Literaturoznawstwo i historiografia*, eds. W. Boleckiego i J. Madejskiego, Warsaw: Wydawnictwo IBL PAN.

Lemann Natalia 2008, *Epicka historiografia we współczesnej prozie polskiej*, Lodz: Wydawnictwo Uniwersytetu Łódzkiego.

Littel Jonathan 2006, *Łaskawe*, trans. M. Kamińska-Maurogeon, Cracow: Wydawnictwo Literackie.

Machocka Aleksandra 2009, „Między interaktywnością a intermedialnością. Książka jako przestrzeń gry", *Homo ludens* No. 1.

Malewska Hanna 1961, *Panowie Leszczyńscy*, Cracow: Znak.

Malewska Hanna 1959, *Listy staropolskie z epoki Wazów*, Cracow: PIW.

Marshall Robert 1990, *In the Sewers of Lvov: a Heroic Story of Survival from the Holocaust*, New York: Macmillan Publishing Company.

Michałowski Piotr 2003, „Strategie skandalu i stereotypy odbioru", *Przestrzenie teorii* No. 2.

Miejsce urodzenia (movie) 1992, director Paweł Łoziński.

Narracja i tożsamość (I). *Narracje w kulturze* 2004a, eds. W. Bolecki, R. Nycz, Warsaw: IBL PAN

Narracja i tożsamość (II). *Antropologiczne problemy literatury* 2004b, eds. W. Bolecki, R. Nycz, Warsaw: IBL PAN.

Neuger Leonard 2009, *Splot. Refleksje nad „Naszą klasą" Tadeusza Słobodzianka*, [in:] T. Słobodzianek, *Nasza klasa Historia w XIV lekcjach*, Gdansk: słowo/obraz/terytoria.

Novik Naomi 2006, *The Temeraire Series*: *His majesty`s Dragon*, London: Del Rey.

O niedźwiedziu co poszedł na wojnę (movie) 2011, director Will Hood, Adam Lavis, TVP and BBC.

"Oprawcy milczą, wywiad z Jonathanem Littellem", *Le Monde*, cited from: www.maxaue.pl [18.12.2012].

Orr Linda 1976, *Jules Michelet, Nature, History, Language*, Ithaca, NY: Cornell University Press.

Pajewski Janusz 1991, *Pierwsza wojna światowa 1914–1918*, Warsaw: PWN.

Pietrasik Zdzisław 2002, „Widok z wieży błaznów", *Polityka* No. 43, http://archiwum.polityka.pl/art/widok-znbsp;wiezy-blaznow,376224.html ds. 19.09.2012.

Pięciak Wojciech 2008, „Historia w oczach psychopaty", *Tygodnik Powszechny* No. 40/2008.

Piwko dla niedźwiedzia (movie) 2008, director Maria Dłużewska, TVP.

Polityka historyczna: historycy–politycy–prasa. Konferencja pod honorowym patronatem Jana Nowaka-Jeziorańskiego, 2005, eds. A. Cichockiej, A. Paneckiej, Warsaw: Wydawnictwo Muzeum Powstania Warszawskiego.

Pomian Krzysztof 2006, *Historia – nauka wobec pamięci*, Lublin: Wydawnictwo UMCS.

Radomski Andrzej 2010, *Internet–Nauka–Historia*, Lublin: Wydawnictwo UMCS.

Ranke von Leopold 2003, *Idea historii powszechnej*, [in:] *Opowiadanie historii w niemieckiej refleksji teoretycznohistorycznej i literaturoznawczej od oświecenia do współczesności*, ed. and trans. J. Kałążny, Poznan: Wydawnictwo Poznańskie.

Ransmayr Christoph 1998, *Ostatni świat*, trans. Jacek Buras, introduction: Andrzej Szczypiorski,Warsaw: Sic!.

Review of the game „Mali Powstańcy" http://www.planszowki.gildia.pl/gry/mali_powstancy_warszawa_1944/mali_powstancy_-_recenzja_gry

Roskowiński Rafał 2008, *Wizna 1939, 40:1*, http://www.wojsko-polskie.pl/articles/view/13197,KOMIKS+%E2%80%9EWizna+1939%E2%80%9D.html

Sapkowski Andrzej 2006, *Lux perpetua*, Warsaw: SuperNOWA.

Sapkowski Andrzej 2004, *Boży wojownicy*, Warsaw: SuperNOWA.

Sapkowski Andrzej 2002, *Narrenturm*, Warsaw: SuperNOWA.

Saramago Jose 2012, *Podróż słonia*, trans. W. Charchalis, Poznan: Rebis.

Saryusz-Wolska Magdalena 2009, *Pamięć zbiorowa i kultura: współczesna perspektywa niemiecka*, Cracow: Universitas.

Sąsiedzi (movie) 2001, director Agnieszka Arnold.

Schama Simon 1991, *Dead Certaines. (Unwarranted Speculations)*, New York: Knopf.

Shtetl (movie), 1996, director Marian Marzyński.

Shusterman Richard 1998, *Estetyka pragamtyczna: żywe piękno i refleksja nas sztuką*, trans. A. Chmielowski, Wroclaw: Wydawnictwo Uniwersytetu Wrocławskiego.

Słobodzianek Tadeusz 2009, *Nasza klasa. Historia w XIV lekcjach*, Gdansk: słowo/obraz/terytoria.

Słomczyński Maciej, Muszyński Beniamin 2011, *Janek. Historia małego powstańca*, Chojnice, www.masz-wybor.com.pl

Solska Ewa 2011, *Komemoracja w społeczeństwie sieciowym. Dyskursywne konsekwencje projektu "Henio on Facebook"*, [in:] *Historia w kulturze współczesnej. Niekonwencjonalne podejścia do przeszłości*, eds. P. Witek, M. Mazur, E. Solska, Lublin: Wydawnictwo UMCS.

Szeja Jerzy 2008, „Nowa forma kultury: wyzwanie pedagogiki?", *Kultura i Historia* No.14.

Tazbir Janusz 2003, „Czytając Hannę Malewską. Panowie Leszczyńscy po latach", *Tygodnik Powszechny* 2003/13.

Tazbir Janusz 1960, „Listy staropolskie. Recenzja", *Nowe Książki* 1960/11.

Topolski Jerzy 1998, *Od Achillesa do Béatrice de Planissoles. Zarys historii historiografii*, Warsaw: Rytm.

Topolski Jerzy 1996, *Jak się pisze i rozumie historię. Tajemnice narracji historycznej*, Warsaw: Rytm.

W ciemności, (movie) 2011, director Agnieszka Holland.

White Hayden 2009, *Proza historyczna*, ed. E. Domańska, trans. P. Borysławski and others, Cracow: Universitas.

White Hayden 2000, *Poetyka pisarstwa historycznego*, eds. E. Domańska, M. Wilczyński, Cracow: Universitas.

Wokół Jedwabnego 2002, eds. P. Machcewicz and K. Persak, vol. 1, Studia, vol. 2, Dokumenty, Warsaw: IPN.

Katarzyna Gutkowska-Ociepa*
University of Silesia

AFTERPOP:
THE ALMOST PERFECT CONVERGENCE

Abstract
This paper focuses on one of the newest notions in Spanish literary theory created by Eloy Fernández Porta in his work *Afterpop. La literatura de la implosion mediatica* (2007). The theorist reaches for the aesthetical accomplishments of postmodernism, avant-pop and cyberpunk in order to analyze them in the context of the new artistic mentality from the beginnings of XXI century. Juggling a multitude of literary techniques and names from various cultural backgrounds such as W. S. Burroughs, Julián Ríos, David Foster Wallace, David Cronenberg or Michael Haneke, Fernández Porta searches for new criteria and new methods of recognizing the complexity and insights of intermediatic, multifaceted and polysemic, implosive "new literature".

Key words: afterpop, polysemic new literature, intermediatic texts, Eloy Fernández Porta

> An error has been detected in your consciousness.
> All source-code is corrupt. Continue?
> OK
> (...)
> The network is monitoring your Digital Being. Create alias?
> OK
>
> Mark Amerika, OK Texts

The notion of the *Afterpop* may seem to some as kind of a terminological provocation as, for instance, the postpostmodernism of *Jürgen* Habermas, yet, whilst used as a powerful tool in the erudite discourse of Eloy Fernández Porta (born in 1974), it becomes a handy metaphor and etiquette for

---

* Philology Department, University of Silesia, Bankowa 12, 40-007 Katowice, e-mail: katarzyna.gutkowska@us.edu.pl

the recent tendencies in the contemporary narrative. One should note that the contemporary novel is considered quite frequently a synecdoche for the whole concept of literature in the framework of Porta's metaliterary reflexions.

According to his observations, in the last decades, plenty has changed in literature and its way of functioning in the society: the widened scope of the impact of the mass media, both verbal and non-verbal, enabled the transition from the postmodern "hypertext" to its latest upgraded version: "intermedial text". The changes went quite deep, since:

> [The] unprecedented expansion of culture, made possible specifically by the exponential growth of technology, has changed the contours of the world: pop culture has not only displaced nature and "colonized" the physical space of nearly every country on earth, but (just as important) it has also begun to colonize even those inner, subjective realms that nearly everyone once believed were inviolable, such as people's memories, sexual desires, their unconsciousness. (...) In fact, this landscape has increasingly become less a literal territory than a multidimensional *hyperreality* of television lands, media "jungles" and information "highways", a place where the real is now a "desert" that is "rained on" by a ceaseless "downpour" of information and data; "flooded" by a torrent of disposable consumer goods, narratives, images, ads, signs, and electronically generated stimuli; and peopled by media figures whose lives and stories seem at once more vivid, more familiar, and *more real* than anything the artist might create. Adapting to this new conditions has been especially difficult for fiction, a print-bound medium that seems especially ill-suited for survival in the global village's electronic system of communication, with its bewildering proliferation of new lingos, databases, and 57 channels (soon expanding to 500). (McCaffery 1995: XIII–XIV)

The cited words come from 1995 and they do not approach the problem hitherto from a more intermediatic point of view that may be found in the Porta's proposal: as one can see, the track leads here "de la metaficción a los metamedia": from the metafiction to the metamedia, the type of texts based entirely on the notion of transgression and the necessity of overcoming formal limitations of the traditionally perceived novel (Humanes Bespín 2007). The genre that seems to be predestined to surrender to the demands of the intermedial poetics without any significant difficulty should be a short story, since:

> [...] el relato breve, tradicionalmente, [...] siempre [...] había sido un objeto cultural desde luego inferior a la novela pero también sujeto a una perceptiva, a una normativa y unos principios más estrictos que los de la novela. Es por eso que a partir de los cuarenta con Borges y después de él con los posmodernistas norteamericanos algunos autores empezarán a coger este objeto literario de vanguardia, en un banco de pruebas y experimentación [...] el ciberpunk a prin-

cipios de los ochenta llega en un momento en el que el cuento, al menos en la tradición norteamericana, ya se ha establecido como género de vanguardia [...] A partir de ahí, el uso de los nuevos medios técnicos, sea cuentos en la red, sea poemas en flash [...] son un factor de transformación dentro de la teoría del relato [...] a mí me parece más importante el tratamiento temático de las nuevas tecnologías en esos relatos, porque si se da un cambio en la concepción de literariedad suscitado por los nuevos medios eso afectará a toda literatura, y probablemente a ese nivel no haya distinción entre la teoría del relato y teoría de la novela. (Humanes Bespín 2007)

[(...) traditionally, a short story (...) had always been a kind of a cultural invention characterized by an obviously inferior status than a novel, nonetheless it was always submitted to the much stricter evaluation, structural norms and rules than the ones referring to the novel. That is why from the forties with Borges and – afterwards – with the American postmodernists, some authors would seize precisely that avant-garde literary object and try to experiment with it [...] Cyberpunk[1] consolidates at the beginnings of the eighties, at a time when a short story, at least in the American tradition, had already gained a position of an avant-garde literary form [...] Since then, the use of the new technical devices, such as on-line story, poems in flash [...] becomes an important factor in the transformation of the theory of the short story [...] what seems most relevant to me is the way of handling the new technologies as a subject in these stories, for the reason that if there is a change in conceiving the notion of the literariness evoked by the new media, it should affect the whole literature and, therefore, there will be no difference as far as a short story or a novel is concerned. (Humanes Bespín 2007)[2]]

Even though the name "work of art" may sound quite odd, inadequate and exaggerated to the generation of Javier Marías, Enrique Vila-Matas & Antonio Muñoz Molina in the context of "afterpop", for the intermediaticly oriented Fernández Porta – it is definitely self-evident. Another member of his coeval group, a novelist, physicist and the author of the "Nocilla Project", the novelistic trilogy and a documentary that completes the three collections: *Nocilla Dream, Nocilla Experience, Nocilla Lab* – Agustín

---

[1] In the article, I define cyberpunk as: a literary current in fantasy, originated in the 1980s. Some theorists claim it began with the appearance of *Neuromancer* by William Gibson in 1984, the bible of the genre. Chief representatives, apart from Gibson, are Rucker, Sterling, Cadigan, Stephenson. The main feature of all cyberpunk works is the description of the interior of the computer network, the electronic reality, which – after Gibson – is called cyberspace. The relevant characteristic of the cyberpunk poetics is the principle "High tech, low life", according to which the main character's living standard is quite low (e.g. he lives in a shantytown) even though it's situated in the world of strongly developed technology. The elements of cyberpunk may be found in Polish fantasy as well: Dukaj, Ziemkiewicz and Wiśniewski. (Marecki 2003: 299, transl. K. G.)
[2] All Spanish and Polish citations in the article were translated by myself, unless indicated otherwise.

Fernández Mallo, speaking of the future of narrative genres, pointed out that a novel:

> (...) pasará por un soporte "que albergue texto música, fotografía y vídeo, y conexión on-line a la Red, y que la novela será una composición de ese tipo, mucho más completa y compleja que el cine incluso." (Azancot 2010)
>
> [will accept the support offered to the text by music, photography, video and a broadband, so that the novel will become a composition much more complex and congeneric, even more that cinema (Azancot 2010)]

His declaration sounds fairly powerful as his "Nocilla Project" encountered wide echoes in the literary world in Spain and has become a foundation for the minting of the generational name of authors appurtenant to the new aesthetics: "los nocilleros" or "los nocilla"[3].

The fragmentary nature of his prose and the managing of the plot as a pretext form for toying with the polimorphic appetite increased the frequency of them being called "los fragmentarios". Fernández Porta and Fernández Mallo more than once have presented together "Nocilla Project" as well as their other avant- and afterpopesque proposals with the usage of multimedial presentations, fragments of movies, images with sonic background, live shows with live music, sometimes even all of it at the same time. Both of them also share a way of understanding the main features and the potential of literature as well as a conviction about the future popularity of the intertextually and intermediaticly enriched *nouvelle* (the short novel format). The ascertainment of the author of *Nocilla Dream* about the short-sightedness and the limitations of the writers who seem to be insufficiently pleased with the new model of the novel and the experimentation of the younger generation of story-tellers also strengthens the foundation for the openness of the afterpop to the newer, more functional and more courageous artistic solutions:

> Hay personas que se creen los garantes o elegidos para salvaguardar un templo sagrado, tarea que, en realidad, nadie, salvo una perversa maquinita que hay en cerebro llamada Super Yo, les ha pedido. Y trasladan esa confusión al terreno moral, de sacerdote. La literatura para ellos es una moral que está siendo violentada. Un puritanismo como otro cualquiera. Nada nuevo bajo el sol. Lo triste es comprobar que hay gente que piensa que aquí no hay sitio para todos. Personalmente, me encanta que se edite literatura que nada tenga que ver con la mía, y cuanta más, mejor. Me parece un signo de buena salud. (Azancot 2010)

---

[3] *Nocilla* is a popular Spanish brand of chocolate & hazelnut spread.

[There are some people who consider themselves the chosen ones, who think that their obligation is to protect the temple, even though they were not asked to do this by anything else than the perverse machine in their brains called Super Ego. They transfer this specific disorientation to the morality sphere. The literature constitutes for them some kind of ethics that seems to be violated. Puritanism as any other. There's nothing new under the Sun. It's sad to know that there is no place for everyone. Personally, I love that there is the literature that's completely different than mine; the more dissimilar, the better. I think it's a sign of a good health. (Azancot 2010)]

The opposition: they-superannuated and us-the open-minded ones is significant, since it is supposed to be a foundation of the concept of afterpop in literature. Nonetheless, the openness of the authors born in the seventies derives from the diametrically opposite set of artistic points of reference. For the "nocilleros" the most relevant ground of relation is contemporary American literature with its autothematic and culture-centered dimension, television (especially the animated TV series such as *The Simpsons* or *Family Guy*), the popular and niche yet accessible music and movie productions based on the multidimensional and polymorphic way of conveying the artistic message (e.g. *Funny Games* by Michael Haneke, where the mentality of the characters, their hierarchies and values are reflected by the conscientiously chosen soundtrack which evokes the ensemble of the stereotyped associations (cf. Fernández Porta 2007: 46)).

Indicating that Enrique Vila-Matas, born in 1948 in Barcelona, one of the best and the most experimenting Spanish novelists at present, despite all the innovations is not a creator of the afterpopesque texts, Fernández Porta revealed that the americocentrism is one of the main features that differs Vila-Matas from the younger authors (Paris has already stopped being the artistic, nostalgically idealised cradle). Furthermore we do not find in the works by the author of *Dublinesque* the appetite inscribed in the afterpopesque standards of intensified fictional pretextuality, even more enhanced, intermediatic intertextuality, biographic transgression in the creation of the *homo duplex* nor, though handled *cum grano salis*, relation with specific science, revealed at the lexical and conceptual levels. In order to exemplify it all in praxis, one could allude to the short characteristic of a novel that has become a starting point for the "fragmentarios" or "afterpoppies":

Nocilla dream, que puede soportar sin pesadumbre la etiqueta indie, es una de las apuestas narrativas más arriesgadas de los últimos años. Proliferan en ella las referencias al cine independiente norteamericano, a la historia del collage, al arte conceptual, a la arquitectura pragmática, a la evolución de los PCs y a la decadencia de la novela. Agustín Fernández Mallo se fija en los outsiders del siglo XXI y sobre todo en la misteriosa conexión entre algunas vidas alternativas y globalizadas que transitan por escenarios de Serie B: rubias de burdel que sueñan con que algún cliente las lleve hacia el Este, ácratas que habitan en extrañas micronaciones, ancianos chinos adictos al surf, un argentino que vive en un apartahotel de Las Vegas y construye un singular monumento a Jorge Luis Borges... Todos ellos atrapados en la metáfora conductora de los desiertos y en la belleza del vacío.[4]

[Nocilla dream, which undoubtedly could be tagged with the indie label, is one of the freshest, daring and graceful novels of the last few years. It's full of references to the independent American cinema, to the history of collage, to the conceptual art, to the pragmatic architecture and to the decadence of the novel. Agustín Fernández Mallo concentrates on the outsiders of the 21st century and especially on the mysterious connection between some alternative and global biographies that pass through the screenplays of Series B: the blonds from the brothel who dream about a client bringing them to the West, anarchists living in the weird micronations, the Chinese senior citizens addicted to surfing, an Argentinean who lives in an apart-hotel in Las Vegas and dedicates himself to the creation of a monument of Jorge Luis Borges... All of them trapped in the leading metaphor of the deserts and the beauty of the emptiness.]

The title of the article as well as the whole concept of the afterpopesque convergence derives from the mini-treatise *Afterpop* with the significant subtitle: *La literatura de la implosión mediática* (Berenice, Córdoba 2007) which concerns the intensified tendency of cumulating extra-literary elements in the interior of fictitious texts. It is a procedure that might be called precisely "mediatic implosion" and it begins to take its toll in the contemporary prose almost on a regular basis. Moreover, it is becoming more and more noticeable not only in the narrative, but also in literary criticism. All in all, the monograph of Fernández Porta is an elaborated, comprehensive, interpretative model of a contemporary work of fiction and, at the same time, a border form which contains the components of the literary criticism, the historical outline of the literary evolution, the theoretical-literary project and a socio-cultural analysis. It constitutes an unconventional, (post)postmodern, erudite and jocose meta-literary hybrid – the only thing missing seems to be an added movie, series of multimedia or even a soundtrack, in spite of the fact that an addition of this sort would not have been a completely new touch in the publishing industry. Sometimes editors decide to add a DVD with a documentary or an interview to the printed version of a book; like in the case of the collection of

---

[4] The description of the essence of the Fernández Mallo's esthetics comes from the webpage of his publisher, Candaya press: http://www.candaya.com/nocilladream.htm.

essays and reviews on Vila-Matas's books: *Vila-Matas. Portátil* (*Vila-Matas. Portable* or, translating it in a more figurative way, *Vila-Matas. On the go*) or they introduce a kind of soundtrack that is somehow supposed to accompany the main text (we can observe these tactics in the edition of an Italian essay-treatise by Alessandro Baricco *Next. Sobre la globalización y el mundo que viene* (Baricco 2002) where some parts have been graphically marked and singled out with a mini-title "bonus track" which then find its explanation in the closing part of the book).

While reading the considerations of Fernández Porta, it is hard not to get hold of an impression that in spite of the gladly adapted new style and the subject area related to the world of the new media, by means of reconciling the extra-literary and ultramodern with the concept of a novel, there is an intricate net of intertextual ties with the universal dimension of the novelistic tradition, especially the Spanish-language one: Julio Cortázar, Jorge Luis Borges or Carlos Fuentes. The new prose is full of tricks and strategies present in the works by the South American literary giants: the perchant for the argumental dissociation, the fragmentariness and the literary magic put in the context of everyday triviality and, also, the creation of the broken identity of "I", the predilection of Borges for the re-production of the relation between the word and the reality as a foundation of the cognoscible world, the obsessive return of the motif of a book and the labyrinth, the lack of chronological linearity and – known e.g. from *Aura* by Fuentes – steering of a discourse towards "You", toying with the fictional truth and false, suppositions and the substantial fact, the corporeality and the intangibility – all of these elements and techniques find a reflection in the new, intermediatic, afterpopesque prose.

The prefix "after" is crucial, since "los poppies" (a name invented by Fernández Porta) belong to the other kind of artists: they do not consider themselves popcultural. The author of *Eros. La superproducción de los afectos* does not deny pop culture the right to scaling the heights of sublimation and exploratoriness, however – similarly to the high, academic postmodernism and its lower, beatnik, Borroughsian postmodernist equivalent – Fernández Porta also differentiates two registers of pop and, therefore, he indicates that the afterpop was created by the more sophisticated version of pop culture, the one penetrating not only the superficial dimension of the individual's and collective existence in a mediatic reality, but also by the tradition of avant-pop that eulogizes the literature as a still powerful artistic tool. All of the fore-mentioned aspects created along the way the new narrative quality: afterpop.

The prior to afterpop style, avant-pop, may be described as:

> doing many kinds of art, mixing the mass culture with the avant-garde or its high register, amalgamating various disciplines and, particularly, the relation with the Internet. The avant-pop artist gladly does the recycling; his favourite creating method is sampling. Usually, the ultimate version of his works is a hypertext, he loves combinating the genres, for instance, the prose with a comic-like style. A piece of art made by an avant-pop artist is a collage of the audio, space and visual forms which show the notable understanding of television, advertisements, video games, clips and the computer programming structure. (Marecki 2010: 220)[5]

The after-pop artist is the one who adds to the avant-pop revelations the specific kind of self-consciousness according to which the avant-pop solutions are merely an overture to the toying with more complex and better developed (meta)media:

> se sitúa en un espacio histórica y simbólicamente posterior: asume que la cultura de consumo tal y como se conoció a lo largo de la segunda mitad del siglo XX no sólo «está en ruinas» sino que, en cierto modo, es el pasado inmediato. En algunos casos llega incluso a asumir que se trata de «un clásico» al que se respeta pero se da muy por sentado – tan por sentado que va desapareciendo-. En este sentido, tal autor da el paso siguiente al que lleva la camiseta de Michael Jackson en broma: ahora no es sólo un icono, por importante que fuera, el que se postula como «pasado» y «fantasmal», sino una estética entera. «Ahora aparezco. Ahora desaparezco. Ahora aparezco para desaparecer y se me perdonarán, espero, ciertas vacilaciones a la hora de intentar promover algo parecido al orden luego de un permisivo caos de años». Estas palabras, con las que empieza el relato de Fresán Apuntes para una teoría del escritor, me parecen muy representativas de

---

[5] One might also be interested in other Polish understandings of the avant-pop aesthetics, for instance, the one presented by Piotr Siwecki who concentrates his attention other aspects of the current:
Banalizm i avant-pop wyrażają wspólne dążenie pisarzy, którym jest nie tyle odnalezienie własnej dykcji jako skrajnie indywidualnego stylu, ile odnalezienie dykcji w bezstylowości kooperacyjnej, czy też raczej kooperacyjnej bezstylowości (eklektyzm, plagiaryzm). Copyright przestaje być sygnałem odrębności twórcy – staje się często kategorią opisującą doświadczenie określonej grupy społecznej, pokolenia, choć jednocześnie pozostaje sygnałem tęsknoty za indywidualizmem nieuwikłanym w konsumerystyczną machinę promocji. (Siwecki 2010: 238)
[Banalism and avant-pop express the common aim of the writers which is not finding their own diction as an utterly individual style but finding diction with a lack of cooperative style or, more likely, cooperative unstyliness (eclectism, plagiarism). The copyright stops being an indication of the distinctiveness of the author; it often becomes a category describing an experience by a specific social group, a generation, although it still constitutes a manifestation of yearning for individualism which puts the consumerisistic promotion machine aside. (Siwecki 2010: 238)]

Afterpop: the Almost Perfect Convergence

la posición en que se sitúa el escritor afterpop. Esta posición se define por una ironía inestable y reconocida que se pone de manifiesto en una serie de continuos deslizamientos entre distintas maneras de abordar el permisivo caos de años de la cultura de consumo. En algunos casos se trata de una actitud retro en la que se describe la cultura pop desde un supuesto futuro; en otros, encontramos un gesto engagé, como si se tratase de una causa que requiere de filiación. [...] el escritor afterpop aparece de manera simbólicamente violenta en esa cultura adoptando posiciones que la problematizan, como la del extranjero, el primitivo o el teórico, de la misma manera, también desaparece de ella, adoptando actitudes que la superan, como la del coolhunter. (Férnandez Porta 2007: 62–63)

[he situates himself in a posterior historical and symbolic space: he assumes that the culture of consumerism, conceived in the second half of the 20th century, is not only in decay, but also – in a way – has become a recent past. In some cases the author even assumes that it concerns the classics as well: respected but treated quite indulgently – so indulgently that it seems to disappear. Thus, the author makes a step that indicates that the T-Shirt of Michael Jackson as a joke is not an icon, even though it's perceived as important, phantasmal and coming from the past, but a total concept of aesthetics. «I exist now. Now – I disappear. Now, I appear in order to disappear and, I hope, my doubts and dilemmas accompanying me while trying to recuperate some state similar to order after the chaos of the years will be forgiven». I find the opening lines from the story by Fresán Apuntes para una teoría del escritor very representative from the position where the after-pop artist situates himself. It is characterised by the recognisable, yet slightly unstable irony that reveals itself in a series of the permanent slides between various ways of handling the indulging chaos of the years of the culture of consumerism. In some cases it is some sort of retro attitude in which pop culture is described from the supposed future; in others, on may find an engagé gesture as if it concerned the matter that requires some kind of affiliation. [...] the after-pop writer appears in this culture in a symbolically violent way, adopting stances which somehow problematize it, as the one of a foreigner, a primitive or a theorist; sometimes he disappears in it as well, adopting attitudes that overpower it, like the one of coolhunter. (Férnandez Porta 2007: 62–63)]

While depicting the variety of pop, Fernández Porta uses a style that "coruscates" with the plentitude of images and the metaphorical-allegorical formulation of the high and low register of culture. The critic transmutes the analysis in a hard-edged, puckish rewriting of the story, evoking literary topoi, tales and the characters approved and easily recognised by the pop-society. Accordingly, we find here the absorption of a poet by the surreal Unicorn, starved to death by the group of poets immersed eagerly in watching the football on television[6] and, thusly, we hear here the echoes

---

[6] Fernández Porta uses a motif here which is present in a short story by Marvin Cohen: *The Saving of Surrealism* Marvina Cohena from 1973. Cf. Fernández Porta 2007: 222–223.

of the mesianistic-redeeming concept of an intellectual, close to the idea of an individual sacrifice for the wellbeing of the masses. There also includes the tabloid's aesthetics, grotesque description of an affair between Mrs Avantgarde and Mr Pop in Paradise City, celebrating in the world of innovations and the technicist creative impulses that lead the artists astray. Pop seems to be here a character of a mentality imbued with the pragmatic sense of art as well as of socially acknowledged rules, pretending – with a thespian skill – that he understands everything, even though in reality it is not the case at all. In the world where Mallarmé decides about the oncoming trends, where the press coverings are written by Jeana-Françoisa Lyotarda himself, the affair between Avantgarde and Pop reaches the bizarre denouement in an ironic image of the persecution of the lovers by the authentic sublimity; the lovers who sincerely want to reconcile the market strategies with an Avant-garde project focused on the representation of the present, yet unpresentable "now"[7]. The "now" strongly related to the understanding of the Modern in the contemporary commercial world:

> Ser moderno en la era del mercado implica, como es sabido, debatirse entre la confianza en la novedad – tecnológica, artística – y la certidumbre de la capacidad que el mercado tiene para reapropiar en su favor los contenidos de la novedad. La respuesta avant-pop a esta problemática no será ya la de ignorar programáticamente / tolerar sociológicamente los productos de la baja cultura ni la de conservar museísticamente los objetos de la alta, sino la de teorizar sobre Los Simpson y descubrir las virtudes del Finnegans Wake en diagonal. En cuanto a la cuestión de la novedad, valga el dictum de Mark Amerika: "Mezcla de vanguardismo alquímico y formación de capital chamánica, el avant-pop no es tu típico movimiento literario". (Fernández Porta, 2007: 228).

> [To be modern in the age of the market implies, as one perfectly knows, struggling between the certainty of the power of the innovation – both technological and artistic – and the confidence about the capacity of the market to reaproppiate the new contents to its own advantage. The answer of the avant-pop to this issue will not be an attempt to ignore programmatically / socially tolerate the products of low culture or to museally conserve the objects of the high culture, but theorize about The Simpsons and revealing the virtues of Finnegans Wake diagonally. As far as the issue of the novelty is concerned, it will be beneficial to cite the words by Mark Amerka: "The Mixture of the alchemic Avant-garde and the shamanistic formation: the avant-pop is not your typical literary movement" (Fernández Porta, 2007: 228)]

---

[7] Fernández Porta alludes to the text by Jean-François Lyotard: *The Sublime and the Avant-garde.* Cf. Fernández Porta 2007: 227.

Afterpop: the Almost Perfect Convergence

Fernández Porta intercepted the notion of the avant-pop from Larry McCaffery who, in turn, took it from the title of an album by Lester Bowie, the trumpeter and the compositor who used to tease the old tunes with his new arrangements and recreations of the well-known melodies: Blueberry Hill and Crazy. McCaffery sensed that Bowie's strategy is similar to the one that could be seen in postmodern literature and that is the reason why he introduced it once and again in the works about the most experimental tendencies in literature at the time. By referring to the musical nomenclature, Eloy Fernández Porta has successfully shown that it makes it quite easy and more specific to notice the new tendencies in the narrative. The music criticism is put in the Polish newspaper on a back burner, respectively the ones about the reviews about cinema and the theatrical ones, even though it is usually busy with incessant experimenting with the sound, required by the moving whirl of the technical abilities. It is very easy to react quicker to the generating of the new names in music criticism and, therefore, it reacts much more rapidly to the necessity of creating the new notions and the revision of the existing ones, thus, gaining the credibility.

The notion of an avant-pop was also taken by Ronald Sukenick who saw in the avant-popesque current not only the literary movement, but also the special and cultural one, expressed par excellence by hyperfiction:

> El texto concebido como agregación de fuentes, formas y registros, crítica a la vez que creación y forma vital más que producto cultural. La hiperficción sería así la forma contemporánea de la tradición retórica, que Sukenick contrapone a la tradición de la lógica en el siguiente sentido: si la segunda propone directrices, convicciones y razonamientos definidos, la primera es un catálogo de recursos, ideas oposicionales y modalidades de expresión. (Fernández Porta, 2007: 230–231)

> [The text conceived as an aggregation of the sources, forms and registers turns critically at the same time as creation and a form a little bit more vital than culture. Serious hyperfiction would be here a contemporary form of the rhetorical tradition, confronted by Sukenick with the logical tradition in a sense that if the second one offers the directions, the convictions and the defined reasons, the first one constitutes a catalogue of the means, contrasting ideas and the modulations of expression. (Fernández Porta, 2007: 230–231)]

Thusly, the "avant-pop gesture" would be a manipulated exploitation of stimuli, information and values of the cultural and market spheres, which would be a cause to a subversively evoked transformation in both a market and an artistic context. The amended statement would be similar to a computer virus turning the society and its habits thoroughly inside out. A consequence of this way of thinking is Mark Amerika's cyberpunk theory according to which an interception of the subversive elements takes place through the internet, data media and all kinds of information technologies. It is to induce an origin of a new model of creation and creator:

> […] el proyecto de un gomi no sensei, un maestro de la basura que construye a partir de los deshechos de la cultura contemporánea, llenando su carrito con una mezcla heterogénea de restos del hipermercado pop, recogiendo la polifonía posmoderna, adorando la idea de indiferenciación, empollando un relato o quizá una novela entera en los confines de una sola unidad sintáctica, apelando a la unidad de atención de un mosquito. (Amerika, Olsen 1995: 14)

> [the project gomi no sensei, the master of rubbish who creates on the basis of the waste of the contemporary culture, filling his trolley with the heterogeneous mixture of the leftovers from hypermarket of pop, collecting the postmodern polyphony, adoring the concept of indistinctiveness, fitting the story or maybe even a whole novel in the limits of one syntactic unit, referring to the attention span typical of a mosquito. (Amerika, Olsen 1995: 14)]

This description better reflects, nevertheless, the essence of the euphoric immersion in the consumptionist creative possibilities typical for "los poppies" while the subject afterpop is a trend exposing different values. When comparing a pop artist with an afterpop artist, Eloy Fernández Porta draws attention to a different – higher – degree of an artistic and a social self-awareness of the afterpop artists and their distinct values hierarchy. It seems that at least for now afterpop is considered a niche trend, still emancipating hence still in a development stage. It is conceivable, that – as time goes by – the afterpop will lose its intermedial freshness, multiplied piecemeal character and so actively built the theoretical superstructure – some critics even made it more distinctive by insisting that the "nocilleros" created more literary texts and less theoretical-essayist ones[8]. And although Fernández Porta does not consider himself a spokesman for the generation of Fernández Mallo, Loriga and Uribe, without a doubt he senses the expediency of their creative intentions – a formal pursuit of the cultural extraverbial spheres, presenting books in multimedial forms and joining them with a monodram happening, provocative playing the older against the newer tendencies as well as with experiments in relation to the plot and style. Even though afterpop is a bit more sublimed version of pop, it is

---

[8] "Menos teoría, menos normativa y disciplina inglesa para los demás, y más novela" [Less theory, less indications and less of an English discipline for the others, more novels]. (Azancot 2010).

concerned with blurring the boundaries between the 'poppy' culture and the high or quasi-high culture, it also serves as a standard in the increasing volume of texts overstepping the traditional genological borders and relying on referrals to different kinds of media and their products of varying levels of sophistication.

The translation of this concept to Polish circumstances in the face of a lack of local holistic interpretations of the tendencies in prose over the last decades would be – it appears – advantageous in many aspects: there are not many Polish prose writers, born mid=seventies, who would dare to formulate a synthetic statement taking all, or at least the majority, of the prosaic tendencies of the current generation of authors in their thirties. An exception to this may be Michał Witkowski's sketch-essay entitled *Recycling (Notatki na marginesie twórczści własneji innych roczników siedemdziesiątych)* (Witkowski 2010: 90–50). Reprinted in the collective volume *Literatura polska 1989–2009. Przewodnik* (2010) prepared by critics and writers connected to the 'Ha!art' circle, Witkowski's text does not constitute an angle, which can be perceived as anywhere near to complete: it is dated 2001, which limits the referenced texts and names mainly to the nineties – the first Polish decade of free market and free media. Therefore at the moment a recycling continuation is missing (*Recycling bis?*): just as broad and precise an analysis of the young prose of the second decade of XXI century, even more so that – although some of the traits of the young literature detailed by Witkowski have survived like for example exploiting the 'pop-fraction' assumptions and creating literature out of literature in various, more or less surprising configurations – there still emerge new tendencies, which situate themselves somewhat against Witkowski's hopes and expectations. In 2001, the author of *Margot* wrote:

> Roczniki siedemdziesiąte przeprowadziły już dosyć sprawną i szybką akcję dekonstrukcji modelu mitograficznego, dlatego pisanie dalej utworów „podgryzających" mitografię, powieść inicjacyjną i nostalgiczną to wyważanie otwartych drzwi. Również ton został już dostatecznie obniżony, sprowadzony na ziemię. Ta pierwsza fala roczników siedemdziesiątych [...] odegrała rolę likwidatorską i mam nadzieję, że na tym się nie skończy. Bo oto po oczyszczeniu terenu otwierają się przed nami ogromne, wspaniałe perspektywy. Taki język, jaki sobie wywalczyliśmy, uwolnieni od konwencji mitograficznych i innych, otwiera nas na prawdziwą, jak najbardziej dzisiejszą rzeczywistość, tę „lodówkę na nóżkach", jak ją pozwoliłem sobie nazwać. Mam nadzieję, że przynajmniej niektórzy z nas opiszą ją świeżym, agresywnym językiem, bez min i manier konwencji, bez stylizowania, i nareszcie zechcą objaśnić, co się pod tą rzeczywistością kryje. (Witkowski 2010: 49–50)

[Writers born in 1970's have carried out a rather dextrous and quick deconstruction of the mythographical model, that is why continuous writing of texts biting into mythography, an initiation and nostalgic novel is like reinventing the wheel. Also the tone has been sufficiently lowered, grounded. The first wave of these authors played a role of a liquidator and I hope it is not going to end there. Because here after clearing the ground the new, great perspectives have emerged. The language we have fought for, freed from mythographic and other conventions, is opening us to a real, contemporary reality, the 'fridge on feet', as I allowed myself to name. I hope, that at least some of us will describe it using a fresh, aggressive langauge, without any masks or convention mannerisms, without stylisation, and at last will explain what exactly this reality is. (Witkowski 2010: 49–50)]

How in the context of expectations of the author of *Barbara Radziwiłłówna z Jaworzna-Szczakowej* should we then treat – to mention at least one of the most famous and important names – much respected and prized creations of Ignacy Karpowicz, in which all types of myth and stylisation often play the role of a compositional-storyline leitmotif? Witkowski's analysis seems a cause, one of the original links of a description of what is technically new in literature, especially in prose. From time to time a statement appears from one of the published authors, like *Lament miłośnika cegieł* by Jacek Dukaj, in which – ironically – he expresses not a hope for crystallisation of the innovative tendencies but rather a yearning for a 19th century realism, prosaic fullness and a coherently developed novel. Beside Przemysław Czaplinski's *Efekt bierności. Literatura w czasie normalnym* (Kraków 2004) or *Powrót centrali. Literatura w nowej rzeczywistości* (Kraków 2007), nobody else proposes a structuring frame useful in interpreting what in the Polish prose in the context of media could actually be perceived as innovative. Maybe it is still influenced by Euro- and Polishcentric attitudes of the prosaics debuting in the last few decades – not many of them reach for texts that have not been yet translated and which are essential in the context of metaprosaic research in the world, like novels and the essays of David Foster Wallace, fashionable in the niche intellectual circles or fickle critical texts by Enrique Vila-Matas. Perhaps this is the reason why afterpop has not arrived in Poland yet. Especially that avant-pop which is – as we know – one of the pillars of afterpop, was not so long ago (in 2010) described by one of the Polish researchers as follows:

obecnie jeden z najpopularniejszych ruchów w sztuce zachodniej. Zrodzony na gruzach postmodernizmu jako mutacja cyberpunka największe triumfy święcił w latach dziewięćdziesiątych. Do Polski dociera z opóźnieniem, podobnie jak z opóźnieniem dotarły do nas elementy, które przyczyniły się do powstania avant-popu, czyli mass media i wysoko rozwinięta technologia. (Marecki 2010: 220)

[Nowadays one of the most popular movements in the western art. Created from the remains of postmodernism as a mutation of cyberpunk it rode high in 1990's. It gets to Poland with a delay, just like with a delay reached here the elements, which were the cause of the emergence of avant pop, namely mass media nad highly developed technology. (Marecki 2010: 220)]

Notwithstanding the clear processual character of adapting the new aesthetics in Poland, Marecki also notices the influence and traits of avant-pop in the works of a few young Polish fiction writers and artists, among others Sławomir Shuty, Wilhelm Sasnal and in the works of a duo Krasnowolski-Tkaczyk (cf. Marecki 2010: 221–225).

It seems that the situation with afterpop may be similar: the Polish authors do need a little bit more time to include in their creative act the possibilities offered by the new media in such a way that they bring their strategies beyond the level of literal references and mechanical copying of the styles present in non-literary communication situations. It is worth noting that the assessment of the potential dynamic accommodation of the afterpop creative approaches is difficult even in the case of such a dominant and resiliently evolving medium in Poland like the internet. Evident at the start of the first decade of 21st century upheaval around the notion of "liternet" or "netart" seems to lose its power – whatever the case may be the hitherto new media are common today to such a degree that they are an integral element of Polish everyday life, whereas they do not bring many expected results in the cultural and artistic areas. In 2003, Marta Cuber stated perspicaciously in the symptomatically entitled text *Internet jako źródło cierpień literatury. O polskiej prozie internetowej (i jednym dramacie)* [Internet as a Source of Suffering for Literature. About the Polish Internet Prose (and one drama)]:

> Polska proza internetowa (i jeden dramat) przypomina naiwne dziecko, które chciałoby zjeść cukierek i jednocześnie zatrzymać go w ręce. Teksty, jakie przeglądałam, starają się bowiem załatwić dwie sprawy nie do pogodzenia (przy ambitnych założeniach): zachować właściwości tradycyjnej literatury i, gdzie można (a raczej, gdzie wypada), błysnąć sieciowym nowatorstwem. W ten sposób jednak nie podobna zostać avant-garde. Poza wszystkim nie proponuje się w nich wiele ciekawego: zarówno na poziomie narracji, jak i fabuły. Nie chciałabym się bawić w prognozowanie, ale wreszcie będzie trzeba polskiemu liternetowi zjeść ten cukierek (przymierzania się do poważniejszej literatury internetowej, jeżeli tylko taka jest możliwa) i kupić nowe, to znaczy zaproponować garść bardziej interesujących pomysłów. Oczywiście, przy założeniu że proza internetowa zamierza rozszerzyć kanał komunikacyjny o czytelników Prousta, Joyce'a czy Llosy… Bo namawianie literatury popularnej (a na tym poziomie zatrzymuje się przynajmniej kilka wymienionych tekstów) do zakupu kolejnych torebek łakoci jest niekonieczne. (Cuber 2003: 92–93)

[Polish internet prose (and one drama) reminds a naïve child who would like to eat a candy and hold it in its hand at the same time. The texts, which I reviewed, are trying to reconcile two issues that cannot be brought together successfully (while keeping an ambitious approach): to retain the characteristics of the traditional literature and, wherever possible (or rather, wherever befitting), show an internet-like innovation. If writing this way, it is not possible to become avant-garde. Moreover they have nothing interesting to offer: both on the level of narration as well as the storyline. I would not like to play a role of a forecaster, however it will eventually come to a point where the Polish liternet will have to eat this candy (while aspiring to a more serious internet literature, if it is at all possible) and buy new ones, which means proposing a few more interesting ideas. Obviously, it all is based on the assumption that the internet prose is going to widen the communication channel to the readers of Proust, Joyce or Llosa… Because persuading the popular literature (an at least a few of the mentioned texts never went beyond this level) to buy more bags of sweets is unnecessary. (Cuber 2003: 92–93)]

The works around which Cuber evolves her harsh evaluation of the Polish liternet, are *Tabu* by Kinga Dunin, *Miłe fantazji początki* by Sławomir Shuty (2001), *Cz@t (drama)* by Krzysztof Rudowski, *S@motność w sieci* (2002) by Janusz. L. Wiśniewski or created along with the internauts *Krótka historia Iwony Tramp* by Krystyna Kofta (2001). These titles have been present on the literary market for over ten years now, however they have never found many Polish liternet successors.

It seems that the Polish scene misses a young researcher of a sharp personality like Eloy Fernández Porta[9], who by juggling daringly with the names of authors from a variety of cultural areas – noting the following as well: W.S. Burroughs, Julian Rios, David Cronenberg or, mentioned earlier, Haneke – and referring to their experiments, theories and intentions, based on principles but gracefully and wittingly defines where the meaning of the literary texts is situated in the panoramic depiction of the current culture. He is opposed to a preconceived and conventional interpreting of texts of young authors, through showing the pop qualities in the plots of the "serious" writers, supported by establishment, like Javier Marías and, at the same time, he focuses on the "afterpop" qualities, innovation in the "los nocilleros" novels, like the ones by Ray Loriga. It needs to be noted that this new formation gained the precious awareness that the literature, attacked from all over by the meaning-making impulses, flexible in relation to the philosophical, ethical, anthropological, theological and ideological concep-

---

[9] Every publication of Fernándeza Porty posterior to the Afterpop… has been received with a great amount of interest, enthusiasm and applause from the critics. One of his recent works: €®O$. *La superproducción de los afectos,* another treatise-essay, in April 2010 was awarded with Premio Anagrama for the best essay of the year.

tions – it does, indeed, according to Fernández Porta, become a place of the convergent media implosion, a continual osmosis and reinterpretation of the cultural and intellectual atoms, which together make the global cultural network. This awareness consecutively opens up incomparably vaster areas for (extra) literary and structural peregrinations.

Bibliography

Amerika Mark 2007, *Meta/Data. A Digital Poetics*, Cambridge, MA: The MIT Press.

Amerika Mark, Olsen Lance 1995: *Smells like Avant-Pop: An Introduction, of Sorts*, [in:] *In Memoriam to Postmodernism*, San Diego: San Diego State University Press, [in:] Fernández Porta Eloy 2007, *Afterpop. La literatura de la implosión mediática*, Córdoba: Editorial Berenice.

Azancot Nuria 2010, «Los fragmentarios, ¿a muerte con los clásicos? Los jóvenes nocilleros se enfrentan a las críticas generales de autores consagrados", *El Cultural*, 12.03.2010, http://www.elcultural.es/version_papel/LETRAS/26783/Los_fragmentarios_a_muerte_con_los_clasicos (28.05.2012).

Baricco Alessandro 2002, *Next. Sobre la globalización y el mundo que viene*, Spanish translation by X. González Rovira, Barcelona: Editorial Anagrama,

Cuber Marta 2003, *Internet jako źródło cierpień literatury. O polskiej prozie internetowej (i jednym dramacie)*, [in:] *Liternet.pl*, ed. Piotr Marecki Cracow: Rabid.

Fernández Porta Eloy 2007, *Afterpop. La literatura de la implosión mediática*, Córdoba: Editorial Berenice.

Hopfinger Maryla 2010, *Literatura i media. Po 1989 roku*, Warsaw: Oficyna Wydawnicza.

Humanes Bespín Ivan 2007, "A mí me gusta hablar de qué actitudes pueden representar a autores distintos o distintos estados de ánimo del mismo autor". Interview with Eloy Fernández Porta, http://www.literaturas.com/v010/sec0707/entrevistas/entrevistas-02.html. (28.05.2012).

Kita Barbara 2003, *Miedzy przestrzeniami. O kulturze nowych mediów*, Cracow: Rabid.

Literatura polska 1989–2009. Przewodnik 2010, ed. P. Marecki, Cracow: Ha!art.

Marecki Piotr (ed.) 2003, *Liternet.pl*, Cracow: Rabid.

Marecki Piotr 2010, *Avant-pop po polsku*, [in:] *Literatura polska 1989–2009. Przewodnik*, ed. P. Marecki, Cracow: Ha!art.

McCaffery Larry (ed.) 1995, *After Yesterday's Crash. The Avant-Pop Anthology*, New York: Penguin.

Siwecki Piotr 2010, *Optymizm warunkowy albo kilka tautologicznych uwag na temat literatury alternatywnej – avant-pop i banalizm jako strategie istnienia literatury w społeczeństwie spektaklu*, [in:] *Literatura polska 1989–2009. Przewodnik*, ed. P. Marecki, Cracow: Ha!art.

Witkowski Michał 2010, *Recycling (Notatki na marginesie twórczości własnej i innych roczników siedemdziesiątych)*, [in:] *Literatura polska 1989–2009. Przewodnik*, ed. P. Marecki, Cracow: Ha!art.

Wójtowicz Ewa 2008, *net art*, Cracow: Rabid.

Beata Śniecikowska*
IBL PAN

TRANSCULTURAL CONVERGENCE?
POLISH POETS AND ARTISTS
AND THE ORIENTAL VERBO-VISUALITY

Abstract
The article concerns different aspects of convergence processes of the traditional Oriental genres in the Polish culture, focusing on haiku, *haiga* and *haibun*. It examines artists' books, visual arts and the artistic websites. The theoretical frame of the research is rooted in the concept of transculturality introduced by Wolfgang Welsch.

The author analyses Polish works of art employing different strategies of combining words and images, thereby showing unexpected similarities between cultures and revealing the artistic changes caused by the choice of different media. The investigation proves that the most interesting compositions uncover unexpected common elements between apparently contradictory traditions, the necessary condition is, however, at least the basic knowledge about the Other.

Key words: verbo-visuality, transculturality, convergence, haiku, *haiga, haibun*

The paper focuses on the concept of transculturality introduced by Wolfgang Welsch (cf. Welsch 1998, Welsch 2004), adapting it to the analyses of different fields of convergence in contemporary Polish culture: employing and transforming old Oriental genres into more hybrid forms appearing on the Internet, becoming parts of artistic exhibitions or being incorporated into artists' books. It is a convergence of a special kind – "transplanting" the genres into the new medial ground must have been preceded by their basic assimilation in the new culture.

The term 'convergence' is used to describe different technological, industrial, social and cultural processes (Jenkins 2007: 9, Jakubowicz 2011: 27).

* IBL PAN, Nowy Świat 72, 00-330 Warszawa, e-mail: beata.sniecikowska@gmail.com

All of them prove important in the analyses concerning the "transplantation" of the foreign literary and artistic genres, which seem utterly incongruent with the Polish tradition. In the paper, however, I concentrate only on the cultural dimensions of the problem, believing they define an interesting field of research for comparative cultural studies. As Jenkins claims, convergence is not just a matter of sophisticated media devices but a process occurring in human minds and human communication (cf. Jenkins 2007: 9).

I am interested mainly in three genres: haiku, *haiga* and *haibun*. The common basis of the three is haiku: a poetic genre strongly related to visual arts (calligraphy, similarities of imagery in haiku and *sumi-e, nanga, ukiyo-e*, shared aesthetic and ethical beliefs of *haijins* and *Zen* painters – cf. Addiss 2005, Śniecikowska 2007: 243–251). In the new cultural environment haiku also tends to be close to visual arts, which is reflected on the level of typography and book illustration (cf. Śniecikowska 2007: 255–262) but also, less obviously, in artistic spatial arrangements (artists' books, haiku-based art exhibitions) and, last but not least, in different multisensory forms spread by means of the Internet.

First and foremost, verbo-visuality of haiku in the new culture manifests itself in strong connections between poems and their illustrations (paintings, photographs, films), which may be compared and at least partly derived from the Japanese art of *haiga*. *Haiga* is a type of *sumi-e* painting illustrating particular haikus or created in the spirit of this poetry (cf. Takeuchi 2005: 198, Addiss 2005: 204, Addiss 2006), usually accompanying the calligraphy of the poem on the same scroll, sheet of paper, screen or fan. Works of *haiga* tend to present one shape or figure (maximally several of them) on a monochrome background, sometimes getting close to abstract art (cf. http://www.japonia.org.pl/?q=node/75, http://www.brooksbookshaiku.com/LidiaRozmus/haiga.html). Some scholars use the term '*haiga*' to describe the whole verbo-visual composition treating it as a kind of word-graphy (cf. Śniecikowska 2005: 79–84; 2013) which cannot be easily split into text and image (Addiss 2006, Watts 1988: 178). In my research I generally follow this path, being aware, however, of certain 'cracks' between the parts in contemporary Western *haiga*, especially ones created by two authors: a poet and a visual artist.

Traditional Japanese haikus were not only accompanied by *haiga* illustrations but they were also parts of *haibun* – a genre interweaving prose and poems, often an itinerary. The prose explained ambiguities of the poems, revealing in what circumstances given haiku was composed and thus suggesting its interpretation. Contemporary Western incarnations of *hai-*

bun, especially online ones, are frequently combined with *haiga* forming various hybrid (in terms of media and genres) verbo-visual compositions.

Originally, only *haiga* were verbo-visual in the strict sense. In case of haiku and *haibun* the relations with visual arts were important but not direct. The introduction of haiku and the related genres to the West[1] is also linked with the expansion of verbo-visuality.

In the paper I wish to trace different manifestations of transculturality in the mentioned spaces of convergence in Polish culture. One may argue that such examination of verbo-visuality of the haiku-related genres does not require implementing the Welsch's term as the well known notions of interculturality and multiculturality may easily suffice. I believe the concept of transculturality – though still possibly "risky and disputable" (Rewers 2007: 119) – enables broader analysis of the investigated phenomena: very remote in time and space and having different philosophical and artistic background. I do not want to treat cultures as isolated monoliths (cf. Welsch 1998, Welsch 2004, Wilkoszewska 2004: 14) as "sharp" opposition of East and West often obscures the actual picture. I am interested in "shading" cultural differences, showing fictitiousness of some seemingly impassable borders, revealing surprising cultural meeting points and describing "the interference of the values and standards of different cultures" (Rewers 2007: 128). Exploring the spaces of convergence of the old Oriental verbo-visual forms is a very good occasion for such a transcultural survey.

Beyond two dimensions

Haiku and artists' books

Some scholars claim haiku poets and publishers outside Japan generally mistreat the poems' layout (cf. Kotlarek 2009: 440), which is, moreover, in a way culturally justified (no comparable calligraphy tradition in the West). The statement is obviously too strong. Visuality of haiku in the West must be perceived first on the basic, typographical level. Roland Barthes rightly emphasizes the importance of the notation of haiku in Western volumes of poetry. He praises the practice of placing a single poem on an otherwise empty page (Barthes 2003: 57). Still, there are numerous typographic ways of publishing haiku. One extreme is the printing asceticism Barthes values

---

[1] The described phenomena are not restricted to Polish culture – analogical processes occur in other Western countries.

so much, the other – pesky, banal orientalisation (quasi-calligraphy, ornaments made of pseudo-ideograms etc. – cf. Śniecikowska 2007). The haiku layout, which we should allegedly forget about in the West, is a field of intensive exploration and experiments. Visuality related to haiku seems to burst from the pages in search for a three-dimensional materialisation. I focus on the process of moving haiku and haiku-related works beyond two dimensions and incorporating them into the field of visual arts.

Let me first examine some contemporary artists' books – artefacts inaccessible for wider public, made by hand in only a few copies[2]. What happens with haiku in such works? What is the bicultural and/or transcultural background for such adaptations?

An assemblage by Katarzyna Szpilkowska *Haiku z plaży* ('Haiku from the beach', http://www.kolekcja.bookart.pl/info/viewpub/tid/4/pid/317) consists of a worn-out wooden box, round pebbles inscribed with single words and a small copy-book in a thick wooden cover. The copy-book contains 19 short poems written on single pages, under each text appears an irregular ink dot (similar ink-blots also appear on the pages without text). These expressive, fingerprint-like dots may be regarded as an Occidental reference to *ensō* – calligraphic Zen symbol of unity, entity, enlightment painted with one stroke of a brush. The blue colour of the ink is also telling: together with the blots and the majuscule handwriting it may be interpreted as referring to childhood, early education, school years and thus to an open, void mind of a child (fundamental Zen condition of self-development).

The relation between pebbles and poems is easy to uncover: texts consist of words written on the stones. Some lyrics are close to the prototypical Western haiku[3]: the perception of the world is full of certain tenderness, poems are filled with empathy to non-human beings and at the same time they are stylistically "fresh" and truly haiku-like[4]. Some poems are, how-

---

[2] The works I describe are parts of the collection of Muzeum Książki Artystycznej (Book Art Museum) in Łódź.
[3] In my research on the Oriental literary forms transferred to the West I use the prototypical genre models, which is useful especially in the description of works meeting only some of the central criteria of the genre. Cf. Śniecikowska (in print).
[4] The examples read: "KAMIEŃ TRWA. / MORZE / ODDYCHA / NIEBIESKO" ('stone lasts. / the sea / breathes / bluely'), "SKÓRA / ŚMIEJE SIĘ / RYBIO" ('skin / is laughing / fishly'), "PTAK PLĄSA – / WIATR / PEŁZA / BEZTROSKO" ('bird is prancing – / wind / crawls / carelessly').
In case of works inaccessible on the Web I quote the original Polish version and give an English translation. Other literary texts appear only in the English translation.

ever, highly incoherent[5] as if they were created with the slightly modified Dadaist method of pulling words (inscribed on pebbles) at random out of the post-avant-garde hat[6].

The connection between texts and the assembled objects is not self-evident, some semantic links are clear enough though. The composition proves riveting as the artist manages to keep balance between the sensual and the intellectual. The assemblage corresponds with the haiku and Zen aesthetics (appreciation of the worn-out, the common, the ordinary; incorporating nature into the work of art). The haikus are visualised, concretised and "sensualised" (the role of touch!) by natural ready-mades (pebbles) and simple but defamiliarised human made objects[7]. Szpilkowska manages to combine Oriental inspirations and the familar if slightly outdated attributes of everyday life (blue ink, copy-book). Cultural diversity is also reflected in the stylistics of the poems: oscillating between genuine poetics of haiku and... delicate pure-nonsense.

Marek Gajewski chooses a totally different way of concretising haiku. His Haiku III (http://www.vebsoft.pl/mgajewski/display_gallery.php?SectionID=4&GalleryID=3&Lang=PL) is a composition created over 24 years (1985–2009) with utmost respect for the cultural and physical "material" of art. The composition resembles a portable altar – triptych. The sides of the "altar" were made of sheets of thick cream paper inscribed with two short Buddhist meditative texts and one haiku (presumably written by Gajewski himself[8]), accompanied by the engravings of the artist. The abstract and semi-abstract prints form lines of ornaments, which at first sight remind of a series of Oriental ink landscape paintings, Egyptian reliefs or... contemporary comics. Some engravings are outlined with regular black circles – such graphical tondos might again be treated as a Western version of *ensō*.

---

[5] Some examples: "SZUMNIE PARSKA / UŚMIECH / RYBA TRWA / PIESZCZOTLIWIE" ('boisterously snorts / the smile / the fish lasts / caressingly'), "UŚMIECH / ODDYCHA / ZIARNIŚCIE / RYBA / TRWA / SZUMNIE" ('smile / breathes / grainily / fish / lasts / boisterously').

[6] Another analogy may be a contemporary American game""Haikubes": a set of 63 dice (each engraved with a word or short phrase) for creating haiku. Cf. http://www.haikubytwo.com/review-haikubes/.

[7] The wooden box (old suitcase?) and an old-fashioned copy-book (poetic travel diary?) may be related with the travelling aspect of haiku and *haibun*.

[8] None of the literary texts employed by the artist is subscribed. The note attached to Gajewski's work provides us with the poets' and writers' names (Bashō – wrongly spelled as "Basko", Buson, Issa, Rajneesh (Osho), Seung Sahn, Gajewski) not attributing them to particular texts.

The middle part of *Haiku III* consists of a fan decorated with lines of engravings (element typical of both Oriental and Western cultures), one of the printing matrices used by an artist and 8 loose sheets of paper with the Polish translations of classical Japanese haiku. Gajewski used hand painted, cooked paper with slightly ragged edges. Its monochrome red surface with blurred patches of colour seems to hide misty landscapes waiting only for a clear shape to appear. And there are several shapes appearing indeed – not painted but written and printed. A text of a haiku is carefully written by hand in horizontal lines along the longer edge at the bottom of each page. A line of engraving – similar to the ones already described – decorates the upper part of the composition. The engravings this time seem close to incomprehensible calligraphy (linear notation makes the impression stronger[9]) or unintelligible abstract *haiga*.

The work is completed by a text hidden on the back side of the "altar", sounding Taoist or Zen, telling of a "Great Man" by the name "I Do Not Know".

At first sight the rich multipart artefact seems very far from simplicity and asceticism of haiku and traditional Japanese aesthetics. It also seems a far cry from what corresponds to them in Occidental cultures. The composition surely reflects the strong belief of Western artists that works inspired by Far Eastern masterpieces deserve rare, precious materials and remarkable layout. Still, *Haiku III* is a coherent, well-thought-out meditative composition. Texts chosen by Gajewski, coming from different times and different places, share the same philosophical background. The visual side of the work is more ecclectic, joining the forms and techniques familiar to Western art (triptych, tondo, composition in lines) with deep Oriental inspirations. The genre name haiku works as a synecdoche (*pars pro toto*) of a greater verbo-visual composition built on similar or corresponding aesthetic and philosophical foundations.

The already described examples of the artists' books show that moving haiku beyond two dimensions is often connected with its recontextualisation. The works are the authors' unique attempts at visual, sensual (the role of touch!) concretisation of poetry. The formula for success is careful blending of forms of Oriental origin and those known from the artists' own culture and own sensual experience. Some genre conventions must be therefore given up.

---

[9] For the Polish reader the first, "classical" anthology of Japanese haiku (*Haiku* 1983), where the translations were taken from, may also be a visual intertext. The book had an eleborate typographical layout – calligraphies played a role of illustrations.

It seems worthwhile to confront the works of Szpilkowska and Gajewski with the book *Motyle* ('Butterflies', 2007, http://www.kolekcja.bookart.pl/info/viewpub/tid/4/pid/120) by Franciszek Bunsch, which is much simplier and at the same time less homogeneous. When the book is closed it looks like a small copy-book in hard back – when open it proves a long strip of paper folded as an accordion, printed and inscribed on one side. What makes the work more unusal are the geometrical paper shapes glued to the edges of the "pages" – the open book is in fact three-dimensional. It is decorated with multicoloured semi-abstract figures resembling butterflies and cob-webs, accompanying haiku poems. Such verbo-visual form seems to correspond to *haiga* and Japanese scrolls *shi-ga-jiku* (*shinga jiku* – cf. Trzeciak 2002: 139) containing both literary texts and paintings. Still, apart from haiku there are also some other lyrical texts having nothing in common with these tiny meditative poems and, last but not least, the textual forms the author names "nowe ('new') gatunki". The polysemous word "gatunki" may be translated as "genres" or "species" – only the latter is the right choice here as "nowe gatunki" proves humorous coinages (resembling the names of insect species) for different human types. Abundance of visual and literary forms, graphical and genological incoherence strongly distract the readers' / viewers' attention not letting them concentrate on haiku themselves. There is no place for synergy of haiku and the alleged *haiga*. Still, looking for deep transcultural links was supposedly not the author's intention. This is clearly reflected in the title of the work, which is *Butterflies* (here: light, careless, small, multicoloured literary beings) and not *Haiku*.

An interesting counterpoint for the already described artists' books, which differently adapt the haiku and *haiga* tradition, is a composition by a *haijin* and *sumi-e* painter Lidia Rozmus. The book *My journey* (Rozmus 2004) / *W podróży* (Rozmus 2005)[10] was published by a regular publishing house, still it may be regarded as an experimental artefact. Rozmus is an author both of the layout and the literary text. The volume is hidden in an elegant, orientalised paper slipcase of untypical shape and ascetic non-chromatic colouring. The main visual motif on the cover is, again, an expressive *ensō* – this time in its traditional form. Painting *ensō* in grey, not black ink may, however, suggest some subtle cultural changes. The book itself stops on the verge of three-dimensionality: accordion-like folded pages annex space, defamiliarising reading experience. You may turn the "pages" normally, still the most natural way of perceiving the whole work

---

[10] The book was first published in English in 2004, a year later a Polish version followed.

is spreading it as a long scroll and reading / watching carefully its both sides. Visual and literary content of *My journey* form a harmonious entity.

The title of the volume refers to Master Bashō, poet-traveller, and his journey diaries. The book interweaves prose and haiku just as classical *haibun*: prose sheds light on the poems, poems illustrate prose. Literary communication is "supplemented" with black and white photographs appearing asymmetrically in the pages and a strip of expressive abstract *sumi-e* painting (resembling an ECG notation) along the "scroll". The photos themselves usually depict single natural shapes (cf. Śniecikowska 2012), just as the works of old Japanese masters of *zenga* or *haiga* (types of *sumi-e*), and semantically go with the literary text. Thus, Rozmus evidently combines the genres of *haibun* and *haiga* in an expressive form she calls *haibun-ga* (cf. Kreis 2002: 8, Walker 2005, Olson 2005).

The author generally follows old Japanese masters, her innovations are at the same time slight and significant. *Sumi-e* is accompanied by photographs, *haibun* and *haiga* are united[11], and a scroll is at the same time a set of pages. The haikus themselves seem very close to the genre prototype without just being uncreative English or Polish imitations of the Oriental texts (on the contrary, you may see traces of modern epiphany in these poems – cf. Śniecikowska (in print), Michałowski 2008).

My journey is an active continuation of the old Japanese genres (cf. Balbus 1983: 145); the books by Szpilkowska, Gajewski, Bunsch cannot be so unambiguously qualified. This does not automatically mean that full three-dimensionality equals formal or generic richness. It is, however, surely connected with greater heterogeneity (especially in case of an assemblage) and more polisensory perception. Three-dimensional works are in a way bolder, more unique and more exposed to incomprehension. They use genres as components but they do not function within genres nor form new ones. *Motyle* ('Butterflies') are a loose Occidental variation partly based on Oriental motifs. *Haiku III* is an attempt at gathering and uniting within one work different visual and textual components referring to haiku. Szpilkowska in a way turns haiku into material objects which she finally uses to form the poems. The ontic status of the three artists' books is to some extent parallel to classical *haiga* (verbo-visual works existing in one / few copies), which is, however, definitely not enough to talk about any traces of transculturality. A proof of transcultural links is, however, the possibilty of coherent and creative combination of textual and visual forms deriving from

---

[11] It is typical of many contemporary works inspired by Japanese culture, especially online ones.

different cultural universes. Still, the basis for such artistic activity must be undoubtedly knowledge about the Other (though in some aspects Similar) and... clear composition of the work (the work by Bunsch being negative example here). Under such conditions even strongly modified Oriental forms may help people of the West capture their own experience.

Art exhibitions entitled haiku

A phenomenon that deserves careful research is numerous art exhibitions employing the term 'haiku' in their titles[12]. Undoubtedly artists and curators perceive the great visual potential of haiku. Some decisions, however, prove highly surprising; tracing transculturality in the presented visual and verbo-visual configurations seems unintelligible. Still, some reveal unexpected parallels between seemingly incomparable pieces of art.

In the recent years the greatest haiku-centred museum enterprise was the exhibition *Czy można przesadzać kwiaty rzepaku? Twórczość mistrzów haiku* ('Is It Possible to Replant Rape Flowers? Works of Haiku Masters') in the Museum of Literature (Muzeum Literatury) in Warsaw (15 Feb 2002 – 15 March 2002). The assumption of this unique project was not only to trace but also to create spaces of convergence and transculturality. From the point of view of the Welsch's theory it seems an ideal arrangement for further studies. The exhibition consisted of pieces of poetry (Polish translations of Japanese haiku, Polish haiku-inspired poetry by Stanisław Cichowicz, Janusz Stanisław Pasierb, Jerzy Harasymowicz, Hieronim

---

[12] The following is a selecton of exhibitions (not analysed in the paper):
 – *Strumień żółtego piasku* ('Stream of Yellow Sand'), Centrum Sztuki i Techniki Japońskiej "Manggha", Sept 2001 (haiku, *sumi-e, bonsai*, cf. Kreis 2002: 7–10).
 – Paula Rettinger, *Haiku*, Cień Klub, Kraków 2003.
 – Janina Kraupe, *Haiku*, Artidotuum Gallery, Kraków, May 2007 (cf. http://artidotuum.pl/wystawy/).
 – *Wystawa Haiku* ('Haiku Exhibition'), Ośrodek Języka i Kultury Japonii w Łodzi, 2010.
 – *Haiku i Wachlarze* ('Haikus and Fans'), Filia nr 29 Miejskiej Biblioteki Publicznej, Lublin, Oct / Nov 2010.
 – Włodzimierz Witalis Tyc, *Podszepty monsunu albo haiku o zakochanych* ('Monsoon Whispers or Haiku on Lovers'), Galeria Chłodna 20, Suwałki, Nov 2010-I 2011.
 It is worth noting the term 'haiku' is also used in the titles of some musical enterprises joining Oriental and European inspirations but not necessarily strongly connected with haiku poetry itself – cf. the following CDs: A. M. Jopek, M. Ozone, Haiku, Music 2011; Brzóska (D. Brzóskiewicz), Emce Kwadrat (M. Adamowicz), Sójka (S. Sojka), Samplaire (W. Chołaściński), *Haiku fristajl*, Polskie Radio 2006.

Stanisław Kreis) and paintings and installations by visual artists of Poland (about 160 works by Adam Bunsch, Jerzy Stajuda, Teresa Pągowska and Koji Kamoji). The works of the visual artists were arbitrarily attributed to different seasons, which may be regarded as an equivalent of the season word *kigo* in haiku.

The curator of the exhibition, Łukasz Kossowski, claims the perception of the world typical of haiku does not have to be deeply rooted in Oriental (Zen) philosophy (Kossowski 2002). Indeed, contemplation of the real, concentration on the sensual, certain empathy do characterise the output of Bunsch exploring "the microcosm of nature", Stajuda creating "tranquil landscapes", Pągowska and Kamoji artistically recording everyday events (Kossowski 2002: no page numbers). Let me add, such contemplative attitude to the observed seems a specific distinguishing mark of modernist art.

Kossowski is right to emphasize the role of the interdisciplinary parallels: silence and understatement in haiku comparable to empty spaces in visual compositions, simplicity and stylistic asceticism in poetry parallel to raw, simple materials used by visual artists (unprimed canvas in Pągowska's paintings, plywood in works of Kamoji, handmade paper in graphics by Bunsch) (Kossowski 2002). Other interdisciplinary links are: contemplative concentration on details of the perceived world, interest in regular, everyday objects and events, focus on material, the use of limited colour range (cf. Hniedziewicz 2001). Each artist subtly, in his or her own manner, finds similarities between Zen aesthetics, haiku and modern Polish art. It does not mean, however, that they always deliberately looked for such correspondences. The produced works may unintentionally dialogue with the seemingly absolutely incomparable tradition of the Orient. The verbo-visual arrangements of the exhibition truly revealed unexpected relations between arts and cultures.

Let me focus on some aspects of the output of the visual artists in question. Colour graphics by Adam Bunsch[13], employing old Japanese technique of woodcut print *ukiyo-e*, present single natural objects, often changing types of paper, showing the same motif in different scenes, depicting different seasons (cf. Kossowski 2002). The "technical" affinity with Japanese culture is self-evident. Special contemplative attention paid to the tiny natural objects makes the graphics in a way similar to haiku[14].

---

[13] Bunsch is the oldest (born 1896) of the painters whose output was presented in the exhibition.

[14] Bunsch was also a painter of Christian religious scenes and author of religious dramas. Such fusion of interests (Christianity and Orient) seems typical of many Western artists. It proves that contamplative art tends to be linked with religion(s).

Linking Bunsch's works with spring also does not seem controversial (especially if we bear in mind spring iconography of some graphics chosen by the curator).

The relations with haiku seem less evident in case of Pągowska's paintings. Lack of obvious links, however, does not preclude deeper similarities. Kossowski describes Pągowska's works as follows:

> The atmosphere of her paintings is of utmost importance: it is intimate, full of erotic tension, allusive. Many of her works may be associated with the synthetic, disciplined and at the same impressive form of Japanese haiku. [...] Such poetics emanates not only from the painted objects. [...] Everything that is redundant is rejected: imitation of three-dimensional space, abundance of colours, intellectual speculation (Kossowski 2002: no page numbers).

Concentration emanating from the canvas, contemplation of the "silent life" of the nearly haptically depicted objects, defamiliarisation of the visual presentation of nevertheless mimetically shown objects may be reminiscent of good, refined haiku (extreme simplicity of the Oriental miniatures is a myth cf. e.g. Żuławska-Umeda 2007). Also the serenity of Pągowska's works resembles in some way the delicate affirmative humour of Japanese haikus (cf. Śniecikowska 2009). The very personal nature of the paintings can also be linked to haiku (cf. Hniedziewicz 2001). Finally, in her late works Pągowska makes use of unprimed canvas, on which, like a *sumi-e* painter, she draws "signs by means of only a couple of strokes of the brush" (Kitowska-Łysiak 2007). However, the practice of alienating the presented phenomena from the reality (e.g. without a natural background) is clearly very remote from the aesthetics of haiku. The same can be said of eroticism mentioned by Kossowski[15]. Let us recall that the purpose of the exhibition was not to show alleged equivalence of paintings and poems (which is anyway impossible), but to highlight certain not necessarily obvious parallels[16]. One last question: should Pągowska's works be associated with the summer? Apart from the iconography of the presented works, the versatility of the artist, multitude of topics which she explores support this metaphorical classification.

A more obvious choice seems to be Stajuda for the autumn. His works are subtle landscapes, which balance on the border of the external and the

---

[15] "Reformed" 20th century Japanese haiku as well as Western haiku do not shun eroticism. The exhibition in the Museum of Literature was, however, definitely devoted to the classical canons of haiku (and works close to them).

[16] Pągowska herself found the concept of the exhibition very positive (Ł. Kossowski pers. comm.), however, the quest for links with haiku was not her artistic intention.

internal. However, this association may also rise controversies. Haikus are clearly mimetic while Stajuda's works transform and deform the visible reality. Still, let us repeat, the point was not to show simple equivalences.

The last part of the exhibition, the winter, was organised visually by the works of Koji Kamoji, a Japanese living for decades in Poland, who is as it were automatically entitled to take a stand on elements of haiku aesthetics in painting. Kamoji is actually known for creating works that relate to haiku (*Haiku-Woda* – 'Haiku Water', *Haiku-Deszcz* – 'Haiku-Rain', cf. Gorządek 2009) and commenting on the genre himself (Kamoji 2006: 29).

Magdalena Hniedziewicz describes thus this part of the exhibition:

> We enter a room where in front of our eyes on the black wall opens the metaphysical landscape of *Nocny deszcz* ('Rain in the Night') of straight forms with clear contours; they are abstract, but at the same time they define a certain [...] space, they are suggestive in drawing one's gaze into the depths of the blackness. In front of the painting, on the floor [...] there is an installation [...]: a sheet of silver-coloured metal with a glass of water standing in the middle. It is difficult to say how the artist succeeded in creating the tension between the dark picture with powerful forms and the elusive silvery-transparent installation; there is some inexpressible metaphysics to it [...]. On the side walls there are paintings. White surfaces seem to exist only thanks to the points and lines on them, which are delicate and barely noticeable from some distance. [...] The paintings of Koji Kamoji seem to realise what Agnieszka Żuławska-Umeda [...] said [...] about haiku: that the words seem to exist only for us to feel the space/silence stretching between them (Hniedziewicz 2001).

Kamoji's works seem to render the nature of winter perfectly, at the same time tangibly and inexpressibly. Emptiness, avoidance of artistic abundance, restricted selection of colours used, a specific hibernation – all this is perfectly in line with the winter haikus of the masters of the genre. Kamoji has obviously gone further than classical *haijins* in the process of abstracting and transferring meanings. Nevertheless, the aesthetic links remain very strong.

Interestingly, Kossowski, a specialist on symbolist painting, did not decide to compare haiku with the paintings of Wojciech Weiss or Jan Stanisławski, which undoubtedly correspond to Japanese aesthetics (cf. e.g. Kossowski 1999, Król 2011, Król 2007, *Ten krakowski Japończyk...*), or exactly that of haiku. The curator looked for more contemporary parallels, less obvious ones. Some of the chosen works are rather allusions to haiku, this relates both to the visual and the literary plane (use of modern haikus, which are far from simple imitation). An exhibition of this kind shows important links between Japanese aesthetics (even in its most austere incarnation) and widely understood modernism. In this way important, though sometimes surprising common areas can be found or created.

We may also wonder about the choice of the exhibition's subheading *The art of* haiku *masters*. The presented literary works are truly classical haikus or works oscillating around the haiku prototype. The visual works cannot be evaluated in this way. The title provokes the viewer to question well-known pieces of art about their potential transcultural connections. The arrangement of the exhibition actually makes one notice at least some parallels. We might consider the whole enterprise as debatable or at least daring, which is perhaps what researching and presenting artistic phenomena is all about.

An astonishing counterpoint for the described exposition is the exhibition of Sławomir Brzoska's works *Płynna tożsamość – haiku* ('Fluid identity – haiku'; 6th Jul – 27th Aug 2011, "Imaginarium" gallery in Łódź). The exhibition in the Museum of Literature featured the literary miniatures as an important element of the presentation, they entered into a consistent (albeit multimedial) dialogue with the 20th century paintings and graphics. The visitor to Brzoska's exhibition may wonder for a long time about the connection between the visual works presented and haiku. Without the author's explanations provided in the form of a leaflet they might not notice the slightest parallel at all.

The exhibition is divided into two parts complementing each other (according to the artist). The first room houses an installation made of three chairs and strands of red and blue wool. Red threads run radially upwards from two of the chairs and blue ones from the third chair. On the "red" chairs there are objects resembling stones wrapped in blue wool, on the "blue" one there is a cuboid (a large book?) covered in red wool. The whole work resembles the refined avant-garde spatial compositions by Naum Gabo. Its alleged relation to haiku seems to be a puzzle. The author explains in the description of the exhibition that the installation

> will relate to the concept of journey through the rhythm of parallel lines. Creating, unwinding, and then after the exhibition coiling back the wool is a process in the course of which I try to be fully aware of every step and the tension of the lines. The process of emergence and destruction is in my understanding identical to breathing, by which I refer to the archaic intuitions of the existence of the Universe. (leaflet)

As we can see, the exhibition room has become the place of maximal meditative experience of the performed activity for the artist. The very meditativeness of the act of creation (not being a contemplation of the external reality) is too little to look for significant similarities to haiku.

The second part of the exhibition is completely incomprehensible in the context of the term appearing in the title. In a separate room on opposing white walls two films are screened and enter into a silent dialogue. The only sound in the room is the vibrating rhythmical music (it sounds much like breathing), which changes very little throughout the show. On the wall opposite the entrance there is a film showing scenes from the life of contemporary Papuans, the other film shows changes of the face of a white man in his forties (the author). The visitors quickly notice the interelation between the films.

At first, the white man has closed eyes and a plain leather necklace on a bare torso. The young Papuans observe him (or rather whatever they had in front of their eyes while the film was shot) intently. The white man's face starts to change, the boys get excited and point something out with their fingers. The man's face is darkening all the time, his features become sharper, and the simple necklace turns into a colourful tribal one. The change is viewed now by adult Papuans too. In the moment of the greatest tension, when the man becomes most similar to the local people, one of the Papuans plays a primitive instrument holding it in his mouth. The viewers, however, still hear the same vibrating music. The change starts to reverse. The Papuans are shown to perform their daily duties. At the end one of the "savages" takes an ancestor's mummy out of a hut and seats it at the table. The face of the man on the other wall is white again, his eyes are open and there is no decoration on his neck at all. Has everyone returned to their roots? Despite the fact that we are very similar? The "fluid identity" from the title is evident here. Yet, where is the haiku?

Nothing follows from the reference to the name of the Oriental genre, save perhaps irritation of the visitors. Haiku is probably supposed to function as a signal of a deep meditative experience, a journey understood as searching for links between cultures. Yet, the parallel between the Japanese short poems, the installation of wool and chairs and the films inspired by the life of the Papuans has a particularly weak basis. Neither will we find any traces of artistic provocation. The enormous cultural load of haiku had been completely missed. Is this due to lack of knowledge? Or was haiku meant as a fashionable catchy word used simply to lure visitors?

We will analyse yet another exhibition enterprise. Malwina Hryńczak entiled her exhibition *Wampiry / Haiku* ('Vampires / Haiku'; Galeria Twórców Galera, Piekarnia Cichej Kobiety, Zielona Góra, Oct-Nov 2010). The shocking combination in the title has the simplest possible explanation: *Vampires* and *Haiku* are two cycles of works presented together. They share the colour patterns (black and white), clear presentation and sensual imagery (surprising cadres, the haptic details shown with the use of chiaroscuro) and the employment of the techniques of photo-montage in computer graphics. The first cycle deals with social exclusion, the different modern forms of "vampirism" (homosexuals, HIV carriers, the mentally ill, ethnic minorities etc.). The second cycle offers a more ambiguous, erudite game with cultural clichés and icons (the thematic incoherence of the exhibition is the first sign of its stylistic weaknesses.

Each of the works of the cycle *Haiku* is composed of three major elements: image, "ideogram" and words. We can see surprising sets or cadres of people, objects and animals. A complementation of this and a supposed "translation" of the strictly figurative parts into a different medium are quasi-ideograms made of bones, symbols, figures etc. Finally, there are texts, the alleged haikus, most of which prove to be epigrams in fact. They rely on puns, some are humorous, others reflexive but we also have provocative and distressing ones.

The first "haiku" is: "There is room / for the shadow…" with a signature: "The sun". The photo-montage shows a cat and a mouse and their shadows on the wall, swapped. This is accompanied by quasi-ideograms looking like abstract avant-garde photograms. Further poems are ascribed to particular figures. For example, Henry VIII "writes": "Women are like roses / – I like to cut them". This "haiku" is matched with a photo-montage of a woman's body divided into parts enclosed by a flower of a rose and two lines of "ideograms" made of a naked woman's silhouette in various poses. A photo-montage showing the smiling face of Princess Diana behind a car wheel is combined with the text: "Winding / are the Lord's paths / Diana" and "ideograms" made of road signs. The distressing couplet "In the sun of the noon / a house of cards" (next to it we can see a house made of cards on a desert and "ideograms" made of playing cards) is signed by Osama bin Laden. In another composition Hitler is looking at crowds of people and "saying": "Enchanted history… I recall these moments". The "Ideograms" are made of tanks, bullets, a helmet, a skull and a swastika. Finally, a rather trivial text: "I got lost… / On the paths of Life" is signed by Death. Next to it we find "ideograms" of bones and a photo-montage – a contour of Death with a photo of a street along which someone is walking.

In sum, we have verbo-visual compositions that are very attractive visually, inventive, sometimes shocking, sometimes transgressing the borders of good taste. In a way they resemble the old European form of emblems with allegorical depictions of people or phenomena combined with a lemma (inscription) explaining the meaning of the image and a subscript (usually an epigram) explaining the link between the image and the lemma[17]. In Hryńczak's work, the role of the lemma is performed by the "ideograms". The compositions prove to be interesting in many ways, intertextual, but very weakly related to haiku (or with *haiga* by extension). The artist seems to treat haiku as a synonym of a poetic miniature with a specific kind of humour to it (cf. her statement at http://cojestgrane.pl/wydarzenie/66718/). The author does not obey any of the key features of the genre, save conciseness. Her humour is also very different from that of classical *haijins* (cf. Śniecikowska 2009). The strongest parallel to Oriental forms is the verbo-visuality of the composition itself. The closeness to European epigrams and emblems is much more evident though, even in the presence of the "ideograms" that feign Oriental signs. The Oriental inspiration without any deeper study has thus produced an enrichment of Occidental forms (epigram, emblem). The alleged convergence of haiku in a new artistic plane is a completely false trail, which does not denounce the value of the work as such, however.

I have described three very different exhibitions which referred to haiku in their titles. It proves, much like in the case of the analysed artists' books, that the most interesting, truly transcultural works obtain when the artist's or curator's activity is supported by knowledge and preceded by deep reflection. Only such output will show fascinating, non-trivial common spheres. However, even the superficial, stereotypical references reveal some parallels between the forms of the Oriental tradition and the searches of Polish modern and post-modern art. The vital element is the stress on presenting the materiality of the works and the striving for verbo-visuality itself.

The Orient in Polish – on the Internet

A particularly interesting domain for investigating the convergence of the Far Eastern verbo-visual genres is the Internet. While browsing through Polish-language websites on haiku, one can quickly encounter forms described as *digital art haiga* (or *digital haiga*), *foto-haiga, foto-filmo haiga*, haiku photography, digital *haibun*. The most important questions to be asked

---

[17] Hryńczak's compositions are remotely related to work by Gajewski (or its part – manually dyed cards with texts of haikus and graphic compositions made of quasi-ideograms). Gajewski's work is deeply rooted in Buddhist aesthetics, graphical forms are absract or semi-abstract. Similarities to emblems will not be found in it.

about these works are related to their innovativeness. What changes with the use of a new medium in comparison to the work's basic model – the "analogue" Oriental form? How do the online compositions compare to earlier (and current) Polish works on paper? How much do the authors make use of the special properties of the Web: the interactivity, hypertextuality, widely understood mulitimediality? In other words – are we dealing with a significant modification of earlier patterns or are we just reading Orientalised "Internet paper"?

It is astonishing (at least at first) how many artists use the form of a blog. The choice seems to result from practical considerations: the ease of starting and running a blog and the possibility of communicating within the web millieu of *haijins* and *haiga* artists. Blogs on haiku usually have several functions (e.g. a diary, a filter; cf. e.g. Gumkowska 2009: 240–241). The posts with haiku or *haiga* are ordered chronologically, the readers can comment on the texts, they also can view the author's profile and, what is very important, follow the links to other Orient-inspired websites. This allows one to learn quickly the abundant Polish-language blogosphere centred on the notion of haiku[18]. This is very important for the literary life, but is in fact an extra-artistic use of the Web (cf. e.g. Cywińska-Milonas 2002: 96–97).

The blogs referred to here are often spacious virtual "open drawers", where the artists keep and at the same time publish literary texts as well as pictures (or photographs) related (or unrelated) to them. The blogs are places where they post their reflections, relations from poetic contests or meetings with the readers, book reviews or upload music or audiovisual files which do not necessarily belong to the category of *film-haiga* (cf. http://rozsypany-czas.blogspot.com/, http://eddie-ad.blogspot.com/, http://haiassneg.blogspot.com/, http://travellingbetweentheworlds.blox.pl/html, http://haikuworld.blox.pl/html/1310721,262146,14,15.html?3,2011, http://haiku2009-publikacje.blogspot.com/). The authors often resort to the mode of incomplete and unfinished message typical of the Web (cf. e.g. Szczęsna 2011: 200, Szczęsna 2009: 68). The poets put their works to scrutiny and quite often modify them according to the readers' comments or allow others to modify them. The Web also opens a plane of specific interpersonal intermedial acts – the internauts co-author *haiga* by combining someone

---

[18] Surprisingly, nearly all comments on the blogs (as well as forums) devoted to haiku and *haiga* are very positive, any criticism that can be found there is always balanced. The poets form a kind of literary club whose unwritten rule is great kindness for other artists' work. They are readers, reviewers and authors at the same time. Thus, open criticism could probably lead to ostracism.

else's poems with visual works (e.g. photographs), which may strongly affect the interpretation of the texts.[19]

Some of the blogs can be considered as open works *in statu nascendi*. For obvious ontic reasons they are not a closed, fully composed artistic whole. Nor are they, however, completely random literary and artistic collections (cf. e.g. http://haiassneg.blogspot.com/, http://haikuofplanet.blogspot.com/). Are they then "most modern *silvae rerum*"[20] (Gumkowska 2009: 231)? Anna Gumkowska is right in her comment that "for the multimedial forms, which by their very nature belong to allogeneous semantic systems, the term *silva rerum* loses meaning" (Gumkowska 2009: 231–232). One must, however, emphasise that blogs on haiku are *silva*-like already at the level of their literary content – in many ways they are close to the old heterogeneous genre of *silva rerum*, as well as to some modern forms of it (cf. Szczepan-Wojnarska 2005: 76–77, Nycz 1984).

Marcin Składanek considers websites to be "domains of paratexts" (Składanek 2010: 399). However, I wish to treat the abundance (mainly to do with the widely understood navigation) of Internet sites relating to the Oriental verbo-visuality as more than just paratextuality. Despite their modest format (commonly that of a blog) the sites are treated by the authors as verbo-visual aesthetic artefacts or even as a kind of multimedial total works of art. This means obviously combining contradictory elements – a blog assumes constant variation; its existence also depends on conditions which are not artistic at all.

Let us also notice that the extent of the "blogginess" may differ. Some sites strive for a kind of formal and functional asceticism – the authors limit the number of external links, sometimes they block the possibility of commenting, pay attention to the visual coherence of the blog, thus making it close to a fully designed author's websites or even a paper publication. However, many Polish sites dealing with haiku are amorphous or downright aesthetically mediocre (cf. e.g. http://eddie-ad.blogspot.com/, http://orston.blogspot.com/). The multifunctionality of the blog allows aesthetic chaos, although it need not generate it.

---

[19] For example, combining Magdalena Banaszkiewicz's poem: "late autumn / in the deserted garden / a flower is rusting" with a photograph by Joanna Lewandowska showing an old rusting balustrade with a flowery motive destroys the creative metaphor (the most interesting element in the quoted haiku). Cf. http://magdajasna.blogspot.com. See also http://joo-dailyhaiku.blogspot.com/search?updated-min=2011-01-01T00:00:00%2B01:00&updated-max=2012-01-01T00:00:00%2B01:00&max-results=50.

[20] Gumkowska refers to the concept of modern *silvae rerum* introduced by Ryszard Nycz (Nycz 1984). They are a type of 20th century heterogeneous literary texts joining different genres and traditions, often fragmentary and employing the technique of *collage*.

Orientalisation

A large portion of the websites presenting haiku, *haiga*, *haibun* are characterised by evident mimetic Orientalisation of the visual and verbal message. The authors try hard to recreate old means of communication with the use of the new egalitarian medium.

Let us now examine one of the most refined Polish verbo-visual compositions – the combination of poems and photographs by Waldemar Frąckiewicz entitled *Krople słońca* ('Droplets of the sun'[21]; http://serwisy.umcs.lublin.pl/w.frackiewicz/KS.htm; the work has also appeared in print[22]). This online volume of poetry or, to be precise, a kind of unfolding scroll with texts and photographs is at the same time close to haiku and *haiga*, but also fairly remote from the spirit of these arts. The composition seems very homogeneous and visually clear (it makes use of black, grey and white only). Moving, concise haikus correspond well with the photographs of nature although they are not simply illustrations to the texts. We encounter numerous understatements here – in the texts themselves and in the vague photographs set against blank spaces (cf. Barthes 2003: 57). The work strongly resembles old verbo-visual *shi-ga-jiku* although photography is a modern way of capturing the world. The digital "scroll" itself is technologically advanced all throughout. However, Frąckiewicz's *photo-haiga* has the mood of Japanese graphic works closely corresponding with haiku (cf. Śniecikowska 2007). They are images of nature most of the time showing one or two shapes against a relatively homogeneous natural background. These are often rather unusual forms, which are based on conceits more than those shown by Japanese painters (which can possibly be attributed to the change of the medium – photography captures anything, making the message "artistic" requires some deautomatisation of perception).

The online volume by Frąckiewicz still has another hidden layer to it. By clicking on a photograph, we get a detailed personal description of it (which matters more considering that not all of them can be easily linked with the haikus), naming the circumstances in which it was taken and not

---

[21] Frąckiewicz has also created other compositions of haiku and photographs, which are not, however, as refined and whose form is more remote from the aesthetics of the Far East. Cf. http://serwisy.umcs.lublin.pl/w.frackiewicz/haiku.htm. See also: http://serwisy.umcs.lublin.pl/w.frackiewicz/hieroglify.htm

[22] 52 pages, size 20 cm x 20 cm (Frąckiewicz 2002). In this format we lose the impression of unfolding a scroll and the hidden exegeses.

infrequently providing a ready interpretation – sometimes lengthy and embedded in various currents of Oriental and Western philosophy. All the aesthetic clarity and understatement suddenly disappear, the range of interpretation or even co-creation of the work left to the reader shrinks drastically. Does this contradict the link to the genre of haiku itself?

The Japanese *haibun* once again proves an important point of reference. Frąckiewicz's interpretations obviously differ from those known e.g. from Bashō's diaries – the Polish author's explications are closer to a treatise or learned exegesis. Nevertheless, the link remains discernible. We are thus confronted with an interesting literary and medial hybrid, a modern online equivalent of two forms related to haiku: firstly, the scroll with poems and pictures (*shi-ga-jiku*, *haiga*) and secondly, the text noting facts, impressions and interpretations related to particular photographs and by extension to the poems (akin to *haibun*)[23]. The oscillation between the genres is enabled by the use of the Web.

Frąckiewicz's work – and its *haiga-haibun* shape – has a paper equivalent. However, this is not the book version of *Krople słońca*, but the aforementioned volume by Lidia Rozmus (Rozmus 2004; 2005)[24]. Thanks to the use of the Internet as the medium Frąckiewicz's composition – unlike Rozmus's book – preserves the aesthetic of *haiga* in pure form. *Haibun* is to an extent an optional element here.

Frąckiewicz has proposed a total work, composed in each and every verbal and visual detail. He did not use the form of a blog, but created a closed self-referring composition, which is not connected by links to the vivid haiku-related blogosphere.

Many other Polish websites are products of the visual and literary Orientalisaton. Having discussed Frąckiewicz's work, we are not surprised to find that the artistically most interesting and most refined sites either completely avoid the blog format or consciously reduce its interactive nature. The template is strongly personalised and the possibility to comment on the texts is blocked (cf. e.g. *foto-haiga* by Dorota Pyra http://rozsypany-czas.blogspot.com/search/label/haiga).

The references to the culture of the Far East in many online *haiga* can be, however, missed by the reader at first as the Oriental elements are

---

[23] The haikus and photographs keeping in line with the aesthetics of haiku can also be seen on the websites of Marek Szyryk (a poet and photographer) http://szyryk.art.pl/. However, in this case we are not dealing with a relation close to *haiga* or *haibun*.

[24] The character of the prose fragments makes Rozmus's work closer to the traditional *haibun*. Her *My journey* / *W podróży* and *Krople słońca* by Frąckiewicz are similar as active continuations of haiku (cf. Balbus 1983: 145).

modified in line with the author's own background. The colourful modern photographs do not show crooked twigs or mountain peaks known from the Japanese ink painting. The composition of the cadre (presenting certain objects on a monochromatic plane) and the focus on the detail make these Polish *haiga* somewhat close to the aesthetics of haiku and its associate visual arts (cf. e.g. Urszula Wielanowska's blog http://jasminum72.blox.pl/html). Another point to make is that it is hard to find truly distinguistished works among these. In the online flood of mediocre *haiga* where landscape photographs are accompanied by imitations of haiku (cf. Michałowski 2008) written in a wave-shaped lines, what attracts attention are works that are at least artistically decent. *Foto-haiga* by Grażyna Kaźmierczak is noteworthy thanks to mere variation of font depending on the semantics and stylistics of the individual haikus. These compositions illustrate a rather obvious fact unknown to Polish paper *haiga*: the choice of the image that accompanies the text (Kaźmierczak sometimes combines one poem with different photographs) clearly changes the reception of the whole verbo-visual work. Jadwiga Gala Miemus (http://poezja.com.pl/?q=node/625) is even more extreme in this respect – some of her poetic conceits are completely incomprehensible without the photographs (it is difficult, for example, to associate on one's own the phrase "rungs leading to eternity" with the shadows of tree trunks on a path to a cemetary).

The visual component might also be just an ornament of the haiku blogs. It sometimes is an interesting decoration of the poetic website (cf. http://zimowehaiku.blogspot.com/), but sometimes it irritatingly simplifies the message for example by the use of a multiplied quasi-Oriental motive (http://entuzjazm.blox.pl/html/1310721,262146,21.html?157645).

It proves again that the key to artistic success, regardless of the medium used, is simply the knowledge supporting the creative intuitions and allowing combinations of literary and visual parts that are in some way similar or complementary.

Naturalisation of the Other – "unity in multiplicity" or incoherent eclecticism?

What seems to be most interesting in the online works discussed here are the processes of strong naturalisation of the Oriental forms in the new cultural environment (cf. Johnson 2011: 130): the introduction of the elements of the Western culture to the works inspired by Japanese art, strong integration of equally valued parts: foreign and native one, and finally indicating or even creating transcultural spaces. In case of *haiga* on the Web (and akin forms) this type of naturalisation concerns first of all the visual sphere. The texts usually have few innovations, they mimic the foreign models (known to the artists from the second hand) without offering deeper Occidental intrusions in the sphere of poetics.

One must consider whether the naturalisation leads to the accomplishment of "unity in multiplicity" (the more so because *haiga* or *film-haiga* combine ingredients of different media) or whether it stops at the level of incoherent eclecticism. It is not hard to guess that for different works this question will be answered differently.

Marek Domagała (Marek Haik) proposed on his blog http://haikuofplanet.blogspot.com an original and simple graphic composition: the individual *haiga* are like postcards that are displayed against an abstract background covered with watercolour stains. The "postcards" themselves imitate thick sepia handmade paper; clear straight lines (as if drawn with a pencil) mark the places of the illutrations to haikus. This means a subtle dialogue with the Oriental aesthetics related to haiku. The structure of the "paper" suggests great attention paid to the material, ideally straight lines in pencil are on the other hand very remote from the expressive brush strokes in the Zen painting and calligraphy[25]. The digital pictures themselves balance between the figurative and the abstract, they use or imitate different techniques (digitally modified photograph, dry pastel, and watercolour). These are techniques typical of the Western art (like drawing in pencil mentioned before) although the works are clearly inspired by Far Eastern aesthetics (exposing the detail, the role of the monochrome background). Domagała succeeds in delicate and well thought-out naturalisation of *haiga* without blurring the origin of the form.

However, the most interesting artefact of the blog is the film (*film-haiga*), an etude with an excellent Orientalising and disturbing soundtrack. The work illustrates or rather construes the text of a haiku (the words appear in a non-random fashion on the screen): "neon snakes / dig in the moonlight / tunnel dreams". The work clearly refers to the tradition of the avant-garde film, the associations with the 1930's cinema of e.g. Len Lye are very strong. At the same time the light snakes flaring up on the screen can be associated with the expressive nearly abstract forms of *sumi-e* ink painting (e.g. *zenga*). The circle of the moon appearing in the film is also

---

[25] These compositions are in many ways close to the cards on which haikus are written in the artist's book by Gajewski.

reminiscent of the Far Eastern culture. The poem itself is the greatest literary experiment in the whole of the blog – it is most metaphorical and remote from the genre prototype. This is a very interesting and so far final point of the development of haiku and *haiga* on the Internet – a very creative work making considerable use of the possibilities of the Web and also proving the possibility of inspiring combination of cultures or, to use Welsch's terms, revealing transcultural shared places[26].

Usually, however, the naturalisation of haiku does not run so smoothly – the "seams" between the forms and traditions are clearly visible and the conspicuous incoherent eclecticism cannot be simply revalued in any post-modernist fashion (cf. Kazimierska-Jerzyk 2008: 94–140). Even in these incoherent compositions one can after all find interesting concepts of verbo-visual combinations, transcultural glimpses showing that different poetics can be reconciled without simple imitation. For example, Mariusz Ogryzko (who like many Polish *haijins* publishes his poems in English – http://haiga.pl/2.html) is able to combine surrealist aesthetics with haikus perfectly capturing Japanese *sabi* (lonelines, emotional distance, acceptance of the inevitable; cf. Watts 1988: 182, Kubiak Ho-Chi 2009: 84–85). A sepia photograph of chairs of various kinds that are placed chaotically on the snow (or sand?) is an illustration to the poem "winter cemetery / I sit near the smallest grave / the brightest". The other pole of the experiment is the creation of haiku ekphrases[27] of Western works of art (including older works). The dialogue of distant forms often proves to be only apparent, some works, however, seem to put each other in an interesting new light (the case of Memling's *Last Judgement* and its haiku ekphrasis – http://sehaikuan.blogspot.com/).

We must also mention as works worth of notice the photographs and computer graphics by Aleksander Litowczak (http://haiga-budzenie.blogspot.com[28]) drawing from differing inspirations, keeping traces of Zen aesthetics (presentation of a detail against a homogeneous background),

---

[26] The experimental character of Domagała's works is clear in comparison with the anachronistic works of Jadwiga Gala Miemus called by the author *filmo-foto haiga* (or *foto-filmo haiga*) http://poezja.com.pl/?cat=10 (a series of films and photographs of nature with a featureless soundtrack, simple imitative haikus approaching the viewer, lack of intriguing tension between the image and the text).

[27] Classical haikus were quite often ekphrastic and intertextual, which is usually forgotten in the West.

[28] I believe the more homogeneous graphics by Litowczak made as illustrations to the haikus of Magdalena Banaszkiewicz (http://budzenie-jasna.blogspot.com/) are much less interesting.

yet lacking its asceticism, far from stylistic refinement (ostensible use of wavy text lines, loud colours). The most interesting of his works are the simple geometric abstractions which do not imitate Oriental works but at the same time fit well into the clear image schemata of *haiga* and haiku. The simple imagery decidedly suffers from ostensible use of fonts and, first of all, the literalness that destroys the poetic message[29]. The combination of geometric abstraction and haiku in itself seems successful (at least potentially). Another interesting feature we find in Litowczak's works is the striving to render graphically the texture of the described materials[30], which is yet another incarnation of the interest in the materiality that we can observe in many of the discussed works. It is also a specific, modernist, link between different aesthetics.

***

The online output of Polish haiku, *haiga, haibun* authors should be to a large extent treated as poetry on… paper. The artists try to make their works as similar as possible to what can be seen in printed volumes. There is usually a two-degree mimesis (however different these degrees are) – the digital medium mimics the traditional paper one, while the stylistics of the texts and graphic compositions is strongly reminiscent of the Oriental (or what haiku and *haiga* authors deem as such). Still, nearly all digital *haiga* and *haibun* are medial hybrids – the authors refuse to resign from the simple functionalities of the Web, which modify the perception of the work. It appears that the *haijins* and *haiga* authors are not, however, particularly interested in exploring the potential of the multimedial, interactive

---

[29] For example, the poem "a table in the garden / into a plate with porridge / a plum petal fell" is illustrated by Litowczak in the following way: on a green background there is a white belt with a red grid (most likely a tablecloth). On the belt there is a yellow circle with a clear edge (the plate) and a small white blot inside (the petal). In another *haiga* the artist chooses more restrained imagery. A fragment of a rhombus touching a horizontal line symbolises a tram ("five o'clock in the morning – / in the blizzard vanishes / a cracking tram"). The ascetic imagery and its suspense are spoilt by the blunt use of stars in the place where the rhombus touches the line.

[30] For example, we can see a nearly tangible blow-up of a sheepskin coat ("a crowd at the bus stop – / the wind pushes in under my coat / together with the frost") or fishnet tights in chiaroscuro ("the bar's nearly empty – / some strange woman / on a seat nearby"), we feel the delicacy of long woolen fibres in nearly abstract coils of thread in a scarf ("the cap and the scarf / the calendar spring / has just come"), we recognize the gust of the wind in the multiplanar, monochromatic computer graphic in chiaroscuro ("six in the morning – / the wind gets on the tram / before a bunch of people").

and hypertextual nature of the Internet. Only few of them are creative in the combination of the media. Is this the craving for reduction of the stimuli, stylistic asceticism or rather a kind of carelessness, application of easy solutions, and simple use of the Web as an ad hoc diary? The second answer seems closer to the truth.

Still, we must admit that many of the blogs to an extent resemble Oriental *haibun* with an addition of the visual component (thus being a type of *haibun-ga*). This makes clear some similarities between the practices of haiku authors creating in different places and epochs. If we reverse the direction of analysis, we might conclude that *haibun* of the Japanese *haijins* (of Bashō's line – cf. Issa 1997) is in a way situated between the form of diary, old heterogenous genre of *silva rerum* and… contemporary heterogeneous literary texts (modern *silvae rerum*)[31].

Transcultural convergence?

In the paper I have described various spaces of convergence of Oriental verbo-visuality, showing more and less successful attempts to implant foreign genres in new cultural and medial areas. We must decide in the end to what extent the convergence is here linked with transculturality. Welsch has observed that for the Japanese, the actual origin of an artefact does not matter. The important criterion is closeness, the ability to "fit in" the Japanese culture. Such works might be nominally foreign, but will be deemed Japanese. (Welsch 2004: 42).

Could this description be applied to the works analysed here? In other words, have haiku, *haiga*, *haibun* become Polish? I believe the answer is to some extent positive, even more so because the Japanese genres re-profiled in the process of genological transplantation prove surprisingly close to the forms of the Occident: diaries, epigrams, aphorisms, emblems, *silvae rerum* and finally (and obviously) illustrations. The most interesting, however, are those compositions that consciously expose various relations between the East and the West. These works have the potential to produce active continuations of the Oriental genres with the Far Eastern schemata complemented with ingredients from the Western culture. Surprising planes of understanding, agreement, similar thinking of art and feeling it can be revealed even by works that combine elements

---

[31] For an account of the links between traditional Japanese aesthetics and the ideas of modernism see Śniecikowska (in print).

which seem completely incompatible, for example, haiku and the poetics of surrealism or the tradition of abstract avant-garde film. Naturally, this is not to say that surrealism or the cinema of the 1930s had much in common with the stylistics and the way of presenting the world in the discussed Oriental genres. Yet, an artist open to diverse stimuli can make use of very heterogeneous inspirations in their creation, for which a common denominator may be found, as it turns out. Still, a necessary condition seems to be the knowledge of the Other in some non-trivial degree (cf. e.g. Said 1978).

Let us recount again that an important link (also in the perspective of transculturality) between the different traditions is the strong striving to unify the word and the image, to transgress the borders between arts and to fuse them. This is very entrenched in the Oriental culture and supported by centuries of e.g. calligraphy or *haiga* painting, in the culture of the West it rose in prominence in modernist times[32]. Its intensity is proven e.g. by the fact of inclusion within the visual arts of forms that were originally only related to them but not strictly verbo-visual (as haiku or *haibun*).

The described phenomena of Polish art of the end of the 20th and the turn of the 21st century undoubtedly derive from the spirit of modernism, in the majority of cases not turning into post-modernism. The technological development enabled their existence in the context of new media without obscuring their pedigree. This perspective allows one to notice numerous common points between modern art of the West and the Orient (cf. e.g. Michałowski 2008: 129–133, 142–144; Johnson 2011; Hokenson 2007, Hakutani 2009), which can be perceived as a specific widely understood transcultural space. Barring the amount of striving to combine different arts, let us enumerate just the following: fragmentariness, specific framing of the presentation, interest in everyday details and the sensual experience of an individual, "sparing" poetics, artistically processed catching of glimpses of epiphany. Last but not least, the very openness to other cultures, which under closer scrutiny may prove surprisingly familiar.

Translated by Jerzy Gaszewski, Beata Śniecikowska

---

[32] The common artistic aims are revealed by the parallels between avant-garde word-graphy and some Oriental (old) and Polish (new) *haiga* compositions. Another noteworthy context is the contemporary movement of liberature. All of these were obviously preceded by the 19th century striving for *correspondance des arts*.

Bibliography

Addiss Stephen 2006, *Interactions of Text and Image in Haiga*, [in:] *Matsuo Bashō's Poetic Spaces*, ed. E. Kerkham, New York: Palgrave Macmillan.

Addiss Stephen 2005, *Haiku i haiga*, [in:] *Estetyka japońska*. vol. 2. *Słowa i obrazy. Antologia*, ed. K. Wilkoszewska, Cracow: Universitas.

Balbus Stanisław 1983, „Stylizacja i zjawiska pokrewne w procesie historycznoliterackim", *Pamiętnik Literacki*, No. 2.

Barthes Roland 2003, *La préparation du roman I et II. Cours et séminaires au Collège de France (1978–1979 et 1979–1980)*, Texte établi, annoté et présenté par Nathalie Léger, Paris: Seuil.

Brzóska (Dariusz Brzóskiewicz), Emce Kwadrat (Marcel Adamowicz), Sójka (Stanisław Sojka), Samplaire (Wojciech Chołaściński) 2006, *Haiku fristajl*, Polskie Radio.

Cywińska-Milonas Maria 2002, *Blogi (ujęcie psychologiczne)*, [in:] *Liternet*, ed. P. Marecki, Rabid, Cracow: Rabid.

Frąckiewicz Waldemar 2002, *Krople słońca. Fotografia. Haiku*, Lublin.

Gorządek Ewa 2009, *Koji Kamoji*, http://www.culture.pl/web/guest/baza-sztuki-pelna-tresc/-/eo_event_asset_publisher/eAN5/content/koji-kamoji, accessed on 13.09.2012.

Grochowski Grzegorz 2000, *Tekstowe hybrydy*, Wrocław: Wydawnictwo Funna.

Gumkowska Anna 2009, *Blogi wobec tradycji diarystycznej. Nowe gatunki w nowych mediach*, [in:] *Tekst (w) sieci*. vol 1. *Tekst. Język. Gatunki*, ed. D. Ulicka, Warsaw: Wydawnictwa Akademickie i Profesjonalne.

Haiku 1983, *Haiku*, trans. A. Żuławska-Umeda, afterword M. Melanowicz, Wroclaw: Ossolineum.

Hakutani Yoshinobu 2009, *Haiku and Modernist Poetics*, New York: Palgrave Macmillan.

Hniedziewicz Magdalena 2001, „Haiku w poezji i w obrazach", *Pismo Krytyki Artystycznej* 2001 No. 35, http://free.art.pl/pokazpismo/nr35/tekst3.html, accessed on 30.10.2007.

Hokenson Jan Walsh 2007, *Haiku as a Western Genre. Fellow-Traveler of Modernism*, [in:] *Modernism*, vol. 2, ed. A. Eysteinsson, V. Liska, Amsterdam / Philadelphia: John Benjamins.

Issa Kobayashi 1997, *The Spring of My Life and Selected Haiku*, trans. S. Hamill, Boston–London: Shambhala.

Jakubowicz Karol 2011, *Nowa ekologia mediów. Konwergencja a metamorfoza*, Warsaw: Wydawnictwo Poltext.

Jenkins Henry 2007, *Kultura konwergencji. Zderzenie starych i nowych mediów*, trans. M. Bernatowicz, M. Filiciak, Warsaw: Wydawnictwa Akademickie i Profesjonalne.

Johnson Jeffrey 2011, *Haiku Poetics in Twentieth-Century Avant-Garde Poetry*, Lanham–Boulder–New York–Toronto–Plymouth: Lexington Books.

Jopek Anna Maria, Ozone Makoto 2011, *Haiku*, Music.

Kamoji Koji 2006, ***, [in:] *Haiku*, ed. and trans. A. Żuławska-Umeda, Bielsko-Biała: ELAY.

Kazimierska-Jerzyk Wioletta 2008, „Strategia rewaloryzacji" we współczesnej refleksji nad sztuką. *Piękno, eklektyzm, epigonizm, infantylizm*, Cracow: Universitas.

Kitowska-Łysiak Małgorzata 2007, *Teresa Pągowska*, http://www.culture.pl/baza-sztuki--pelna-tresc/-/eo_event_asset_publisher/eAN5/content/teresa-pagowska, accessed on 2.09.2012.

Kossowski Łukasz 2002, *Czy można przesadzać kwiaty rzepaku? Twórczość mistrzów haiku*, katalog wystawy w Muzeum Literatury im. Adama Mickiewicza, 15 Feb – 15 March 2002, Warsaw.

Kossowski Łukasz 1999, *O inspiracjach japońskich w sztuce polskiej*, in *Chopin – Polska – Japonia. Wystawa z okazji 80 rocznicy nawiązania stosunków oficjalnych między Polską a Japonią oraz Roku Chopinowskiego*, Warsaw.

Kostyrko Teresa 2004, *„Transkulturowość" w ujęciu André Malraux – przyczynek do pojmowania terminu*, [in:] *Estetyka transkulturowa*, ed. K. Wilkoszewska, Cracow: Universitas.

Kotlarek Magdalena 2009, *Haiku – Akunin – Przekład*, [in:] *Między oryginałem a przekładem*, vol. XV. *Obcość kulturowa jako wyzwanie dla tłumacza*, ed. J. Brzozowski, M. Filipowicz--Rudek, Cracow: Księgarnia Akademicka.

Kozyra Agnieszka 2010, *Estetyka zen*, Warsaw: Wydawnictwo Trio Biblioteka Fundacji im. Takashimy.

Kreis Hieronim 2002, *Od autora*, [in:] idem, *Strumień żółtego piasku*, Cracow: Wydawnictwo Tyniec.

Król Anna 2007, *Obraz świata, który przemija. Inspiracje sztuką Japonii w malarstwie Jana Stanisławskiego i jego uczniów / An Image of a Floating World in the Paintings of Jan Stanisławski and his Studets*: Cracow: Centrum Sztuki i Techniki Japońskiej Manggha.

Król Anna 2011, *Japonizm polski / Polish Japanism*, Cracow: Centrum Sztuki i Techniki Japońskiej Manggha.

Kubiak Ho-Chi Beata 2009, *Estetyka i sztuka japońska. Wybrane zagadnienia*, Cracow: Universitas.

Michałowski Piotr 2008, *Haiku wobec epifanii nowoczesnej*, [in:] idem, *Głosy, formy, światy. Warianty poezji nowoczesnej*, Cracow: Universitas.

Nowa wystawa w Muzeum Literatury, „Biuletyn Kulturalny" (28.02.2002), www.msz.gov.pl/files/file_library/42/20020225p_6978.doc, accessed on 30.10.2007.

Nycz Ryszard 1984, *Sylwy współczesne: problem konstrukcji tekstu*, Wroclaw: Ossolineum.

Olson Marion, "My journey" by Lidia Rozmus, Modern Haiku 2005, Vol. 36.1, http://www.modernhaiku.org/bookreviews/Rozmus2004.html.

Rewers Ewa 2007, *Transkulturowość czy glokalność? Dwa dyskursy o kondycji post-ponowoczesnej*, [in:] *Dylematy wielokulturowości*, ed. W. Kalaga, Cracow: Universitas.

Rozmus Lidia 2005, *W podróży*, Evanston: Deep North Press.

Rozmus Lidia 2004, *My journey*, Evanston: Deep North Press.

Said Edward W. 1978, *Orientalism*, New York: Pantheon Books.

Shusterman Richard 2008, *Body Consciousness. A Philosophy of Mindfulness and Somaesthetics*. Cambridge: Cambridge University Press

Shusterman Richard 2003, "Entertainment: A Question for Aesthetics", *British Journal for Aesthetics* 43 (3).

Shusterman Richard 1997, "Somaesthetics and the Body/Media Issue", *Body and Society* 3 (3).

Składanek Marcin 2010, *Parateksty w środowiskach informacyjnych mediów interaktywnych*, [in:] *Pogranicza audiowizualności*, ed. Andrzej Gwóźdź, Cracow: Universitas.

Szczepan-Wojnarska Anna M. 2005, *Sylwiczny i intymistyczny charakter blogów*, [in:] *Język @ multimedia*, ed. A. Dytman-Stasieńko, J. Stasieńko, Wroclaw: Wydawnictwo Naukowe Dolnośląskiej Szkoły Wyższej Edukacji TWP we Wrocławiu.

Sopyło Małgorzata 2008, *Estetyka książki elektronicznej*, Novae Res, Gdynia: Wydawnictwo Innowacyjne.

Szczęsna Ewa 2011, *Dyskurs internetowy a literacki*, [in:] *Komparatystyka dzisiaj*, vol. 2. *Interpretacje*, ed. E. Kasperski, E. Szczęsna, Warsaw: Dom Wydawniczy Elipsa.

Szczęsna Ewa 2009, *Wprowadzenie do poetyki tekstu sieciowego*, [in:] *Tekst (w) sieci*, vol. 1. *Tekst. Język. Gatunki*, ed. D. Ulicka, Warsaw: Wydawnictwa Akademickie i Profesjonalne.

Szura Magdalena Antonina 2003, *Czy blog może być literaturą?*, [in:] *Liternet.pl*, ed. P. Marecki, Cracow: Rabid.

Śniecikowska Beata (in print), „Oryginały czy imitacje? Wokół „najprawdziwszych" polskich haiku", *Pamiętnik Literacki*.

Śniecikowska Beata 2013, *Słowografia / Word-graphy*, sensualnosc.ibl.waw.pl.

Śniecikowska Beata 2009, *"In the Beginning Was... Laughter" – Humour in the Japanese and Polish Haiku Poetry*, [in:] *Humor. Teorie, praktyka, zastosowania / Humour. Theories, Applications, Practices*, Vol. 2/2: *Making Sense of Humour*, eds. S. Dżereń-Głowacka, A. Kwiatkowska, Piotrków Trybunalski: Naukowe Wydawnictwo Piotrkowskie.

Śniecikowska Beata 2007, *"Between Poem and Painting, between Individual and Common Experience – the Art of Haiku in Japan and in Poland"*, *Art Inquiry. Recherches sur les Arts* 2007, vol. IX (XVIII).

Śniecikowska Beata 2005, *Słowo – obraz – dźwięk. Literatura i sztuki wizualne w koncepcjach polskiej awangardy 1918–1939*, Cracow: Universitas.

Takeuchi Melinda 2005, *Wiersze i obrazy*, [in:] *Estetyka japońska*, vol. 2. *Słowa i obrazy. Antologia*, ed. K. Wilkoszewska, Cracow: Universitas.

Ten krakowski Japończyk... Inspiracje sztuką Japonii w twórczości Wojciecha Weissa / That Krakow Japonist. Japanese Art. Inspirations in the Work of Wojciech Weiss 2008, Cracow: Centrum Sztuki i Techniki Japońskiej Manggha.

Trzeciak Przemysław 2002, *Idea i tusz. Malarstwo w kręgu buddyzmu chan/zen*, Warsaw: Prószyński i S-ka.

Walker Rachel 2005, *Lidia Rozmus: Sumi-e Painter's Haiku*, http://performance.millikin.edu/haiku/writerprofiles/WalkerOnRozmus.html; accessed on 19.02.2103

Wallis Mieczysław 2004, *Wybór pism estetycznych*, ed. T. Pękala, Cracow: Universitas.

Watts Alan W. 1988, *Zen w sztuce*, [in:] *Buddyzm*, eds. J. Sieradzan, W. Jaworski, M. Dziwisz, Cracow: Krakowskie Wydawnictwo Prasowe RSW „Prasa–Książka–Ruch".

Welsch Wolfgang 2004, *Tożsamość w epoce globalizacji – perspektywa transkulturowa*, [in:] *Estetyka transkulturowa*, ed. and trans. K. Wilkoszewska, Cracow: Universitas.

Welsch Wolfgang 1998, *Estetyka i anestetyka*, in *Postmodernizm. Antologia przekładów*, ed. R. Nycz, Cracow: Wydawnictwo Baran i Suszczyński.

Welsch Wolfgang 1998, *Transkulturowość. Nowa koncepcja* kultury, [in:] *Filozoficzne konteksty rozumu transwersalnego. Wokół koncepcji Wolfganga Welscha*, Part 2, ed. R. Kubicki, trans. and ed. B. Susła, J. Wietecki, Poznan: Wydawnictwo Fundacji Humaniora.

Welsch Wolfgang 1997, *Aesthetics beyond aesthetics*, [in:] *Undoing aesthetics*, London: SAGE Publications.

Wilkoszewska Krystyna 2008, *Doświadczenie estetyczne – strategie pragmatyzacji i zaangażowania* [in:] *Nowoczesność jako doświadczenie. Dyscypliny, paradygmaty, dyskursy*, eds. A. Zeidler-Janiszewska, R. Nycz, Warsaw: Wydawnictwo Szkoły Wyższej Psychologii Społecznej „Academica".

Wilkoszewska Krystyna 2004, *Ku estetyce transkulturowej. Wprowadzenie*, [in:] *Estetyka transkulturowa*, ed. K. Wilkoszewska, trans. K. Wilkoszewska, Cracow: Universitas.

Wilkoszewska Krystyna 1999, *Estetyki nowych mediów*, [in:] *Piękno w sieci. Estetyka i nowe media*, ed. K. Wilkoszewska, Cracow: Universitas.

Żuławska-Umeda Agnieszka 2007, *Poetyka szkoły Matsuo Bashō*, Warsaw: Neriton.

Haiku web pages

http://artidotuum.pl/wystawy/, accessed on 18.09.2012.

http://budzenie-jasna.blogspot.com/, accessed on 12.09.2012.

http://cojestgrane.pl/wydarzenie/66718/, accessed on 2.10.2102.

http://eddie-ad.blogspot.com/, accessed on 15.09.2012.

http://entuzjazm.blox.pl/html/1310721,262146,21.html?157645, accessed on 2.08.2012.

http://haiassneg.blogspot.com/, accessed on 19.09.2012.

http://haiga.pl/2.html, accessed on 6.10.2012.

http://haiga-budzenie.blogspot.com, accessed on 2.10.2012.

http://www.haikubytwo.com/review-haikubes/, accessed on 10.09.2012.

http://haiku2009-publikacje.blogspot.com/, accessed on 30.09.2012.

http://haikuofplanet.blogspot.com/, accessed on 4.10.2012.

http://haikuworld.blox.pl/html/1310721,262146,14,15.html?3,2011, accessed on 3.09.2012.

http://jasminum72.blox.pl/html, accessed on 15.09.2012.

http://joo-dailyhaiku.blogspot.com/search?updated-min=2011-01-01T00:00:00%2B01:00& updated-max=2012-01-01T00:00:00%2B01:00&max-results=50., accessed on 2.09.2012.

http://magdajasna.blogspot.com, accessed on 24.09.2012.

http://orston.blogspot.com/, accessed on 2.09.2012.

http://poezja.com.pl/?cat=10, accessed on 1.10.2012.

http://poezja.com.pl/?q=node/625, accessed on 14.10.2012.

http://rozsypany-czas.blogspot.com/, accessed on 14.10.2012.

http://rozsypany-czas.blogspot.com/search/label/haiga, accessed on 10.10.2012.

http://sehaikuan.blogspot.com/, accessed on 13.10.2012.

http://serwisy.umcs.lublin.pl/w.frackiewicz/haiku.htm, accessed on 20.08.2012.

http://serwisy.umcs.lublin.pl/w.frackiewicz/hieroglify.htm, accessed on 2.06.2012.

http://serwisy.umcs.lublin.pl/w.frackiewicz/KS.htm, accessed on 2.06.2012.

http://szyryk.art.pl/, accessed on 15.06.2012.

http://travellingbetweentheworlds.blox.pl/html, accessed on 1.09.2012.

http://www.brooksbookshaiku.com/LidiaRozmus/haiga.html, accessed on 12.06.2012.

http://www.isp.uz.zgora.pl/index.php?option=com_content&view=article&id=300&Itemid=449, accessed on 3.10.2012.

http://www.japonia.org.pl/?q=node/75, accessed on 6.09.2012.

http://www.kolekcja.bookart.pl/info/viewpub/tid/1/pid/6, accessed on 8.07.2012.

http://www.kolekcja.bookart.pl/info/viewpub/tid/2/pid/15, accessed on 8.07.2012.

http://www.kolekcja.bookart.pl/info/viewpub/tid/2/pid/16, accessed on 8.07.2012.

http://www.kolekcja.bookart.pl/info/viewpub/tid/4/pid/120, accessed on 10.06.2012.

http://www.kolekcja.bookart.pl/info/viewpub/tid/4/pid/317, accessed on 8.07.2012.

http://www.vebsoft.pl/mgajewski/display_gallery.php?SectionID=4&GalleryID=3&Lang=PL, accessed on 29.07.2012.

http://zimowehaiku.blogspot.com/, accessed on 12.09.2012.

https://plus.google.com/photos/108591924668579813559/albums/5272690246302443393?banner=pwa, accessed on 3.09.2012.

Bogusława Bodzioch-Bryła*

Jesuit University Ignatianum

FROM AN E-NARRATIVE POEM TOWARDS AN INTERACTIVE WORK OF ART. MEDIA CONVERGENCE ILLUSTRATED WITH *DOWN* BY ZENON FAJFER AND *THE SURPRISING SPIRAL* BY KEN FEINGOLD

Abstract

The text, using the example of a work belonging to the literary style *(Spoglądając przez ozonową dziurę* [Detect Ozone Hole Nearby] by Zenon Fajfer) and the interactive art (the installation *The Surprising Spiral* by Ken Feingold) analyses the idiosyncracy of works positioning themselves at the borderland of media and literature, works both literary (textual, narrative and poetic) as well as media ones (changeable, iconic, set in a computer program, double-indirect), paying attention to the meaningfulness of the disciplines borderland (in this case literary and media studies). The author stresses the reasonableness of the question asked by Katarzyna Bazarnik, whether, by accident, the "Darwinian" evolution of species continues. In the author's opinion, based on her observation of works belonging to the literary style and the discussed work *The Surprising Spiral* by Ken Feingold, this question should get a positive answer. And possibly, as an effect of initiation, which has already happened, we will soon be entering the museum-gallery space not only in order to look but also to read.

Key words: liberature, Zenon Fajfer, Ken Feingold, borderland of media and literature, new media

> The sheet of paper is not transparent, not in the least. This is only an illusion. We can no longer pretend that it is not here. It is. It has always been. It was and it had a nice smell. If I wanted a transparent page, I would use a transparent sheet.

---

* Institute of Culture Studies, Jesuit University Ignatianum in Krakow, Kopernika 26, 31-501 Krakow, e-mail:bogusiabb@interia.pl

> If I want a fully transparent page, I will print my text on a transparency and bind it in glass. The text will hover in the air, and the reader will be able to look at its members as if (possibly) God looks at us through the ozone hole.
>
> What will I bind it in? In glass? Why not? Who said that a book must always look like «a book»? After all, this is only a convention that everybody follows automatically. […] The book may even look like a bottle. What's more, it *may be* a bottle. *But Eyeing Like Ozone Whole* (2004) is a book like any other. But a book that cannot look otherwise. Because its form is dictated by the text. […]
>
> The creative act (often) begins from reflection on the structure of the book, and the act of reading (always) begins from taking the book in hand. A different book structure is tantamount to a different physics. The invisible text is meta-physics. Somewhere in between there is the reader who learns to read anew. (Fajfer 2010: 107–109).

This is what the introduction to the text discussing the issue of changes in a literary work of art at the turn of the 21st century[1] might be but for the fact that the artists, changing the physical form of a book, moved one step forward. Zenon Fajfer performed a contamination of a literary work of art having certain properties typical for e.g. the World Wide Web, while Ken Feingold inserted a literary text and the form of a codex into the boundaries of an interactive installation-work. The following text concentrates on two, in my opinion, tightly related works: the electronic version of Zenon Fajfer's *DOWN* published on the CD *Primum Mobile* attached to the paper volume *ten letters* containing versions of poems prepared in the form of an audiovisual presentation as well as on the interactive and at the same time deeply narrative example of a work of art – Ken Feingold's installation entitled *The Surprising Spiral*.

A few words about the term convergence

The conflict of two presently observed culture trends – convergence and participative culture – has changed the world of media and will certainly define its development over the next decades – Mirosław Filiciak writes (Filiciak 2006: 170). Media scholars have already been stressing the com-

---

[1] And considering some experiments of the group OPOJAZ representing Russian formalism, also at the turn of the 20th century.

plexity of the convergence phenomenon resulting in multi-faceted understanding of it for the last few years.

> Fragmentation seems in some way to be one of the important features of new media. Yet at the same time one of the buzzwords of the new media explosion has been 'convergence' – the idea that at some point the technologies of media would all come together. Television, online video delivery, Internet communications and telecommunications combined in one 'black box' that will look something like a phone. However this vision has been widely challenged as devices and platforms have proliferated and instead *content* has converged (see Jenkins 2006: 15). Convergence however has at least two other meanings in this context. The first is the merger of media corporations in an attempt to provide a horizontal integration of different media products across a range of platforms. Thus the acquisition of MySpace by Rupert Murdoch's Fox Interactive in 2005 means not only that Fox have a foothold in the social networking market but that they can find new markets for the Fox back catalogue online as well as using the social network as a site for the development of new media products which may have a life in TV and cinema. 'Win / win' situations. (Lister, Dovey, Giddings, Grant, Kelly 2009: 202).

The conclusion drawn from these observations could be that the phenomenon of convergence may be found not only in the process of various media joining but also, and first of all, in the consequences of the joining, i.e. in the emerging of new and so far non-existent qualities.

Henry Jenkins significantly extends the meaning of the term, stating that the convergence phenomenon should be related to the mental state of contemporary culture participants who live in the world determined by new technologies transforming.

> [...] the convergence is most importantly occurring *not* in the labs of technologists or the boardrooms of corporations but in the minds of the audience. It is we who are convergent – moving freely across a range of media platforms making connections between story worlds where the convergent activity has to do with the ways we make meaning of a fragmented media landscape, «convergence represents a cultural shift as consumers are encouraged to seek out new information and make connections among dispersed media content (Jenkins 2006: 3).

This is all very contradictory – we seem to be living through a period where the conflicts and opportunistic alliances of business interests produce a very dynamic system in which we experience fragmentation *and* convergence occurring concurrently. It is as if we are experiencing centripetal *and* centrifugal forces as outcomes of the same rapidly spinning wheel of media business and innovation. We can explain this in part by reference back to Anderson's Long Tail idea. The big media businesses who produce the 20 percent of products commanding 80 percent of sales at the head of the demand curve are not going away". (Lister, Dovey, Giddings, Grant, Kelly 2009: 202-203).

Some researchers signalise a new type of threat brought about by the discussed phenomenon:

> Convergence can be understood as a way to bridge or join old and new technologies, formats and audiences. Such cross-media joining and borrowings may feel disruptive if we assume that each media has a defined range of characteristics or predetermined mission. Medium-specific approaches risk simplifying technological change to a zero-sum game in which one medium gains at the expense of its rivals. A less reductive, comparative approach would recognise the complex synergies that always prevail among media systems, particularly during the periods shaped by the birth of a new medium expression(Jenkins, Thornburn 2003: 3).

In scientific literature also general-culture convergence consequences as well as the necessity to change certain habits and to create new tools adequate for examining and describing new culture qualities created as a result of convergence get stressed:

> The old either-or oppositions (co-optation vs. resistance) have long dominated debates between political economy and cultural studies. Approaches derived from the study of political economy may, perhaps provide the best vocabulary for discussing media convergence, while cultural studies language has historically framed our understanding of participatory culture. Neither theoretical tradition, however, can truly speak to what happens at the intersection between the two (Jenkins 2003: 292).

Another fact pointed at is that the emergence of the convergence phenomenon forces the necessity of asking new questions concentrating on the peculiar nature of the old and new information and communication technologies (ICT):

> We need, then, to ask a number of questions of the modernist and avant-garde calls for new media to define itself as radically novel. Do media proceed by a process of ruptures or decisive breaks with the past? Can a medium transcend its historical contexts to deliver an 'entirely new language'? Do, indeed, media have irreducible and unique essences (which is not quite the same as having distinguishing characteristics which encourage or constrain the kind of thing we do with them)? These seem to be especially important questions to ask of new digital media which, in large part, rely upon hybrids, convergences and transformations of older media. (Lister, Dovey, Giddings, Grant, Kelly 2009: 62).

These questions turn out to be important also in relation to works of art and the especially interesting conclusions seem to be the ones based on the observation of works which use the convergence phenomenon in order to arise in a particular form – an entity happening at the borderland of a literary and media text. Maryla Hopfinger in her book *Literatura a media. Po 1989 roku* (Hopfinger 2010), mentioning the literary context of media convergence, writes about a literary book moving beyond its traditional structure and about looking for new media for the content layer, first in the traditional form and then as new information and communication technologies, i.e. about literary-formal experiments which do not constitute *differentia specifica* of our time but reach back into the history of a literary book. The phenomena sources, according to Hopfinger, brought about formal experiments, which vividly intensified in certain moments of the history-literary and history-cultural process. Summing up the change which happened in the position and reception of literature after the breakthrough of 1989 the researcher stresses that the contemporary communication scene is cumulative while the dominance of audiovisual messages does not exclude the functioning of the earlier shaped forms of expression. However, it changes their place in the new configuration and the functions which they have today. It is thus impossible to claim that we are dealing with a break with communication experiences. There is a law of continuity and change in the way culture functions and the law expresses itself at the so called communication scene where all earlier forms and ways of communication between people meet: media as well as all the old and new communication practices – face-to-face communication, press and the radio, the cinema and television, painting and music, literature and television, professional, amateur, analogue and digital photography, a comic and postcards, various types of records, landline and mobile phones, computers and the Internet. These and other still new media and practices join those already present ones on the scene while the old ones usually disappear (Hopfinger 2010: 22).

Bogusława Bodzioch-Bryła

Literary consequences of media convergence, i.e. about the possible reception of an e-narrative poem and problems related to it[2]

Zenon Fajfer, the author of *Detect Ozone Hole Nearby*, exploits the possibilities offered by a hypertext strikingly cautiously, choosing only those which best harmonise with the idea his poetry contains[3]. Let us analyse the way the poem we are concerned with emerges in front of a reader's eyes: at first, four subsequent letters appear on the screen and constitute the word *DOWN*. Each letter turns out to be the beginning of a next word. After the development of all of the letters an inscription appears which comprises the title of the work: *Detect Ozone Hole Nearby*. The title alternately winds up and unwinds on the screen getting farther or closer to the reader's eyes.

---

[2] This article was originally written in Polish and referred to the Polish version of Zenon Fajfer's poem *Detect Ozone Hole Nearby*. The literary translation of the poem into English made by Katarzyna Bazarnik, Zenon Fajfer and Finn Fordham, in the official published version, significantly differs from the original poem. Even considering the peculiar process of translation, which follows its own rules and is never literal, it actually constitutes a separate literary work to a larger extent than a literal translation. Preparing the article for translation into English turned out to be more problematic than one might expect, therefore the author of the article (having consulted the translator of the article, the translator of the poem and also, indirectly, the author of the poem) has decided to use a risky solution and to explain it to the readers. Only this gives her a chance to show the attractive, emanative way of unveiling Z. Fajfer's poem in front of readers' eyes and of making its analysis and interpretation in a traditional article at the same time. So, in the main text of the article the print screens of the English literary translation of Fajfer's poem made by Katarzyna Bazarnik, Zenon Fajfer and Finn Fordham taken from the CD *Primum Mobile* were attached, which shows the electronic version of the poem, its appearance and changes in subsequent screens. The analytical and interpretational part of the article will be based on the word-for-word translation of the poem (made by Katarzyna Bazarnik) which will consequently be placed under some print screens (because this basic version of the poem is the subject matter of the article). This "literal" translation has never been published before and was used only as a draft for preparing the literary translation.
The author would also like to thank Katarzyna Bazarnik and Zenon Fajfer for giving her access to the aforementioned close to the original version of the poem translation and for their permission to publish it in this article.

[3] It is undoubtedly difficult to give an account of the process of "happening", "becoming" or rather the emergence of the discussed work in the form of a traditional description because it is difficult to cite this transforming unity. So in order to make the picture of the piece and its appearance on the screen at least a little bit clearer the most convenient solution is to make print screens of the poem.

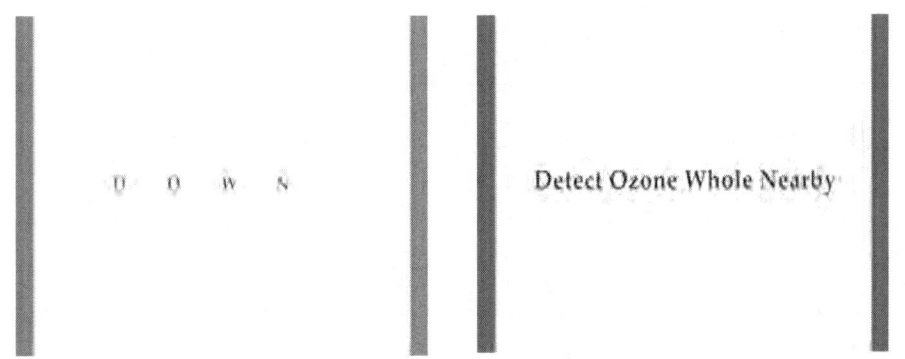

Photo 1. *Detect Ozone Hole Nearby*   Photo 2. *Detect Ozone Hole Nearby*

Next, gradually, a text appears on the screen and it then covers its whole space creating a record:

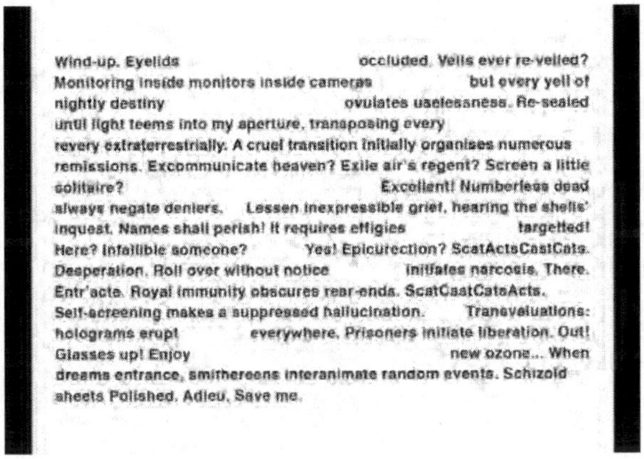

Photo. 3. *Detect Ozone Hole Nearby*

Over./Done./Finished. Lower the eyelids./Close the eyelids. Once again? From one screen/monitor to another. Taking off of the curtains. Or a scream. But. Futile despair. Yapping of fate and time. A hermetic case/glass box (?). Until someone opens it. Disperses the dream. Fills in the skyling's[4] eye with the breath. In order for it to see to dead initials. Or in order for it to smash the screen. Who would dare smash the screen/monitor? Hide somehow? Beg/prey/refuse mercy in another voice?[5] Offend the majesty of the treacherous screen? Screw the fun of playing with puppets? What finesse! The spring cull, an act of inexpressible altruism.

---

[4] A pun on "niemowle" = a baby, and "niebo"= "sky, heaven"
[5] Another fantastic pun on the phrase "łaski odmawiac", which here means "refuse mercy" and "say prayers" or rather "prey grace/mercy"

Find gun shells. Or [finger]prints. Proof [to be used] for defending the framed one, irrefutable/unquestionable alibi. Does the barrel bluff? Wound the sniper's eyes[6]. Now! *AktTakTkaKat*[7]. Will you hit the target, the infallible being? [So exciting that] you have got an erection/epicurection? So little, but what torture/suffering. Or better without any warning. *TkaTakKatAkt*. Entr'cte. Love, lowe, lohe, loshe[8]. Covering naked arses with [the privilege of] immunity. Emotional interpretation. Grow indifferent, distance oneself. Another screen/monitor: I am a spectator/viewer.

An eruption of suppressed fantasy. Reverse parts/roles. Are there any other parts? The victim becomes a tyrant, the director an ordinary actor, the walk-on a cameraman. Or a non-engaged screenaziwriter. Stop the camera! A sip of refreshing ozone.

Scenario three, the aleatoric one. The throne of the skyling, an interactive scene of nappy changing. Adieu. Before they will wipe their arse with me. Or you'd better put the bottle away. Here. Or perhaps there. Anew. And? And nothing? Rather unimpressive acting/playing. The final episode. You come up and push the atelier bottle. And set me free?

[Katarzyna Bazarnik, Literal translation of *Detect Ozone Hole Nearby*, *The visible upper layer of the text*. A draft of the literal version of the translation of *Detect Ozone Hole Nearby*, an equivalent of the third screen (Photo 3)].

The next lines of the created work get bolded and overshadowed. Afterwards, some characters disappear and, in consequence, the screen looks like this:

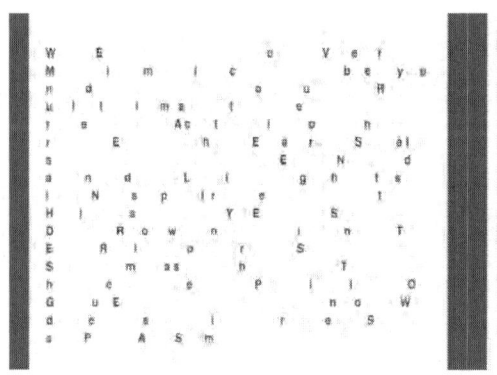

Photo 4. *Detect Ozone Hole Nearby*   Photo 5. *Detect Ozone Hole Nearby*

---

[6] In the original a pun "otrzy": this sounds like "oczy" = eyes, but the spelling indicates O_3, i.e., "O three", or the chemical formula for ozone.

[7] Onomoatopeic transformation of 3 letters that form 4 words; the sound effect and the anagrammatic transformation are more important than sense.

[8] Another pun on the word "milosc"=love. Mi=me, imlosc=them-love, namlosc=us-love. A bit like "history", "herstory", "theirstory", "ourstory".

The widened text pulls itself together with a crash creating another record (Photo 5). At the moment when the text slides together a loud crash of broken glass can be heard.

The characters change their positions again, some of them disappear. The process is accompanied by the sound of glass pressed. Additionally, at the bottom right hand corner of the screen, a small, at first hardly visible red point appears. It grows creating an inkspot resembling a bloodstain. The spot grows while the next parts of the text disappear.

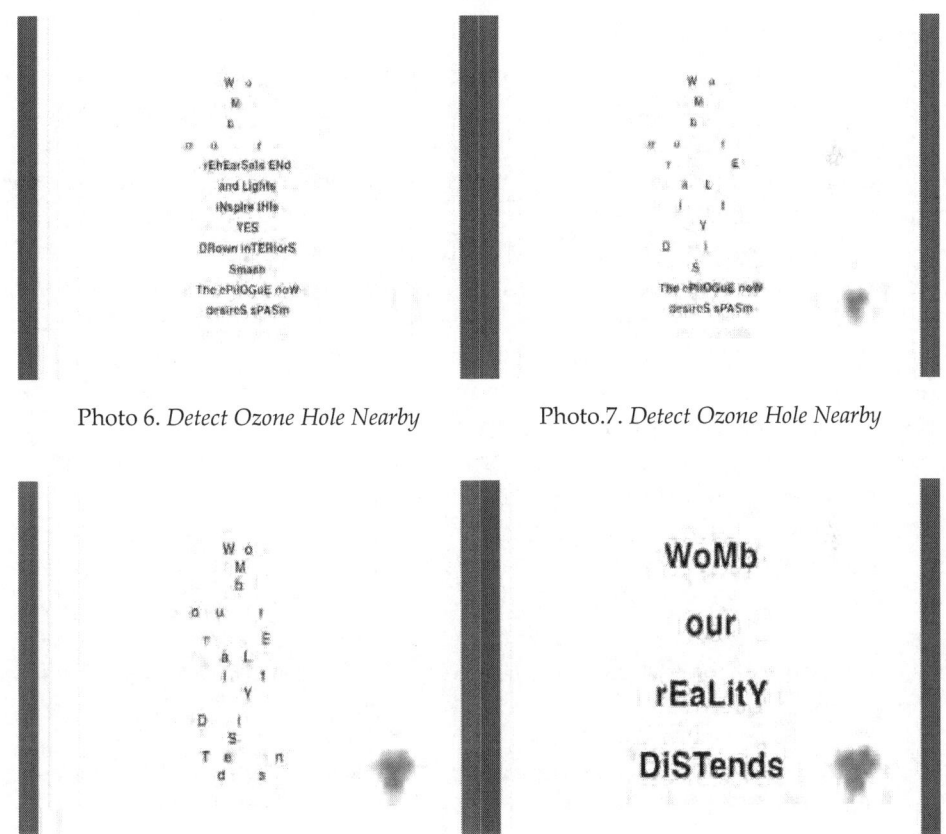

Photo 6. *Detect Ozone Hole Nearby*   Photo.7. *Detect Ozone Hole Nearby*

Photo 8. *Detect Ozone Hole Nearby*   Photo 9. *Detect Ozone Hole Nearby*

The next step of transformation consists in the disappearing of the parts of the text which were written in lower case, in consequence of which the piece cramps till the moment the only thing left on the screen is the record "word" which gradually grows.

Photo 10. *Detect...*   Photo 11. *Detect...*   Photo 12. *Detect*

The red spot disappears, gradually colouring the text. Then the image itself disappears. In the final stage of the work transformations one can hear a female voice saying the expression "word".

It is necessary to add that the poem is accessible in two versions – an electronic one and the so called "material" one (entitled *But Eyeing Like Ozone Whole*) because it is rather difficult to differently label a piece written down on a rolled transparency and hidden in a bottle. The narrative poem in a bottle encompasses the content compatible with the record presented in the third slide mentioned (Photo 3), though with a slightly different layout. Also, the reader encounters a bigger difficulty than in the case of the e-narrative poem. One has to put an effort into reading the text in two ways: first, the full content printed on a transparency, and then, to put only the printed fonts together in a cohesive way, which turns out to be rather inconvenient for eyesight[9].

It is difficult to escape the impression that it is impossible to attempt at interpreting a work without considering an author's explanation of its genesis and its final form despite the explanation being verbalised much earlier (long before the creation of the work, in the context of work on *Oka-leczenie*):

> I wanted to describe the inexpressible: birth and death. I wanted to touch the very moment of leaving and arriving, the two poles of the great mystery.
>
> What is, however, left to the writer who does not believe in the adequacy of language or the mere magic of silence? I was without an idea for a long time until 1993 when my father died and soon afterwards my son was born. For over

---

[9] It is necessary to add that the text turns out not to be open to forms of use unpredicted by the author, e.g. an attempt at making a xerox copy of it for academic didactic use failed: the transparency broke in a few places and the poem fell into pieces. Moreover, it is really hard to take it out of the bottle in such a form.

forty days I was living in a very strange state; I had an impression as if both of them were somewhere near. Finally, when I witnessed the birth, when I saw how that which had remained hidden for so long was emerging, I realized that my text should be hidden, too. I grew certain that neither death nor birth can be expressed in any other way, if they can be expressed at all.

I wanted to achieve perfect iconicity: I wanted to leave invisible for the reader what is invisible for us in everyday experience. I felt that only if I were to leave it like that, would it remain true. Invisible, and yet – let us add – seeable. […] But this would only be possible with the use of some new dimension of text, some new form, a form that would enable words to be placed in another space, or to put it more precisely, enable the *creation* of that space.

I pondered on various ways of encrypting words […]. The form that seemed so promising was something that I called emanationism: a kind of Chinese-box acrostic consisting of several layers of contracted text. It differs from the traditional acrostic insofar as one should read the initials of words (to be precise, all words from each subsequently emerging layer) and not only the first letters of each verse. All its layers form a multidimensional structure that can be reduced to a non-dimensional point.

How does it all work? Let us imagine a text whose words begin to disappear and only their initial letters stay. These letters form a new text out of which another text emerges through an analogous process, and the process continues up to the point when the whole work contracts to one word like an imploding star.

I would like to demonstrate how it actually works, using as an example «Ars poetica» (2004), a poem which I wrote ten years later, and which exists also in an electronic version". (Fajfer 2010: 97–98).

It is impossible to interpret the poem in a linear way. This kind of reading would impose a kind of interpretational violence. A strategy where certain flashes of meanings are caught and where some tracks initiated this way are continued as well as wondering through succeeding screens offered by the author seems to be more sensible. It is also suggested by the lyrical I writing: "Emotional interpretation. Grow indifferent, distance oneself".

We are dealing with a work about a poem emerging, about a narrative poem as well as a new life being born. The use of contaminations of terms "baby" (in Polish "niemowlęcie") and "sky/heaven" (in Polish "niebo") which creates a sort of pun on words "skyling" (in Polish "niebowlęcie") ("Fills in the skyling's eye with the breath") may be treated as an element stressing the divine particle in existence and a reference to the biblical creation act ("breathed into his nostrils the breath of life"), which may signalise a new life coming from the beyond. A significant role is also played by other contaminations in the poem: "lowe, lohe, loshe" ("Entr'cte. Love, lowe, lohe, loshe"), "screenaziwriter" ("The victim becomes a tyrant, the director an ordinary actor, the walk-on a cameraman. Or a non-engaged screenaziwriter"). It may be acknowledged that the neologisms created by means of contamination substitute a metaphor in Fajfer's writing. They compose a kind of screen within a screen and their ambiguity makes transfers between meanings. Those contaminations attract attention to the very issue of ambiguity, to the gradual meanings completion, to their overlapping, in a way heralding what will happen in a moment by means of screens changing and opening, completing the already existing contents and with new ones unveiling for the reader together with another sequence of images.

Fajfer juxtaposes two categories: ambiguity and the possibility of meaning extension described by the lyrical I as "taking off the curtains" against unambiguity, closure and limitation ("A hermetic case/glass box (?). Until someone opens it. Disperses the dream").

The openness of the narrative poem, visible in the transforming structure, is also signalised on the level of meanings of the work in the stressed changeability of roles between the sender and the receiver, the creator and the reader ("Reverse parts/roles. Are there any other parts? The victim becomes a tyrant, the director an ordinary actor, the walk-on a cameraman. Or a non-engaged screenaziwriter. Stop the camera! [...] Scenario three, the aleatoric one. [...],/an interactive scene of nappy changing. Adieu...").

The clarity of the text got disturbed by the author in a controlled way. He introduced an element of chaos and mixing in order to point at the moment when the text stops having a meaning as a record and starts to have an effect as a visual whole (See photo 13).

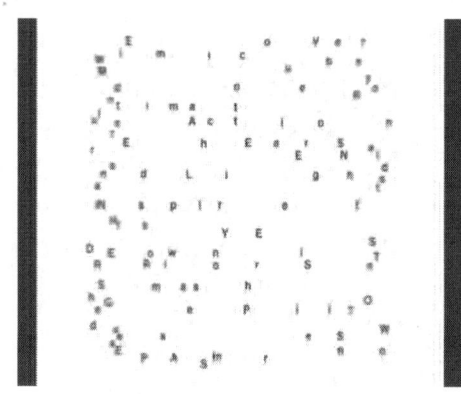

Photo 13.

This is the moment when it is impossible to notice a written sense in the screen. It is only possible to look at the jumbled characters as at a picture, and let us repeat, at a picture of chaos. This state is an answer to the discomfort triggered by the feeling of suppression and constraint which should be overcome ("Futile despair. Yapping of fate and time. A hermetic case/glass box (?). Until someone opens it. Disperses the dream", "the majesty of the treacherous screen", "So little, but what torture/suffering"), which happens in the work in various ways and in its various layers (of reception and construction). We are facing a transition ("From one screen/monitor to another. Taking off of the curtains"), a smashing of a monitor ("Who would dare smash the screen/monitor?"), a systematic transformation of senses ("*AktTakTkaKat* – an onomatopoeic transformation of 3 letters that form 4 words in Polish, "Love, lowe, lohe, loshe"), an unexpected swapping of roles ("Another screen/monitor: I am a spectator/viewer. An eruption of suppressed fantasy. Reverse parts/roles. Are there any other parts? The victim becomes a tyrant, the director an ordinary actor, the walk-on a cameraman. Or a non-engaged screenaziwriter"). The consequence of such a liberation is the aforementioned eruption ("Or a scream/? [So exciting that] you have got an erection/epicurection, An eruption of suppressed fantasy/ You come up and push the atelier bottle. And set me free?") As well a temporary chaos and a division of meanings.

A full interpretation or explanation of the Web text can by no means be made because its inexplicability is made innate there by the author. Also its structure is in principle based on it[10].

Literary and media qualities in an emanative poem

The work may be considered important on the grounds of the medium Fajfer chose resigning from those he has used so far – the non-traditional and innovative ones in form, nevertheless placing themselves more on the side of the "old media" (where the meaning of the term must be separated from the one commonly used in media studies because the matter the artist

---

[10] One might certainly go further in analytical and interpretational action, however in the limited length of the article there would not be then enough space for mentioning other, equally important aspects of the work. Therefore the analysis and interpretation of the poem is deliberately left incomplete and open, with only certain interpretational threads outlined.

used as the basis of his work, inter alia glass[11] or paper[12] used in an unconventional way, are undoubtedly special examples of untypical means of recording) and he uses an interactive carrier. It is the very carrier that another issue worth stressing can be ascribed to, because the artist, choosing an interactive medium, has decided, unlike one might assume, not to use all the possibilities it offers. He has not given up on an, in a way, traditional flat layout of the text on the page, using the branching structure of a hypertext[13] only to a limited extent. This is one of the reasons why one should not use the expression "an open work" but rather "a half-closed work".

The duality of the work seems to be obvious – it is embedded in both literary and in media spheres as Fajfer's poem is a literary work of art happening at the borderland of media and literature. Apart from the determinants of its literariness and poeticality (artistic means, a poetic function) there are visible typical media qualities, just to mention a few: the dynamic changeability of the transforming message, its being iconic (the significance of a picture) understood on two levels: as creating a graphically meaningful whole out of letter characters (the shape of the record, especially with reference to photos 4, 5, 6, 8, 9, and 11) but also as using graphic signs and pictures (e.g. the growing red spot, photos 6, 7, 8, 9, 10, and 11) or as the colouring expression "word" emerging while the red spot disappears (photo 11). The other media qualities are: basing the work in a computer program and its double indirectness made through a new medium[14] (as a kind of double indirectness which reaches the level of the content of the work)[15].

---

[11] E.g. in the case of the material – glass edition of *But Eyeing Like Ozone Whole* (2004), as well as the second ("amended") edition in a carton pack (Fajfer, 2009)

[12] See e.g. *Oka-leczenie* by K. Bazarnik and Z. Fajfer. (Bazarnik, Fajfer 2009)

[13] Like e.g. Sławomir Shuty did (in his hipertextual novel *Blok* which may be read according to the topographic direction of the text (based on the structure of floors and flats his characters live in) or through classical hyperlinks; http://www.blok.art.pl/), by Radosław Nowakowski (in his novel *Koniec świata według Emeryka*), etc.

[14] In the case of Fajfer's poem one may ascertain that we are dealing not only with language double indirectness but also with an additional kind of complexity – a structure double indirectness which is not a binary structure but a rhizomatic or branching one. Therefore it is not enough to discuss only double indirectness but it is necessary to talk about double indirectness and densing or interweaving. Up to a point, because like I have stated before, Fajfer reduced the hypertextual character of the work for the sake of a certain, so to speak, controlled opening.

[15] Because traditional literature was also double indirect through the paper and print format but that double indirectness did not spread over the level of meanings of the work (only works belonging to the specific poetry group [calligrams], futurists' experiments and other references to them were an exception) and books were thought about in terms of content and meaning.

Fajfer undertakes polemics with some of the new media qualities pointed by Lev Manovich (Manovich 2006: 91–118)[16]. It is hard to argue with the numerical representation, the issue of modular structure of individual objects or with transcoding but the issue of automation may be dubious here because Fajfer did not rely on a computer program in terms of creating the message. The reader can at most make the work run and is also able to stop it but eliminating human participation from the creative act or depriving the work of intentionality (at the creative process stage) is out of the question. The work was created as an intentional production and is an effect of the very intentionality. Fajfer's poem cannot exist in variations or in various versions (the recipient is not able to create variants of the literary message[17]) and will thus not become its creator or the creator's partner because a dialogue is possible only on the interpretational level (only its interpretations can be variable).

Discussing Fajfer's work it is possible to talk about, at most, an interesting dialogue of literature with new media, a certain kind of a literary romance which, taking the strength of fascination with media into consideration, starts to wear the characteristics of a strong relationship[18].

---

[16] Describing the language of new media Lev Manovich mentions the following of its properties:
– numerical representation (all new media objects are numbers written in a digital form); a picture or a shape may be recorded as a mathematical function; the object may be algorithmically processed; they are programmable; objects here consist of 'discreet", discontinuous elements);
– structure modularity of objects (each of them consists of independent parts all of which consist of smaller, also independent elements and so on, up to the level of indivisible pixels, 3D points or textual characters. Removing one of the elements [adding a new one or an exchange] does not radically violate the whole message structure);
– automation (creating a message may, up to a certain extent, be given to e.g. computer programs without a direct human influence, which is a way of [partial] elimination of intentionality from the creative process);
– variability (fluidity, changeability); the final, once and forever fixed representation of the message does not exist. It is not like in a traditional written text, a classical film or video. Theoretically, countless variations may be created. They are message "variations" and a computer user entering the dialogue becomes a message creator and the creator's partner;
– transcoding (a certain "translation" of culture texts into the language understood by the computer; this way two levels influence each other – the computer and culture ones; a researcher does not exclude the option that the former influences the latter one: this is how e.g. new media genres or a new message content come into being and how the organisation of media understood as institutions changes);

[17] Unless we recognise the "material" version (a narrative poem closed in a glass bottle) and the electronic one as variations.

[18] Similar conclusions will refer to Fajfer's works *Ars poetica* and *Immanent treatise*

To be specific, it must be admitted that some of the properties indicated by Manovich actually materialise only in the recipient's mind. Considering Fajfer's work as a whole and treating the work itself and the potential interpretations it generates as equally important, one might undoubtedly call it a new media work.

Fajfer exploits the possibilities offered by a hypertext extremely carefully, choosing only these which best correspond with the ideas presented in his poetry[19]. His work constitutes a clearly limited whole, each time "happening" the same way. It is spatial, however, in a totally different way. It is more, so to speak, going into itself or between particular levels (openings, screens) of the same text rather than between different texts constituting a whole. Anyway, there are no links between particular levels (screens) in the work; they may be read, contrary to appearances, according to the linear sequence of openings. The issue should not be understood in categories of a deficiency because this trick was used by the author on purpose and a structure thought-out this way goes hand in hand with the idea the poem contains or is even subordinate to it. The screen motif occurs in the text very often ("From one screen/monitor to another", "/in order for it to smash the screen", "Who would dare smash the screen/monitor?", "Offend the majesty of the treacherous screen?") – Fajfer writes and consistently starts making subsequent screens work showing the reader how one can see (read) the work in the original version[20] and then in the one extended with other images. Each successive "opening" of the poem changes its sense and, significantly extending it, attracts attention to the aspect of speech which is absent in the preceding version.

---

[19] What proves that the author's choices are fully justified and deliberate is one of his statements explaining the reasons for using the emanative poem form. Fajfer writes: "it is wrong to treat emanationism simply as a writing technique. What is created through it is a totally new literary form whose structure is not semantically neutral (unlike, e.g. the structure of the sonnet), but pregnant with important meanings: from epistemological and ontological to cosmogonic ones. In emanational prose and poetry, every single letter of text is shown and seen from a new perspective; hackneyed words and motifs regain their freshness. Such notions as time, space, hero, plot, narrator and the lyrical «I» take on a totally new dimension in the process of literary emanation, writing off as fiction gloomy prophecies about the exhaustion of literature soaked in self-reflexivity. On the contrary, I believe that together with emanationism literature is entering a new, subtler phase of existence, and *Oka-leczenie* marks only the beginning of this process. When writers get used to this technique, when they familiarize themselves with its benefits and learn to overcome technical conditions, masterpieces will appear that are not dreamt of not only in philosophy. (Fajfer 2010: 40–41)

[20] Being aware that the term "original version" is not entirely adequate as there are no "next versions" but rather intersecting or overlapping levels or layers of the work.

Even though the hypertext form used by Fajfer turns out to be closed (or, as it was said before, at most half-closed) by means of the aforementioned deliberate limiting, the work itself is left open. Moreover, this openness should be recognised as the crucial quality of that type of works. This is by no means a novelty in literature. A smaller or bigger element of openness has appeared in the most famous attempts at defining a literary (poetic) work as well as a work of art. Just to mention some examples – the notion of indefinite place used by Roman Ingarden, Umberto Eco's open work category or Robert Escarpit's theory of susceptibility to betrayal. In the light of these observations all efforts put into telling the whole truth about a poem seem to be interpretational violence. In the case of works using new media as a medium the aforementioned openness gains a more literal and radical character; it stops touching only the issue of the possibility of interpreting the tropes and the text itself and it starts to be proved by the structure of the work which stops being laminal (structuralism) and starts being hypertextual and rhizomatic, as the sense of the work got located in such an existence basis (a branching medium).

Where should one search for tools to interpret literary works settled at the literature and media borderland? In the theoretical tools resource of literary or media studies? A clear answer to this question does not exist. In principle – somewhere "in between". The essence of the problem is that the artistic matter has undoubtedly managed to get ahead of its description tools because in a theoretical description we are in a way still confined to the tools of literature and film studies. And considering the fact that film studies rely to a large extent on the literary work theory – the situation gets markedly limited.

Katrzyna Bazarnik, making her attempt at literary-theoretical extra defining of liberature, apart from the genre qualities typical for works belonging to this group, points at some properties located between the literary and media works[21], i.e. the use of non-verbal and typographic means of expression subjected to the verbal expression and helping it; the spacial structure of the text, often resulting in an unconventional book form; iconicity, both pictorial and diagrammatic (iconicity of structures); self-reflexivity or metatextuality; hybridity/polimediality; interactivity and ergodic quality, i.e. a situation in which the reader determines the shape of narration; materiality; medium specificity (where exploiting specific features of a medium an intermedial translation is impossible since transporting the text onto a different carrier distorts the work) (Bazarnik 2010: 159–163).

---

[21] Emphasising, however, that the group of qualities is blurred, therefore to classify a work as liberature it is not necessary to identify all of them in a given work.

"Would, then, *ten letters* be a model prototype of e-liberature, an example [...] of usefulness of even this term, and does it mean that the "Darwinian" evolution of genres would be going on?" – Katarzyna Bazarnik asks (Bazarnik 2010: 163). Taking the work I am going to discuss in a moment into consideration, i.e. *The Surprising Spiral* by Ken Feingold – the answer to the question asked by her should probably be given a positive answer.

The Surprising Spiral by Ken Feingold as an example of a total work falling between a work of art and a literary work[22]

A work written by Ken Feingold in 1991 entitled *The Surprising Spiral* is an extremely interesting example of an artistic experiment constituting, in my opinion, an eminent example of old and new media convergence introducing, in effect, a new artistic and literary quality. The author himself writes about his work:

> *The Surprising Spiral* is an interactive artwork, utilizing a computer controlled videodisc, computer graphics, digitized sounds and texts, and synthesized voices, embedded within sculptures. The work responds to the form of the viewer/participant's engagement. The viewer's ability to interact and direct the flow of images and sounds allows him or her to "play" the piece, to seek or escape from finding a destination, or to enjoy its labyrinthine paths. There are two sculpture/interface objects through which a viewer can interact with the work. One is a large, hollow handmade book (13"x 15"x 6") in which are encased replicas of human hands. In a cut out in the center of the cover is embedded a transparent touch screen, which appears to be the glass "cover" of the book. On this touch screen are fingerprints, placed above the fingertips of the larger hand within the book. When a viewer touches any of the fingerprints, various things can happen: there are always sound responses to these touches, usually speech; the video can change to another location in the world, or an animated text might be evoked. In any case, a turn is taken in the labyrinth[23].

---

[22] *The Surprising Spiral* by Ken Feingold was also my analysis subject in my article *Pomiędzy naturą a simulacrum. O przekraczaniu natury w sztuce interaktywnej, na przykładzie dzieła The Surprising Spiral Kena Feingolda oraz instalacji Christy Sommerer i Laurenta Mignonneau* where I paid attention to contemporary artists using elements of nature in the process of creating a work of art.

[23] See: http://wro05.wrocenter.pl/thesurprisingspiral_pl.php. The description comes from a website promoting the International Media Art Biennale Wroclaw 2005. Access date: 03.08.2012.

The work has a complex cause and effect structure, and a touch that the viewer makes might have an immediate visual response, happen a short time later, or much later. I wanted these to mirror our daily cause and effect experiences. That is, sometimes we see the results of an action immediately, very soon, much later, etc. No two viewers will see the same flow of images or hear the same sounds in the same sequence, and the actions of previous viewers will also affect the structure found by another viewer. On the spine of the book is the title *La Espiral Sorprendente*, the title of the work in Spanish. It is homage to Borges and Paz, the writers who inspired this work.

Photo 14. Ken Feingold, *The Surprising Spiral* (1991)[24].

The other interactive object is also a book, an actual book of Octavio Paz, *The Monkey Grammarian*. Embedded in the cover of the book is a casting of a man's lips, and between the lips a faint red light glows. When a viewer holds their fingertips upon the lips, one hears texts from the book spoken aloud. When the hand is removed, the text ceases, and the mouth falls silent again. If no one does anything to interact with the work for a length of time, it follows a path of images that lead to one of the looped "nature" images. At this point, the work will also clear its memory of the touches previous viewers have made, and it begins anew when touched again. These objects are set upon furniture sculptures made by author, and these stand upon a painted wooden platform[25].

---

[24] See: http://wro05.wrocenter.pl/thesurprisingspiral_pl.php. Access date: 03.08.2012.
[25] Ibid.

Photo 15. Ken Feingold, *The Surprising Spiral* (1991)[26].

How to interpret such a work? According to Feingold's suggestions it may be stated that:

> The work is about the simultaneous sensations of ecstasy and emptiness which arise from the labyrinthine nature of traveling, of being in motion; the mind reflecting upon itself and upon the organization of languages, thoughts and perceptions. Images flow from one place in the world to another, a continuous movement of the passenger, the one walking through, passing through; the view of the world along the path, with no end in mind. These are images that I recorded from 1979 to 1991, in the USA, India, Japan, Argentina, Thailand, Scotland, Sri Lanka, utterly without any conception of cinematic mise en scene. They are the remains, the visual and auditory residuum of what has been passed by, moved through. As a reverse side, moments of the camera's fixity which have observed what we think of as "nature", that is, time outside of our own determinations, events unfolding oblivious to human purposes, the temporal order which marks our own passage through time, whether we are in motion or not[27].

Piotr Zawojski presented an interesting analysis of the installation. The researcher notices that it is just a model version of a realisation representing the first generation of artists attempting at creating an interactive narrative work (though not a linear or multilinear one) appealing through stories generated by interactors-users. Those stories cannot repeat, their sequenc-

---

[26] Photo source: http://www.medienkunstnetz.de/works/the-surprising-spiral/ Access date: 15.07.2012.

[27] Webpage source: http://wro05.wrocenter.pl/thesurprisingspiral_pl.php. Access date: 15.07.2012.

ing is based on modules suggested by the artist but these modules may each time be randomly composed in the reception process. A narrative character is in this case a result of a certain kind of game a user participates in by means of interface(s). Referring to the mythical "book" of the world as a labyrinth, citing Borges and Paz – the writers under whose patronage the work was created, the artist designed a multithreaded, branching navigation route over pictures recorded during travels around the world, using also an excerpt of the feature film *L'immortelle* by Robbe-Grillet, some documents, commercials, computer animations, as well as various sound effects, words and passages spoken in several languages (Zawojski 2005)[28]. Some passages of *El mono grámatico* by Octavio Paz can be heard when the second interface is used. Zawojski stresses that, like in *The Book of Sand* by Borges, the travel here resembles a hypertextual navigation. Borges, creating the concept of an infinite book called it *The Book of Sand* because neither the book nor sand have a beginning or the end. "A line consists of an infinite number of points; a plane consists of an indefinite number of lines; a supervolume – of an infinite amount of a volume…" Borges writes and these words accurately characterise the idea behind Ken Feingold's work (Ibid.).

Jorge Luis Borges whose output Feingold refers to by means of placing the Spanish title on his own work, describes a "Total Book", a divine one which transforms into a monstrual or devilish one in the short story *The Book of Sand*. The description of it, stressing contradictions and its paradoxical nature, corresponds with the multiple dimensions of *The Surprising Spiral*:

> It was a clothbound octavo volume that had clearly passed through many hands. I examined it; the unusual heft of it surprised me. On the spine was printed Holy Writ, and then Bombay.
>
> «Nineteenth century I'd say», I observed.
>
> «I don't know», was the reply.
>
> «Never did know».
>
> The characters were unfamiliar to me. The pages, which seemed worn and badly set, were printed in double columns, like a Bible. The text was cramped, and composed into versicles. At the upper corner of each page were Arabic numerals. I was struck by an odd fact: the even-numbered page would carry the number 40,514, let us say, while the odd-numbered page that followed it would be 999. I turned the page; the next page bore an eight-digit number. It also bore a small

---

[28] http://www.zawojski.com/2006/04/19/galaktyka-post-gutenberga/. Access date: 15.07.2012.

illustration, like those one sees in dictionaries: an anchor drawn in pen and ink, as though by the unskilled hand of a child.

It was at that point that the stranger spoke again. "Look at it well. You will never see it again". There was a threat in the words, but not in the voice. I took note of the page, and then closed the book. Immediately, I opened it again. In vain I searched for the figure of the anchor, page after page. To hide my discomfiture, I tried another tack.

«This is a version of Scripture in some Hindu language, isn't that right?»

«No», he replied.

Then he lowered his voice, as though entrusting me with a secret.

«I came across this book in a village on the plain, and I traded a few rupees and a Bible for it. The man who owned it didn't know how to read. I suspect he saw the Book of Books as an amulet. He was of the lowest caste; people could not so much as step on his shadow without being defiled. He told me his book was called the Book of Sand because neither sand nor this book has a beginning or an end».

He suggested I try to find the first page. I took the cover in my left hand and opened the book, my thumb and forefinger almost touching. It was impossible: several pages always lay between the cover and my hand.

It was as though they grew from the very book.

«Now try to find the end».

I failed there as well.

«This can't be», I stammered, my voice hardly recognizable as my own.

«It can't be, yet it is», the Bible peddler said, his voice little more than a whisper.

«The number of pages in this book is literally infinite. No page is the first page; no page is the last. I don't know why they're numbered in this arbitrary way, but perhaps it's to give one to understand that the terms of an infinite series can be numbered any way whatever».

Then, as though thinking out loud, he went on.

«If space is infinite, we were anywhere, at any point in space. If time is infinite, we are at any point in time».

His musings irritated me.

«You», I said, «are a religious man, are you not?»

«Yes, I'm Presbyterian. My conscience is clear.

I am certain I didn't cheat that native when I gave him the Lord's Word in exchange for his diabolic book». […]

I showed no one my treasure. To the joy of possession was added the fear that it would be stolen from me, and to that, the suspicion that it might not be truly infinite. […] I examined the worn binding and the covers with a magnifying glass, and rejected the possibility of some artifice. I found that the small illustrations were spaced at two-thousand-page intervals. I began noting them down in an alphabetized notebook, which was very soon filled. They never repeated themselves. (Borges; http://www.annecoale.com/web4pics/bookofsand.pdf).

An absurdity, a paradox, ("It can't be, yet it is" [Ibid.]) and an oxymoronic quality ("The number of pages in this book is literally infinite. [Ibid. Underlined by B.B-B.]) Are the categories linking both works in question and traceable both in the context of Feingold's work and Borges' prose. As one can see, the peculiarity of the book is stressed in the text in various ways. The artist offers a certain game with the reader, not only deconstructing the eternal truths, but also suggesting that the text of *The Book of Sand* should be read in a similar way: "I was struck by an odd fact: the even-numbered page would carry the number 40,514, let us say, while the odd-numbered page that followed it would be 999. I turned the page …" – Borges writes transforming the sacred book into an infernal and "monstrual" one not only in the symbolic plane, through reversing the page number (999 changes into 666), but also in the mental one: "I felt it was a nightmare thing, an obscene thing, and that it defiled and corrupted reality. I considered fire, but I feared that the burning of an infinite book might be similarly infinite, and suffocate the planet in smoke" (Ibid.).

Photo. 16. Ken Feingold, *The Surprising Spiral* (1991)[29]

According to P. Zawojski, the work – installation *The Surprising Spiral* by Ken Feingold also refers to the problem of interface development, and, to be more specific, tactility. Faingold mentions that one of the reasons of his interest in touch screens was an inscription placed in a catalogue designed by Marcel Duchamp. It was a catalogue of an exhibition entitled *Le Surréalisme* prepared by Feingold and Andre Breton in 1947. On the cover of the book one could see an artificial woman's breast while on the reverse it was written in French Prerie de Toucher – Please touch… A physical relationship, closeness, a direct contact – this is a book moved into a technological

---

[29] A photo by Anna Mrogowicz from the vertical portal culture.pl: http://www.culture.pl/baza-sztuki-pelna-tresc/-/eo_event_asset_publisher/eAN5/content/wro-miedzynarodowe-biennale-sztuki-mediow. Access date: 15.07.2012.

dimension. When touched it activates a totally new, labyrinthine and hybrid reality. But to make it open for us and to get immersed in it we must go through the experience of a book (Zawojski 2005).

The Surprising Spiral is a textual and narrative work and at the same time it is hypertextual and rhizomatic. Paying attention to its quite important quality (on wchich, to the same extent as on its physical materiality and audiovisuality, it is based) which is its language character, one might risk stating that we are dealing not only with a variation of a hypertextual, interactive and media work but, in the first place, a textual and literary one.

Photo 17 and 18. Ken Feingold, *The Surprising Spiral* (1991)[30]

Dorota Hartwich stresses the language-experimental aspect of the discussed object. In her report from an exhibition *Inna książka. Książka i tekst poza książką w dobie nowej komunikacji* [31]she emphasizes that a language experiment of this kind illustrates how:

> language gets independent from reality, escapes from grammar rules, skips logic laws and functions according to its own principles. It is no longer a reflection of the world, it loses, as Michel Foucault would say, its transparence; *signifiant* leaves *signifié,* words – even if they enable us to see things through them – are not their «analogons». *The tree I'm writing about is not the tree I see* – says the

---

[30] The source of photographs: http://catalogue.nimk.nl/site/?page=%2Fsite%2Fart.php%3Fdoc_id%3D2813. Access date: 15.07.2012. See also the work documentation prepared by the author: http://catalogue.nimk.nl/site/?page=%2Fsite%2Fart.php%3Fdoc_id%3D2813. Access date: 05.09.2012.

[31] (which was held in May 2005 in Muzeum Narodowe in Wrocław as a special event of XI Międzynarodowe Biennale Sztuki Mediów WRO 05. (International Media Art. Biennale WRO 05).

voice in Ken Feingold's installation *The Surprising Spiral* [...]. In his installation Feingold also liberates words [...]; the author of the work adopts a consciously developed artistic strategy [...]. Feingold emancipates a written word – a text, extracting it from its primary environment, i.e. from a book. He constructs an interactive book without a text..." (Hartwich)[32]

The text which is created by each subsequent interactor and all of them together because the former one can influence what the latter one hears or sees. "Feingold eliminated only written words from the book. Spoken words are present and function beyond the book – they can be, again through touching, «brought out» form the mouth replica placed on the authentic volume by Octavio Paz (*The Monkey Grammarian*). Random pictures of reality triggered by a hand movement are assigned to a text read aloud" (Ibid).

We are therefore dealing with a special kind of work placing itself at the borderland of mediality (installation work) and textuality (book work) with a form evading any attempts of defining or classifying. A media or multimedia work is based on an individually changed structure of an aesthetic situation. The elements involved in it are an interactive artefact (i.e. an object), and interactor (a combination of the functions of a receiver and a user), an interface, an interactive process and the work itself (which is neither an artefact nor an interface). It is a work in which the property is not limited to the sphere of perception but conditions it itself, its ontic status and structure; a work truly interactive, displaying its properties and functioning only when the user behaves in an active way, using the object as a tool to achieve one's aims; a work created only in the process of reception and interaction, it is processual and lasts as long as the interaction develops and as long as the interactor decides to break the contact with the work. It is a work where not only a fully concentrated observation, contemplation or experiencing a *catharsis* from a secure distance matters but rather a work where a deed, a specific action influencing the object must be a response of a receiver. It is a form leading a receiver to a co-participation, joining a dialogue, not only on the level of interpretation but mainly in the sphere of actions; a form engaging not only the receiver's eyesight and hearing but often touch as well (Kluszczyński 2001: 85–99).

Feingold's work uses most of the expression means named by Kluszczyński. In spite of partly imitating a traditional medium with its appearance it is actually based on a computer carrier, uses a film, sound, a photo as well as written and spoken words (to be more specific: written

---

[32] ttp://odra.okis.pl/article.php/371. Access date: 15.07.2012.

words transported into their spoken version). The work constitutes a representation of multimedia art. It is related to and directly evolves from the development of computer technology (multimediality – a complex compound and multi-faceted communication with a computer). Kluszczyński suggests that it should be called interactive multimedia art or hypermedia art. The latter term draws attention to the hypertextual quality of a work which does not follow a linear order typical for textual structures but is based on a multi-level structure of a hypertext with a free multi-directional navigation through its numerous levels.It is worth mentioning that Kluszczyński distinguishes the so called classical kind of multimedia art as an effect of a broad understanding of a medium category (which may refer to each form of expression), art determined by co-occurrence of several different forms of artistic expression within one work. What is interesting, *The Surprising Spiral* is a link between the first and the second meaning scope of the discussed term. Its physical, tangible form imitating a book links it with the classical kind of multimedia art. One can not only read or hear it but also admire it. If not beautiful like a heavy, lavishly hardbacked book volume may be, the opening of which promises a surprise (what is more, it is exposed on a heavy wooden pedestal or a reading stand), it certainly is physically interesting and is able to catch a viewer's eye.

Photo 19. Ken Feingold, *The Surprising Spiral* (1991) [33].

---

[33] Photo from the website of WWW Center for Art and Media ZKM in Karlsruhe: http://on1.zkm.de/zkm/werke/SurprisingSpiral Access date: 15.07.2012.

An interactive reading in a gallery space?

Here is the place where the question whether this is the future of literature should be asked. Will literature start moving towards literary representations characterising total works – material and textual at the same time, but also hypertextual, rhisomatic and media-like -according to the democratisation, digitalisation and the audiovisual nature of literary culture recently described by Maryla Hopfinger? Like *The Surprising Spiral*? The initiation has already happened and may cause the highlighting of a certain, one must admit, extremely interesting and promising trend in the area of contemporary art. The trend would undoubtedly change the amount of time the reader spends in a museum because one would enter the museum-gallery space not only to look but also to read. This is also because apart from *The Surprising Spiral* other examples of this type can be named, e.g. *Text Rain* (from 1999) by the duet Camille Utterback and Romy Achituv[34] and *Beyond Pages* (1995), a work created by Masaki Fujihata[35].

What is the real difference between Feingold and Fajfer? Both Fajfer and Feingold call for a holistic approach to work. In both cases we deal with not only a textual message but also with the significance of the physical constitution of the object and influence upon (and message derived from) the work. In the case of *The Surprising Spiral* it is simply a work (an interactive installation) using the physical and material character of an artefact and becoming an interface to a larger extent.

I am obviously aware of the risk lying in juxtaposing works belonging to such different creative environments as interactive art and e-liberature. Through this controversial juxtaposition I intended to attract attention to the fact that narrative works exist in the sphere of fine arts and literature and they constitute a clear example of new qualities emerging in effect of media and literature convergence. Both of them, however, and each one for a different reason, struggle against someone who wants to interpret them (*The Surprising Spiral* does so because it does not generate consistent narration and constitutes at most an artistic evidence for the world's textuality or intertextuality; in Fajfer – due to his overcontrolled and closed constitution both on the level of structure and content; cyber narrative poems (not mentioned in this article) – usually due to the limited amount of con-

---

[34] See e.g.: http://camilleutterback.com/projects/text-rain/. Access date: 05.09.2012.
[35] See e.g.: http://www.youtube.com/watch?v=flXXXhe9diY. Access date: 05.09.2012.

tent). A demanding reader, receiver or interactor would expect a literary potential from the senses generated by them – a literary potential which might face the potential of the literary content of the culture of printing. As literature scholars we will have to stick to awaiting the emergence of a cybernetic work (which would find its place somewhere between *The Surprising Spiral* by Feingold, cybernetic poems by Bromboszcz and a content comparable to *The Name of the Rose* by Umberto Eco). So far, however, our appetites have not yet been satisfied.

Translated by Dorota Ślęzak

Bibliography

Bazarnik Katarzyna, Fajfer Zenon 2009, *Oka-leczenie*, Cracow: Korporacja Ha!art.

Bazarnik Katarzyna 2010, *Liberatura czyli o powstawaniu gatunków (literackich)*, [in:] Z. Fajfer, *Liberatura czyli literatura totalna. Teksty zebrane z lat 1999–2009. Korporacja*, Cracow: Korporacja Ha!art.

Bodzioch-Bryła Bogusława 2006, *Ku ciału post-ludzkiemu… Polska poezja po 1989 roku wobec nowych mediów i nowej rzeczywistości*, Cracow: Korporacja Ha!art.

Borges Jorge Luis, *The Book of Sand*, trans by A. Hurley, http://www.annecoale.com/web4pics/bookofsand.pdf.

Eichenbaum Borys 1972, *Problemy stylistyki filmowej*, trans. B. Grabowska, [in:] *Estetyka i film*, ed. A. Helman, Warsaw, as cited, [in:] W. Osadnik 1986, *Lingwistyka i filmoznawstwo. Krytyczna ocena tendencji lingwistycznej w badaniach nad filmem*, Katowice: Wydawnictwo UŚ.

Fajfer Zenon 2010, *W stronę liberatury*, [in:] idem, *Liberatura czyli literatura totalna. Teksty zebrane z lat 1999–2009*, ed. K. Bazarnik, Cracow: Korporacja Ha!art.

Fajfer Zenon 2010,*Liberature or total literature. Collected Essays 1999-2009*, trans. and ed. K. Bazarnik, Cracow: Korporacja Ha!art.

Fajfer Zenon 2009, *Spoglądając przez ozonową dziurę*, Cracow: Korporacja Ha!art.

Filiciak Mirosław 2006, *Wirtualny plac zabaw. Gry sieciowe i przemiany kultury współczesnej*, Warsaw: Wydawnictwa Akademickie i Profesjonalne.

Godzic Wiesław 1984, *Film i metafora. Pojęcie metafory w historii myśli filmowej*, Katowice: Wydawnictwo UŚ.

Hartwich Dorota 2005, *Litera na wolności*: http://odra.okis.pl/article.php/371. Data dostępu: 15.07.2010.

Hendrykowski Marek 1994, *Słownik terminów filmowych*, Poznan: Wydawnictwo „Ars Nova".

Hopfinger Maryla 2010, *Literatura i media. Po 1989 roku*, Warsaw: Oficyna Naukowa.

Jakobson Roman 1989, *O stosunku między znakami wizualnymi i audytywnymi*, [in:] idem, *W poszukiwaniu istoty języka* I, ed. M. R. Mayenowa, Warsaw: PIW.

Jakobson Roman 1972, *Upadek filmu?*, [in:] *Estetyka i film*, ed. A. Helman, Warsaw: Wydawnictwa Artystyczne i Filmowe, as cited, [in:] W. Osadnik 1986, *Lingwistyka i filmoznawstwo. Krytyczna ocena tendencji lingwistycznej w badaniach nad filmem*, Katowice: Wydawnictwo UŚ.

Jenkins Henry 2006, *Convergence Culture*, New York and London: New York University Press.

Jenkins Henry 2003, *Quentin Tarantino's Star Wars? Digital Cinema, Media Convergence and Participatory Culture*; [in:] *Rethinking Media Change. The Aesthetics of Transition*, eds. D. Thorburn and H. Jenkins, Cambridge MA: MIT Press.

Jenkins Henry, Thornburn David 2003, *Introduction*, [in:] *Rethinking Media Change. The Aesthetics of Transition*, eds. D. Thorburn and H. Jenkins, Cambridge MA: MIT Press.

Jeżyk Łukasz 2010, *Widzieć, wierzyć, wiedzieć. Dwadzieścia jeden liter Zenona Fajfera*, [in:] Z. Fajfer, *Liberatura czyli literatura totalna. Teksty zebrane z lat 1999–2009*, Cracow: Korporacja Ha!art.

Kluszczyński Ryszard W. 2001, *Światy multimediów*, [in:] *W świecie mediów*, ed. E. Nurczyńska-Fidelska, Cracow: Universitas.

Lister Martin, Dovey Jon, Giddings Seth, Grant Iain, Kelly Kieran 2009, *New Media: A Critical Introduction*, London, New York; http://www.philol.msu.ru/~discours/images/stories/speckurs/New_media.pdf.

Manovich Lev 2006, *Język nowych mediów*, Warsaw: Wydawnictwa Akademickie i Profesjonalne.

Miczka Tadeusz 1995, *Kino jako poezja optyczna. Próby futuryzacji kinematografu w Polsce w latach 1918–1939*, [in:] *Kino – Film: poezja optyczna?* ed. J. Trznadlowski, Wroclaw: Wydawnictwo Uniwersytetu Wrocławskiego.

Nowakowski Radosław 2005, *Koniec świata według Emeryka*; http://www.emeryk.wici.info/

Paz Octavio 1974, *Małpa gramatyczna*, trans. Krystyna Rodowska; http://www.grupaphp.com/phpspiskiiplotki/sip008.php.

Preikschat Wolfgang 1994, *Wideo jako metafora*, [in:] *Prędkość i przyjemność. Kino i telewizja w dobie symulacji elektronicznej*, ed. A. Gwóźdź, Kielce: Wydawnictwo Szumacher.

Rek Jan 1994, *Między filmem a literaturą. Szkic do portretu Łódzkiego Ośrodka badań nad filmem*, [in:] *Film: Obraz – Język – Wyobraźnia – Idea*, ed. J. Trznadlowski, Wroclaw: Wydawnictwo Uniwersytetu Wrocławskiego.

Shuty Sławomir 2002, *Blok*; http://www.blok.art.pl/

Stern Anatol 1959, *Film w poezji*, [in:] *Wspomnienia z Atlantydy*, Warsaw: Wydawnictwa Artystyczne i Filmowe.

Tynianow Jurij 1972, *Prawa kina*, trans. B. Grabowska, [in:] *Estetyka i film*, ed. A. Helman, Warsaw, as cited, [in:] W. Osadnik 1986, *Lingwistyka i filmoznawstwo. Krytyczna ocena tendencji lingwistycznej w badaniach nad filmem*, Katowice: Wydawnictwo UŚ.

Zawojski Piotr 2005, *Galaktyka post-Gutenberga*, "artPapier", No. 12.

Zawojski Piotr 1998, *Cyfrowe obrazy fotograficzne – pomiędzy bytem wirtualnym a rzeczywistym*, [in:] *Intermedialność w kulturze końca XX wieku*, ed. A. Gwóźdź, S. Krzemień-Ojak, Białystok; http://www.fil.us.edu.pl/film-i-media/zawoj/PZCyfob.htm. Data dostępu: 15.07.2012.

Other links

http://www.zawojski.com/2006/04/19/galaktyka-post-gutenberga/
http://catalogue.nimk.nl/site/?page=%2Fsite%2Fart.php%3Fdoc_id%3D2813
http://on1.zkm.de/zkm/werke/SurprisingSpiral
http://oneartworld.com/artists/K/Ken+Feingold.html?atab=works&image=2806
http://wro05.wrocenter.pl/thesurprisingspiral_pl.php.
http://www.culture.pl/baza-sztuki-pelna-tresc/-/eo_event_asset_publisher/eAN5/content/wro-miedzynarodowe-biennale-sztuki-mediow.
http://www.medienkunstnetz.de/works/the-surprising-spiral/
http://www.newsweek.pl/Europa/jedno-pioro-jest-ptakiem,43818,2,1.html

BIBLIOGRAPHICAL NOTES

Peter Gärdenfors, PhD, (b. 1949)

Professor in Cognitive Science at Lund University since 1988. Adjunct professor at University of Technology Sydney since 2012.

Main current research interests are concept formation, cognitive semantics, and the evolution of cognition. His publications include the following books: Knowledge in Flux: Modeling the Dynamics of Epistemic States, MIT Press, 1988. Conceptual Spaces, MIT Press, 2000. How Homo Became Sapiens: On the Evolution of Thinking, Oxford University Press, 2003. The Dynamics of Thought, Springer Verlag, 2005, The Geometry of Meaning: Semantics Based on Conceptual Spaces, MIT Press 2014. Member of the Royal Swedish Academy of Letters, History and Antiquities since 1996. Member of Academia Europaea since 1999. Member of Leopoldina Deutsche Akademie für Naturforscher since 2004. Member of the Royal Swedish Academy of Science since 2009. Member of the Prize Committee for the Prize in Economic Sciences in Memory of Alfred Nobel since 2011.

William Powers

William Powers is the author of the *New York Times* bestseller, *Hamlet's BlackBerry*. Widely praised for its insights on the digital future, the book grew out of a paper he wrote as a Shorenstein Fellow at Harvard's John F. Kennedy School of Government. The book has been selected as the Common Read at a number of U.S. colleges and universities and published in many other languages including Chinese, Korean, Polish, German and Russian. He is currently a research scientist at the Laboratory for Social Machines at the MIT Media Lab, developing new technologies to solve problems in governance, journalism and other sectors of the public sphere. A former *Washington Post* staff writer, he is a two-time winner of the U.S. National Press Club's Rowse Award for best American media commentary. In recent years, he has spoken at South By Southwest, the Aspen Ideas Festival and many other conferences and organizations.

Jarosław Płuciennik, PhD, (b. 1966)

Professor Ordinarius of the Humanities at Chair of Theory of Literature, at the Institute of Contemporary Culture, University of Lodz, Poland with specialization in literary culture, cognitive semiotics, and new media of reading. He published among others 7 books, co-edited several volumes, both in Polish and English. He is Pro-Vice-Chancellor for Curricula and Quality Assurance and Enhancement at the University of Lodz, the Editor-in-Chief of the Problems of Literary Genres, and the Head of the Chair of Theory of Literature at the Institute of Contemporary Culture, University of Lodz, Poland. He studied and did research in Lund, Sweden, and Cambridge, UK, and Bolzano, Italy. He was a guest lecturer at University of Warsaw, University of Lund, and Music Academy in Lodz. His recent interests are: cognitive domains related to senses in translations, iphonology, e-learning, m-learning, comparative analysis of cognition across all media.

Michał Wróblewski, PhD, (b. 1985)

Affiliated at Chair of Theory of Literature, at the Institute of Contemporary Culture, University of Lodz. Thesis defence in 2014: *The Graphic Novel - a Study of the Genre in the Perspective of Cognitive Science*. Author of several publications and translations in relation to genre studies, popular culture, theory of literature and cognitive semiotics. He has published, among others, in "Przestrzenie Teorii", "Teksty Drugie" and "The Problems of Literary Genres", in which he also works as an editor. Currently he is involved as the prime contractor in international educational projects - The iProfessional (Erasmus Multilateral Projects), Supporting Boys Reading (Erasmus+), Digitally Competent Youth: DIGI.COM/YOUTH (Erasmus+). He acts also as an assistant of project manager - in the interdisciplinary team iPro UŁ for Open Educational Resources and ICT skills at the University of Lodz.

REVIEWER
Danuta Ulicka

LINGUISTIC EDITOR
Stephen Dewsbury
Michał Wróblewski

TYPESETTING
Munda – Maciej Torz

COVER DESIGN
Łukasz Orzechowski

COVER IMAGE
Graphics by Paweł Więckowiak

First Edition. W.07036.15.0.K

Publisher's sheets 24.8; printing sheets 25.25